SURVIVANCE

NARRATIVES OF
NATIVE PRESENCE

EDITED BY GERALD VIZENOR

UNIVERSITY OF NEBRASKA PRESS · LINCOLN AND LONDON

© 2008 by the
Board of Regents
of the University of Nebraska
"Aesthetics of Survivance"
© 2008 by Gerald Vizenor
All rights reserved
Manufactured in the
United States of America
⊚
Library of Congress
Cataloging-in-Publication Data
Survivance :
narratives of Native presence /
edited by Gerald Vizenor.
p.   cm.
Includes bibliographical
references and index.
ISBN 978-0-8032-1083-7
(pbk.: alk. paper)
1. Indians of North America
—Social conditions.
2. Indians, Treatment of
—North America.
3. Indians of North America
—Public opinion.
4. Public opinion
—United States
5. Indian literature.
6. American literature
—Indian authors
—History and criticism.
I. Vizenor, Gerald Robert,
1934–
E98.S67S87 2008
305.897—dc22
2008021780

Designed and typeset in
Charlotte Sans &
Dirty Headline by
R. W. Boeche.

The application of the name Indians to the native peoples and tribes of the New World is an erroneous usage, originating in the belief that the Spanish discoverers of America that they had reached the eastern shores of Asiatic countries already partially known. As it happens, the name is now, even apart from the addition of Americans, customarily applied to the aborigines of the Western hemisphere, while it is used with far less frequency as a collective name for the inhabitants of the great country of the East known from the remotest times in India.

Entry for Indians, America,
Encyclopedia Britannica, ninth ed.

In one of their traditions it is stated that "when the white man first came in sight of the 'Great Turtle' island of Mackinaw, they beheld walking on the pebbly shores, a crane and a bear who received them kindly, invited them to their wigwams, and placed food before then." This allegory denotes that Ojibways of the Crane and Bear Totem families first received the white strangers, and extended to them the hand of friendship and rites of hospitality, and in remembrance of this occurrence they are said to have been the favorite clans with the old French discoverers.
William Warren, *History of the Ojibway Nation*

As the reader will have understood, I borrow from these two traditions: from theory of literature, the reflections on general notions, principles, and criteria; from literary theory, the criticism of literary good sense and the reference to formalism. Providing recipes, then, is not the point. Theory is not method, technique, cuisine. On the contrary, the purpose is to become skeptical of all recipes, to eliminate them by reflection. My intention, then, is not in the least to facilitate things, but to be vigilant, suspicious, skeptical, in a word: critical or ironic. Theory is a school of irony.
Antoine Compagnon,
Literature, Theory, and Common Sense

CONTENTS

1. AESTHETICS OF SURVIVANCE

Literary Theory and Practice

GERALD VIZENOR

> *When a language dies, a possible world dies with it. There is no survival of the fittest. Even where it is spoken by a handful, by the harried remnants of destroyed communities, a language contains within itself the boundless potential of discovery, or re-compositions of reality, of articulate dreams, which are known to us as myths, as poetry, as metaphysical conjecture and the discourse of law.*
>
> George Steiner, *After Babel*

The theories of survivance are elusive, obscure, and imprecise by definition, translation, comparison, and catchword histories, but survivance is invariably true and just in native practice and company. The nature of survivance is unmistakable in native stories, natural reason, remembrance, traditions, and customs and is clearly observable in narrative resistance and personal attributes, such as the native humanistic tease, vital irony, spirit, cast of mind, and moral courage. The character of survivance creates a sense of native presence over absence, nihility, and victimry.

Native survivance is an active sense of presence over absence, deracination, and oblivion; survivance is the continuance of stories, not a mere reaction, however pertinent. Survivance is greater than the right of a survivable name.

Survivance stories are renunciations of dominance, detractions, obtrusions, the unbearable sentiments of tragedy, and the legacy of victimry. Survivance is the heritable right of succession or reversion of an estate and, in the course of international declarations of human rights, is a narrative estate of native survivance.

Fourth Person

Charles Aubid, for instance, declared by stories his native presence, human rights, and sovereignty. He created a crucial course and sense of survivance in federal court and defied the hearsay of historical precedent, cultural ethnologies, absence, and victimry.

This inspired storier was a sworn witness in federal court that autumn more than thirty years ago in Minneapolis, Minnesota. He raised his hand, listened to the oath for the first time in the language of the Anishinaabe, Chippewa, or Ojibwe, and then waved, an ironic gesture of the oath, at United States District Judge Miles Lord. Aubid testified by visual memory, an inseparable sensibility of natural reason, and with a singular conception of continental native liberty. His stories intimated a third person other than the apparent reference, the figurative presence of a fourth person, a sui generis native discourse in the oral language of the Anishinaabe. That native practice of survivance, the storied presence of a fourth person, a visual reminiscence, was repudiated as hearsay, not a source of evidence in common law or federal court precedent.

Aubid was a witness in a dispute with the federal government over the right to regulate the *manoomin*, wild rice, harvest on the Rice Lake National Wildlife Refuge in Minnesota. Federal agents had assumed the authority to determine the wild rice season and to regulate the harvest, a bureaucratic action that decried a native sense of survivance and sovereignty.

Aubid, who was eighty-six years old at the time, testified through translators that he was present as a young man when the federal agents told Old John Squirrel that the Anishinaabe would always have control of the *manoomin* harvest. Aubid told the judge that the Anishinaabe always understood their rights by stories. John Squirrel was there in memories, a storied presence of native survivance. The court could have heard the testimony as a visual trace of a parol agreement, a function of discourse, both relevant and necessary.

Justice Lord agreed with the objection of the federal attorney that the testimony was hearsay and therefore not admissible and explained to the witness that the court could not hear as evidence what a dead man said, only the actual experiences of the witness. "John Squirrel is dead," said the judge. "And you can't say what a dead man said."

Aubid turned brusquely in the witness chair, bothered by what the judge had said about John Squirrel. Aubid pointed at the legal books on the bench, and then in English, his second language, he shouted that those books contained the stories of dead white men. "Why should I believe what a white man says, when you don't believe John Squirrel?" Judge Lord was deferential, amused by the analogy of native stories to court testimony, judicial decisions, precedent, and hearsay. "You've got me there," he said, and then considered the testimony of other Anishinaabe witnesses.[1]

Monotheism is hearsay, the literary concern and ethereal care of apostles, and the curse of deceivers and debauchery. The rules of evidence and precedent are selective by culture and tradition, and sanction judicial practices over native presence and survivance.

Charles Aubid created indirect linguistic evidence of a fourth person by visual reminiscence. His stories were intuitive, visual memories, a native sense of presence, and sources of evidence and survivance.

Native Humanist

Ishi, the native humanist, endured by survivance and natural reason in two worlds. He was named by an academic, not by vision, a lonesome hunter rescued by situational chance. Native names are collective memories, but his actual names and sense of presence are obscure, yet his museum nickname, more than any other archive nomination, represents to many readers the cultural absence and tragic victimry of Native American Indians in California.

The spirit of this native hunter, captured almost a century ago, has been sustained as cultural evidence and property. Ishi was humanely secured in a museum at a time when other natives were denied human and civil rights.

Alfred Kroeber, the eminent anthropologist, read the newspaper reports and contacted the sheriff who "had put the Indian in jail not knowing what else to do with him since no one around town could understand his speech or he theirs," writes Theodora Kroeber in *Alfred Kroeber: A Personal Configuration*. "Within a few days the Department of Indian Affairs authorized the sheriff to release the wild man to the custody of Kroeber and the museum staff. [Thomas] Waterman arrived in the city with him and Ishi was soon settled" in one of the rooms in the anthropology museum "furnished earlier" by Phoebe Apperson Hearst. Theodora Kroeber continues,

> The whole staff concentrated on learning to communicate with him,
> meanwhile trying to reassure him and to protect him from the curiosity

*of the crowds who daily tried to get a closer look at him. It was during
those first days Kroeber gave him the name Ishi, which means* man *or*
one of the people *in Yana, thus satisfying the popular need to call
him by name and saving Ishi the embarrassment of telling of his actual
private name to a stranger and hearing it used by other strangers, such
use of a personal name being taboo to California Indians.*[2]

Ishi was named the last of the Stone Agers, and overnight he became the
celebrated survivor of cultural genocide. He was alone but never contemptuous, or servile, and his stories were never given to nihility or victimry. He
was a native humanist in exile and a storier of survivance.

Ishi had endured the unspeakable hate crimes of miners, racial terrorists,
bounty hunters, and government scalpers. Many of his family and friends
were murdered: they were the calculated victims of cultural treason and ra-
pacity. Truly the miners were the savages. Indeed, California natives barely
survived the gold rush, the cruelties of colonial missions, partitionists, and
poisoned water. Only about fifty thousand natives, or one in five, were alive
in the state at the turn of the twentieth century.

Ishi never revealed his sacred name or any of his nicknames, but he never
concealed his humor and humanity. Lively, eager, and generous, he told tricky
wood duck stories to his new friends. This gentle native lived and worked for
five years in the museum of anthropology at the University of California.

Ishi was "at ease with his friends," writes Theodora Kroeber. He "loved to
joke, to be teased amiably and to tease in return. And he loved to talk. In telling a story, if it were long or involved or of considerable effect, he would per-
spire with the effort, his voice rising toward a falsetto of excitement."

Saxton Pope, the surgeon at the medical school located near the museum, notes that Ishi "amused the interns and nurses by singing" his songs. "His
affability and pleasant disposition made him a universal favorite. He visited
the sick in the wards with a gentle and sympathetic look which spoke more
clearly than words. He came to the women's wards quite regularly, and with
his hands folded before him, he would go from bed to bed like a visiting physician, looking at each patient with quiet concern or with a fleeting smile that
was very kindly received and understood."

The Bureau of Indian Affairs sent a special agent to advise Ishi that he could
return to the mountains or live on a government reservation. Kroeber writes

that Ishi "shook his head" and said through the interpreter that he would "live like the white people from now on. I want to stay where I am. I will grow old here, and die in this house." And by that he meant the museum. Ishi was clearly a native of survivance.[3]

Ishi created a sense of natural presence in his stories, a native presence that included others. He was a visionary, not a separatist, and his oral stories were assertions of liberty. This native humanist was amused by the trace of time on a wristwatch and by the silence of scripture. He was a tricky storier in exile.

Ishi was in exile by name, by racial wars, and by the partisans of cultural dominance. He was a fugitive in his own native scenes, pursued by feral pioneers and malevolent miners, yet he endured without apparent rancor or mordancy and created stories of native survivance.

The pioneers were separated from animals and natural reason by monotheism and the biblical covenants of human dominion over nature. Ishi was a humanist more at home in nature than a museum; clearly he was a man of natural reason, a mature storier and healer, and unlike the pioneer predators, he seemed to embrace the merits of a democratic and civil society.

Ishi is not his native name, but we imagine his presence by that museum nickname. Ishi is in our visions, and he persists by that name in our memory. We bear his exile as our own, and by his tease and natural reason we create new stories of native irony, survivance, and liberty.[4]

Higher Civilization

The Cherokee Phoenix, one of the first native newspapers, was established in 1828. Native newspapers "grew slowly" and were "considered an oddity until the last two decades of the nineteenth century," notes Daniel Littlefield in the *Encyclopedia of the North American Indians*. These early native "newspapers were aimed primarily at the American public as well as the local population and promoted an image of 'civilization' to the outside world."[5]

I discovered that image of civilization in the *Progress*, a weekly newspaper published by my distant relatives more than a century ago on the White Earth Reservation in Minnesota. I was inspired by the dedication of the editor and the news stories that created a singular sense of native presence and survivance.

I was a graduate student at the time, more than forty years ago, at the University of Minnesota. During my early research on native writers, tribal leaders, and treaties at the Minnesota Historical Society, a generous reference librarian directed me to the original bound volumes of the *Progress*, the first newspaper published on the White Earth Reservation.

I was transformed, inspired, and excited by a great and lasting source of a native literary presence and survivance. The newspaper countered the notion of a native absence and instead sustained a personal source of solace and enlightenment as well as a unique historical identity. I slowly, almost reverently, turned the fragile pages of the newspaper and read stories and notes by and about my distant relatives.

The *Progress* was founded by Augustus Hudon Beaulieu, the publisher, and Theodore Hudon Beaulieu, the editor. They were directly related to Alice Beaulieu Vizenor, my paternal grandmother, and my great uncle John Clement Beaulieu.

Reading the newspaper that afternoon at the Minnesota Historical Society was truly transformational, a moment that still lasts in my stories and memory, in spite of the unreasonable, dismissive response by the faculty graduate advisor. He refused to accept my historical, descriptive content analysis of the reservation newspaper because, he said, it was not an acceptable subject of graduate study. My advisor apparently considered reservation newspapers mere hearsay and not historical precedent.

The *Progress* announced one spring morning in the first issue, March 25, 1886, that the "novelty of a newspaper published upon this reservation may cause many to be wary in their support, and this from a fear that it may be revolutionary in character." The declaration continues with a sense of native survivance: "We shall aim to advocate constantly and withhold reserve, what in our view, and in the view of the leading minds upon this reservation, is the best for the interests of its residents. And not only for their interests, but those of the tribe wherever they now are residing."

I was persuaded and motivated by the advocacy of the editor, the gestures to the "leading minds" on the reservation, and imagined my presences as a writer for the newspaper. I worried at the same time about the fragile condition of the newsprint.

> *The main consideration of this advocacy will be the political interests,*
> *that is, in matters relative to us and to the Government of the United*

*States. We shall not antagonize the Government, not act, in the pre-
sentation of our views, in any way outside of written or moral law.*

*We intend that this journal shall be the mouth-piece of the commu-
nity in making known abroad and at home what is for the best interests of the tribe. It is not always possible to reach the fountain head
through subordinates, it is not always possible to appeal to the moral sentiment of the country through these sources, or by communication through general press.*

*We may be called upon at times to criticize individuals and laws, but
we shall aim to do so in the spirit of kindness and justice. Believing that
the "freedom of the press" will be guarded as sacredly by the Government on this reservation as elsewhere, we launch forth our little craft,
appealing to the authorities that be, at home, at the seat of government, to the community, to give us moral support, for in this way only
can we reach the standard set forth at our mast-head.*

The *Progress* was dedicated to "A Higher Civilization: The Maintenance of
Law and Order."

I was amused by the words "fountain head," the source or originator, but
the sense was ironic, an "appeal to the moral sentiment of the country." I was
impressed by the dedication of the editor to "moral law" and, in my view, moral agency. Rightly the editor argued, it is not possible to communicate to the
government "through subordinates." I was already involved in the discourse of
reservation politics and civilization by the first few issues of the newspaper.

The *Progress* was confiscated by federal agents shortly after the newspaper was distributed on the White Earth Reservation. Theodore and Augustus Beaulieu, both tribal members, were ordered by federal agents to leave
the reservation. They avoided the agents and found sanctuary in the mission
church. The Benedictine priests at the time were active in reservation politics
and obviously endorsed the publication of a newspaper for the community.

The *Progress* was first published on March 25, 1886. The second issue was
published on October 8, 1887, more than a year after federal agents seized
the press and property of the newspaper and after a subcommittee testimony and favorable hearing in federal court. T. J. Sheehan, the United States Indian Agent, a malevolent federal appointee, was an obsessive denier of native
liberty, and he would not tolerate freedom of the press on the reservation

without his approval. Sheehan wrote to the editor and publisher that they had "circulated a newspaper without first obtaining authority or license so to do from the honorable Secretary of the Interior, honorable Commissioner of Indian Affairs, or myself as United States Indian Agent."

Practically every means of communication by federal agencies about natives was ironic, and in this instance the mere use of the word "honorable" was an invitation to mockery. The honorific names of secretaries, commissioners, and federal agents are an eternal summons to ridicule and tricky invectives. The honorable political appointees are obvious contradiction, and those who carried out the policies of dominance are the agents of irony, the measures of dishonor and venality.

The mockery of federal agents has always been a native theme in stories. These practices of mockery are not the same as the cultural tease of acceptance. I read about the abuses of the federal agent on the reservation, and my mockery increased by the page. The *Progress* endured, truly an honorable declaration of native survivance and liberty.

Sheehan asserts in his formal letter that publisher Augustus Beaulieu "did scheme and intrigue with certain chiefs on White Earth Reservation without the knowledge of myself and the Indians of this agency, for the said chiefs to proceed to Saint Paul, Minnesota, for the purpose of signing a power of attorney for the Mississippi Indians, deputizing a person to act as an attorney for the Indians in certain business interests affecting the welfare of the Indians on White Earth Agency, all of which I considered revolutionary to the United States Government and a detriment to the welfare of these Indians."

Sheehan continues,

> Whereas you have at different times advised the full and mixedblood Indians to organize and "kick" against the rule established by myself as United States Indian agent, for the suppression of card playing, or other games which may be detrimental for the Indians on this agency. . . .
>
> Whereas, Theodore H. Beaulieu has written and caused to be printed in a newspaper adjacent to White Earth Reservation, false and malicious statements concerning the affairs of the White Earth Reservation, done evidently for the purpose of breaking down the influence of the United States Indian agent with the Indians of White Earth Agency.

Sheehan unwisely continued to devalue the ideas and interests of the "leading minds" of the reservation until his capricious manner resulted in an official investigation by a subcommittee of the United States Senate. The subcommittee convened a hearing about a year after the *Progress* was confiscated by federal agents.

Clement Hudon Beaulieu was the first witness to testify on Tuesday, March 8, 1887, before the subcommittee of the Committee on Indian Affairs. Clement was the father of publisher Augustus Beaulieu and uncle of editor Theodore Beaulieu.

The *Progress* published the second issue of the newspaper on October 8, 1887, more than a year after the editor and publisher were ordered removed from the reservation by federal agents and six months after an investigation by the subcommittee of the Senate Committee on Indian Affairs.

Theodore Beaulieu wrote the following on the front page of the second issue:

> In the month of March last year, we began setting the type for the first number of The Progress and were almost ready to got to press, when our sanctum was invaded by T. J. Sheehan, the United States Indian Agent, accompanied by a posse of the Indian police. The composing stick was removed from our hands, our property seized, and ourselves forbidden to proceed with the publication of the journal. We had, prior to this time, been personally served with a written notice from Mr. Sheehan detailing at length, surmises beyond number as to the character of The Progress, together with gratuitous assumptions as to our moral unfitness to be upon the reservation, charging the publisher with the voicing of incendiary and revolutionary sentiments at various times.
>
> We do not believe that any earthly power had the right to interfere with us as members of the Chippewa tribe, and at the White Earth Reservation, while peacefully pursuing the occupation we had chosen. We did not believe there existed a law which should prescribe for us the occupation we should follow. We knew of no law which could compel us to become agriculturalists, professionals, "hewers of wood and drawers of water," or per contra, could restrain us from engaging in these occupations. Therefore we respectfully declined obeying the mandate,

at the same time reaching the conclusion that should we be restrained we should appeal to the courts for protection.

We were restrained and a guard set over our property. We sought the protection of the courts, notwithstanding the assertion of the agent that there would be no jurisdiction in the matter.

The United States district court, Judge Nelson in session, decided that we were entitled to the jurisdiction we sought. The case came before him, on jury trial. The court asserted and defended the right of any member of a tribe to print and publish a newspaper upon his reservation just as he might engage in any other lawful occupation, and without surveillance and restrictions. The jury before whom the amount of damage came, while not adjudging the amount asked for, did assess and decree a damage with a verdict restoring to us our plant. . . .

Now that we are once more at sea, fumigated and out of quarantine, and we issue from dry dock with prow and hull steel-clad tempered with truth and justice, and with our clearance registered, we once more box our compass, invite you all aboard, and we will clear port, set sails to favorable breezes, with the assurance that we will spare no pains in guiding you to a "higher" civilization.

The *Progress* was not the first paper to be published on a federal reservation, but it was the first tribal newspaper to be seized capriciously by federal agents. The *Progress* continued weekly publication for about two years and then changed the name to the *Tomahawk*. The editor and publisher remained the same.

Theodore Hudon Beaulieu, the feisty editor, strongly opposed the federal allotment of reservation land, the provisions of the Dawes General Allotment Act of 1887. One front-page report, for instance, was introduced by this verbose feature headline: "Is it an Indian Bureau? About some of the freaks in the employ of the Indian Service whose actions are a disgrace to the nation and a curse to the cause of justice. Putrescent through the spoils system."[6] The *Progress* created a sense of presence, survivance, and native liberty by situational stories, editorial comments, reservation reportage, and the resistance of the editors denied a measure of arbitrary federal dominance, historical absence, and victimry.

Natural Estates

The native stories of survivance are successive and natural estates. Survivance is an active resistance and repudiation of dominance, obtrusive themes of tragedy, nihilism, and victimry.

The practices of survivance create an active presence, more than the instincts of survival, function, or subsistence. Native stories are the sources of survivance, the comprehension and empathies of natural reason, tragic wisdom, and the provenance of new literary studies. Native storiers of survivance are prompted by natural reason, by a consciousness and sense of incontestable presence that arises from experiences in the natural world, by the turn of seasons, by sudden storms, by migration of cranes, by the ventures of tender lady's slippers, by chance of moths overnight, by unruly mosquitoes, and by the favor of spirits in the water, rimy sumac, wild rice, thunder in the ice, bear, beaver, and faces in the stone.

Survivance, however, is not a mere romance of nature, not the overnight pleasures of pristine simulations, or the obscure notions of transcendence and signatures of nature in museums. Survivance is character by natural reason, not by monotheistic creation stories and dominance of nature.

Survivance stories create a sense of presence and situational sentiments of chance. Monotheism takes the risk out of nature and natural reason and promotes absence, dominance, sacrifice, and victimry.

Survivance is a practice, not an ideology, dissimulation, or a theory. The theory is earned by interpretations, by the critical construal of survivance in creative literature, and by narratives of cause and natural reason. The discourse on literary and historical studies of survivance is a theory of irony. The incongruity of survivance as a practice of natural reason and as a discourse on literary studies anticipates a rhetorical or wry contrast of meaning.

Antoine Compagnon observes in *Literature, Theory, and Common Sense* that theory "contradicts and challenges the practice of others" and that ideology "takes place between theory and practice. A theory would tell the truth of a practice, articulate its conditions of possibility, while an ideology would merely legitimate this practice by a lie, would dissimulate its conditions of possibility." Theory then "stands in contrast to the practice of literary studies, that is, literary criticism and history, and it analyzes this practice" and "describes them, exposes their assumptions — in brief, criticizes them (to criticize is to separate, discriminate)," writes Compagnon. "My intention, then, is not in the least to facilitate things, but to be vigilant, suspicious, skeptical, in a word: critical or ironic. Theory is a school of irony."[7]

Bear Traces

The presence of animals, birds, and other creatures in native literature is a trace of natural reason, by right, irony, precise syntax, literary figuration, and the heartfelt practice of survivance. Consider a theory of irony in the literary studies of absence and presence of animals in selected novels by Native American Indians. The creation of animals and birds in literature reveals a practice of survivance, and the critical interpretation of that literary practice is theory, a theory of irony and native survivance. Verbal irony is in the syntax and ambiguous situations of meaning, absence and presence, as one concept turns to another.

The Anishinaabeg, for instance, are named in "several grand families or clans, each of which is known and perpetuated by a symbol of some bird, animal, fish, or reptile," observes William Warren in *History of the Ojibway Nation*. The *ajijaak*, or crane totem, is the word for the sandhill crane, a dancer with a red forehead and a distinctive wingbeat. "This bird loves to soar among the clouds, and its cry can be heard when flying above, beyond the orbit of human vision." Warren, an Anishinaabe historian, declared more than a century ago that native crane leaders in "former times, when different tribes met in council, acted as interpreters of the wishes of their tribe."[8]

Keeshkemun, an orator of the crane totem at the turn of the nineteenth century on Lake Superior, encountered a British military officer eager to enlist native support for the French and Indian War. Michel Cadotte translated the stories of the orator. Keeshkemun created an avian presence by his totemic vision and natural reason.

"I am a bird who rises from the earth, and flies far up, into the skies, out of human sight; but though not visible to the eye, my voice is heard from afar, and resounds over the earth," said Keeshkemun.

Englishman, "you have put out the fire of my French father. I became cold and needy, and you sought me not. Others have sought me. Yes, the Long Knives found me. He has placed his heart on my breast. It has entered there, and there it shall remain."[9]

Metaphors are persuasive in language, thought, and action. "Our ordinary conceptual system, in terms of which we both think and act, is fundamentally metaphorical in nature" and "not merely a matter of language," observes George Lakoff and Mark Johnson in *Metaphors We Live By*. "Metaphor is one of our most important tools for trying to comprehend partially what cannot be comprehended totally: our feelings, aesthetic experiences, moral practices, and spiritual awareness. These endeavors of the imagination are not devoid of rationality; since they use metaphor, they employ an imaginative rationality."[10]

Metaphors create a sense of presence by imagination and natural reason, the very character and practice of survivance. The critical interpretation of native figurations is a theory of irony and survivance. The studies of oratory and translation, figuration, and native diplomatic strategies are clearly literary and historical, text and context, and subject to theoretical interpretations.

N. Scott Momaday, for instance, has created a literary landscape of bears and eagles in his memoirs and novels. "The names at first are those of animals and of birds, of objects that have one definition in the eye, another in the hand, of forms and features on the rim of the world, or of sounds that carry on the bright wind and in the void," declares Momaday in *The Names*. "They are old and original in the mind, like the beat of rain on the river, and intrinsic in the native tongue, failing even as those who bear them turn once in the memory, go on, and are gone forever."[11]

Clearly metaphors provide a more expansive sense of signification and literary survivance than simile. John Searle argues in "Metaphor" that the "knowledge that enables people to use and understand metaphorical utterances goes beyond their knowledge of the literal meaning of words and sentences." Searle declares that a "literal simile" is a "literal statement of similarity" and that "literal simile requires no special extralinguistic knowledge for its comprehension."[12]

Metaphor is that "figure of speech whereby we speak about one thing in terms which are seen to be suggestive of another," observes Janet Martin Soskice in *Metaphor and Religious Language*. The "greatest rival of metaphor, simile, in its most powerful instances does compel possibilities. Simile is usually regarded as the trope of comparison and identifiable within speech by the presence of 'like' or an 'as,' or the occasional 'not unlike.'" Simile, she argues, "may be the means of making comparisons to two kinds, the comparison of similars and dissimilars, and in the latter case, simile shares much of the imaginative life and cognitive function of its metaphorical counterparts." However, simile cannot "be used in catachresis," the excessive or misuse of words. Simile cannot create the lexicon, as does "dead end" or the "leaf of a book."[13]

James Welch, for example, created a precise sense of presence, a landscape by simile. "Tumble weeds, stark as bone, rocked in a hot wind against the west wall," and, "I was as distant from myself as a hawk from the moon," he writes in *Winter in the Blood*.[14]

"I have this bear power. I turn into a bear every so often. I feel myself becoming a bear, and that's a struggle I have to face now and then," Momaday tells Charles Woodward in *Ancestral Voices*.[15] Momaday became a bear by visionary transformation, an unrevealed presence in his novel *House Made of Dawn*. Angela, the literary voyeur, watches Abel cut wood, "full of wonder, taking his motion apart. . . . She would have liked to touch the soft muzzle of a bear, the thin black lips, the great flat head. She would have liked to cup her hand to the wet black snout, to hold for a moment the hot blowing of the bear's life." Later, they come together in the bear heat of the narrative: "He was dark and massive above her, poised and tinged with pale blue light."[16]

Another writer, Leslie Silko, encircles the reader with mythic witches, an ironic metaphor of survivance in *Ceremony*. The hardhearted witches invented white people in a competition, a distinctive metaphor that resists the similative temptations of mere comparison of natives with the structural extremes of dominance and victimry:

> The old man shook his head. "That is the trickery of the witchcraft," he said. "They want us to believe all evil resides with white people. Then we will look no further to see what is really happening. They want us to separate ourselves from white people, to be ignorant and helpless as we watch our own destruction. But white people are only tools that the witchery manipulates; and I tell you, we can deal with white people, with their machines and their beliefs. We can because we invented white people; it was Indian witchery that made white people in the first place."[17]

Louise Erdrich creates tropes in her novel *Tracks* that are closer to the

literal or prosaic simile than to the metaphors that inspire a sense of presence and survivance. She names moose, bears, cats, and other animals, but
the most common is the dog. For instance, she "shivered all over like a dog,"
and she "leaned over the water, sucking it like a heifer," and his "head shaggy and low as a bison bull."[18]

David Treuer also creates a few animals and birds in his novel *The Hiawatha*:
deer, mallards, and a goose kill in the city. Conceivably, only the curious,
astray, and then dead deer, an erudite sacrifice, was necessary. That scene
in the first few pages becomes the singular metaphor of the novel, a sense
of absence and melancholy. Any sentiments of native survivance are overturned by woe and mordancy. The omniscient narrator alleges that "memory always murders the present."[19] Many of the scenes are heavy, overbooked
irony. The natives and other characters, however, arise with glory and gran-
deur as construction workers on a skyscraper, a material metaphor of survivance, but once grounded they are separated, dissociated, tragic, and en-
ervated by cultural dominance, nihility, and victimry. "The earth would treat
them with the same indifference as loose steel, a dropped hammer, a wind-
blown lunch," writes Treuer. "This was the secret: the building wanted to stay
standing, to grow, to sway but hold on, and so did they." The "tower wanted to be noticed and admired, as did the Indian crew. Its bones of steel and
skin of glass were treated roughly by the wind, heat, and ice as were their
skin and bones."[20]

March, the streets are "dirty with sand," and homeless men reach out to
touch a wild deer astray in a "church parking lot." Truly a tensive scene as
the men reach out in silence to warm their hands on the deer, hesitant, and
the deer walks untouched through a "channel of men." Then heedless, one
man placed his hand on the deer, and in an "instant it was running." The men
"hook their fingers" on the fence "and watch the deer bound down the weedy
and trash-strewn slope to the freeway and into the traffic."[21]

Treuer, who slights the distinct character of native literature, pronounces
the deer dead in five pages and evokes a weighty metaphor of want and victimry. The scene of the deer astray in rush hour traffic is obvious, portentous.
The intention of the author is clear—a dead deer. The choice disheartens
and yet appeases by the familiar simulations of sacrifice. That emotive scene
provokes the pity and sympathy of some readers, those who may concede

the simulations of victimry. Surely other readers might imagine the miracu-
lous liberty of the deer by natural reason and survivance.

The Hiawatha closes in a second-person crescendo of nihility. "You move
stones with your feet but there is no impression, no remnant of your life, your
action. Whatever you do is not accommodated, it is simply dropped onto
the hard earth you pass. You will be forgotten. Your feet, your hands are not
words and cannot speak. Everything we accumulate—our habits, gestures,
muscles trained by the regimen of work, the body remembering instead of
the mind—it is of no use."[22]

House Made of Dawn by N. Scott Momaday, as a comparison, ends with a
song, a sense of presence and native survivance. Abel "was alone and running
on. All of his being was concentrated in the sheer motion of running on, and
he was past caring about the pain. Pure exhaustion laid hold of his mind, and
he could see at last without having to think. He could see the canyon and the
mountains and the sky. He could see the rain and the river and the fields beyond. He could see the dark hills at dawn." Abel "was running, and under his
breath he began to sing. There was no sound, and he had no voice; he had
only the words of a song. And he went running on the rise of the song. *House
made of pollen, house made of dawn.*"[23]

Treuer declares in *Native American Fiction: A User's Manual* that native fiction, "if there is such a thing," should be studied as literature, and by "applying ourselves to the word, and, at least at the outset of our endeavors, by ig-
noring the identity of the author and all the ways the author constructs his
or her authority outside the text, we will be better able to ascertain the true
value of that text."

The "true value" of any text is elusive as truth is only the ironic intention
of the author and forevermore of the consciousness of the reader. Treuer
creates a fallacy of the "true value" of literature, and he seems heartened by
the implied death of the author and by the strains of formalism and erstwhile
New Criticism. Yet he does not appear to be haunted by the wake of literary intentionalism or the implied intentions of the native author. "Over the
past thirty years, Native American fiction has been defined as, exclusively,
literature written by Indians," he notes. The sentiment, however, that "Native American literature should be defined by the ethnicity of its producers (more so than defined by anything else) says more about politics and

identity than it does about literature. This is especially true, and especially clear, when we see that our books are constructed out of the same materials available to anyone else. Ultimately, the study of Native American fiction should be the study of style."[24]

Treuer shows his own intentional fallacy that counters silky ideas about literature, style, and identity. The symbol of a broken feather enhances the cover of his book, a trace of image and identity politics, and the biographical note that he is "Ojibwe from the Leech Lake Reservation in northern Minnesota" implies that he would rather favor being read for his ethnicity.

So if there is *only* literature by some dubious discovery of the "true value" of the cold, white pages of style, then there is no sense of native presence and survivance. Treuer teases the absence of native survivance in literature, but apparently he is not an active proponent of the death of the author. Surely he would not turn native novelists aside that way, by the ambiguities of cold print, only to declare as a newcomer his own presence as a native author.

Tragic Wisdom

Native American Indians have resisted empires, negotiated treaties, and as strategies of survivance, participated by stealth and cultural irony in the simulations of absence in order to secure the chance of a decisive presence in national literature, history, and canonry. Native resistance of dominance, however serious, evasive and ironic, is an undeniable trace of presence over absence, nihility, and victimry.

Many readers consider native literature an absence not a presence, a romantic levy of heroic separatism and disappearance, while others review native stories as cryptic representations of cultural promises obscured by victimry. The concurrent native literary nationalists construct an apparent rarefied nostalgia for the sentiments and structures of tradition and the inventions of culture by a reductive reading of creative literature. The new nationalists would denigrate native individualism, visionary narratives, chance, natural reason, and survivance for the ideologies that deny the distinctions of native aesthetics and literary art. Michael Dorris, the late novelist, argued against the aesthetic distinctions of native literature. Other authors and interpreters of literature have resisted the idea of a singular native literary aesthetic.

Native literary artists in the furtherance of natural reason create the promise of aesthetic sentiments, irony, and practices of survivance. The standard dictionary definitions of *survivance* do not provide the natural reason or sense of the word in literature. Space, time, consciousness, and irony are elusive references, although critical in native history and literary sentiments of the word *survivance*.

The sectarian scrutiny of essential individual responsibilities provokes a discourse of monotheist conscience, remorse, mercy, and a literature of tragedy. The ironic fullness of original sin, shame, and stigmata want salvation, a singular solution to absence and certain victimry. There is a crucial cultural distinction between monotheism, apocalypticism, natural reason, and native survivance.

Dorothy Lee observes in *Freedom and Culture* that the "Dakota were responsible for all things, because they were at one with all things. In one way, this meant that all behavior had to be responsible, since its effect always went beyond the individual. In another way, it meant that an individual had to, was responsible to, increase, intensify, spread, recognize, experience this relationship." Consider, for the "Dakota, to be was to be responsible; because to be was to be related; and to be related meant to be responsible."

Personal, individual responsibility in this sense is communal and creates a sense of presence and survivance. Responsibility in the course of natural reason is not a cause of nihility or victimry. "The Dakota were responsible, but they were accountable to no one for their conduct," writes Lee. "Responsibility and accountability had nothing in common for them. Ideally, everyone was responsible for all members of the band, and eventually for all people, all things."

Yet Lee declares no "Dakota was accountable to any one or for any one. Was he his brother's keeper? Yes, in so far as he was responsible for his welfare; no, in so far as being accountable for him. He would never speak for him, decide for him, answer prying questions about him. And he was not accountable for himself, either. No one asked him questions about himself; he gave information or withheld it, as he own choice. When a man came back from a vision quest, when warriors returned, they were not questioned. People waited for them to report or not as they pleased."[25] Original, communal responsibility, greater than the individual, greater than original sin, but not accountability, animates the practice and consciousness of survivance, a sense of presence, a responsible presence of natural reason and resistance to absence and victimry.

Survivance is, of course, related to the word *survival*, and the definition varies by language. *The Robert and Collins dictionnaire français-anglais, anglais-français* defines *survivance* as a "relic, survival; cette coutume est une survivance de passé this custom is a survival *ou* relic from the past; survivance de l'âme survival of the soul (after death), afterlife." *The New Shorter Oxford English Dictionary* defines *survivance* as the "succession to an estate, office, etc., of a survivor nominated before the death of the previous holder; the right of such succession in case of survival." And the suffix *ance* is a quality of action, as in *survivance, relevance, assistance*. The *American Heritage Dictionary* defines *ance* as a "state or condition" or "action," as in *continuance*. Survivance, then, is the action, condition, quality, and sentiments of the verb *survive*, "to remain alive or in existence," to outlive, persevere with a suffix of *survivancy*.

The word *survivance* has been used more frequently in the past few years since the publication of *Manifest Manners: Narratives on Postindian Survivance* and *Fugitive Poses: Native American Indian Scenes of Absence and Presence*. "Survivance is an active sense of presence, the continuance of native stories, not a mere reaction, or a survivable name," I wrote in *Manifest Manners*. "Native survivance stories are renunciations of dominance, tragedy, and victimry. Survivance means the right of succession or reversion of an estate, and in that sense, the estate of native survivancy."[26]

The word *survivance* has been used in the titles of many essays and at least one recent book. Anne Ruggles Gere, for example, used the word in the title of her essay "An Art of 'Survivance,' Angel DeCora of Carlisle" *American Indian Quarterly*, 2004. Rauna Koukkanen, "'Survivance,' in Sami and First Nation Boarding School Narratives," *American Indian Quarterly*, 2003.

Survivance, the word, is more commonly used in the political context of francophone nationalism and the Québécois in Canada. Other instances of the word include "Cadjins et creoles en Louisiane. Histoire et survivance d'une francophonie" by Patrick Griolet, reviewed by Albert Valdman in *Modern Language Journal*, 1989.

Ernest Stromberg in the introduction to his edited essay collection *American Indian Rhetorics of Survivance* declares that "'survivance' is the easiest to explain," but he does not consider the compound history of the word. "While 'survival' conjures images of a stark minimalist clinging at the edge of existence, survivance goes beyond mere survival to acknowledge the dynamic and creative nature of Indigenous rhetoric."[27] Stromberg does not cite, consider, or even mention any other sources, expositions, or narratives on survivance. His rhetoric on survivance is derivative.

Clifford Geertz uses the word *survivance* in a structural sense of global differences, the "recurrence of familiar divisions, persisting arguments, standing threats," and notions of identity. Geertz writes in *Available Light* that a "scramble of differences in a field of connections presents us with a situation in which the frames of pride and those of hatred, culture fairs and ethnic cleansing, *survivance* and killing fields, sit side by side and pass with frightening ease from the one to the other."[28] Survivance, printed in italics in his personal essay, is understood only in the context of an extreme structural binary.

"Each human language maps the world differently," observes George Steiner in *After Babel: Aspects of Language and Translation*. He relates these "geographies of remembrance" to survivance. "Thus there is, at the level of human psychic resources and survivance, an immensely positive, 'Darwinian' logic in the otherwise battling and negative excess of languages spoken on the globe. When a language dies, a possible world dies with it. There is no survival of the fittest. Even where it is spoken by a handful, by the harried remnants of destroyed communities, a language contains within itself the boundless potential of discovery, or re-compositions of reality, of articulate dreams, which are known to us as myths, as poetry, as metaphysical conjecture and the discourse of law."[29]

Steiner considers the aesthetic experience of survivance in the responses of readers, listeners, and viewers to music, painting, and literary art. "Responding to the poem, to the piece of music, to the painting, we re-enact, within the limits of our own lesser creativity, the two defining motions of our existential presence in the world: that of the coming into being where nothing was, where nothing could have continued to be, and that of the enormity of death," he writes in *Real Presences*. "But, be it solely on a millennial scale, the latter absolute is attenuated by the potential of survivance in art. The lyric, the painting, the sonata endure beyond the life-span of the maker and our own."[30]

Jacques Derrida uses the word *survivance* once in a collection of essays and interviews, *Negotiations: Interventions and Interviews*. The interviewers for the monthly review *Passages* followed up a point about Karl Marx and Marxism and asked Derrida if he would be "surprised if there were some kind of return—in a different form and with different applications—of Communism, even if it is called something else? And if what brought it back were a need within society for the return of a little hope?"

Derrida responded that "this is what we were calling justice earlier. I do not believe there will be a return of Communism in the form of the Party (the party form is no doubt disappearing from political life in general, a 'survivance' that may of course turn out to have a long life) or in the return of everything that deterred us from a certain kind of Marxism and a certain kind of Communism." Derrida seems to use the word survivance here in the context of a relic from the past or in the sense of an afterlife.[31]

Derrida in *Archive Fever* comments on a new turn of forms in the recent interpretations of *Moses and Monotheism* by Sigmund Freud, the "phantoms out of the past" compared to the form of a "triumph of life." Derrida observes that the "afterlife [survivance] no longer means death and the return of the specter, but the surviving of an excess of life which resists annihilation."[32]

Derrida would surely have embraced a more expansive sense of the word *survivance*, as he has done with the word *différance*. Peggy Kamuf points out in *A Derrida Reader* that the suffix *ance* "calls up a middle voice between the active and passive voices. In this manner it can point to an operation that is not that of a subject or an object," a "certain nontransitivity."[33] Survivance, in this sense, could be the fourth person or voice in native stories.

Notes

1. Gerald Vizenor, *Fugitive Poses: Native American Scenes of Absence and Presence* (Lincoln: University of Nebraska Press, 1998), 167–68.

2. Theodora Kroeber, *Alfred Kroeber: A Personal Configuration* (Berkeley: University of California Press, 1970), 81.

3. Gerald Vizenor, *Manifest Manners: Narratives on Postindian Survivance* (Lincoln: University of Nebraska Press, 1999), 126–37.

4. Gerald Vizenor, "Mister Ishi: Analogies of Exile, Deliverance, and Liberty," in *Ishi in Three Centuries*, ed. Karl Kroeber and Clifton Kroeber (Lincoln: University of Nebraska Press, 2003), 363–72.

5. Daniel Littlefield, Jr., "Newspapers, Magazines, and Journals," in *Encyclopedia of North American Indians*, ed. Frederick Hoxie (New York: Houghton Mifflin, 1996), 328.

6. Gerald Vizenor, *The People Named the Chippewa* (Minneapolis: University of Minnesota Press, 1984), 78–94.

7. Antoine Compagnon, *Literature, Theory, and Common Sense* (Princeton NJ: Princeton University Press, 2004), 9, 12.

8. William Warren, *History of the Ojibway Nation* (Minneapolis: Ross and Haines, 1957), 34, 47, 88. Warren, the first Anishinaabe historian, was born May 27, 1825, at La Pointe, Madeline Island, Lake Superior. He was an interpreter, elected as a member of the Minnesota Territorial Legislature. He died on June 1, 1853. History of the Ojibway Nation was first published by the Minnesota Historical Society in 1885. The crane totem, *ajijaak*, is also known as the "echo makers."

9. Warren, *History of the Ojibway Nation*, 368, 373. See also Gerald Vizenor, *Interior Landscapes: Autobiographical Myths and Metaphors* (Minneapolis: University of Minnesota Press, 1990), 4–6. The Long Knife is a name for the Americans. The name is a translation of *gichimookomann* (*gichi*, big or great; *mookomaan*, knife), a descriptive metaphor of the first contact with white men who carried swords.

10. George Lakoff and Mark Johnson, *Metaphors We Live By* (Chicago: University of Chicago Press, 1980), 3, 193, 229, 235.

11. N. Scott Momaday, *The Names: A Memoir* (New York: Harper and Row, 1976), 3.

12. John Searle, "Metaphor," in *Metaphor and Thought*, ed. Andrew Ortony (New York: Cambridge University Press, 1979), 93, 105, 123. Searle observes, "The question, 'How do metaphors work?' is a bit like the question, 'How does one thing remind us of another thing?' There is no single answer to either question, though similarity obviously plays a major role in answering both. Two important differences between them are that metaphors are both restricted and systematic; restricted in the sense that no every way that one thing can remind us of something else will provide a basis for metaphor, and systematic in the sense that metaphors must be communicable from speaker to hearer in virtue of a shared system of principles."

13. Janet Martin Soskice, *Metaphor and Religious Language* (Oxford, UK: Clarendon, 1985), 15, 58–60.

14. James Welch, *Winter in the Blood* (New York: Harper and Row, 1974), 1–2.

15. Charles Woodward, *Ancestral Voices: Conversations with N. Scott Momaday* (Lincoln: University of Nebraska Press, 1989), 17.

16. N. Scott Momaday, *House Made of Dawn* (New York: Harper and Row, 1968), 31–33, 64.

17. Leslie Silko, *Ceremony* (New York: Viking Penguin, 1977), 132–33.

18. Louise Erdrich, *Tracks* (New York: Harper and Row, 1988), 10, 37, 54, 60, 89.

19. David Treuer, *The Hiawatha* (New York: Picador, 1999), 8.

20. Treuer, *Hiawatha*, 79.

21. Treuer, *Hiawatha*, 5.

22. Treuer, *Hiawatha*, 310.

23. Momaday, *House Made of Dawn*, 212.

24. David Treuer, *Native American Fiction: A User's Manual* (Saint Paul MN: Grey-wolf, 2006), 3–4.

25. Dorothy Lee, *Freedom and Culture* (1959; repr., Prospect Heights IL: Waveland, 1987), 60–61, 65.

26. Vizenor, *Manifest Manners*, vii.

27. Ernest Stromberg, ed., *American Indian Rhetorics and Survivance: Word Medicine, Word Magic* (Pittsburg: University of Pittsburgh Press, 2006), 1.

28. Clifford Geertz, *Available Light* (Princeton NJ: Princeton University Press, 2000), 250.

29. George Steiner, *After Babel: Aspects of Language and Translation*, 3rd ed. (1975; repr., New York: Oxford University Press, 1998), xiv. The word survivance was not used in the first edition.

30. George Steiner, *Real Presences* (Chicago: University of Chicago Press, 1989), 209–10. Steiner observes that it is the "aesthetic which, past any other mode accessible to us, is the felt configuration of a negation (however partial, however 'figurative' in the precise sense) of mortality. Imaging to ourselves the fictive situation or personae in the text, recomposing perceptually the objects or visage in the painting, making audition resonant to the music via an inner complementarity, at once conceptual and bodily, we remade the making."

31. Jacques Derrida, *Negotiations: Interventions and Interviews* (Stanford CA: Stanford University Press, 2002), 111–12.

32. Jacques Derrida, *Archive Fever: A Freudian Impression* (Chicago: University of Chicago Press, 1996), 60.

33. Peggy Kamuf, ed., *A Derrida Reader: Between the Blinds* (New York: Columbia University Press, 1991), 59.

2. WHY IT'S A GOOD THING
GERALD VIZENOR IS NOT AN INDIAN

KARL KROEBER

Survivance, originally a good English word roughly synonymous with *surviv-al*, became obsolete in the nineteenth century. Gerald Vizenor revived it a couple of decades ago, injecting into the old word red coloring and teasing connotations. He uses *survivance* to subordinate *survival*'s implications of es-cape from catastrophe and marginal preservation; *survivance* subtly reduc-es the power of the destroyer. He seizes on *survivance*'s older sense of *succes-sion*, orienting its connotations not toward loss but renewal and continuity into the future rather than memorializing the past. This refashioning of the commonest word in all discourse on the history of American native peo-ples — *survival* — epitomizes Vizenor's inadequately appreciated but most sig-nificant contribution to the remarkable resurgence of native cultures during the past half century.

All his work aims to repair a peculiarly vicious consequence of genocid-al attacks on natives of the Americas: an inducing in them of their destroy-ers' view that they are mere survivors. By accepting this white definition of themselves as victims, natives complete psychologically the not-quite-entire-ly successful physical genocide. Survivance rejects this imposed internalizing; it offers natives modes of personal and social renewal attained through wel-coming unpredictable cultural reorientations. These reorientations promise radically to transform current native life without requiring abandonment of the enduring value of their precontact cultural successes.

This is a difficult position for any native to assume because all American native communities were subjected to genocidal assaults that, unlike those visited on the Jews or the Armenians in the twentieth century, in a majority of cases completely succeeded. Whole peoples and cultures and languages were exterminated, and for the rest the destruction was very nearly total. Those who remained had almost to think of themselves as survivors and to feel a moral imperative to assert the special value of their traditional cultures that had been so savagely attacked. All the native writers responsible for the "Native American Literary Renaissance" of the past forty years have in one fashion or another celebrated traditional cultures even when demonstrating some native success in our postmodern world. The high quality of this American native writing has tempted many sympathetic whites (including me) to support this view, especially because there is so much in traditional native cultures to admire. But disturbing little sensations, like the faint sound of carpenter ants at work, have increasingly gnawed at the edges of my sympathy.

Look at the work of D'Arcy McNickle, for example. Nobody fought harder for the recovery of native rights on the ground of truly, not sentimentally, reconstructed native traditions. Yet both his novels, *The Surrounded*, a forerunner of the Native Literary Renaissance launched by Momaday, Welch, Silko, and Vizenor among others, and his posthumously published *Wind from an Enemy Sky*, which assisted materially in the early struggles of that renaissance, raise troubling questions about survival. The emotional pain evoked by the honesty of these fictions concentrates in McNickle's narrative imagining of the dubious viability of *any* traditional native culture: it is significant that *Wind From An Enemy Sky* tells of the destruction an *imaginary* tribe. Vizenor is the only contemporary native writer who has thought through the implications of McNickle's dark vision, which begins with facts of victimization and rises to question even the possibility of survival.

McNickle's novels, which develop perspectives present in several earlier native fictions, such as Yellow Bird's *Joaquin Murieta* and Pokagon's diversely ambiguous *Queen of the Woods*, come into my mind because I sense some loss of energy and innovativeness in most recent native fiction. And recent critical writing by natives has displayed equivalently disturbing symptoms of a new defensiveness, such as claims that only natives are capable of truly understanding American native literatures and that only they are capable of devising appropriate methods of critique for native writing. This tactic, which earlier native creative writers and critics alike avoided, has proved self-defeating with other "ethnic minorities," and for American natives it is particularly dangerous because they derive from so many spectacularly diverse cultures. The logic of the claim (leaving aside strains it puts on the science of genetics, as in the case of cross-bloods) would exclude, say, a Cherokee as an appropriate commentator on a Comanche novel, unless the claim is broadened to refer to some generic "Native Americanness." But this broadening in effect accepts the white generalizing classification of all American natives as "indians." Vizenor more adroitly than any other native writer has rejected and condemned that sneaky classification. He insists that there are now no real indians. Indians are counterfeit people, simulations created by whites to complete intellectually the genocidal terrorism they have practiced so enthusiastically since 1492.

It took me a long time to understand fully the hazards and significance of Vizenor's enterprise. Here I'll say little about its dangers because my immediate purpose is to increase appreciation for the value of Vizenor's insights, which make him one of the most important native writers of the late twentieth century. His persistent claim that indian is an unreal construct of white colonialism, a stereotype that blocks authentic native survivance, dramatizes the historical fact that for most natives alive today continuity with their traditional cultures has been irretrievably disrupted. The primary personal evidence of this disruption is language loss. Vizenor understands how terrible is the burden on a native who is aware of being linked through family to an ancient, impressive, and admirable culture and yet may have no means by herself directly to take advantage of that heritage. She must in all likelihood rely on the research of her culture's destroyers to recover knowledge of its finest capabilities and accomplishments.

Vizenor confronts this gruesome irony (lamentably not unusual in world history) by means of unusual linguistic inventiveness. His language is English—twisted against itself to accommodate alien imaginings of a native mind. His stories are founded on verbally turning upside down actual social circumstances of natives in the contemporary white world. His "characters," therefore, are less individualized personalities than personifications of specific native adaptive remodelings of white colonialism's mechanisms of oppression. Vizenor's fictional rhetoric is sustained by continuously inventive diversions, expansions, and ironizings of traditional English vocabulary. His wordplay is entirely different from twentieth-century Euro-American linguistic experimentation popularized by Joyce, the surrealists, and postmodern literary

critics. Vizenor, for example, seldom puns or deploys Derridean spelling dis-
tortions. He prefers a simultaneously subtler and more outrageous shape-
shifting of conventional connotations of familiar words or phrases. Sovereignty in his writing is suddenly no longer the attribute solely of great political
entities (such as the U.S.A.) but equally of a small band of enterprising and
comically idiosyncratic natives — or, even more startling, of a single visionary native. His nearest analogue as a verbal tactician among Western writers
is Rabelais, whose Abbey of Thélème, a "true" monastic order fostering individual liberation and sovereignty, seems a prototype of the social arrange-
ments favored by all of Vizenor's ebullient "postindians."

Vizenor demonstrates how an American native may reanimate his pre-in-
dian heritage by refashioning the English language that has been imposed on
him — to the advantage of both native and English. His fundamental rhetorical strategy is to seize key verbal sites of white racism and oppression and to
turn them into bases for reconstituting the colonizer's language and social
prejudices so as to empower new native imagining. Probably his most spec-
tacular exercise of this strategy is *The Heirs of Columbus* in which he imagines
Samuel Eliot Morrison's "Great Mariner," who inexplicably committed the
stupidest navigational error in human history, as excusable, and even lov-
able, because summoned by a native shaman "silent hand-talker" to become
for contemporary postindians a vehicle for their articulation of a New World
imaginative sovereignty.

Vizenor's fiction always focuses on discoveries, frequently of surprising aspects of familiar phenomena. His fictions characteristically take place in a future emerging out of the present in order to cast serious events into a comic mode that welcomes the unexpected at the expense of the supposedly
predetermined. He consistently refuses to be trapped in a tragic vision because that for American natives means taking upon themselves an enemy's
definition of them as victims imprisoned in an irrecoverable past. Through
playing tricks with his oppressor's language to upset his sociopolitical power structures, Vizenor reawakens the individual visionariness that he identifies as uniquely characterizing New World natives.

Often to their short-term political disadvantage, North American native
peoples have never wholeheartedly embraced any generic "nativeness," which
in fact, constitutes only a feeble sovereignty. They retain a healthy respect for

the particularity of each of their cultures, even at times putting contempt for traditional red enemies ahead of anger against invading whites. Although this particularizing seems disastrous for tribal peoples with small populations, especially as the number of native speakers diminishes, it is healthy because it provides the necessary specific focusing for processes of imaginative reconstitution that are the only secure foundation for native survivance. Against the colonialist simulations of indians (nowadays most dangerously sliding into ecological formulations, such as the indian as a repository of "natural wisdom," which does nothing but turn the noble savage green), natives must assert *counterimaginings* to create their authentic presence as what Vizenor calls postindians. Such imaginative self-recreation is accomplished primarily through storytelling because indian was and is a stereotypic substitute for actual natives created by white storytelling, often in the modes of scientific history and anthropology, like camp followers trailing behind military massacres and the deliberate bureaucratic obliteration of native languages. Vizenor refers to himself as a native storier and insists on the necessity of narrative chance for establishing postindian realities because, as Tom Stoppard put it, the "unpredictable and the predetermined unfold together to make everything the way it is." These words are from *Arcadia*, a very funny and a powerfully emotional drama, but one resolutely not tragic. Its final beautiful image of past and present dancing together both elegantly and awkwardly directs us to the comedic core of Vizenor's visionary conception of red survivance in white America.

As a native dispossessed of his language, Vizenor turns for recourse to the trickster, whom Vizenor perceives not as a characterological figure but what he calls a comic holotrope. This figure of speech can manifest the creative force within individuals that allows them to escape from crippling burdens of the traditions they depend upon for their sense of personal and communal identity. Vizenor dramatizes natives' skill in individual visionariness to resist becoming victims *even of their own culture*. A major function of the traditional native trickster, for example, is to help individuals to adapt constructively the tense interplay between traditional conventions and idiosyncratic personality to ever-changing circumstances, both natural and social. Vizenor's transformations are directed specifically against the manifest manners of white colonialism through trickster language brought up to date to exploit subversive possibilities in the self-contradictions of English. This trickster storytelling liberates natives from both their current victimization by white culture and the subtler self-limiting impulse to accept themselves as representative survivors of cultures dead just as Latin is a dead language. For these purposes the protean rhetorical figure of the trickster is perfect, not alone because it is not a major trope of elite Western fiction but also because the trickster's core narrative turns on some form of self-victimization, although always at the end escaped, recovered from, or made socially re-creative through some process of self-transformation, usually carrying with it with significant linguistic effects, often the bestowal of names.[1]

The native trickster has many names, and Vizenor commonly orients his stories by inventive namings. A person's name embodies what someone else chooses to call him and therefore primarily manifests the *namers'* attitudes and purposes. So far as the name is socially adopted, it becomes a means through which the individual may socialize himself. In traditional native cultures names commonly identified an individual's role in tribal history. In native cultures an individual's activities frequently brought about changes in his name that reflected changes in his social circumstances. Vizenor's survivance narratives appropriately reverse this process: a name launches the emergence of a new personality or an innovative social or political function. The contemporary storier creates a new nativeness expressing an imaginative reformulation of a specific cultural past by nativizing a present-day social situation.

Vizenor titled an early collection of essays *The Everlasting Sky: New Voices from the People Named the Chippewa*. Chippewa was a name applied by whites to Vizenor's people who named themselves Anishinaabe. The reality of his people's self-identification he recovers from the obscuring simulation of Chippewa by articulating beneath the "Everlasting Sky" Anishinaabe voices that are new. "New" here translates the traditional Anishinaabe *oski*, meaning "for the first time." So contemporary voices and voices from the distant past become equally innovative for white readers hearing them both for the first time. Vizenor's title thus turns to new purposes the positive force of King Arthur's curious antiepitaph, "The Once and Future King." And so far as Vizenor's title is recognized as not only recalling a cherished past but also as carrying the promise of a vital future (necessarily still unimagined and surprising), it implies the healing of wounds and the spreading out of laughter and good cheer, again recalling Rabelais's liberative, life-renewing purposes.

Vizenor writes to heal. He encourages recognition that authentic sovereignty depends on a healthiness free from the twentieth century's twinned diseases of dominance and victimry. He is no casual optimist, but he believes that, if American natives can free themselves from a simulated existence as indians, stop defining, and even celebrating, themselves as survivors, they can attain a psychological and communal sovereignty that will benefit not only themselves but also whites. For although Vizenor writes from a native position, he always addresses white Americans as directly as natives, and although he never minimizes divisive difficulties nor passes over the enduring hurtfulness of colonialist injustices, his manner is persistently comedic, his tone hopeful, his target curing wounds, not exacerbating animosities. He has no concern with another world, only with the immediate, practical future of this one. His imagining, although drawing skillfully and subtly upon ancient oral tradition, is expressed in admirable prose for an audience of postmodern readers. His work exemplifies the mindset essential to survivance. His books transpose into contemporary circumstances the renewing purpose animating all major traditional Native American religious ceremonies. These ceremonies culminate in joyousness — the person, the people, the earth that is their home restored together so as to carry the past forward into an as-yet-undetermined future with a vigorous confidence — usually expressed by earth-pounding dancing to the ceaseless beat of blood-enlivening drums.

Given this commitment, it is not surprising that Vizenor has written several times with perception and humor of Ishi, although never as a purely historical figure, Vizenor always imagining Ishi alive and well and very much in control of his own life. Vizenor's Ishi quietly yet mischievously upsets white professionals by turning their solemnities into vital absurdities —, even while he engages their admiration and their affections.

The history of Ishi's life from which Vizenor's imagining takes off pivots on the early morning of August 29, 1911, when workers coming to a slaughterhouse near Oroville, California, found an emaciated native crouching against the slaughterhouse fence. They called the sheriff, who for the starving man's protection, housed him in the country jail, where a variety of local natives tried unsuccessfully to communicate with him in their indigenous languages. The sheriff contacted Alfred Kroeber, senior professor of anthropology at the

University of California, who sent his colleague Thomas Waterman to Oroville. There Waterman succeeded in communicating with the native through
the use of the Yana language, recognizing that the latter was a member of
the southernmost Yana group, the Yahi, who were thought to have been exterminated by white settlers in 1870.

After the gold rush in the early 1850s, increasing numbers of whites established farms and ranches by seizing the territory of several northern California tribal peoples near Mt. Lassen, displacing, killing, and enslaving the natives. Only the Yahi actively fought back, although they had no weapons but
their light hunting bows; they appeared to have been wiped out by a series
of carefully planned massacres of Yahi men, women, and children in 1870. But
a small group of about forty Yahi in fact escaped and went into hiding in the
rough back country of the Sierras. For forty years this little group with ever-
dwindling numbers carried on their centuries-old way of life in concealment
from the knowledge of any whites. The last of the group, who had lived this
hidden life since early boyhood, was the man found in Oroville

Alfred Kroeber gained permission from the Bureau of Indian Affairs in Washington DC to have this man, by journalists turned into a national celebrity as
"The Last Wild Indian in America," brought by train to San Francisco. There,
he was housed in the Phoebe Apperson Hearst Museum, of which Kroeber was
director and given a salaried position, with free access to the facilities of the
University Hospital next door. There the man lived, worked, traveled about,
and made friends in San Francisco and the Bay area until his death from tu-
berculosis in 1916. At the museum he was given a name by Kroeber (not only
to satisfy demands of newspapermen but also so he could put the Yahi on the
university payroll) since like many American natives he would not make public his given tribal name. The name Kroeber chose was Ishi, meaning "man" in
the Yahi language, a choice Ishi cheerfully accepted and even learned to write
(for payroll purposes). For some months Ishi aroused tremendous popular
interest, with newspapers printing many stories about the "Stone Age" native's experiences in the twentieth-century world and with crowds of people
coming to the museum to see him wearing Western dress and for whom he
frequently demonstrated some of his native skills such as arrow-point and
bow making and use of the fire drill.[2]

Ishi certainly seems a survivor and a victim if ever there was one. Yet Ishi from the first quietly but adamantly refused to play the role of victim. He practiced survivance. He cherished his native culture, its beliefs, its customs, and its stories, historical and imaginative, sacred and entertaining. He was always eager to tell the anthropologists about traditional Yahi life, to sing Yahi songs, tell Yahi stories, although he would never speak about his personal experiences during the forty years of concealment. His enthusiasm as an expositor of Yahi culture is revealed by his behavior shortly after his arrival in San Francisco. On the afternoon of September 6 he started talking into a phonograph, telling a long story about Wood Duck that he finished the morning of the next day. This recording required fifty-one wax cylinders and was then the longest oral narrative ever phonographically recorded. In the next two weeks he recorded songs and stories on another sixty-five cylinders.

Although in later years Ishi told and recorded more, his enthusiastic readiness for these first performances reveals his astonishing capacity to cope with his daunting circumstances. He had, after all, just entered an utterly strange world of white people whom he had known only from a distance as cruel and merciless enemies. Their world was full of terrifying strangenesses: newspapers, cameras, electricity, automobiles, tall buildings, cable cars, and all the technological mechanisms of twentieth-century culture, along with what must have been to him most oppressive, masses of people. Ishi had lived almost his entire life in natural surroundings in the company of no more than two score low-voiced, exquisitely polite people. San Francisco in 1911 was a raucous, booming metropolis of nearly half a million go-getters. Yet, despite his profound and unwavering commitment to all the traditions of the Yahi, Ishi plunged into this utterly alien life with both enthusiasm and aplomb.

Thousands of people wanted to hear about Ishi and if possible to see him. When on the Friday of his first week in San Francisco he was taken to a vaudeville show, he became the center of attention, for performers as well as audience. Yet he conducted himself in what must have been for him an unbelievably weird situation with genial dignity. On Sunday afternoons at the museum, which had now become his home, people flocked to see him and to admire his skills, such as flaking arrow points. He would seem trapped in the position of a living exhibit. However, Ishi in his courteously restrained manner subverted his white-prescribed role: for instance, he would act as a generous host, presenting a finished arrow point as a gift to one of the onlookers. It was an act of noblesse oblige. During his first months at the museum the university officials and the Bureau of Indian Affairs debated how Ishi could best be provided for in the future, but Ishi by unobtrusively establishing himself both as useful and at home in the museum while making friends with the entire staff effectively settled the issue for his "protectors." The life that he led in San Francisco to a remarkable degree he determined for himself.

He never ceased to cherish and celebrate his traditional Yahi culture. He thought and behaved always in accordance with its beliefs and social manners. And he loved nothing so much as to talk about that life. The interest of the anthropologists, resident and visiting, in his Yahi language, of which he was the last speaker, seems to have been of especial importance to him. That he never became really fluent in English appears in part to have been his deliberate choice. He made the linguists come to his language — it was their job to figure out the proper English equivalents. While they labored to translate, he savored the beloved sounds that rearticulated the moral and imaginative achievements of his Yahi heritage.[3]

Yet Ishi learned enough English not merely to travel around the city and East Bay area, making use of streetcars, cable cars, and ferries, but he also learned enough of the language to make many white friends, children as well as adults. One can only faintly imagine Ishi's moments of loneliness, what must have been dark plunges back into remembrance of his terrible losses. But he never let these thoughts dominate him. With unfailing curiosity he explored the strange life of the city, adapting it to his preferences, enjoying things and people in his own way and thereby becoming a person others liked for himself, not for his celebrity status. He remained, of course, the only Yahi in the world, but the reports of those who came to know him are unanimous in speaking of him as never being self-pitying and never seeming in the least need of pity. All of the many who knew him personally speak of him as reserved but vividly responsive, a dignified but friendly man with an innate considerateness which made him a valued companion.[4]

It is significant, however, that not a few people today, including some contemporary anthropologists who have put themselves forward as champions of indians, would imprison Ishi within the stereotypical role of victimized survivor. In editing the book *Ishi in Three Centuries*, my brother and I discovered with surprise that these professionals wanted to learn nothing about Ishi's

life in San Francisco except what might be interpreted as evidence of his suffering, debasement, and alienation. They seemed offended by the accumulating evidence that fascinated us of the surprising diversity and complexity of Ishi's social experiences in twentieth-century San Francisco. To these
academics I owe a sharpened awareness of the difference between survivance and survival.

But the importance of Ishi's practice of survivance goes beyond revelations
of current academic ethnic profiling as it opens profound questions about
relationships between individuality and culture. Ishi displays how intensity of
commitment to one's primary culture may enable, rather than disable, an individual's positive engagement with another, even alien, culture. His Yahi heritage strengthened and refined personal qualities that allowed Ishi to adapt
swiftly and productively to situations that were completely foreign to Yahi
traditions. It is this paradoxical power of a culture to equip an individual to
go beyond its limits that Vizenor identifies as the root source of survivance.

This power is perhaps most vividly manifested in oral cultures, such as all
those native to North America. Oral cultures are perpetually being recon-
stituted through narrative discourse because they exist as cultures primarily only as individuals speak. There are relatively few physical embodiments
but multitudes of verbal enactments of an oral culture, in which linguistic
and cultural systems are almost totally integrated. Core beliefs and commit-
ments are dynamically renewed chiefly through verbal performances, that is,
the imaginative sharing of traditions by storytelling. The core is thus constantly being remade, made differently, as traditional words are rearticulated and heard now in a configuration of circumstances that had never previ-
ously existed.

Speech always requires an individual speaker, so uniqueness is built deeply
into such cultures. This characteristic is why Vizenor observes that conventional descriptions of native cultures too often exaggerate their communal
character. His point is that the communal strength of native societies concentrates on empowering individuals. This apparent paradox in fact makes possible survivance as something more "natural" to a native than mere survival.

Vizenor recognizes, as too few professional students of culture do, that all
tradition, however valuable, also exerts a dangerous repressive force. That
force was often resisted by American natives, who successfully sustained their

cultures through the exercise of a remarkable adaptability, a readiness to change exemplified by woodlands tribal peoples taking advantage of the introduction of horses to become within a couple of generations buffalo hunters on the open prairies. Equally important, as Vizenor repeatedly emphasizes, was the native high valuation of individually experienced dreams, visions, and shamanistic trances. These last, for example, are built on an individual psychically breaking away from the community and venturing beyond ordinary parameters of behavior so that a shaman's continuous and profoundest risk is being unable to return to ordinary life. This experience illustrates that the vital center of the native community is always the power of individuals, what Vizenor aptly calls a "visionary sovereignty."

This sovereignty helps to explain the extraordinary fecundity of trickster stories throughout native societies. Trickster stories, with which Vizenor has consistently associated his own art, affirm a culture by bringing to bear against one or more of its accepted traditions a bizarrely deviant individual act that compels intensified evaluations of conventionalized practices and beliefs. This enhanced awareness (which Vizenor perceives as provoked by a culture's capacity to tease, a quality too little appreciated by ethnologists) revitalizes the potentially inert oppressiveness of conventions through either modification or reaffirmation, perhaps most often both together. This is why the trickster is always, whether culture-creator or culture-contestor, distinctively individualized, distinguishing himself either as creator or contestor from identification with what he makes or remakes, what he challenges or invents. The trickster therefore to many ethnologists has appeared puzzling because he is simultaneously both central and marginal to his culture. And this is why the trickster is never simply a "character" but a figure of speech, a deliberate anomaly of language. The trickster is an anomaly that gives vitality to a traditional, inherited system of language, sustaining the system by exercising its capacity for constructively challenging and revising itself. The trickster thus is a function of language's self-reconstructive power that can only be realized through speech of an individual. The trickster is a deliberate, conscious exploitation of the productive tension between linguistic system and speech act in which inheres the potent livingness of every language to self-transform so as to accommodate to changing natural or social circumstances.

Anthropology and cultural history could benefit significantly from attending more closely to Vizenor's identifying visionary and trickster stories as crucial means for survivance for postindians, natives who reject the false romance of victimry, with its implicit evocation of the sterile oppositions of savagery and civilization. It is especially worth noticing that Vizenor's approach allows him, uniquely among contemporary native writers, to produce predominantly comedic works. This practice situates him squarely in the principal mode of traditional American native storytelling, a huge proportion of which was ironically humorous in character and nearly all of which in one fashion or another aimed to heal individual and community. Tragedy is not the primary mode of native North American storytelling and may indeed be a peculiarly specialized and rare feature of but a few societies.

Human culture is a proactively adaptive developmental power that has enabled our species to succeed spectacularly in evolutionary competition. Culture is literally life enhancing for human beings. Still it can be most effective only if it retains its liberating qualities, facilitating our capacity to change ourselves as well as to change our environment. And among the many kinds of social creatures that have inhabited and do inhabit the earth, only human societies succeed by *nurturing* individuality in all its constituent members. This behavior is why healthy societies are full of laughter — for a society of individuals is a wonderful comic paradox. Only humans are capable of communal laughter, the sharing of intense subjective pleasure in perceiving our own dangerous foolishness, and it is a perception that produces frequently wiser, more life-enhancing thinking and behavior. Because Vizenor's survivance offers us this perspective, it appears a conception of at least as much value to later immigrants to the New World as to the earlier ones whom we (and they) think of as "natives" — a term, however, superior to *indians*. The latter is a term that is ultimately infected with its own fascinating inauthenticities and that, if we are lucky, may someday call forth a Postvizenorian commentator.

Notes

1. Tricksterism also enables Vizenor to participate, even while inverting a primary form of postmodern literature, in the first-person narrative, most conspicuous in the now wildly popular falsified (not merely fictional) memoir. Vizenor recognizes (as ethnologists and folklorists have generally failed to do) that traditional trickster narratives are never in the first-person form because they manifest the dependence of the native community on *visionary* individuality, which is a unique realization

of communal desires and ideals.

2. Theodora Kroeber's *Ishi in Two Worlds* (1961; repr., Berkeley: University of California Press, 2005) is the fundamental account of Ishi's life and has been the starting point for all subsequent discussions of Ishi's experience and its significance, along with the book from the same press she later edited with Robert Heizer, *Ishi the Last Yahi: A Documentary History* (Berkeley: University of California Press, 1979).

3. Many of the contrasting parallels between Ishi's story and Primo Levi's deeply moving account of his year in Auschwitz brilliantly illuminates the differences between survival and survivance. An instance is Levi's heart-rending account of his desperate need to remember and translate for a French prisoner in the camp portions of *The Divine Comedy*. See Primo Levi, "The Canto of Ulysses," in *Survival in Auschwitz*, trans. Stuart Wolf (New York: Simon and Schuster, 1990), 109–116. The revealing contrast with Ishi is how Dante's poem, although profoundly meaningful to Levi, as a printed artifact of another man's imagining embodies the subtle separation of Western individuals from their technological culture. Ishi's retelling of oral stories, communally created and preserved through individual performances, literally reenacted his culture. There was no way that Ishi's memory could fail because it was his culture.

4. Ishi's warm friendships with several children are of special interest. For example, see the memoir of Fred Zumwalt Jr. in *Ishi in Three Centuries*, ed. Karl Kroeber and Clifton Kroeber (Lincoln: University of Nebraska Press, 2003), 1–12. This volume offers a broad spectrum of commentary on Ishi's life by both whites and Native Americans and includes scientific and historical information about him and Native Californians that has emerged since the original publication of *Ishi in Two Worlds*. It also offers translations and analyses of stories recorded by Ishi. Richard Burrill's *Ishi in His Second World: The Untold Story of Ishi in the Greater San Francisco Bay, September 4–December 31, 1911* (Susanville CA: Anthro Company, 2006) is built around the gathering of a number of recollections of Ishi by San Franciscans who personally knew him.

3. NATIVE SURVIVANCE IN THE AMERICAS

Resistance and Remembrance in
Narratives by Asturias, Tapahonso, and Vizenor

HELMBRECHT BREINIG

Survivance lies in the word. It is language; it is the verbal and imaginary construction of an adequate reality that makes survivance more than physical survival. *Webster's Third International Dictionary* defines the term as meaning (1)"survival" and (2)"the right of succession (as to an office or estate) of a survivor nominated before the death of the incumbent or holder." But in Gerald Vizenor's *Fugitive Poses* the term carries new connotations: "Survivance, in the sense of native survivance, is more than survival, more than endurance or mere response; the stories of survivance are an active presence."[1] Referring to Derrida's theory of presence, Vizenor speaks of Native oral stories as "creations of fugitive motion, a sense of presence that must be heard, and these oral creations are evermore; otherwise, our presence and restitution of sound and seasons would be traced to the sinecures of literature."[2] In written literature, on the other hand, "the trace of that native presence is an absence, a causal notion or representation in the silence and distance of pictures and print."[3] However, as for Derrida presence and absence are inevitably linked, and this linkage applies to survivance as well. Its meaning can never be simply present, and its place in the chain of signifiers makes it carry echoes of older and other connotations.

Thus in French the term *survivance* means "relic" or "leftover." And, sure enough, it can also refer to cultural survival, as when Kwame Anthony Appiah employs it with reference to the struggle of the Québécois for cultural survival. Important for him is not "the maintenance of a francophone ethnic identity — not *survivance* — but equality of citizenship in a francophone state."[4] If for Vizenor survivance should gain more weight than Appiah accords a mere "ethnic identity," if it is to be more than *Survival This Way*, to quote the title of Joseph Bruchac's collection of interviews with American Indian poets, then there must be traces of "the right to succession," as in "the native stories of survivance are successive and natural estates."[5] And when Vizenor continues that "survivance is an active repudiation of dominance, tragedy, and victimry," we are made to wonder what that third syllable, "ance," may evoke, if not endurance.[6] I take it that *remembrance* and *resistance* are part of that active presence in life and in literature.

Survivance as Violent Resistance: Asturias
Survivance lies in the word, and as Native survivance it should be studied not only in the United States and Canada but also as it can be achieved by that majority of the indigenous population of the Americas living south of the U.S. border. The conflicts there may be even more drastic than in the north. With thousands of victims even in recent years, resistance may take forms that have been replaced elsewhere by tribal schools, litigation, and casinos.

Let us look at a radical example in which survivance as resistance may even connote death, nay, suicide killing. In Miguel Ángel Asturias's story "¡Americanos Todos!" (We are all Americans!), the Guatemaltecan tour guide Emilio Croner Jaramillo, called Milocho, is immensely popular among American tourists. He has acquired U.S. citizenship and, after a stormy affair with the blonde Californian beauty Alarica Powell, is dreaming of a future life with her in the United States. However, the CIA-sponsored invasion of Guatemala by foreign mercenaries in the 1954 coup that toppled the democratically elected Arbenz government prevents his return from the coast to Guatemala City. He witnesses the bombing of the indio and mestizo villages near the coast by American airplanes whose national identification symbols had been removed and the massacre of the Indian population of whole villages suspected of sympathizing with the "Communists." Although no Mayan himself but a light-skinned mestizo, he identifies with the poor population of his native country and particularly the indios who are once again being robbed of life, property, and cultural identity.

Sometime later, Milocho is once again guiding American tourists through the Guatemaltecan highland. Alarica has rejoined him, and their plans for a

touring business connecting the American East and West coasts have ma-
tured. But when she teases him about the passivity of even the majestic volcanoes that in the colonial past destroyed the cities of the conquistadors, his
memories of the massacred Indians and his feelings of guilt for having done
nothing to defend his country, nay, for being "an American" himself rise up,
and he drives the bus full of gringos into a deep gorge, killing all aboard. In
his death plunge he shouts the ironic leitmotif phrase of the story, "We are
all Americans!" — a phrase which before had been uttered even by the Guatemaltecan military officers, who in the service of the United Fruit Company
and the CIA, had led the coup against their own government.

Is Milocho, the suicide killer, then a case of Native survivance? Yes, he is
when we see his growing awareness of the ironies of his own situation and his
growing engagement with the political and social conditions of his country,
past and present, as part of a resistance that is not limited to acts of physical revenge but entails a mental and emotional identification with those who
have been victimized for centuries and, what is more, an imaginary transcendence of the state of helplessness. The series of surreal images rushing through
Milocho's mind reveals him as capable of transforming reality in line with traditional Mayan beliefs concerning the creative power of the word without literally following Mayan symbology. He thus becomes a representative of the
author who in his rage and frustration fictionalized the events of the coup in
his collection of eight stories, *Week-end en Guatemala* (1956). These stories
form a series comprising "¡Americanos Todos!" and culminating in an imaginary overthrow of the new rulers by the masked masses during the native
feast of Torotumbo. That this event never took place in reality and that, indeed, it took decades of guerilla resistance against a brutal military dictator-
ship until some kind of political compromise could be reached — a first level
of national reconciliation including elements of a recognition of indigenous
rights — does not diminish the function of these texts in demonstrating how
the imagination can overcome victimization.

Week-end en Guatemala, like many of the works of the Nobel laureate Asturias, is available in many languages but, to my knowledge, not in English.
Survivance can be made difficult by breakdowns in intercultural communication, which in turn may perhaps be traced back to ideological constraints.
The situation of the indigenous population of Guatemala became known to

many only when the Quiché Rigoberta Menchú won the Nobel peace prize in 1992, although possibly even before with the publication of her autobiographical and testimonial book *I, Rigoberta Menchú: An Indian Woman in Guatemala* (1983). This book is one of the texts singled out by Doris Sommer in her discussion of the "resistant text." Menchú's testimonial ends with, "I continue to hide what I think no one else knows. Not even an anthropologist, nor any intellectual, no matter how many books he may have read, can know all our secrets."[7] Menchú's aggressive rejection of the reader makes sense because, in order to reach the outside world, she has to lower her guard, to write in Spanish rather than Quiché or some other Mayan dialect, and for that matter has to write rather than speak. Thus, just as it is important that she should make us aware of the desperate plight of the indigenous population of her country, just so is it important that she should still try to shield her culture from the acquisitive glance of the outsider. "The less apprehension in/by Spanish, the better; it is the language that the enemy uses to conquer differences. For an Indian, to learn Spanish can amount to passing over to the other side, to the Ladinos, which simply means 'Latin' or Spanish speakers. One paradox that Rigoberta has to negotiate in her politics of cultural preservation is the possibility of becoming the enemy because she needs Spanish as the lingua franca in a country of twenty-two language groups. . . . And those of us who do read her are either intellectually or ethically unfit to know secrets."[8]

Thus survivance in this context depends on speaking and on withholding speech, on the participation in two apparently incompatible and incommensurate systems of communication. Asturias's Milocho realizes that he has already done what Menchú is trying to avoid: he has become the enemy. None of the tourists takes his innuendoes about the power of the mythic volcanoes seriously. The rejection of the intruders can therefore function only by radical negation of any kind of mediation and cultural translation. When the tourists finally confront the Other, it is the abyss that is about to kill them. By the same act Milocho kills the enemy in himself.

Asturias's own position in this quandary is difficult to identify. His essentialist and often racist 1923 university thesis, "El problema social del indio," recommended an influx of European blood in order to move the indigenous population out of its supposed stasis. Under the impact of his subsequent anthropological studies in Paris, he turned into an ardent admirer of the Maya tradition and pointed out his Indian roots on his mother's side. His claim of a Mayan identity has been accepted by some and declared a myth by others.[9] However, the question of blood quantum as a measure of Native identity may be even more problematic in Latin America than in the United States and Canada. In a country like Guatemala even the mestizo (Ladino) part of the population will have more indigenous ancestors than many or even most Native Americans and First Nations persons can lay claim to.

The "pure" *indígenas* make up between 44 and 60 percent of the thirteen million Guatemaltecans, language being the main dividing criterion, with even bilingual Native people often being counted among the Ladinos. In a country where large-scale massacres of the Native population took place even in the last part of the twentieth century, the elements of survivance may be different from those shaping the lives of the northern neighbors. Survival in terms of life, property, language, and traditional farming culture may require more drastic divisions between "friend" and "foe." And yet, by identifying with the indigenous population and by taking responsibility for its survival, Asturias fulfills exactly the central criterion for a Native identity named by Gerald Vizenor: "Now, my view is this: that identity is a choice, but identity is a responsibility. And it's not who people are by their fractions or their quantum; it's who people are by their responsibility with peers and families and communities."[10]

Thus as an Indian by choice Asturias will have to pursue a route different from the one chosen by Menchú. As a contribution to Native survivance, he cannot write a resistant text. Instead, in his best work such as *Hombres de maíz* (Men of Maize) (1949), he develops a new form of literature, a literature of high complexity achieved by what has come to be called "magic realism," a literature intended to make Western readers aware of the strange world of the Maya.

Hombres de maíz deals with the conflict between the "Men of Maize," the subsistence-farming, traditionally living Maya, and the *maiceros*, slash-burning Ladino tenant farmers growing corn for their own and especially the land-owners' profit. It is vaguely set in the early decades of the twentieth century, but the struggle of resistance depicted here has continued to the present day. However, the novel does not really try to make us familiar with this strange world.

In this case one can adapt Sommer's argument that "unlike elitist and esoteric forms of exclusion, which address a limited circle of initiated ideal readers, no initiation is possible into a resistant text."[11] While initiation into the
complexities of this elitist text is possible for a proper readership, this step
does not take us into the secrets of tribal culture and beliefs. On the one
hand, Asturias, in spite of his extensive Mayan studies, could hardly claim to
be more than an outsider there. On the other hand, I think that he wanted
the Other to appear in its radical strangeness. Thus the numerous intertex-
tual references to the *Popol Vuh* and other traditional Mayan texts flesh out
the story with cultural material but are not meant to be a repository of anthropological information in a way that would make the person best versed
in Mayan lore the ideal reader. Sitler is right in arguing that "*Hombres de maíz*
is a novel filled with acts of extreme violence and the most notable of the violent activities in the work are performed by its Maya characters."[12] But this
violence need not be read as an indication of Asturias's continuing racism.
Rather, this novel, which more than any of his others enhanced his literary
reputation, bridges the gap between the cultures not by way of creating understanding but of acceptance. As Ronald Daus has pointed out correctly,
Asturias's magic realism does not try to reproduce the workings of "the native mind" and its magic world view (a world view the author avowedly did
not share) but instead evokes it by inventing what in his eyes might best
symbolize this type of thinking, notably by a dazzling display of (surrealism-
schooled) images and stylistic devices: "Gran amarilla se puso la tarde. El cer-
ro de los sordos cortaba los nubarrones que pronto quemaría la tempestad
como si fuera polvo de olote. Llanto de espinas en los cactos. Pericas gemi-
doras en los barrancos. ¡Ay, si caen en la trampa los conejos amarillos! ¡Ay,
si la flor del chilindrón, color de estrella en el día, no borra con su perfume el
olor del Gaspar, la huella de sus dientes en las frutas, la huella de sus pies en
los caminos, sólo conocida de los conejos amarillos!"[13]

The Yellow Rabbits of maize are here put into the context of an almost over-
rich nature imagery. In the scene from which the passage is taken, the Native
leader Gaspar Ilóm is about to be poisoned by an emissary of his opponent,
the army colonel. But in this invocation of tutelary spirits that I have quoted, who speaks or thinks these warnings and wishes? Is it the Mayan gods
and spirits? The shamans fighting on Gaspar's side? The narrative voice of

the novel and hence, in a sense, the author? It is just as impossible to unravel the connotative wealth of the language as to locate the point of view. Survivance by the word in this novel lies not so much in the wishful thinking of the ending in which the natural order is restored — contrary to historical probability — but in the surplus of the imagination displayed in the text. While no direct intercultural translation from the indigenous to the dominant society is possible, Asturias seems to believe in a kind of transfer by evocation. As it were, the spirit of the Native culture is meant to survive in a modern (and modernist) cultural context as part of a *mestizaje* containing an (undefined) space even for the alien traditions of the *indígenas*. Survivance is here a result of hybridity, with survivance by resistance remaining a fiction, but a fiction that can help to create a greater, transcultural awareness.

Survivance as Remembrance: Tapahonso

Survivance as resistance entails survivance as remembrance. Both texts by Asturias discussed here are in a sense historical fictions, but only in a limited sense. *Week-end en Guatemala* is about very recent history and tells the events mainly from the perspective of those victimized, albeit along with some ironic demonstrations of the motivation of the aggressors and with a projection into an imaginary future. *Hombres de maíz*, though very vaguely referring to events in the early twentieth century, is placed in an almost mythic, dreamlike present of no time and all time, a cyclic time frame clearly referring to tribal views. In contrast, the North American texts I want to study now directly take issue with the dominant ways of writing history. Of course, minority writers are not alone in this project.

Poststructural theory has done much to question totalizing notions of history and thus helped to destroy the claim to superior truth of historical narratives in Western societies. Indeed, as Michel de Certeau ironically puts it, "History is probably our myth."[14] Hayden White's studies in the constructedness and literariness of historiography have made the "fictionality of history" a common concept. But it is the study of colonialism in which the political implications of "History" have become most obvious. As Robert Young's *White Mythologies* amply demonstrates, Derrida's deferral of meaning, Foucault's studies of repressed alterity, and other approaches have not only dismantled the claims of (post-)Hegelian history but thereby also facilitated the recognition of the complementarity of history and colonialism.

Current postcolonial theory locates the subversive potential of the Other in the hybridity of both the metropolis and the periphery, with Third World and migration models forming the basis for this type of thinking. The case of Native American literature is related but also different. To see it as just another example of the *Empire Writes Back* paradigm is to ignore the fact that here the empire is located both within the societies of the Americas and within the individual writer. Anishinaabe critic Kimberly M. Blaeser takes up Vine Deloria's characterization of Native American literature "as presenting a 'reflective statement of what it means and has meant to live in a present which is continually overwhelmed by the fantasies of others of the meaning of past events.' . . . Indeed, any discussion of literary representation of history in the Americas finds it[s] center in the notion of possession, not merely physical possession of the land and its resources, but ideological possession, because to a large degree the two have gone hand in hand: those who control the land, have controlled the story (the his-story) of the land and its people."[15]

The relationship between the traditional indigenous communities in Guatemala and the dominant society may still be characterized by a model of largely unmitigated binary difference, with *mestizaje* mostly being seen as opposed to, rather than connected with, the Native population. A writer like Asturias embodies the elite with only a limited degree of actual hybridity in his self-construction. The situation in North America is often significantly different from that in Guatemala but not harmonious either. Contemporary Native American and First Nations literature reveals that David Hollinger's concept of postethnicity as the freedom of the individual to choose between a variety of ethnocultural affiliations may be too optimistic even in the United States and therefore less adequate than Vizenor's own notion of the *postindian* that both acknowledges the existence and the inadequacies of the Columbian "simulation" *indian*.[16] The simultaneity of absences and presences in the context of interethnic relations and discourses and the omnipresent practice of binary differentiation in spite of its shortcomings result in a network of tensions. They belong to the sphere of what I have called *transdifference*, the simultaneous relevance of conflicting properties or affiliations. I quote from a recent paper that explains the concept at length, including its relevance to intercultural studies:

> The term transdifference *refers to phenomena of a co-presence of*

different or even oppositional properties, affiliations or elements of semantic and epistemological meaning construction, where this co-presence is regarded or experienced as cognitively or affectively dissonant, full of tension, and undissolvable. Phenomena of transdifference, for instance socio-cultural affiliations, personality components or linguistic and other symbolic predications, are encountered by individuals and groups and negotiated in their respective symbolic order. As a descriptive term transdifference allows the presentation and analysis of such phenomena in the context of the production of meaning that transcend the range of models of binary difference. It is not to be confused with de-differentiation (as in concepts of synthesis, syncretism, transculturation) or with a temporalized deferral of difference (différance).[17]

Neither de-differentiation as aimed at by Asturias nor radical difference as postulated by Menchú can be called adequate intercultural models in North America. Navajo writer Luci Tapahonso is a case in point for the widespread existence of transdifferent positionalities. Although she has grown up in a traditional community and although Navajo is her first language, she is part of the U.S. cultural elite as well. Her short text "In 1864" approaches the history of the traumatic defeat of the Navajos by the U.S. cavalry and their subsequent forced Long Walk to a kind of concentration camp at Bosque Redondo in the form of storytelling as an oral and communal procedure. "In 1864" is a narrative poem, or a poeticized story, about a car trip to the Bosque Redondo area and the stories and reminiscences told on the way; the free poetic form successfully serves the purpose of suggesting the rhythm and rhetoric of oral narration. The family in the car—a very common storytelling situation among the Navajos today—becomes a synecdoche for the tribal community moving both into the future and returning to the scene of past trials. The opening lines establish the positive value system against which to judge the experience of the Long Walk and the camp life at Bosque Redondo:

While the younger daughter slept, she dreamt of mountains,
the wide blue sky above, and friends laughing.[18]

The first storyteller is the poem's speaker. She remembers the experience of a Navajo electrician who worked in that area and who at night heard the voices of the spirits of those held captive there in the 1860s. He sang and prayed for them but found himself unable to stay on:

> The place contained the pain and cries of his relatives,
> the confused and battered spirits of his own existence.[19]

The second story is the remembrance of the great-grandmother, a survivor of the Long Walk, as told by an aunt. In this story we get a summary of the events: the rounding up of the people, the killing of the flocks, the fear of the soldiers, and the people killed on the way. The poet consoles her crying elder daughter by reminding her that at Bosque Redondo the Navajos also learned some cultural skills, such as the making of fry bread, now considered traditional Navajo food, the use of coffee, and the type of clothing that became a kind of Navajo national costume and can sometimes still be seen today:

> They decorated their dark velvet
> blouses with silver dimes, nickels and quarters.
> They had no use for money then.
> It is always something to see — silver flashing in the sun
> against dark velvet and black, black hair.[20]

The text accordingly represents the following cultural elements: a Navajo aesthetics that is also an ethics — (beauty and thus harmony based on a capacity to transform even the utilitarian), a poetics — (oral talk as an "active presence" and the exchange of storytelling voices as the basis for literary texts), and a model of history, in which history consists of the collective memory of firsthand experience uniting the family and "the people." The poem's narrative selection is based on communal values taught in "the old stories that the holy people had given us."[21] The past is relevant only inasmuch as it is present to the living. Its purpose is to establish identity in the homological structures of family ties and story relationships; the phrase "we are related" here has a double significance. Reality experience and value system are religiously informed, but the narrative remains oral history and does not blend into myth because in Tapahonso's opinion the sacred stories must not be retold. Unlike Menchú her rejection of outsiders is not put forth in the story but is implied by silence where other Native writers have tried a variety of forms to transform myth into literature. In this story of victimization and trauma, survivance as resistance is achieved by countering the dominant history by words of remembrance that are different in form and content. But with the exception of a few Navajo words, the text is in English. While Tapahonso more than others writes decidedly for her own group of origin, her narrative transformation of history and history telling lets us realize some of the remaining tension of transdifference between the cultures to which she belongs even though the elements of transculturation she mentions — fry bread and coffee, for instance — may represent successful hybridization. It should not go unmentioned that blue jeans have largely replaced velvet dresses: like any intercultural phenomenon, situations of transdifference are not static.

Survivance as Irony: Vizenor

Remembering that Gerald Vizenor called Native oral storytelling a way of creating an active presence, one may wonder how his own work relates to both the oral tradition and the dominant forms of history writing. Isn't Vizenor the postmodernist whose historical novel *The Heirs of Columbus* is an extremely writerly metahistorical collage of any number of narrative genres and modes, of quotations from numerous sources past and present, of fiction and non-fiction? Isn't his success in this masterful narrative largely due to the way he transgresses not only the boundaries of conventional historical narratives but also the content of history, the events considered as formative for a given society or even for mankind, by adding elements of fantasy and of science fiction-like projections into the future? Is it not due to his wonderful wit and humor even in the face of the sad and tragic? Such questions come to mind when we open his very recent book *Bear Island: The War at Sugar Point* (2006). This work recounts a largely forgotten incident in the struggle between Native Americans and the American government, but it does so in an unexpected form, that of the verse narrative. Again, it is not blank verse or some form of bardic long line that Vizenor finds adequate for his story but an extremely short, two-stress line that he likes to call "imagist." But if the shortness of the line may indeed remind one of imagist poetry or haiku (of which Vizenor has written a large number), who has ever heard of an imagist or haiku poem running to more than eighty pages? Once again, Vizenor manages to surprise his readers.

Bear Island is a narrative about an episode in the Indian Wars after those wars were over. It is about an episode that remarkably ended with a Native victory. The book's cover blurb has it this way:

> Drawing on the traditions of Anishinaabe storytelling, acclaimed poet Gerald Vizenor illuminates the 1898 battle at Sugar Point in Minnesota in this epic poem. Fought between the Pillagers of the Leech Lake Reservation (one of the original five clans of the Anishinaabe tribe) and U.S. soldiers, the battle marked a turning point in relations between the government and Native Americans. Although outnumbered by more than three to one, the Pillager fighters won convincingly.
>
> Weaving together strands of myth, memory, legend, and history, Bear Island lyrically conveys a historical event that has been forgotten not only by the majority culture but also by some Anishinaabe people.

This description is both correct and misleading time and needs commenting upon because it does not do full justice to the range of surprises Vizenor has in store for us. Certainly, Vizenor is an accomplished and acclaimed poet, but he is much better known as a novelist, essayist, and critic. That he should choose verse for a historical narrative is an element of estrangement. According to Abrams's *Glossary of Literary Terms*, in "its strict use . . . the term epic or heroic poem is applied to a work that meets at least the following criteria: it is a long narrative poem on a great and serious subject, related in an elevated style, and centered on a heroic or quasi-divine figure on whose actions depends the fate of a tribe, a nation, or the human race."[22] With these criteria in mind then, *Bear Island* can hardly be called epic: the incident was too small, the characters are too commonplace, and the style, although often poetic, is not elevated.

The ironic dissonance between "battle" and "Sugar Point" may owe its existence to historical and geographical chance, but Vizenor makes the most of it by phrasing his subtitle *The War at Sugar Point*. The "war" lasted for little more than a day and took place among the potatoes and cabbages of the Pillager chief whom the soldiers had been sent out to capture because he had rejected his second arrest on trumped-up charges of neglecting a court summons. Bugonaygeshig, or in English "Hole in the Day," the clan chief and central character of the narrative, had called for assistance and received the aid of nineteen Anishinaabe men, whom the U.S. Third Infantry confronted with more than seventy soldiers. These latter had just returned with glory from the Spanish-American War. If that conflict was a "splendid little war," as Secretary of State John Hay called it, how is one to call the War at Sugar Point? Nonetheless, there was serious fighting, glorious for the Anishinaabe, disastrous for the Army. While the Native warriors got away unhurt, the Third Infantry suffered heavy casualties: six men killed and eleven wounded, too many casualties to think of this poem as a mock-epic. Rather, Vizenor points to the ironies of an armed conflict that left a number of recent immigrants, most of them from Germany, dead because the issue had been blown up out of all proportions by U.S. authorities who could think only in terms of control over "the Indians." Irony also arises inasmuch as some of the casualties were the result of ignorance or braggadocio and inasmuch as virtually nothing but the exercise of petty authority was at stake for the whites while for the Anishinaabe this was an issue of clan loyalty, land rights, and the right to live in a traditional manner and according to traditional values. A further irony is that the fighting started when an Army rifle fell and a shot was discharged accidentally, but in a larger sense the whites had had it coming.

The Anishinaabe involved later got away with light sentences, indicating that a turning point in Native-white relations had indeed been reached, although it was to take many decades before substantial changes in U.S. Indian policy would be achieved. And, indeed, an end of the injustice is still not in sight. Consequently, while the symbolic value of the incident is significant, its nature as an event of historical importance may be doubted, as can be seen from the fact that it had been forgotten not only by "the majority culture" but also by part of the Native population because as an event of countervictimization it did not fit into either side's pattern of viewing history.

To call this text lyrical would be inadequate if the term carried only its usual connotations of musical language and a strong expression of personal emotion in a small poetic form. Compared to Asturias's metaphors, Vizenor's imagery is modest and his language terse, while his anger and sorrow are expressed in a highly controlled manner:

> *supreme portraits*
> *courts and congress*
> *brushed aside*
> *the constitution*

native rights
worthy resistance
steadily dishonored
by wicked grafters
stories bent
against nature
federal marshals
paid by law
for arrest reports
false warrants
captured natives.[23]

But the language is powerful, musical in a simultaneously modern and archaic way. In its hammering two-beat rhythm it reminds me of the angry short lines of parts of Ezra Pound's Mauberley cycle. So if survivance is resistance, it is resistance not only as a physical act — the content of this narrative — but as a resisting of conventions and conventional expectations. Once again, Vizenor is changing the landscape of literature. He resists cultural amnesia by resurrecting this story of a battle fought long ago. He makes the small subject large by its historical and ethical implications. He chooses the large genre of the epic only to make it small by the quasi-imagistic short line, which he makes large again by its cultural echoes of the small form and imagist or haiku-like metaphors of the traditional poetry of the Anishinaabe. Indeed, certain passages might be cut from the text and thereby acquire the poetic concision of a haiku or a short imagist poem:

the red sumac
brighten memories
hands and eyes
against the stones

or further down the page:

kingfishers
cut from a bough
dragonflies
break at sunrise

first shimmer
in the eyes.[24]

There is nothing of the flamboyance of Asturias in this text, none of the grandiose gestures, but the way Vizenor handles language opens up a world of spaces and interspaces. The fact that he uses no punctuation and no upper-case letters has enormous transformative effects. Hole in the Day thus becomes "hole in the day," and we may wonder what a hole in the day may signify. Bugaunak or Bagwana, a former Anishinaabe hero of the Pillager clan who miraculously survived a battle with the Dakota in Vizenor's translation of the name becomes "By My Heart" or rather "by my heart." As such and without quotation marks, the name startles the reader into wondering: is this a reference to something close to the author's or narrator's heart — which the story undoubtedly is — and can it indicate something he knows by heart, like something from the traditional cultural archive?

Still there are other passages that show Vizenor at his best as a harsh, unrelenting critic of white colonialism:

> *duty bound*
> *ushers and scalpers*
> *pocket stories*
> *traduce the dance*
> *native stories*
> *scenes of presence*
> *at the mercy*
> *of pious scorn*
> *wicked chantey*
> *confederate cruelty*
> *bounty and hue*
> *of wonted genocide*
> *by first light*
> *outgunned*
> *at sugar point*
> *forever in the book.*[25]

In a way it is Vizenor's aim to retrieve and return the stolen stories. At the same time, he pillories the aggressors' arrogance by putting it "forever in the book."

This phrase encapsulates the proud claim of the literary writer that art as a special area of the culture of memory cannot only resist the forgetfulness of the public in both the colonizing and the colonialized society but can in fact call the events back to life. What has been lost through the omnipresence of the discourse of victimization can thus be turned into another victory.

The keyword here is art. To resurrect the story of the Battle at Sugar Point, it would be sufficient to write an article in a journal or mention the incident in a history book. But to make it live requires more. This need is made clear by Vizenor's method of multiple narration. All we need to know in terms of standard history is already told in Jace Weaver's foreword. It is told again and enriched in the author's "Introduction: The War at Sugar Point" by information about the Anishinaabe belief system, the clans, the traditional courage of the Pillagers, the efforts of the tribe to remain independent in the context of the wars on the North American continent, the fight with the Dakota, and the greater historical context. This way we can associate Hole in the Day's behavior with the trickster tradition but also with his role as leader and healer. The armed conflict itself is related partially by quotations from historical and journalistic sources.

Thus it is not the *what* but the *how* of narration that makes the long poem stand out as the story of survivance as "an active presence." As in traditional oral texts, there is much repetition, in part by the technique of the leitmotif, for instance the recurrent mention of the city dock at Walker Bay where the

> *pale indian agents*
> *heave an empire*
> *of stray discoveries*
> *over the dock.*[26]

The poem's six cantos therefore are not simply chapters in an ongoing narrative but form overlapping and interreferential poetic units that give the narrative a bardic quality that one had not expected from its brevity and its concise verse language.

While the text in no way appears as a rewritten myth, the oral tradition as "creations of fugitive motion, a sense of presence that must be heard" thus makes its appearance, after all. Transdifference of poetic art indeed. Imagism is in Pound's words a poetry based on the "Image" as "a vortex or cluster of fused ideas and . . . endowed with energy," a poetry "that should be at least as well written as good prose," with emotion as "an organiser of form, not merely of visible forms and colours, but also of audible forms."[27] In *Bear Island* Imagism in Pound's sense meets with Anishinaabe oral texts alluded to, for instance, by the repeated quotation of the image "summer in the spring" from a well-known Anishinaabe song.[28] Those texts are tribal and therefore quite different in their cultural function from Imagism as a highly sophisticated literary project, but they are also remarkably similar in the way emotion organizes sound and form. The text thrives on such ambivalences, for instance that of English versus Anishinaabe, prose versus verse, and historical factuality versus imagination.

Vizenor's anger is directed against those who contributed to the destruction of land, culture, and intercultural exchange, then and now, and this anger encompasses those soldiers who stole cultural artifacts and paid with their lives. His anger is visible and audible on just about any page — in vain does one look for the rich humor informing his novels. Humor is mentioned as part of the Native oral tradition but hardly enacted except, say, in the mention of the necklace of spent shells Hole in the Day would wear for the rest of his life or the "bloody potatoes / and wounded cabbages" that might indeed contribute to the laughable in a mock-heroic poem by Swift or Pope but here carry a gruesome irony.[29]

Nonetheless, it is important to remember that the "cross-blood" Gerald Vizenor is writing from both sides of the dividing line. In a sense his anger does not stem only from a Native position but also from that of a descendant of European immigrants having turned against the shortsightedness of his "ancestors," and in this sense he knows what Menchú, in Sommer's words, means by "becoming the enemy." But other than Menchú, his position is not primarily one of difference but of transdifference, not in the sense of overcoming but of living with difference, with the tension of what will not dissolve in a brew of harmonious hybridity.

Sam McKegney's doubts about the applicability of the term *survivance* to political analysis and critique seems to me unfounded. He writes, referring to a paper by Colin Samson that "if conducting our analysis through the imperfect vehicle of language dooms us to, at best, perpetually misrepresenting and, at worst, perversely simulating 'the real,' how can we adeptly address political problems affecting 'the real experience[s]' of Native North Americans? . . . To take survivance seriously, critics must be willing to intercede in the semiotic fog of Beaudrillardian [sic] simulation and make explicit the connections between the hyper-reality of text and the political and social reality of Indigenous North America."[30] Vizenor's poem shows how in view of all the fluidity and relativity of "the real" we can and must opt for a version that will make the world a better place for all involved.

It is therefore logical that Vizenor's allegiance to the Native side should not prevent him from opting for the white version of the story rather than the Anishinaabe one. The introduction mentions both:

> *Pinckney reported that nineteen armed Natives waited at the tree line. The soldiers expeditiously occupied the cabin and vegetable garden of Hole in the Day at Sugar Point. The war started by chance that morning when a recruit stacked his rifle but forgot to engage the safety. Another man stumbled against the rifles, the stack collapsed, and the unsecured weapon sent a bullet skipping across the ground toward where the Ojibwe lay hiding. Stories from the Indian side tell of several soldiers firing at a canoe-load of women who were on their way to beg release of the captives on the steamer.*[31]

In the poem Vizenor mentions the latter version once again but sticks to the official story, presumably because he does not want to heighten the heroics of defending home and family but to emphasize the ridiculous banality of the start of the fight and hence the irony of the event. Hole in the Day's necklace thus leads to

> *native survivance*
> *remembrance*
> *a defeated army*
> *overcome by winchesters*
> *and fierce irony.*[32]

The irony is history's but also the author's who demonstrates in this text that survivance by resistance cannot depend on physical resistance alone but needs the imaginative and poetic transformation, the "active repudiation of dominance, tragedy, and victimry," to make it "an active presence" that can contribute to steering the current course of events.

Survivance lies in the word. For the more than forty million indigenous people in the Americas and for the untold millions of mixed bloods, it may mean
different things: different actions to be taken, different shades of identity
to be formed. But it is language, the spoken and the written word, through
which survivance becomes real.

Notes

1. Vizenor, *Fugitive Poses*, 15.
2. Vizenor, *Fugitive Poses*, 63.
3. Vizenor, *Fugitive Poses*, 63.
4. Appiah, *Ethics of Identity*, 103.
5. Vizenor, *Fugitive Poses*, 15.
6. Vizenor, *Fugitive Poses*, 63.
7. Menchú, *Rigoberta Menchú*, 377.
8. Sommer, "Resisting the Heat," 418–19.
9. For example, see Sitler, "Asturias."
10. Vizenor, Interview, 159
11. Sommer, "Resisting the Heat," 422.
12. Sitler, "Remnants of Racism," 5.
13. Asturias, *Hombres de maíz*, 18.
14. de Certeau, *Writing of History*, 21.
15. Blaeser, "New 'Frontier,'" 37–38.
16. Vizenor, *Fugitive Poses*, 15.
17. Breinig and Lösch, "Transdifference," 105
18. Tapahonso, "In 1864," 7.
19. Tapahonso, "In 1864," 8.
20. Tapahonso, "In 1864," 10.
21. Tapahonso, "In 1864," 10.
22. Abrams, *Glossary of Literary Terms*, 49.
23. Vizenor, *Bear Island*, 47–48.
24. Vizenor, *Bear Island*, 21.
25. Vizenor, *Bear Island*, 16.
26. Vizenor, *Bear Island*, 29.
27. Pound, "Affirmations," 345.
28. Vizenor, *Bear Island*, 49.
29. Vizenor, *Bear Island*, 86.
30. McKegney, "Trickster Poetics," 83.
31. Vizenor, *Bear Island*, 7–8.
32. Vizenor, *Bear Island*, 86.

Bibliography

Abrams, M. H. *A Glossary of Literary Terms*. 3rd ed. New York: Holt, Rinehart and Winston, 1971.

Appiah, Kwame Anthony. *The Ethics of Identity*. Princeton NJ: Princeton University Press, 2005.

Ashcroft, Bill, Gareth Griffiths, and Helen Tiffin, eds. *The Empire Writes Back: Theory and Practice in Post-Colonial Literatures*. London: Routledge, 1989.

Asturias, Miguel Ángel. *Hombres de maíz*. 1949. Reprint, Buenos Aires: Editorial Losada, 1963.

——. *Week-end en Guatemala*. 1956. Reprint, Buenos Aires: Editorial Losada, 1968.

Blaeser, Kimberly M. "The New 'Frontier' of Native American Literature: Dis-Arming History with Tribal Humor." In *Native American Perspectives on Literature and History*, edited by Alan R. Velie, 37–50. Norman: University of Oklahoma Press, 1995.

Breinig, Helmbrecht. "Hybrid Retrospections: Myth, Fiction, History and the Native American Historiographic Short Story." In *Re-Visioning the Past: Historical Self-Reflexivity in American Short Fiction*, edited by Bernd Engler and Oliver Scheiding, 313–41. Trier, Germany: Wissenschaftlicher Verlag Trier, 1998.

Breinig, Helmbrecht, and Klaus Lösch. "Transdifference." *Journal for the Study of British Cultures* 13, no. 2 (2006): 105–22.

Bruchac, Joseph, ed. *Survival This Way: Interviews with American Indian Poets*. 1987. Reprint, Tucson: University of Arizona Press, 1990.

Daus, Ronald. "Miguel Ángel Asturias." In *Lateinamerikanische Literatur der Gegenwart in Einzeldarstellungen*, edited by Wolfgang Eitel, 297–329. Stuttgart: Kröner, 1978.

de Certeau, Michel. *The Writing of History*. Translated by Tom Conley. New York: Columbia University Press, 1988.

Deloria, Vine, Jr. "Foreword." In *New and Old Voices of Wah'kon-tah: Contemporary Native American Poetry*, edited by Robert K. Dodge and Joseph B. McCullough, ix–x. New York: International Publishers, 1985.

Hollinger, David. *Postethnic America: Beyond Multiculturalism*. 1995. Reprint, New York: Basic Books, 2000.

Immerman, Richard H. *The CIA in Guatemala: The Foreign Policy of Intervention*. Austin: University of Texas Press, 1982.

McKegney, Sam. "From Trickster Poetics to Transgressive Politics: Substantiating Survivance in Tomson Highway's Kiss of the Fur Queen." *Studies in American Indian Literatures* 17, no. 4 (2005): 79–113.

Menchú, Rigoberta. *I, Rigoberta Menchú: An Indian Woman in Guatemala*. Edited by Elisabeth Burgos-Debray. Translated by Ann Wright. 1983. Reprint, London: Verso, 1984.

Pound, Ezra. "Affirmations — As for Imagisme." In *Selected Prose 1909–1965*, 344–47. London: Faber, 1973.

Schoultz, Lars. *Beneath the United States: A History of U.S. Policy toward Latin America.* Cambridge MA: Harvard University Press, 1998.

Sitler, Robert K. "Miguel Ángel Asturias: 'Gran Lengua' of the Maya: A Myth That Will Not Die." *South Eastern Latin Americanist* 41, nos. 3–4 (1998): 1–8.

———. "Remnants of Racism in Miguel Ángel Asturias' Hombres de maíz." Paper presented at the twelfth Mid-America Conference on Hispanic Literature, University of Colorado–Boulder, 1995. http://www.stetson.edu/~rsitler/CV/remnants.docMyth.doc (accessed January 12, 2008).

Sommer, Doris. "Resisting the Heat: Menchú, Morrison, and Incompetent Readers." In *Cultures of United States Imperialism*, edited by Amy Kaplan and Donald E. Pease, 407–32. Durham NC: Duke University Press, 1993.

Tapahonso, Luci. "In 1864." In *Sáanii Dhataaffl — The Women Are Singing: Poems and Stories*, 7–10. Tucson: University of Arizona Press, 1993.

———. Interview with Helmbrecht Breinig and Klaus Lösch. In *American Contradictions: Interviews with Nine American Writers*, edited by Wolfgang Binder and Helmbrecht Breinig, 111–23. Hanover NH: Wesleyan University Press, 1995.

———. "The Moon Is So Far Away: An Interview with Luci Tapahonso." By Andrea M. Penner. *Studies in American Indian Literatures* 8, no. 3 (1996): 1–12.

Vizenor, Gerald. *Bear Island: The War at Sugar Point.* Minneapolis: University of Minnesota Press, 2006.

———. *Fugitive Poses: Native American Indian Scenes of Absence and Presence.* Lincoln: University of Nebraska Press, 1998.

———. Interview with Helmbrecht Breinig and Klaus Lösch. In *American Contradictions: Interviews with Nine American Writers*, edited by Wolfgang Binder and Helmbrecht Breinig, 143–65. Hanover NH: Wesleyan University Press, 1995.

Wearne, Philip. *Return of the Native: Conquest and Revival in the Americas.* Philadelphia: Temple University Press, 1996.

White, Hayden. *The Content of the Form: Narrative Discourse and Historical Representation.* Baltimore: Johns Hopkins University Press, 1987.

———. *Tropics of Discourse: Essays in Cultural Criticism.* Baltimore: Johns Hopkins University Press, 1978.

Young, Robert. *White Mythologies: Writing History and the West.* London: Routledge, 1990.

4. ON SUBJECTIVITY AND SURVIVANCE

Rereading Trauma through *The Heirs of Columbus*
and *The Crown of Columbus*

DEBORAH L. MADSEN

> *We measure who we are from what we have done to the Indians.*
>
> Gerald Vizenor, *Landfill Meditation*

> *Survivance stories honor the humor and tragic wisdom of the situation,
> not the market value of victimry. . . . Stories of survivance are a sure
> sense of presence. . . . Most of my stories are about survivance. No
> matter the miseries, most of the characters in my stories take on the
> world with wit, wisdom, and tricky poses. My stories are not the trag-
> ic mode, not the themes of heroic ruin, destruction, and moral weak-
> ness. My storiers are tricky not tragic, ironic not heroic, and not the
> comfy representations of dominance.*
>
> Gerald Vizenor, *Postindian Conversations*

In this essay I take as my starting point dominant Western theories of trauma
that deploy paradigms of trauma therapy that are based on the "recovery"
of a singular and homogenous subjectivity. The cultural bias of this assumption that reassimilation or reintegration of a fragmented ego must necessarily be the object of therapy becomes clear in the context of Gerald Vizenor's
concept of survivance. Survivance places productively in question the stability and desirability of this notion of selfhood in a Native American Indian context. The Western understanding of trauma emerges as a narrative of
dominance, but it is revealed as such only when we substitute the term *survival* of trauma with that of *survivance* in the face of historical trauma. In what
follows, I want to ask how does a postindian subject, such as Gerald Vizenor

describes, survive? Is recovery from historical trauma either desirable or possible? And how is Native subjectivity situated in relation to the dominant American multiculture within the context of postcontact historical trauma? My texts for this investigation are two prominent but very different Anishinaabe, Chippewa, or Ojibwe novels written in anticipation of the Columbian quincentenary: Gerald Vizenor's *The Heirs of Columbus* (1991) and Louise Erdrich and Michael Dorris's *The Crown of Columbus* (1991). The latter novel offers us a survivor narrative, while in contrast, Vizenor's work offers a narrative of survivance.

Trauma in the Ruins of Representation

The implicit assumption in my title is that texts by Native American writers such as Gerald Vizenor and Louise Erdrich are "trauma narratives," that is, these writers engage, whether deliberately or not, in the representation of historical trauma as a consequence of their status as self-identified Native American Indian, tribal, Anishinaabe writers. The fact that they have each written a significant text addressing the Columbian quincentenary, the anniversary of the beginning of the European invasion of the New World, is assumed similarly to address the trauma consequent upon that invasion for Native people. These assumptions raise the highly problematic and contested questions of what constitutes trauma, who defines it, how it is represented in literary texts (and indeed in language itself), and what interests are served by contemporary definitions of literary trauma.

The Jungian clinician Emmett Early, for instance, argues that trauma is recognized as a contemporary problem because, unlike conditions in the past, it is only in the present that trauma is sufficiently *uncommon* to be seen as something outside the norm. Indeed, it is only in the current, fourth edition of the *Diagnostic and Statistical Manual* that the definition of trauma as an overwhelming experience outside the realm of normal human experience has been revised. However, theorists like the feminist clinician Laura Brown point out that the definition of trauma as belonging to a specific pathology that is defined within the context of patriarchal culture serves to hide the traumatizing conditions experienced as everyday life by members of oppressed groups: the poor, women, and marginalized ethnic groups including Native Americans. She argues that "to admit that these everyday assaults on integrity and personal safety are sources of psychic trauma, to acknowledge the absence of safety in the daily lives of women and other nondominant groups, admits to what is deeply wrong in many sacred social institutions and challenges the benign mask behind which everyday oppression operates."[1] This acknowledgement, that trauma itself is subject to appropriation by dominant discourses that serve interests other than those whose lives are most at risk, is a troubling realization but one that cuts to the heart of the problematics of trauma in a Native context.

To see Native Americans as a group that is by definition traumatized is to acknowledge the inadequacies and partialities of current definitions of trauma that emphasize the experience or witnessing of, or confrontation with, an event that is sudden and unexpected, which provokes a response of intense fear, helplessness, or horror. An understanding of trauma such as this fails to account both for the inherited nature of certain forms of historical trauma and equally for the traumatic nature of everyday life for vulnerable people who daily confront with fear and helplessness the absence of safety or security in their lives. Reading Native American texts as trauma narratives can help us to read back against the grain of contemporary trauma theory to an enriched understanding of how the discourses of trauma operate in our contemporary multicultural or intercultural society.

The degree of trauma suffered by Native American tribal communities in the wake of Columbus cannot be overestimated. As Anishinaabe scholar Lawrence W. Gross points out, a number of distinguishing features of the historical trauma experienced by Native American peoples must be recognized:

> First, the stress is society-wide in nature. The stress does not simply involve a small segment of the population, as might be the case with combat veterans experiencing post-traumatic stress disorder. Instead, everyone in the culture is affected to one degree or another. Second, the stress strikes at both the personal and institutional levels. As such, some features are expressed in the lives of individual people. However, an apocalypse causes the collapse of societal institutions, which normally function to circumvent and/or minimize stress in the wake of a shock to the culture and assist in the recovery process.[2]

Gross goes on to argue that "an understanding of the comic vision can help explain how Anishinaabe culture is recovering in the wake of what I call 'Post Apocalypse Stress Syndrome.' Along with many other Native American peoples, the Anishinaabe have seen the end of our world, which has created tremendous social stresses. The comic vision of the Anishinaabe is helping us overcome that trauma and helps explain how we are managing to survive."[3] He further shows how the comic vision of Gerald Vizenor and Louise Erdrich, like that of other contemporary Anishinaabe writers, contributes to the survival of the community by bringing the Old World into the New, by playing with cultural traditions old and new, within the context of trickster narratives. I will discuss the work of Vizenor and Erdrich below, but first I want to outline what I see as the urgent necessity of reading contemporary trauma theory through the lens of Native American literature and culture.

The emergent mainstream of trauma theory is dominated by the work of theorists like Cathy Caruth, Shoshana Felman, Dori Laub, and Ruth Leys, theorists whose thought is broadly shaped by psychoanalytic and poststructuralist theories of language and subjectivity. The work of these writers emphasizes the unknowability of trauma except in language, which is always shifting, deferring, and multiplying meaning. I have written elsewhere about the incommensurability of the notion of experience assumed by Cathy Caruth but refused by Native writers such as Paula Gunn Allen.[4] Here I want to suggest that the notion of trauma as fundamentally unknowable serves the interests of what Gerald Vizenor calls the "cultures of dominance." At the same time, this conceptualization identifies the fragmented and multiple subjectivity with trauma by implicitly positing the healed or surviving or posttraumatic self as unified, self-identical, coherent, and singular. Normality is identified (though never explicitly) with a unified, reintegrated, or whole sense of self because the disunified, fractured self is what signifies the unknowable fact of trauma. In a Native context the therapeutic aim of restoring the patient to a condition of cultural productivity similarly serves the interests of assimilation. If we ask whose cultural productivity is to be restored then the imperative to assimilate socially is clearly conflated with the concept of psychic integration or assimilation.

I want to question the assumption that healing necessarily means the transition to a condition of psychic assimilation or wholeness by reading against this understanding of trauma the fictional deployment of the Anishinaabe tribal trickster figure. Kali Tal is uncompromisingly clear in her assessment of the brand of trauma theory that refuses this style of reassessment: "To be an American critic and to turn one's eyes to Europe, to the Holocaust for an example of a traumatized population *while at the same time* steadfastly refusing to look at any aspect of the African American experience (or, for that matter, the experience of Native Americans) is to perpetuate the racist and Eurocentric structures that were responsible for the traumatization of those populations in the first place."[5]

Jonathan Boyarin makes a similar point in his comparison between the situation of European Jews and American Native people: each is eulogized from afar in order to displace anxieties about traumatic histories that are too close to home.[6] It is urgent then that Western theory not only learn from tribal discourses but also that Western theorists learn to resist the discourses of dominance by listening to Native engagements with the historical experience of trauma.

The assumption that healing is equated to the reintegration of psychic trauma through therapy — that the aim of therapy is assimilation — derives in the work of influential scholars like Dominick LaCapra from the Freudian legacy. LaCapra's widely cited essay "Trauma, Absence, Loss" (1999) emphasizes the processes of acting out and working through. Freud describes these concepts in seminal texts such as "Remembering, Repeating and Working-Through" (1914) and "Mourning and Melancholia" (1917). In the latter essay Freud distinguishes the "normal" process of mourning, which integrates loss, from the pathological condition of melancholia. The latter involves the loss of ego that, unlike mourning, cannot simply be overcome after a lapse of time. Melancholia involves compulsive repetition of an absent because traumatic past moment, possession by this traumatic past, and a narcissistic identification with the lost object. The melancholic subject is split in multiple directions between the past and present, caught in nostalgic longing, and trapped in denial. In contrast to melancholia, according to LaCapra "mourning brings the possibility of engaging trauma and achieving a reinvestment in, or recathexis of, life that allows one to begin again."[7]

Mourning is not a passive process of forgetting; rather, mourning is an active process of engaging and accepting the fact of loss. Michael Hardin in his essay on Gerald Vizenor's novel *Heirs of Columbus* addresses this issue of

forgetting: "For a Native American to forget the wars the United States government fought against his/her ancestors, to forget the countless times they
were forced from their homelands and massacred, to forget the European diseases which killed more than the weaponry, or to forget the other devasta-
tions on the native populations resulting from Western colonization, would
serve to free the individual from the burden of a victimizing past, but it would
also free the victimizer from responsibility."[8] Forgetting is not an option; in
Freudian terms even the attempt simply to forget involves repression, melancholia, and the regressive cycle of acting out the symptoms of trauma. The
repressed will always return. However, mourning itself is a complex and ambivalent condition in the Native American context.

In the "literatures of dominance" mourning of a "lost" tribal world takes
the form of the myth of the Vanishing American and other cultural narratives
that Vizenor in *Interior Landscapes* and elsewhere so accurately names "terminal creeds."[9] Mourning, with its acceptance and integration of the lack of
that which can never be retrieved, is an appropriate response, as Hartwig
Isernhagen acutely observes, only "once improvement appears impossible."[10]
That is, when loss is accepted as an irretrievable loss rather than as a potentially recuperable absence, then mourning and the reintegration of the ego
can take place. The acceptance of loss, an acknowledgement that things cannot get better, like the assimilation of the self to the culture of dominance,
is clearly an undesirable location for the Native American subject. To write
out of mourning, however, to write *against* mourning and the assimilated self,
is a strategy that resists the passive position of the victim and the hopeless
victim at that.

It is here that Vizenor's concept of survivance offers a vital alternative. In
Fugitive Poses (1998) he writes that "survivance, in the sense of native survivance, is more than survival, more than endurance or mere response; the
stories of survivance are an active presence. . . . The native stories of survivance are successive and natural estates; survivance is an active repudiation
of dominance, tragedy, and victimry."[11]

Survivance then is not passive survival but an active resistance as well; it is
the refusal of the "manifest manners" of dominance, which posits insistently
Native people as "Vanished," or as tragic victims, or as ig/noble savages frozen in a mythical past, or even as ecowarriors in an idealized New Age future.

Vizenor observes that the fact that "postindians renounce the inventions and final vocabularies of manifest manners is the advance of survivance hermeneutics."[12] Survivance hermeneutics allow us to read back against dominant theories of historical trauma, to read trauma in the "ruins of representation" that are the remnants left once the imposed fictions of "Indianness" are stripped away from the dominant simulation of "indian" presence.

Vizenor's postindian tricksters possess the power, among other things, to disrupt the flow of dominance in both space and time, as is amply demonstrated in *Heirs of Columbus* with such reversals of causality as Columbus's return home to, rather than discovery of, the New World. Reverse causality is important in the context of trauma theory because Freud's theory of acting-out, like Caruth's theory of trauma's "belated temporality," presumes a linear relationship between past and present that permits the possibility of entrapment in a traumatic past.[13] Postindian tricksters deconstruct the very opposition between past and present, defying linear thinking, just as they refuse the opposition between victim and aggressor.

Vizenor explains that underlining this healing deconstructive power are "my storytellers, my characters [who] have the power to heal through a good story, through the ecstatic concentration of energy and with a special genetic signature which is a shamanic power: they can heal and transform the wounded of this civilization. I have turned around the Columbus story to serve healing rather than victimization; there is much to be gained politically from victimization, but there is more to be gained from the power of a good story that heals, and I think my story heals the victims in a poetic and imaginative way."[14] By refusing the status of the victim, one who mourns an unrecuperable loss, while at the same time refusing to reintegrate loss into a unified and "whole" subjectivity, Vizenor's ironic, trickster storytellers embrace a positive multiplicity of being, a subjective diversity that counters the manifest manners of Western theories of trauma that would otherwise impose upon Native people fugitive poses, the masks of indian psychic health, a pretence of self-coherence that serves the fantasies of dominance rather than the practices of survivance.

Throughout his writings Gerald Vizenor describes the trickster as a force who heals and balances the world. The trickster does not unify, does not resolve and remove contradiction, fragmentation, or multiplicities. He holds them in balance. In the introduction to *Narrative Chance* (1989) Vizenor writes that "monologic realism and representation in tribal literatures . . . is a 'bureaucratic solution' to neocolonialism and the consumption of narratives and cultures."[15] The transformation of symptoms into monological therapies is the objective of conventional Freudian approaches to trauma. However, as I indicated above, such a transformation in Native American terms can easily become the adoption of images of what Vizenor calls, deliberately in lowercase italics, the *indian*: images that cater to the needs of traumatizing dominant discourses. Of course, the pathology and suffering that arise from a profound sense of dislocation, a "between worlds" condition, and of alienation from two distinct cultures, is also symptomatic of the trauma described by contemporary theorists. How to embrace subjective diversity without succumbing to alienation is the challenge faced by Native peoples.

The figure of the postindian represents resistance and survival, Native survivance beyond tragedy, victimry, and simulations of the indian that can represent false healing in the culture of dominance. The postindian at once exposes the hermeneutic lack or absence that is constitutive of stereotypical constructions of the indian but at the same time inscribes a trace of what it is that is absent: "Native American Indians are the originary storiers of this continent, and their stories of creation, sense of imagic presence, visionary memories, and tricky survivance are the eternal traces of native modernity. . . . Native stories are an imagic presence, the actual tease of human contingencies, but indians are immovable simulations, the tragic archives of dominance and victimry. Manifest manners favor the simulations of the indian traditionalist, an ironic primitive with no cultural antecedence."[16]

This trace, or excess of meaning that exceeds the absence that is the indian, is revealed in what Vizenor calls in the essay "Shadow Survivance" the "postindian turns in literature." In the absence of the singular indian and with the consequent "closure of dominance," the traces or shadows of tribal survivance appear, along with the potential for a different kind of healing: "The traces are shadows, shadows, shadows, memories, and visions in heard stories."[17] The repetition of the word *shadow* indicates the multiple and diverse nature of these traces that exist outside the constraints of narratives of dominance. Shadows image the hermeneutic excess, the multiple significances, of language understood as a performative utterance. Language does not passively represent or mirror but rather acts to organize our knowledge of ourselves and our world in ways that can be variously traumatizing or healing: "We are shadows, silence, stones, stories, never the simulation of light in the distance."[18] This understanding is participatory, multiple and never fixed. Shadow traces are subject to Derridean différance, as Vizenor makes explicit: always different, always deferred, always-already in creative transformation. Almost Browne, the eponymous trickster hero of the story that opens *Landfill Meditations* (1991), learns from his grandmother to read the living "crossblood" words that are everywhere: "in snow, trees, leaves, wind, birds, beaver, the sound of ice cracking; words are in fish and mongrels. . . . My winter breath is a word, we are words, real words, and the mongrels are their own words."[19] Shadow traces in these living words facilitate survivance as a way of exceeding the confines or boundaries of language, especially when language is articulated by the "dead voices" of social science, anthropology, or history.

Vizenor writes against the traumatizing, monolithic "terminal creeds" perpetuated in social science discourses; these destructive stereotypes of Native American people are embedded in the institutional understandings of Indianness that Ishi, the "museum Indian," iconizes in Vizenor's writings. These monologic Western epistemologies perpetuate trauma, and it is these that Vizenor sets out to subvert with irony, wicked humor, and a language that refuses to render monologic meanings. As Elvira Pulitano observes, "Vizenor's style is not linear, progressive; it does not follow the logic of cause and effect. Rather, it embraces chance, celebrates play, relishes ambiguity, breaks rules, confounds expectations, invites involvement."[20] Vizenor uses language creatively to engage the reader; the trickster liberates the subject to self-knowledge, but that subjectivity is not singular and monolithic. The self is always multiple and subject to liberating transformation because closure is always-already subject to différance: hermeneutic distinctions and deferrals of meaning. Such closure as we know is found in terminal creeds in "the terminal vernacular of manifest manners, and the final vocabularies of dominance."[21]

In an interview, Vizenor said that his writing is many things but "it's not a monologue": it is a dialogue in which the reader is compelled to take an actively creative role.[22] This emphasis upon the plural, on existence and identity in the plural, appears in *Dead Voices* (a novel published in 1992, the actual year of the Columbian quincentenary) in the chapter "Bears." This chapter includes a lengthy meditation on the significance of stories that have been lost by "wordies," or Europeans, who are left only with the desire of tribal stories: "We never had any trouble remembering to use plural pronouns, but most wordies could not understand who we were talking about. They saw the old woman but not the bear. We are one and the same. There's a trickster in the use of words that includes the natural world, a world according to the we, and the we is our metaphor in the wanaki game."[23] Monologic discourses are addressed by "I," but as Vizenor writes in a 1989 essay, "The author, narrator, characters and audience are the signifiers and comic holotropes in trickster narratives."[24] "We" are all in this together in Vizenor's *dia*logic or even *multi*logic style of writing.

In the essay "Eternal Haven" in *Manifest Manners*, Columbus is accused of imposing pronouns on Native people and, in so doing, creating the first simulated indians: "He is the deverbative trickster, the one who landed in two pronouns, the he and you."[25] In this way Columbus excludes Native people from the category of "we" and relegates them to absence, just as Vizenor does in return to Columbus when he addresses him combatively as "You."[26] Columbus is the false trickster, trapped in the static Manichean oppositions of the dominant discourse. As Vizenor writes in *Fugitive Poses*, "The sovereignty of motion is mythic, material, and visionary not mere territoriality, in the sense of colonialism and nationalism. Native transmotion is an original natural union in the stories of emergence and migration that relate humans to an environment and to the spiritual and political significance of animals and other creations. Monotheism is dominance over nature; transmotion is natural reason, and native creation with other creatures."[27] In *Heirs of Columbus* Vizenor transforms Columbus's transatlantic territorial "motion" into native "transmotion" as Columbus is called across the seas by a New World shaman. Vizenor's cross-blood transformations in story after story and book after book offer imaginative affirmations of a diverse selfhood. The multiple personality of the semiotic trickster figure is described in *Landfill Meditations* as "a character in stories, an animal, or person, even a tree at times, who pretends the world can be stopped with words, and he frees the world in stories."[28]

The necessity of rereading Western understandings of trauma from this perspective of survivance is emphasized by mental health professionals, such as Eduardo Duran who in two important books underlines the fact that Western therapies simply do not work in a Native American Indian context. Suicide rates among Native American people remain higher than among non-Natives, as do rates of such disorders as alcoholism, schizophrenia, psychoses, neuroses, personality disorders, and drug dependence. Duran comments, with ironic understatement, that "evidence indicates that Native Americans may not be receiving responsive mental health services, and . . . past and present mental health services for Native Americans are inadequate."[29] Orthodox therapies and views of both illness and healing must be revised, Duran argues, from the perspective of traditional, or indigenous, therapeutic practices. Though Duran seeks ultimately to harmonize what he calls orthodox and traditional therapies, the hybrid and polyvalent strategies that he proposes as steps toward this assimilation are reminiscent of the revaluation of multiplicity or diversity that I see as the most fundamentally valuable aspect of survivance for rereading Western concepts of trauma. I don't want to suggest that fragmentation or alienation are beneficial conditions for anyone; however, multiple discourses and identities, held in creative balance, offer a way of avoiding the dangers of subjective assimilation to terminal creeds.

Two Anishinaabe Columbiads

In the following section I want to explore the potential for the revision of understandings of historical trauma through two very different literary approaches: Vizenor's narrative of survivance *Heirs of Columbus* and Louise Erdrich and Michael Dorris's survival narrative *Crown of Columbus*. Above, I quoted Vizenor's comment in *Manifest Manners* that "we are shadows, silence, stones, stories, never the simulation of light in the distance."[30] This simulation of light is the opposite to tribal shadows but at the same time offers the possibility for imagining both that which is feared and also that which is desired. The story "Feral Lasers" in *Landfill Meditations* demonstrates the power of holograms to create the images of colonizers that terrify tribal people on the reservation and also images of wild animals stampeding the interstate that terrify Anglo-Americans.

In contrast to these images of fear, *Heirs of Columbus* has a laser show in which Almost Browne's recreation of the Admiral is accompanied by the broadcast of a favorable court decision on tribal sovereignty to which the narrator adds that "the notion of sovereignty is not tied to the earth, sovereignty is neither fence nor feathers," the loudspeakers boomed over the headwaters that night. "The very essence of sovereignty is a communal laser. The *Santa Maria* and the two caravels are luminous sovereign states in the night sky, the first maritime reservation on a laser anchor."[31] The communal laser creates an image of Columbus to add to the gallery of figures: Jesus Christ, Joan of Arc, Crazy Horse, and the Statue of Liberty, all figures of communal fictions. Indeed, the laser images projected onto the sky echo the holotropic status Vizenor attributes to the tribal trickster himself: "a comic holotrope, the whole figuration; an unbroken interior landscape that beams various points of view in temporal reveries."[32]

Like the trickster figure, sovereignty is an effect of language, a rhetorical creation that is no less real for that. Indeed, in the legal dispute between the heirs of Columbus and the Brotherhood of American Explorers, the judge sets aside the "common rules of evidence" in favor of imagination and concedes that "the laser shows and wild presentation of virtual realities . . . as the new sources of tribal realities, could be used to appeal a conviction."[33] And Binn Columbus demonstrates her power of imagination, after the judge has stored a secret memory in a box, by recreating from laserlike blue radiance the panther that the judge remembered. The laser show at the end of the novel, as Stone Columbus engages the wiindigoo in the moccasin game, returns "home" seven key figures (Jesus Christ, Columbus, Crazy Horse, Black Elk, Louis Riel, Filipa Flowers, and Pocahontas) to the statue of the Trickster of Liberty. This restoration signifies the balance but not the resolution of good and evil that ends the narrative.

This idea of return is central to *Heirs of Columbus*, in which Vizenor transforms the Admiral into a cross-blood Indian, a descendant of Mayans, and the so-called discovery thus becomes a homecoming. This transformation is a subversive rewriting of the legacy of Columbus. Iping Liang argues in her essay on opposition play in the novel that "Vizenor enacts a tribal discourse of encounter in the comic and communal sign of the trickster figure of Admiral Columbus. By turning the Admiral into a cross-blood Jewish Mayan trickster, Vizenor transforms the tragedy of clash into a comedy of trickstering."[34]

However, I think it is debatable whether the Admiral is indeed a healing trickster. In his sexual liaison with Samana Columbus does undergo transformation "to become a woman, a bear, a hand talker" while she becomes androgynous.[35] But the consequence of this liaison, besides establishing the lineage of Columbus, is for him alienation from himself. He, and not Samana, is traumatized by this encounter as the next day he watches himself sail away: "His bones were lost on a mission, his soul was scorned and abandoned with the histories of the Old World."[36] So Columbus is rewritten in this novel as the victim of a traumatic history. As Hardin comments,

> By altering and pre-empting history, Vizenor determines who has the authority to label someone as "victim"; this also creates the potential for the individual to free him/herself from a binary past which does not allow for anything outside of the conqueror/conquered dichotomy. In his second interview with Laura Coltelli, he states, "I don't consider Columbus a good story and I don't consider it healthy after such a long time to continually tell a bad story that victimizes me." . . . Vizenor is playing the trickster here: in Heirs of Columbus, he makes Columbus a "good story" by rewriting it, by making it about someone other than Christopher Columbus.[37]

Thus in Vizenor's storied transformation the trauma of contact becomes a story of survivance, of changing the world, rather than a story of conquest and of possessing the world. In *Postindian Conversations* (1999) he tells A. Robert Lee that "my idea, you see, is that natives probably landed generations earlier in Europe and the Mediterranean. Natives, in fact, might have taught people everywhere how to build pyramids, how to do all sorts of things. . . . Columbus was a cross-blood, a descendant of the ancient natives, and he was teased by this inheritance to return to his ancestral homeland."[38] This homeland is represented as the tribal New World of the Stone Nation. In this place there are no passports to reify identity into a singular concept; it emerges that Stone himself is not an enrolled tribal member because his father refused "the political reductions of identities."[39] In this tribal New World diversity of identity, of subjectivity, is encouraged.

Heirs of Columbus can be read within a trilogy of "heirship" texts—that also includes *Bearheart: The Heirship Chronicles* (1978, 1990) and *The Trickster of Liberty: Tribal Heirs to a Wild Baronage* (1988). So Iping Liang reads the three works to good effect. She explains that "by reading *The Heirs* [*of Columbus*] in relation to the other two heirship stories, I argue that they delineate

a range of trickster play in the tribal geography that crosses the biographical home in the White Earth Reservation in the headwaters of the Mississippi River; the mythical home in the Chaco Canyon in the Southwest; and the
utopian home of Point Assinika in the international waters forming the border between Canada and the United States."[40]

In *Heirs of Columbus* the Admiral not only comes home, he comes together in the New World, as he is physically reassembled by tribal shamans. This
achievement is a key "acting-out" for Columbus, a healing—through reintegration that happens only through tribal mediation. The narrative offers
other instances of acting-out earlier historical trauma, as when Felipa travels
to London to attend a masque that repeats the celebration held in honor of
Pocahontas, exactly four hundred years before, a masquerade that is mock-
ingly repeated later by Caliban the mongrel who acts as a waiter to entertain
tribal children in "brocaded velvet and a wide elaborate lace collar, and pretended to be Pocahontas in London."[41] Another instance is Stone's establish-
ment of the new sovereign nation, which is a repetition of Columbus's voyage: the "Santa Maria Ferry was the flagship of the tribal armada; two ferries
and seven barges were close behind in Puget Sound."[42] This episode displays
the significance of this ferry voyage: "Columbus Takes Back the New World
at Point Roberts."[43] These instances of acting-out do not bring about therapeutic healing or the assimilation of trauma into a stable subjectivity. Felipa
is killed the day following the masque, and although Stone moves in the direction of healing by establishing the new sovereign tribal nation, it is a complex healing strategy that he pursues.

As Helen Jaskoski notes in her review of *Heirs of Columbus*,

> *A look at the philosophy embodied in works like* The Heirs of Colum-
> bus *shows it to be above all provisional in nature. "Terminal creeds"
> receive Vizenor's scorn in many of his works, and conversely the Trick-
> ster, whose being is ever provisional, contingent, and metamorphic,
> engages and fascinates him. But accepting provisionality as principle
> is a contradiction: to say "there are no absolutes" is to affirm an ab-
> solute, while to suggest a provisional formulation ("maybe there are
> some absolutes?") moves toward inanity. This contradiction vibrates
> at the heart of* The Heirs of Columbus *(and other works), and ac-
> counts, I think, for its self-reflexive, self-conscious self-subversion: no*

> *position can be at the center of the discourse, no character — not ex-*
> *cluding the supposedly omniscient narrative voice — can have more*
> *than momentary, provisional credibility.*[44]

In this novel the very idea of identity is provisional and contingent. Co-lumbus created the indian as a European simulation born of the "culture of death." As Vizenor writes in *Fugitive Poses*, "The *indian* has no native ances-tors; the original crease of that simulation is Columbian."[45] Hardin elaborates, "Stone Columbus wants to eradicate the very idea of racial identity in Assini-ka; the constructs of identity are no longer to exist. The healing, tribal sto-ries are the important thing: stories of Columbus and Pocahontas, wiindigoo and the blue moccasins."[46] The deconstruction of singular understandings of identity is contextualized by the opposition between "terminal blood quan-tum creeds" and the genetic signature of survivance that the heirs have taken from Columbus.[47] The narrative emphasizes both the talismanic animal iden-tities possessed by each of the heirs and the genetic "stories in the blood" that heal. Both visible disguises and invisible identities are represented, like the shamanic shadow in three dimensions that is captured on video by the Brotherhood of American Explorers and shown in court. The witness Mem-phis de Panther advises the judge that "the trouble with humans is they be-lieve their disguises are real, but not imagination, or their dreams."[48] Belief in only the visible, in a single visible identity, is a terminal creed promoted by the culture of dominance.

Throughout the novel singularities are deconstructed in favor of the im-portance of balance, that is, of keeping opposites in a creative tension and necessarily without resolution. The healing property of the survivance sig-nature is described in these terms by the scientist Pir Cantrip: "These four letters are held together in a signature by their opposites, the biochemical codes are bound by their own opposition, and here is where the shaman and the trickster touch that primal source of humor, imagination, and the stories that heal right in the antinomies of the genetic code."[49] The children who are the intended beneficiaries of this new genetic technology, the "lonesome mutants of a chemical civilization," will also be healed by biochemistry.[50] But only shamans and tricksters have the power to "stimulate the trickster oppo-sition in the genes, the ecstatic instructions, and humor in the blood."[51] The power of opposition is distinct from the negative influence of separation, as

Stone explains, "We heal with opposition, we are held together with opposition, not separation, or silence, and the best humor in the world is pinched from opposition."[52] Resolution is death; assimilation into singularity and the surrender of diversity is also death. Consequently at the end the novel offers no resolution beyond the return of all the wounded tribal people, living and dead, among them Columbus and Pocahontas to the New World of Assinika. The wiindigoo advises that the game never ends; the balance of opposed forces that brings tribal healing never ends but must always be renewed, and rewon.

Vivian Twostar, the protagonist of *Crown of Columbus*, thinks of herself not in terms of diversity but of amalgamation into a singular identity, as one of "the lost tribe of mixed bloods, that hodgepodge amalgam of hue and cry that defies easy placement."[53] This amalgamation, she claims, gives her the freedom of self-creation; she has "a million stories, one for every occasion, and in a way they're all lies and in another way they're all true."[54] In this respect Vivian finds kinship with the Columbus she imagines, another "between cultures" person whom she envisions speaking many languages, each with a foreign accent; only in the mid-Atlantic could he find the global perspective to which he could feel that he belonged. This kinship, this sympathy that bridges five hundred years of New World history, underpins the narrative strategy of this novel and its interpretation of post-Columbian history.

The entry for Louise Erdrich in Gale's *Authors and Artists for Young Adults* includes the following comment on *Crown of Columbus*: "Ultimately acknowledging the destructive impact of Columbus's voyage on the Native American people, they [Vivian and Roger] each vow to redress the political wrongs symbolically by changing the power structure in their relationship. In the end, as Vivian and Roger rediscover themselves, they rediscover America."[55] What kind of America do these two characters rediscover? It is not the "America-as-inheritance" that Vizenor's heirs of Columbus claim from the U.S. government. Even when Vivian tells herself that she wants Columbus's diary in order to prove his recognition of tribal sovereignty, thus to win back America for tribal people, she also acknowledges that she is motivated by the greed of discovery. This motive is rather different to that which moved the native Dartmouth student who centuries before deliberately hid the pages of Columbus's diary that indicate the location of the precious crown. This action, the student declares across time in the note included with the pages, is intended to take back that which was taken from him: his land and his life. The contrast between these two characters is significant, indicating as it does that, while the narrative is prepared to acknowledge a counternarrative to the dominant story of Columbus's discovery, the novel's major characters are engaged in a rather different set of issues.

In *Crown of Columbus* Erdrich and Dorris endorse a fundamentally multicultural, or even what Stanley Fish calls a boutique multiculturalist, position on American intercultural relations. The narrative appeals repeatedly to a notion of common humanity that underlies the superficial differences of ethnicity and this notion informs the novelistic representation of Columbus and his "discovery." Vivian tries to imagine a world in which Columbus had never existed and realizes that "if it hadn't been Christopher [*sic*] it would have been somebody else at about the same time — perhaps even somebody worse."[56] The cozy familiarity of referring to Columbus as Christopher signals the proximity that Vivian projects between the two of them. She concedes that Columbus was a slave trader but that is balanced against the slave trading of the Cobb family, an ancestor of whom swapped slaves in part for the original of Columbus's diary, the object of her quest. Vivian's son Nash confesses that he wants to help resolve the mystery of Columbus's treasure in order to make "a connection to the past."[57] Such a bridge is precisely what this novel tries to build: to make a connection to the past by revealing the "common humanity" that links Columbus with present-day Native Americans like Vivian and her son. When Vivian tries to trick Cobb by confessing to an invented need to validate her knowledge of Columbus by reading his original diary, she recognizes, as she says, that "the language I used was that of another time, another place. It was the vocabulary of the colonizer. Discovery. Possession. How different *was* I from the construct I fabricated?"[58]

This commonality, or lack of difference between the European colonizer Columbus and the Native woman Vivian, is made possible by the multicultural nature of the contemporary world described through the character of Nash: "a small place, all parts connected, where an Indian using an ancient Asian art can break into an old European box, witnessed by someone who grew up in Australia."[59] This transnational perspective serves to underline what is common among people of diverse times and places. What is emphasized is not the diversity, however, but the shared characteristics of human beings whether they are Indian, Asian, European, or Australian. In contrast to *Heirs of Columbus*, which resists at every turn the concept of assimilation, of commonality, in favor of creatively balanced oppositions, *Crown of Columbus* seeks the timeless and cultureless human nature of contemporary liberal thought.

Crown of Columbus is therefore a novel about survival, not survivance. Vivian Twostar resists writing the story of 1492 told from the Native's perspective, which is what the editor of the Dartmouth alumni magazine wants her to write. And, in fact, this story is the one that Michael Dorris has written in his young-adult novel *Guests* (1994). But this counternarrative is the story that Vivian tells her students: the story of the decimation of Native communities by disease and the superior force of European armaments. She asks them to close their eyes and project themselves into the past and to imagine living in a tribal community under European assault: "The well-tended faces looked sad, sorry for themselves."[60] Nash similarly describes himself within the context of victimry as "an improbable exception, a survivor of survivors of survivors."[61]

Where Vizenor plays with the idea of difference, although at the same time expressing a profound skepticism toward racial difference, Erdrich and Dorris articulate what is essentially a more pessimistic view of the differences that divide Native people from Anglo-Americans and Europeans. This dissimilarity is evident even in the most obvious aspects of the two novels. Where Vizenor brings Columbus back to the New World, to the Reservation, literally as bones but also in the flesh of his heirs, Erdrich and Dorris take their protagonists to the island scene of Columbus's landing in order to reenact the "discovery," which in their narrative really is represented as a "discovery" in contrast to Vizenor's trickier notion of "return."

The discovery of Columbus's crown is an obvious repetition of the discovery motif, but the concept of repetition is a structuring principle of the narrative. As Roger boards the boat in Florida bound for Eleuthera, he is conscious of repeating Columbus's voyage but in reverse; he is pleased by the thought of "the parallel . . . to the Admiral's own voyage, though of course we debarked from the opposite shore."[62] Yet once on the island, it is Vivian who places them in the position of intruders, conquerors. Like Columbus, each is seeking vindication: "We seemed suddenly like predators, parasites. . . . We had come to Eleuthera to steal away some fantasy of our own. . . . What did we have to do with the pulse of life in this place?"[63] These repetitions even enter the novel's characterization: at one point Vivian imagines Roger as Columbus and herself as his mistress, Beatriz Peraza.[64] In fact, however, the plot of the novel plays more on the Pocahontas myth, with Roger Williams as the New England Captain who requires rescue by the enamored Indian princess. To be sure, this take is the Disney version of the Pocahontas story, and at one point Vivian even jokingly wonders whether Cobb sees their arrival on the island as "Pocahontas and John Smith go to Hawaii."[65]

Where the novel documents in painstaking detail the strategies by which Vivian and Roger negotiate the complexities of selfhood within their multicultural relationship, Vizenor's Columbiad engages in the complex process of deconstruction of the very categories of self versus other so that otherness becomes an opposed but inseparable part of the self. Commenting on Doctor Pir Cantrip's Dorado Genome Pavilion, Jaskoski writes that "when science addresses the genetic code, 'survivance' is no longer a matter of inheritance, but of intellectual manipulation. There are no genes for 'race,' and the concept deconstructs as one more fiction available for pernicious misunderstanding."[66]

By deconstructing the notion of race, of genetic racial specificity, Vizenor neither rejects nor endorses the allied idea of cultural identity, unlike Stone Columbus who "would accept anyone who wanted to be tribal, 'no blood attached or scratched.' "[67] Instead, the narrative holds in balance, on the one hand, the ideas of "stories in the blood," the inherited power of tribal identity that pulled the Admiral across the ocean and, on the other hand, the trickster desire of Stone to "make the world tribal, a universal identity, and return to other values as measures of human worth."[68] What Arnold Krupat calls the democratizing of the metaphoric tribal signature through the emphasis upon shared values permits Vizenor to deconstruct these terminal creeds and "'tragic' closures of birth and blood."[69] At Point Assinika racial identity can be changed with genetic implants, but healing requires the special power of shamans and tricksters.

In connection with blood identity and inheritance, both novels mention parthenogenesis. Vizenor refers to parthenogenesis as a strategy for separatist feminists with whom, like the abused children who flock to Point Assinika for healing, his narrator expresses sympathy. Parthenogenesis in Erdrich and Dorris's novel is, however, purely personal, the spiteful response of Roger Williams to his exclusion from Vivian's pregnancy: "Let Vivian present her baby to the world as a product of parthenogenesis, let her titillate the Women's Studies Program with her brave unmarried motherhood."[70] Roger goes on to describe his work, his poetry, as a refuge not so much from his disappointment or hurt but as from the denial of parenthood that parthenogenesis represents to him. And parenthood clearly signifies a child that will memorialize him: an heir.

Memorialization, whether through a child or an epic poem, is what Roger Williams seeks and this memorialization is also what the novel itself achieves. What this narrative finally remembers is the way in which Columbus's contact with the peoples of the New World made Europe a smaller place, as the island girl Valerie discovers. After her contact with Vivian, for the first time in her life she becomes aware of the sea and of the possibility of crossing it just like Columbus did. Vivian, the Native woman, is here the agent of contact and the breeder of discontent. *Crown of Columbus* memorializes the Columbus in all of us and the "us" by implication that motivated Columbus and all that followed in his name. Where Vizenor brings Columbus's bones into the present as a dead yet powerful presence in the contemporary world, Erdrich and Dorris take us back to 1492 to acknowledge that in his time and place we would have done just the same as Columbus did. This recognition is why Roger, scion of generations of elite New England families, is able to complete Vivian's article on Columbus for the Dartmouth alumni magazine: the difference between him and a Native woman such as Vivian has been eroded by the relentless pressure of the narrative toward common humanity. In this context such superficial differences as gender, ethnicity, and class are purely incidental. Roger becomes Native just as we become Columbus in our timeless human essence.

Let me return to the questions with which I began: how does a postindian subject, such as Gerald Vizenor describes, survive? Is recovery from historical trauma either desirable or possible? And how is Native subjectivity situated in relation to the dominant American multiculture within the context of postcontact historical trauma? Benjamin Burgess in his 2006 essay on *Heirs of Columbus* focuses upon the traumatic impact of the historical narrative of Columbus's "discovery" and "conquest" of the Americas and the potential for healing possessed by some kinds of storytelling. Euro-American culture, he argues, tells stories that make people sick; Anishinaabe culture, in contrast, tells stories to heal:

> Indigenous people, when confronted with the dominant narrative become sick with anger because their pain, the very real historical trauma, is ignored. Euroamericans that celebrate Columbus become sick with fear that their celebrations of civilization over savagery will be negated by Indigenous protests. In the film Bimaadiziwin: A Healthy Way of Life, Sonny Smart, a Bad River Ojibwe, explains the meaning of aakozi, the Ojibwe word for "he/she is sick." He says that an older man told him that the literal translation is "to be out of balance." He goes on to say that "one of the things that can create aakozi could be physical, could be spiritual, intellectual process too, [and] emotional." The last two causes are relevant to this discussion because the dominant narrative sets in motion an intellectual and emotional response.[71]

This understanding of balance as a healthy response to historical trauma informs all of Vizenor's writing; in *Heirs of Columbus* it is clear that the balance of opposites is the only therapeutic strategy that permits a postindian subject to survive. By collapsing opposites into a single collective and reductive category like common humanity, a narrative such as *Crown of Columbus* resolves opposition but at the risk of promoting indian identities. Recovery, in these terms, is no recovery at all. Vizenor offers us a literal recovery of Columbus by subverting the dominant narrative of the Admiral's life and heritage, but this recovery involves neither forgetting nor memorialization, neither melancholia nor mourning, but a creative strategy of writing a route out of mourning through irony, subversion, and outrageous reimaginings that are always provisional, always-already under erasure and in need of renewal.

What is offered as recovery in *Crown of Columbus* is a more conventional working through of loss, through patterns of repetition that lead ultimately to assimilation and reintegration into the contemporary American multiculture. Susan Farrell defends the novel against its hostile initial reviews by describing it as a postmodern narrative. She sees the celebration of multiculturalism as "a conscious strategy, one that not only reminds readers that Indians and contemporary Americans are not mutually exclusive groups but also presents an irreverent, trickster-like mixing of cultures as the key to the survival of Native Americans."[72]

Indeed, this mixing of cultures, this multiculturalism functions, in the novel, as a form of cultural orthodoxy that has supplanted the melting pot and even the salad bowl, replaces them with a house of many nations, like the one Vivian and Roger build at the novel's end. This house, in which each family member has a space in which to be different and yet to remain defined by the encompassing space of the house, symbolizes the happy ending for these protagonists and by extension the national family of New World Americans who can rest guiltless in the knowledge that some kind of justice has been achieved. But in this house there is no mixing of cultures. Roger will eat the Navajo chili that Vivian serves him while Vivian will listen to the Bach that Roger favors, and yet her Native grandmother will live in an add-on room where Roger does not have to listen to her. There is no healing balance in this house or in the story that created it; all opposition is subsumed into a common humanity that Roger, in the last named narration, endorses: "Human nature is no different now than it has ever been: the present is a sponge that sucks history dry."[73] Not surprisingly, the final narrative segment, like the first, is narrated by an anonymous third-person voice; the novel is framed by the voice of "humanity."

This fictional validation of American multiculturalism and the Columbus-in-us-all might represent a comforting Native literary response to the Columbian quincentenary (according to Robert Silberman, worth 1.5 million dollars as an advance to Erdrich and Dorris from a major U.S. media conglomerate), and certainly it is consonant with the dominant direction of contemporary trauma theory with an emphasis upon the reintegration of the ego through working-out strategies of historical repetition. However, in Native terms such reintegration risks acceptance of terminal creeds that depend upon such liberal solutions to historical injustice as multiculturalism and, Vivian Twostar's recourse, international legal bureaucracy. These strategies invite precisely the tragedy and victimry that Gerald Vizenor's work is devoted to negating. The American multiculture can perhaps promise survival but not survivance. Rereading against the direction of liberal multiculturalism and contemporary

trauma theory through the lens of texts like *Heirs of Columbus*, the desirability of recovery as the move to a singular and homogenous subjectivity is profoundly put in question. The preservation of difference not sameness, of
provisionality not stability, and of balance not resolution and Freudian "wholeness" emerges as a desirable condition for Native people who must live every
moment with the evidence of their traumatic history and with the everyday
assaults on their integrity and personal safety that are ongoing sources of
psychic trauma. How to live *not* in sadness, "sorry for themselves" like Vivian
Twostar's Dartmouth students, but rather how to live in a condition of resistance and survival, of Native survivance, beyond tragedy, victimry, and simulations of the indian, apart from false healing in the culture of dominance,
this lesson is one that can only be learned by rereading theory and literature
through the lens of Native literatures of survivance.

Notes

1. Brown, "Not Outside the Range," 105.
2. Gross, "Anishinaabe Culture and Religion," 450.
3. Gross, "Anishinaabe Culture and Religion," 437.
4. Madsen, "Of Time and Trauma."
5. Tal, "Remembering Difference"; emphasis in original.
6. Boyarin, "Europe's Indian, America's Jew."
7. LaCapra, "Trauma, Absence, Loss," 713.
8. Hardin, "Trickster of History," 26–27.
9. Vizenor, *Interior Landscapes*, 235.
10. Isernhagen, "Mourning as a Creative Strategy," 281.
11. Vizenor, *Fugitive Poses*, 15.
12. Vizenor, *Fugitive Poses*, 167.
13. Caruth, "Unclaimed Experience."
14. Coltelli, "Gerald Vizenor," 103.
15. Vizenor, *Narrative Chance*, 6.
16. Vizenor, *Manifest Manners*, 16.
17. Vizenor, *Manifest Manners*, 63.
18. Vizenor, *Manifest Manners*, 64.
19. Vizenor, *Landfill Meditations*, 8.
20. Pulitano, *Native American Critical Theory*, 164.
21. Vizenor, *Manifest Manners*, 68.
22. Blaeser, *Gerald Vizenor*, 162.
23. Vizenor, *Dead Voices*, 39.
24. Vizenor, "Trickster Discourse," 188.

25. Vizenor, *Manifest Manners*, 107.

26. See Vizenor, *Manifest Manners*, 107–8.

27. Vizenor, *Fugitive Poses*, 183.

28. Vizenor, *Landfill Meditations*, 24.

29. Duran, *Archetypal Consultation*, 2.

30. Vizenor, *Manifest Manners*, 64.

31. Vizenor, *Heirs of Columbus*, 62.

32. Quoted in Owens, *Other Destinies*, 251.

33. Vizenor, *Heirs of Columbus*, 65.

34. Liang, "Opposition Play," 124.

35. Vizenor, *Heirs of Columbus*, 40.

36. Vizenor, *Heirs of Columbus*, 40.

37. Hardin, "Trickster of History," 26.

38. Vizenor and Lee, *Postindian Conversations*, 128–29.

39. Vizenor, *Heirs of Columbus*, 156.

40. Liang, "Opposition Play," 133.

41. Vizenor, *Heirs of Columbus*, 145.

42. Vizenor, *Heirs of Columbus*, 122.

43. Vizenor, *Heirs of Columbus*, 123.

44. Jaskoski, Review, 82.

45. Vizenor, *Fugitive Poses*, 15.

46. Hardin, "Trickster of History," 43.

47. Vizenor, *Heirs of Columbus*, 132.

48. Vizenor, *Heirs of Columbus*, 72.

49. Vizenor, *Heirs of Columbus*, 134.

50. Vizenor, *Heirs of Columbus*, 134.

51. Vizenor, *Heirs of Columbus*, 144.

52. Vizenor, *Heirs of Columbus*, 176.

53. Erdrich and Dorris, *Crown of Columbus*, 123.

54. Erdrich and Dorris, *Crown of Columbus*, 123.

55. Gale, "Louise Erdrich," n.p.

56. Erdrich and Dorris, *Crown of Columbus*, 23.

57. Erdrich and Dorris, *Crown of Columbus*, 160.

58. Erdrich and Dorris, *Crown of Columbus*, 200.

59. Erdrich and Dorris, *Crown of Columbus*, 369.

60. Erdrich and Dorris, *Crown of Columbus*, 85.

61. Erdrich and Dorris, *Crown of Columbus*, 364.

62. Erdrich and Dorris, *Crown of Columbus*, 174.

63. Erdrich and Dorris, *Crown of Columbus*, 226.

64. Erdrich and Dorris, *Crown of Columbus*, 112.

65. Erdrich and Dorris, *Crown of Columbus*, 219.

66. Jaskoski, Review, 83.
67. Vizenor, *Heirs of Columbus*, 162.
68. Vizenor, *Heirs of Columbus*, 162.
69. Krupat, "Stories in the Blood," 170, 174.
70. Erdrich and Dorris, *Crown of Columbus*, 50.
71. Burgess, "Elaboration Therapy," 35n3.
72. Farrell, "Colonizing Columbus," 121.
73. Erdrich and Dorris, *Crown of Columbus*, 375.

Bibliography

Blaeser, Kimberly M. *Gerald Vizenor: Writing in the Oral Tradition*. Norman: University of Oklahoma Press, 1996.

Boyarin, Jonathan. "Europe's Indian, America's Jew: Modiano and Vizenor." *boundary 2* 19, no. 3 (Autumn 1992): 197–222.

Brown, Laura. "Not Outside the Range." In *Trauma: Explorations in Memory*, edited by Cathy Caruth, 100–12. Baltimore: Johns Hopkins University Press, 1995.

Burgess, Benjamin V. "Elaboration Therapy in the Midewiwin and Gerald Vizenor's *The Heirs of Columbus*." *Studies in American Indian Literatures* 18, no. 1 (Spring 2006): 22–36

Caruth, Cathy. "Unclaimed Experience: Trauma and the Possibility of History." *Yale French Studies* 79 (1991): 181–92.

Coltelli, Laura. "Gerald Vizenor: The Trickster Heir of Columbus: An Interview." *Native American Literatures Forum* 2–3 (1990–91): 101–15.

Dorris, Michael. *Guests*. New York: Hyperion, 1994.

Duran, Eduardo. *Archetypal Consultation: A Service Delivery Model for Native Americans*. New York: Peter Lang, 1984.

Duran, Eduardo, and Bonnie Duran. *Native American Postcolonial Psychology*. Albany NY: SUNY Press, 1995.

Early, Emmett. *The Raven's Return*. Wilmette IL: Chiron, 1993.

Erdrich, Louise, and Michael Dorris. *The Crown of Columbus*. London: HarperCollins/Flamingo, 1991.

Farrell, Susan. "Colonizing Columbus: Dorris and Erdrich's Postmodern Novel." *Critique* 40, no. 2 (Winter 1999): 121–35.

Fish, Stanley. "Boutique Multiculturalism or Why Liberals are Incapable of Thinking about Hate Speech." *Critical Inquiry* 23 (Winter 1997): 378–95.

Gross, Lawrence W. "The Comic Vision of Anishinaabe Culture and Religion." *American Indian Quarterly* 26, no. 3 (Summer 2002): 436–59.

Hardin, Michael. "The Trickster of History: *The Heirs of Columbus* and the Dehistorization of Narrative." *MELUS* 23, no. 4 (Winter 1998): 25–45.

Isernhagen, Hartwig. "Mourning as a Creative Strategy: The Native American

Renaissance and the Reconstruction of Home as a Type of Diaspora." In *Cultural Encounters in the New World*, edited by Harald Zapf and Klaus Lösch, 281–99. Tübingen, Germany: Gunter Narr Verlag, 2003.

Jaskoski, Helen. Review of *The Heirs of Columbus*, by Gerald Vizenor. *Studies in American Indian Literatures*, 2nd ser., 4, no. 1 (Spring 1992): 79–83.

Krupat, Arnold. "Stories in the Blood: Ratio- and Natio- in Gerald Vizenor's *The Heirs of Columbus*." In *Loosening the Seams: Interpretations of Gerald Vizenor*, edited by A. Robert Lee, 166–77. Bowling Green OH: Bowling Green State University Press, 2000.

LaCapra, Dominick. "Trauma, Absence, Loss." *Critical Inquiry* 25 (Summer 1999), 696–727.

Liang, Iping. "Opposition Play: Trans-Atlantic Trickstering in Gerald Vizenor's *The Heirs of Columbus*." *Concentric: Studies in English Literature and Linguistics* 29, no. 1 (January 2003): 121–41.

Gale. "Louise Erdrich." *Women's History*. http://www.gale.com/free_resources/whm/bio/erdrich_l.htm (accessed July 10, 2006).

Madsen, Deborah. "Of Time and Trauma: The Possibilities for Narrative in Paula Gunn Allen's *The Woman Who Owned the Shadows*." In *Transatlantic Voices: Interpretations of Native North American Literatures*, edited by Elvira Pulitano, 111–28. Lincoln: University of Nebraska Press, 2007.

Owens, Louis. *Other Destinies: Understanding the American Indian Novel*. Norman: University of Oklahoma Press, 1992.

Pulitano, Elvira. *Toward a Native American Critical Theory*. Lincoln: University of Nebraska Press, 2002.

Silberman, Robert. "Opening the Text: *Love Medicine* and the Return of the Native American Woman." In *Narrative Chance: Postmodern Discourse on Native American Indian Literatures*, edited by Gerald Vizenor, 101–20. Norman: University of Oklahoma Press, 1989.

Tal, Kalí. "Remembering Difference: Working against Eurocentric Bias in Contemporary Scholarship on Trauma and Memory." In *Worlds of Hurt: Reading the Literatures of Trauma*. Rev. ed. http://freshmonsters.com/kalital/Text/Worlds/Chap3.html (accessed March 29, 2007).

———. *Worlds of Hurt: Reading the Literatures of Trauma*. Cambridge, UK: Cambridge University Press, 1996.

Vizenor, Gerald. *Bearheart: The Heirship Chronicles*. Minneapolis: University of Minneapolis Press, 1990.

———. *Dead Voices: Natural Agonies in the New World*. Norman: University of Oklahoma Press, 1992.

———. *Fugitive Poses: Native American Indian Scenes of Absence and Presence*. Lincoln: University of Nebraska Press, 1998.

———. *The Heirs of Columbus*. Hanover NH: Wesleyan University Press, 1991.

———. *Interior Landscapes: Autobiographical Myths and Metaphors*. Minneapolis: University of Minnesota Press, 1990.

———. *Landfill Meditations: Crossblood Stories*. Middletown CT: Wesleyan University Press, 1991.

———. *Manifest Manners: Postindian Warriors of Survivance*. Hanover NH: Wesleyan University Press, 1994.

———, ed. *Narrative Chance: Postmodern Discourse on Native American Indian Literatures*. Norman: University of Oklahoma Press, 1989.

———. "Trickster Discourse: Comic Holotropes and Language Games." In *Narrative Chance: Postmodern Discourse on Native American Indian Literatures*, edited by Gerald Vizenor, 187–211. Norman: University of Oklahoma Press, 1989.

———. *The Trickster of Liberty: Tribal Heirs to a Wild Baronage*. Minneapolis: University of Minnesota Press, 1988.

Vizenor, Gerald, and A. Robert Lee. *Postindian Conversations*. Lincoln: University of Nebraska Press, 1999.

5. PLAYING INDIAN

Manifest Manners, Simulation, and Pastiche

YING-WEN YU

The term *Indian* according to the *Merriam-Webster Dictionary* has several meanings. It refers to a "native or inhabitant of India or of the East Indies" or to "a person of Indian descent." It also means an "American Indian," "from the belief held by Columbus that the lands he discovered were part of Asia." Moreover, it is "one of the native languages of American Indians." The definition of *American Indian* is "a member of any of the aboriginal peoples of the western hemisphere except often the Eskimos; *especially*: an American Indian of North America and especially the U.S." Therefore we have to point out that *Indian* and *American Indian* are colonial terms that have been used to designate native peoples of different tribes since Columbus's "discovery" of the American continent. The term *Indian* for Gerald Vizenor implies manifest manners and is "an occidental misnomer, an overseas enactment that has no referent to real native cultures or communities."[1]

In this chapter I intend to use Vizenor's discussion on what *Indian* means to scrutinize the representation of *Indian* from Jean Baudrillard's viewpoint on simulation. Vizenor's manifest manner is in fact a simulation proposed by Baudrillard, which implies the absence of *Indian* and is "without a referent to an actual tribal rememberance."[2] Moreover, in the capital society, or as Fredric Jameson suggests, the "late capital society," the simulated *Indian* representation has become commodified and therefore lacks the relation to the history and culture. However, in the capital society people tend to believe the representation of the simulated *Indian* that souvenirs, novels, and movies with *Indian* flavor make popular. Ironically, viewing or possessing the products does not make people understand native culture or history; on the contrary, these items are collected as museum exhibits for the purpose of nostalgia. The so-called *Indian* has become commodity production, even a fragmented pastiche that lacks depth in relation to the history of any sort. Within the framework of the following discussion, I use Vizenor's works as examples to show how he alternates the *Indian* representation with his ironic portrayal of *Indians* in order to criticize and to make ridicule the commodified and simulated *Indian*.

As Vizenor states, "The word [*Indian*] has no referent in tribal languages or cultures."[3] The term's generalization not only erases the uniqueness of each tribe, but it also labels the so-called *Indian* as the Other. N. Scott Momaday claims in *Everlasting Sky* that "the Indian has been for a long time generalized in the imagination of the white man. Denied the acknowledgement of individuality and change, he has been made to become in theory what he could not become in fact, a synthesis of himself."[4] In other words, *Indian* does not refer to the actual native tribes. On the contrary, it represents the false homogeneity of the dominant culture, namely the western white culture. According to Vizenor, "The word Indian, and most other tribal names, are simulations in the literature of dominance."[5]

In the contemporary debates over tribal identity, integrity, and authenticity, *Indian* is still the term that has been generalized by ethnographers, historians, and colonial misnomers to refer to individual native tribes. In the history of American literature, the earliest accounts of natives were, in fact, written almost entirely by nonnatives from an outsider's point view, with "tribal words and concepts translated into a foreign language — English."[6] English, Vizenor argues, "has been the linear tongue of colonial discoveries, racial cruelties, invented names, the simulation of tribal cultures, manifest manners, and the unheard literature of dominance in tribal communities."[7] The constructed *Indian* is viewed as the Other in the dominant culture and literature. It is, according to Vizenor, a simulated nonentity that insinuates the obvious simulation and ruse of colonial dominance, namely manifest manner: "Manifest manners are the course of dominance, the racialist notions and misnomers sustained in archives and lexicons as 'authentic' representations of indian culture. Manifest manners court the destinies of monotheism, cultural determinism, objectivism, and the structural conceits of savagism and civilization."[8]

Vizenor claims that the *Indian* simulation of manifest manners continues through "the surveillance and domination of the tribes in literature," which he regards as "the ruins of representation."[9] The manifest manners of the literature of dominance will threaten tribal survivance, including cultures as well as creative voices. Vizenor points out that the tribal cultures considered in the linear representation of time, place, and person are actually manifest manners. Moreover, of the three kinds of manifest manners, Vizenor considers "nationalism. . . [to be] the most monotonous simulation of dominance" because "some tribes are simulated as national cultural emblems, and certain individuals are honored by the nation and the tribe as *real* representations."[10] For this reason individual tribal names and languages become nouns and pronouns. Vizenor writes in *The People Named the Chippewa* that the colonial term *Chippewa* is different from the tribal word *Anishinaabe*, the language used by the Anishinaabe people: "In the language of the tribal past, the families of the woodland spoke of themselves as the Anishinaabeg until the colonists named them the Ojibway and Chippewa. The word Anishinaabeg, the singular is Anishinaabe, is a phonetic transcription from the oral tradition. Tribal people used the word Anishinaabeg to refer to the people of the woodland who spoke the same language. The collective name was not an abstract concept of personal identities or national ideologies. Tribal families were the basic political and economic units in the woodland and the first source of personal identities."[11] It is ironic that the manifest manners of performance are honored more than the real native peoples. Tribal identities thus have been misconstructed as the Other and authenticated as simulation.

In the chapter "Terminal Creeds at Orion" in *Bearheart*, Vizenor, in using the term *terminal creeds*, proposes that the fragile identities as *Indians* have been dreadfully shaken.[12] He utilizes the scene of conversation between the people of Orion and Belladonna, a native girl, to suggest that *Indian* is an invention. Belladonna is asked to explain the so-called tribal value and the meaning of *Indian*. She applies the stereotypical representation of *Indian* to the meaning of the two terms:

> We are tribal and that means that we are children of dreams and visions. Our bodies are connected to mother earth and our minds are part of the clouds. Our voices are the living breath of the wilderness. . . . I am different than a whiteman because of my values and my blood is different. . . . We are different because we are raised with different values. . . . Tribal people seldom touch each other. . . . We do not invade

the personal bodies of others and we do not stare at people when we
are talking. Indians have more magic in their lives than whitepeople. . . .
An Indian is a member of a recognized tribe and a person who has In-
dian blood. . . . My tribal blood moves in the circles of mother earth
and through dreams without time. My tribal blood is timeless and it
gives me strength to live and deal with evil.[13]

Belladona, influenced by the manifest manner of the dominant culture, believes that there are essential differences between *Indians* and white people.
She internalizes the ideas unconsciously. Therefore the people of Orion say,
"You speak from terminal creeds. Not a person of real experience and critical
substance."[14] After listening to Belladonna's talk on the *Indians*, these people
point out that her explanations about the *Indian* is nothing more than an invention: "Indians are in invention. . . . You tell me that the invention is different than the rest of the world when it was the rest of the world that invented
the Indian. An Indian is an Indian because he speaks and thinks and believes
he is an Indian, but an Indian is nothing more than an invention."[15]

The story of "Terminal Creed" indicates that the public, including natives
and whites, are profoundly influenced by the terminal creeds and the invented notion of *Indians*. Belladonna's lecture on *Indian* not only fails to define
the term but also makes her interpretation elusive. The example of Belladonna shows that *Indian* is no longer a word with reference to the tribal; on the
contrary, it has become a pronoun to indicate all Native Americans. The favor
of the nonentity pronouns are "neither the source, causes, nor tribal intentions; autobiographies, memories and personal stories are not the authentic representations of either pronouns, cultures, or the environment."[16] As a
believer of terminal creeds, Belladonna is blind to the rules relinquishing "her
responsibility for growth," and becomes, as one character says, "her own victim."[17] Vizenor finds that the threat of death by terminal creeds is particularly ominous for Native Americans; as Blaeser indicates, "He devotes much of
his writing to delineating the 'invented indian.' "[18] Vizenor by mediating between the invented *Indian* and terminal creeds makes clear that the failure
for tribal people to outwit the imposed stereotypes would allow them to be
captured as *Indians* imprisoned by words and stereotypes.

In *Manifest Manners* Vizenor elaborates on his idea of *indians*.[19] *Indian*, according to Vizenor, is the absence of the real natives and the simulation of

tragic primitivism. Natives, on the other hand, are the actual storiers of motion and presence. In order to exemplify this difference, Vizenor applies Rene
Magritte's painting, *Ceci n'est pas une pipe* (This Is Not a Pipe) in order to suggest that the images we perceive, whether in books or on the screen, are not
natives but a mere simulation without actual reference. Magritte's painting
is included in the collection called *The Betrayal of Images* and is a representation of what we understand pipe to be. However, by capturing the essential *pipeness* in the painting, Magritte aims to show the differences between
the conceptual *pipeness* and the visual representation of a pipe. Utilizing the
painting as an example, Vizenor suggests that there is a gap between stereotypical representations of *Indian* and the real native, which, contrary to *Indian*, is of "*actual* action," "imagic presence," and "the actual tease of human
contingencies."[20] Thus the "portrait" of *indian* familiar to the public "is not
an Indian."[21] Vizenor's repetitive statement that "this portrait is not an Indian" challenges tribal representations and provokes further discussion on the
idea of simulation in light of Baudrillard's *Simulacra and Simulations*.

In *Simulacra and Simulation* Baudrillard points out that the simulation is a
product of contemporary consumer culture and imperialistic western science and philosophy, especially ethnography. In the consumer society, desires, which are stimulated by the dominant cultural discourses, mandate human needs. People are precoded with the simulation of what they desire so
that they process the relation to the world through the images. The world is
thus made in the simulated images of people's desire. For example, the image
of simulated *indian* is the product of such consumer culture, and the *indian*
simulation gradually stands for native cultures. Vizenor points out that "the
most romantic representations of natives are the advertisements of cultural dominance, not the natural sources of motion and sovereignty."[22] The *Indian*, as he puts it, is "a case of cultural nostalgia of the presence of tradition
in a chemical civilization; on the other hand, the *indian* is the very absence
and inexistence of reason and literature."[23] A consumer society provides a
precession of simulacra such as the simulation of *Indian*, which is a parade
of images projecting a life that consumers are encouraged to live. Therefore
the boundary between the real and the simulation, according to Baudrillard,
is blurred: "It is no longer a question of imitation, nor of reduplication, nor
even of parody. It is rather a question of substituting signs of the real for the

real itself. . . . Never again will the real have to be produced. . . . A hyperreal henceforth sheltered from the imaginary, and from any distinction between the real the imaginary, leaving room only for the orbital recurrence of models and the simulated generation of difference."[24]

Simulation is no longer the pure reflection of the reality. It gradually takes the place of reality and thereby becomes its own pure simulacrum. *Indian*, like simulation, also replaces the tribal real with its simulated reality. As a seemingly authentic experience becomes even harder to conceive, simulation, willed or not, rules the perception. All we can see are "hyperreal simulations of Indian, created from a model without actual origin or reality."[25] Moreover, following Baudrillard's discussion, Vizenor reaches his idea on simulation: "The simulations are the practices, condition, characteristics, and the manifold nature of tribal experiences. The simulations would include tribal documentation, peer recognition, sacred names and nicknames, cultural anxieties, cross-blood assurance, nationalism, pan-tribalism, new tribalism and reservation residence."[26] Vizenor considers that the simulation is everywhere and has taken the place of the real so that people can only learn or know from the false reality — the dead reality. Baudrillard indicates that "everywhere we live in a universe strangely similar to the original — things are doubled by their own scenario. But this doubling does not signify, as it did traditionally, the imminence of their death — they are already purged of their death, and better than when they were alive; more cheerful, more authentic, in the light of their model, like the faces in funeral homes."[27]

The "death" is in fact created by ethnologists according to Vizenor and Baudrillard. For Baudrillard in order for ethnology to live, its object must die because by dying the object takes its revenge for being "discovered" and because with its death it defies the science that wants to grasp it.[28] In "Heirs of Patronia" in *Hotline Healer*, Almost Browne, the novel's protagonist, is interviewed by an anthropologist, who is amused by Almost's tricky stories, including his birth by chance and the mongrel healers and so on. Instead of appreciating the stories for their humor and imagination, the anthropologist writes that the tricky stories "could be an overstated sense of mythic presence, as [Almost Browne] never revealed the sacred location."[29] In order to make fun of the anthropologist, Almost tells her different stories and tries to show contradictions in them to see if she can make sense of them. However, the cultural anthropologist is so "dedicated, . . . and without a trace of irony, she recorded his stories as true representations of native traditions."[30]

Thus the anthropologist, as well as other scholars, tries to discover the native traditions from a racialist point of view, which is also the manifest manners, so as to produce a hierarchy of values. Almost Browne exaggerates the influence of manifest manners and overturns the simulation with his ironic stories, representing the *Indians* in the primitive stage of life and treating them like fossils. Baudrillard observes that "the Indian thus returned to the ghetto, in the glass coffin of the virgin forest, again becomes the model of simulation of all the possible Indians *from before ethnology*. . . . These Indians it has entirely reinvented—Savages who are indebted to ethnology for still being savages: what a turn of event, what a triumph for this science that seemed dedicated to their destruction! Of course, these savages are posthumous: frozen, cryogenized, sterilized, protected *to death*, they have become referential simulacra, and science itself has become pure simulation."[31]

Both Belladonna and the anthropologist's beliefs are static and even dead. As Louis Owens comments in the afterword to *Bearheart*, the attempts of terminal creeds to "impose static definitions upon the world" are "destructive, suicidal, even when the definitions appear to arise out of revered tradition."[32] The simulation of *Indian* not only, as Baudrillard says, "threatens the difference between the 'true' and the 'false,' the 'real' and the 'imaginary,'" but also destroys "every referential, of every human objective, that shattered every ideal distinction between true and false, good and evil."[33] The simulation or the stereotypical representations reiterate throughout history and culture. Subsequently, Baudrillard suggests that "[the capital] does nothing but multiply the signs and accelerate the play of simulation."[34]

In "Cultural Logic of Late Capitalism" Jameson scrutinizes postmodern culture as late capitalism; it is a "'culture' has become a product in its own right; the market has become a substitute for itself and fully as much a commodity as any of the terms it includes within itself."[35] Therefore the product consumed is in fact "a whole new culture of the 'image' or the simulacrum" and "that strange new thing pastiche slowly comes to take [its] place."[36] Subsequently the representation becomes a source for the production of false social and cultural knowledge. The lack of the depth in history and culture and the production of the simulacrum is what Jameson calls "pastiche":

> Pastiche is, like parody, the imitation of a peculiar or unique, idiosyn-
> cratic style, the wearing of a linguistic mask, speech in a dead language.
> But in a neutral practice of such mimicry, without any of parody's ulte-
> rior motives, amputated of the satiric impulse, devoid of laughter and
> of any conviction that alongside the abnormal tongue you have mo-
> mentarily borrowed, some healthy linguistic normality still exists. Pas-
> tiche is thus blank parody, a statue with blind eyeballs: it is to paro-
> dy what that other interesting and historically original modern thing,
> the practice of a kind of blank irony, is to what Wayne Booth calls the
> "stable ironies."[37]

Therefore following Vizenor's manifest manners are Baudrillard's simulation
and Jameson's pastiche; these three terms in truth reveal that there is no such
thing as *Indian* since it is just a pose without origin.

In early Native American works two contrasting stereotypes of *Indian*
arose—the noble savage and the murdering barbarian. Blaeser suggests
that "eventually, when the tribal people no longer posed any kind of military
threat and the mythical American Eden was rapidly becoming civilized, romantic images of Native American . . . began to capture the popular imagination. The fictional noble savage became a means for satisfying the age-
less human longing for knowledge of the mythical lost past, for contact with
man in his most pristine state."[38] Not only within the field of literature but
also in the movie or television industry, *Indians* are portrayed according to
the rules. Take the movie *Dances with Wolves*, for example, which is considered "a marvelous piece of propaganda" that "exemplifies the strengths of
the American Myth of the Frontier in which white males dominate their surrounding, and Indians and women are present only as props, as means to an
end."[39] Owens further explains that "Indians in movies have always had two
roles: blood-thirsty savage or noble companion. In both of these roles, the
one unchanging obligation of the Indian is to die by the movie's end. These
three expectations—savagism, nobility, and death—delineate neatly the
role of the indigenous Native in the Euroamerican imagination, and they are
expectations founded upon a metanarrative that insists upon the mythic
and tragic 'otherness' of Native Americans. Above all, the media have always
been careful not to portray the Indian as a living, viable inhabitant of contemporary America."[40]

Dances with Wolves not only fails to present the native experience but also valorized the commercially accepted images of *Indians*. The representation of *Indians* does not correspond to the past. On the contrary, as Jameson suggests, "The past as 'referent' finds itself gradually bracketed, and then effaced altogether, leaving us with nothing but texts," and therefore *Indian* becomes an image, a text, and worse, an exhibit waiting to be dissected. As Jameson says, "The producers of culture have nowhere to turn but to the past, the imitation of dead styles, speech through all the masks and voices stored up in the imaginary museum of a now global culture."[41]

The representations of the stereotypical and the simulation of *indian* are constructed socially and culturally by the manifest manners in the capital society that will perpetuate a sense of hostility between the natives and the simulated *indians*. *Indians* not only appear in the literary works but also emerge in the mass media such as television programs and movies. Because of the threat of cultural genocide and forced assimilation, native Americans have to present the tribal lives according to the standard of the white culture. They can only survive and gain acceptance by becoming white or fulfilling the fantasy or stereotype imposed by the white society. Owens writes that "media representations of Indians as romantic, noble, savage artifacts who inhabit an unchanging past are important weapons in this war of eradication. As long as the world is encouraged to imagine that 'real' Indians exist only in the past, it will be easier to ignore the presence of actual Indian people living today in reservation communities."[42] The simulated *indian* representation that arbitrarily signifies the real native is, however, referred to as a nonentity of reference. Scholars and tourists turn to the invented images of *Indian* and thus create images of the *Indian* that fit their imagination.

Sadly, native people can only be accepted in the white world by pretending to be the idealized *Indian*. If native people mistake the invented image for the real, they will gradually become a romantic simulation. The invented *Indian* does not and cannot exist outside the pages of a book except as a simulation. The simulated *indian* has already lost the track of history or of culture; as Jameson puts it, it is "the consumption of sheer commodification as a process."[43] The commercialized *Indian*, without the reference, is oftentimes the target that Vizenor attacks.

In "Heirs of Patronia" in *Hotline Healers*, Almost Browne and his cousin begin their adventure selling blank books in the city and on campus. They promote blank books and claim that they are written by native authors in order to make money. Browne knows very well that people are more interested in the invented *indian* images than the reality of native cultures. Browne and his cousin sell books including *The Way to Rainy Mountain* by N. Scott Momaday, *Faces in the Moon* by Betty Louise Bell, and *Bone Game* by Louis Owens. Moreover, "Almost never hesitated to sign the books as the author, and now and then he would sign another author's name for the association value."[44] He even "boldly signed *The Map of Who We Are* by Lawrence Smith in the name of Maxine Hong Kingston. On the title page of *The Light People* by Gordon Henry, he signed as the novelist Ishmael Reed."[45]

The selling of the blank books is so successful that Browne and his cousin can sell hundreds of copies in a single day. In fact, what people purchase is not the books but the productions, which "proceed by first creating a demand through marketing and then producing the product to meet the demand."[46] The business also indicates that the blank books with names of famous native American writers have become a desired commodity, which characteristic encourages people to buy. Moreover, Almost, by signing the names of ethnic writers on certain books, demonstrates people's ignorance concerning writings of different ethnic cultures. What people buy is nothing but *indian* simulations; consequently the *indian* has become a commodity. Jameson concludes that "appropriately enough, the culture of the simulacrum comes to life in a society where exchange value has been generalized to the point at which the very memory of use is effaced, a society of which Guy Debord has observed, in an extraordinary phrase, that in it 'the image has become the final form of commodity reification.' "[47]

Almost Browne and his cousin also sell blank books on campus "in front of the literature and humanities [building]," where students and teachers are eager to buy them.[48] The latter are not only interested in the books but also "curious about reservation natives in a mobile book business."[49] The books are so popular that "more university courses require empty titles."[50] The relation between the need and demand is thus created through a false reality.

As Jameson points out, pastiche is to satisfy the demand of the society: "The exposition will take up in turn following constitutive features of the postmodern: a new depthlessness, which finds its prolongation both in contemporary 'theory' and in 'beyond historical time.' "[51] Therefore the *indian* simulation under western aesthetic judgment is an "archive" and a "tradition in museum."[52] For example, in "Heirs of Patronia" Thomas King, a well-known native Canadian writer, arrives at the barony of Patronia with a "cultural trunk" in his car.[53] The trunk is "packed with fake native costumes and fantastic turkey feather head dresses that were used in various posed pictures of anthropologist."[54] The *indian* customs are the false representation of natives. When native people put them on, they are regarded as members of primitive tribes, removed from civilization. They become the imprinted pictures in the museum for scholars to study. According to Jameson, it is "understood that the nostalgia film was never a matter of some old-fashioned 'representation' of historical content, but instead approached the 'past' through stylistic connotation, conveying 'pastness' by the glossy qualities of the image."[55] The archive reading of *indians* is a deconstruction of the native in literature and history. Jameson explains that "this omnipresence of pastiche is not incompatible with a certain humor, however, nor is it innocent of all passion: it is at the least compatible with addiction — with a whole historically original consumers' appetite for a world transformed into sheer images of itself and for pseudoevent and spectacle."[56] According to Vizenor and Jameson, the "simulated leaders in the cities who wore bone, beads, and leather, and strained to be the representations of traditional tribal culture" are nothing but pastiche and spectacle.[57]

Influenced by Baudrillard, Vizenor makes use of the former's term *simulation* to further his discussion on simulated *indian*. By exaggerating the manifest manners imposed upon the native culture, Vizenor demonstrates people's obsessions about the simulated *indian* so that the presence of natives gradually vanish. What takes place is the manifest manners, simulation, and pastiche. All three terms point out a fact that the origin has gone, and what is left is just fragmented and depthless images. However, these incomplete images constitute as clichés disguised as knowledge in order to satisfy the need of the audience. As Owens suggests, "The Indians are vanishing under a literal and metaphorical blanket of whiteness as their doom closes in."[58] With Vizenor's idea on manifest manners, Baudrillard's on simulation, and Jameson's on pastiche, *indian* is not only a nonentity but also a problematic term, especially in the postmodern capital society. However, Vizenor's resistance turns the term into language play and at the same time provides it with a new definition.

Notes

1. Vizenor, *Manifest Manners*. By italicizing *Indian* I second Vizenor's critical point that *Indian* is the absence of natives without reference. It is a concept that is imposed by the literature of dominance, namely the values of the white dominant society, and that shows the stereotypical representations of native peoples. *Indian*, as Vizenor suggests in *Manifest Manners*, is "a primitive simulation," which is "the actual absence — the simulations of the tragic primitive" (xii–xiii).

2. Vizenor, *Manifest Manners*, 8.

3. Vizenor, *Manifest Manners*, 11.

4. Quoted in Vizenor, *Everlasting Sky*, 21.

5. Vizenor, *Manifest Manners*, 10.

6. Blaeser, *Gerald Vizenor*, 53. Outsiders refer mainly to the Anglo-American colonizers who tended to believe tribal people were primitive and lacked written languages.

7. Vizenor, *Manifest Manners*, 105.

8. Vizenor, *Manifest Manners*, vii.

9. Vizenor, *Manifest Manners*, 4.

10. Vizenor, *Manifest Manners*, 59–60.

11. Vizenor, *People Named the Chippewa*, 13.

12. Terminal creeds are the manifest manners imposed on the natives by the western culture. Vizenor writes in *Manifest Manners* that "foundational theories have overburdened tribal imagination, memories and the coherence of natural reason with simulations and the cruelties of paracolonial historicism. Anthropologists, in particular, were not the best listeners or interpreters of tribal imagination, liberation or literature" (75). Therefore terminal creeds are not survivance, the native real, but the inscriptions of the literature of dominance.

13. Vizenor, *Bearheart*, 193–96.

14. Vizenor, *Bearheart*, 196.

15. Vizenor, *Bearheart*, 195.

16. Vizenor, *Manifest Manners*, 96.

17. Blaeser, *Gerald Vizenor*, 52.

18. Blaeser, *Gerald Vizenor*, 52.

19. Refusing the use of capitalized *Indian*, Vizenor applies the lower-case italicized *indian* to designate the "simulation, a derivative noun that means an absence" (*Fugitive Poses*, 15).

20. Vizenor, *Manifest Manners*, xi–x.

21. Vizenor, *Manifest Manners*, 18.

22. Vizenor, *Hotline Healers*, 5.

23. Vizenor, *Fugitive Poses*, 38.

24. Baudrillard, "Precession of Simulacra," 2.
25. Vizenor, *Manifest Manners*, 4.
26. Vizenor, *Manifest Manners*, 59.
27. Baudrillard, "Precession of Simulacra," 11.
28. Baudrillard, "Precession of Simulacra," 7.
29. Vizenor, *Hotline Healers*, 23.
30. Vizenor, *Hotline Healers*, 23.
31. Baudrillard, "Precession of Simulacra," 8.
32. Quoted in Vizenor, *Bearheart*, 249.
33. Baudrillard, "Precession of Simulacra," 3, 22.
34. Baudrillard, "Precession of Simulacra," 22.
35. Jameson, "Cultural Logic," 10.
36. Jameson, "Cultural Logic," 6, 17.
37. Jameson, "Cultural Logic," 17.
38. Blaeser, *Gerald Vizenor*, 53.
39. Owens, "Two-Socks Hop," 115.
40. Owens, "Two-Socks Hop," 117.
41. Jameson, "Cultural Logic," 18, 17.
42. Owens, "Two-Socks Hop," 130.
43. Jameson, "Cultural Logic," 10.
44. Vizenor, *Hotline Healers*, 24–25.
45. Vizenor, *Hotline Healers*, 25.
46. Leitch, *Theory and Criticism*, 1730.
47. Jameson, "Cultural Logic," 18.
48. Vizenor, *Hotline Healers*, 25.
49. Vizenor, *Hotline Healers*, 25.
50. Vizenor, *Hotline Healers*, 27.
51. Jameson, "Cultural Logic," 21.
52. Vizenor, *Fugitive Poses*, 50.
53. Vizenor, *Hotline Healers*, 25.
54. Vizenor, *Hotline Healers*, 25.
55. Jameson, "Cultural Logic," 19.
56. Jameson, "Cultural Logic," 18.
57. Vizenor, *Manifest Manners*, 149.
58. Owens, "Two-Socks Hop," 126.

Bibliography

Baudrillard, Jean. "The Precession of Simulacra." In *Simulacra and Simulation*, translated by Sheila Faria Glaser, 1–42. Ann Arbor: University of Michigan Press, 1994.

Blaeser, Kimberly M. *Gerald Vizenor: Writing in the Oral Tradition*. Norman: University of Oklahoma Press, 1996.

Jameson, Fredric. *Postmodernism: The Cultural Logic of Late Capitalism.* Durham NC: Duke
    University Press, 2003.
Leitch, Vincent B., comp. and ed. *The Norton Anthology of Theory and Criticism.* New
    York: Norton, 2001.
Owens, Louise. "Apocalypse at the Two-Socks Hop: Dancing with the Vanishing Amer-
    ican." In *Mixedblood Messages: Literature, Film, Family, Place,* edited by Louis
    Owens, 113–31. Norman: University of Oklahoma Press, 1998.
Vizenor, Gerald. *Bearheart: The Hiership Chronicles.* Minneapolis: University of Min-
    neapolis Press, 1990.
———. *Everlasting Sky: Voices of Anishinabe People.* St Paul: Minnesota Historical So-
    ciety Press, 2001.
———. *Fugitive Poses: Native American Indian Scenes of Absence and Presence.* Lincoln:
    University of Nebraska Press, 1998.
———. *Hotline Healers: An Almost Browne Novel.* Hanover NH: University Press of New
    England, 1997.
———. *Manifest Manners: Narratives on Postindian Survivance.* Lincoln: University of
    Nebraska Press, 1994.
———. *The People Named the Chippewa: Narrative Histories.* Minneapolis: University
    of Minnesota Press, 1984.

6. WILLIAM APESS

Storier of Survivance

ARNOLD KRUPAT

> Survival is a response; survivance is a standpoint, a worldview, and a presence.
>
> Gerald Vizenor, *Postindian Conversations*

My contribution to this volume takes up three of the many overlapping dimensions of Gerald Vizenor's concept, survivance as "a standpoint, a worldview, and a presence" in the work of the nineteenth-century Pequot minister, activist, and writer Rev. William Apess.[1] As a "standpoint, a worldview, and a presence," survivance, as we may quote Vizenor, produces stories that "are an active presence"; survivance "is an active repudiation of dominance, tragedy, and victimry."[2] In regard to what Vizenor has called the "wild ironies of survivance," he notes that his own narratives of survivance are "an aesthetic restoration of trickster hermeneutics, . . . stories of liberation, . . . without the dominance of closure."[3] I want to look at the way in which two Apess texts, "An Indian's Looking-Glass for the White Man" and *Eulogy on King Philip*, powerfully illustrate these comments. Specifically I want to show how these texts work, first, to avoid victimry by substituting for it the ongoing agency and activity of the Native; second, how complementary to this avoidance, they insist on Indian presence rather than absence; and third, how they thus rewrite tragic narratives in the ironic mode. In the second of these texts, as I hope to show, Apess writes against a very specific narrative of dominance. I will offer what used to be called close readings of these texts while contextualizing them historically as fully as I can.

Apess could not, of course, have read Vizenor, and although Vizenor has read Apess, I don't think he was especially focused on Apess in the years in which he elaborated the concept of survivance. As for myself, having read both Vizenor and Apess for a good many years, I am surprised to find only now how extraordinary the confluence is between aspects of the work of the nineteenth-century Pequot and the twentieth- and twenty-first century Anishinaabe writer. To an almost uncanny degree, they meet on the ground of what Vizenor has variously defined as survivance.

For any who may not yet be familiar with William Apess, I'll quickly summarize some of what is known. Apess was born in Colrain, Massachusetts, in 1798. Early in his life he was put in the care of his alcoholic grandparents who beat him severely and then sold him as an indentured laborer when he was only four or five years old. Apess eventually ran off from his master's house and participated in the unsuccessful American attack on Montreal in the War of 1812. He had taken up drinking in the army, and after leaving it in 1815, he wandered about and held a number of odd jobs. In 1813 he had a religious experience, and he turned to evangelical Methodism to help him regain control of his life. He was baptized into the church in 1818 and ordained a minister in 1829. By 1834, however, he had left Methodism to found his own "Free and United Church."

It was around this time that Apess went to Cape Cod to work on behalf of the Mashpee tribe whose rights had been much curtailed by the state of Massachusetts. Although he contributed substantially to the Mashpees's achievement of a greater degree of sovereignty, for reasons not yet fully established, he fell out of favor with them. Twice in January of 1836, Apess delivered a eulogy on the Wampanoag leader called King Philip to an audience in Boston, with the first and longer version being published within the year.[4] In January of 1839 Apess and his second wife Elizabeth moved to New York City where he died four months later of "apoplexy" — perhaps a cerebral hemorrhage but almost surely from the unfortunate administration of botanic remedies given him by a physician.[5]

Apess's first publication was a book-length autobiography, *A Son of the Forest: The Experience of William Apes, a Native of the Forest* (1829), the first such text by a Native American to be produced without the participation of a translator, amanuensis, or editor. Apess followed this work with an abbreviated version of his life story along with short biographies of his first wife and four other Native converts to Christianity in *The Experiences of Five Christian*

Indians of the Pequ'd Tribe (1833). The original edition of this book concluded
with an extraordinary essay called "An Indian's Looking-Glass for the White
Man," a powerful indictment of what Apess called color prejudice and what
we would today call racism (the second edition of 1837 omitted this essay).
Apess's account of his activism on behalf of the Mashpee is documented in
his 1835 *Indian Nullification of the Unconstitutional Laws of Massachusetts Relative to the Marshpee Tribe, or, The Pretended Riot Explained.* In 1836 Apess published the last of his works, the text of his eulogy for King Philip, whom he
claimed as a distant ancestor. My focus in this essay will be on "An Indian's
Looking-Glass" as a text directed against American racism as it most particularly oppresses American Indians and on the *Eulogy on King Philip*, which develops the attack on racism but adds nothing less than a revisionary history
of America.[6] Apess's texts, as I hope to show, are, in Vizenor's phrase, "survivance stories," insisting on the active presence of Native people. They reject
the dominant society's comic narrative of its own "progress" and its complementary tragic narrative of the Indian's decline, insisting that should it come
to be the case that Native people vanish from the east and from the earth,
their story could only be an ironic one of might unjustly making right.[7] Apess
is writing at a time when president Andrew Jackson's "removal" policies most
immediately threaten the Cherokees of Georgia while also threatening other tribal nations, thus the reference to the east. The *Eulogy of King Philip*, as I
will try to show, is offered not only to contest these sorts of stories but also
to contest a very specific narrative, one that is decidedly what Vizenor would
call a narrative of dominance.

From roughly the 1830s to the 1850s and after, American thought about Indians was dominated by — to borrow a phrase from Reginald Horsman — the
discourse of scientific racism. In the sketchiest of summaries, we may note
that this discourse divided humanity into distinct races and ranked those races in relation to their achievement of or capacity for civilization. As Roy Harvey Pearce documented the matter more than half a century ago, the white,
"civilized" American male defined himself positively against an invented, ideologically constructed Other that denominated the Indian as "savage."[8] But
to state the obvious, although Native Americans, persons indigenous to the
Americas, had existed for millennia, there were no "Indians" or "savages" until Europeans created them.

The discourse of savagism and of scientific racism, positing the white, male, Christian capitalist as the crown of creation, operated according to an evolutionary logic well before Darwin's publications (from 1856 to 1871). Although there were exceptions, most mainstream Euro-American writers in the nineteenth century believed that Indians were racially incapable of rising to civilization and that as a race they would inevitably have to vanish. A considerable number of poems, plays, sermons, government publications, narrative fictions, indeed texts of every historically available genre again and again employed the rhetoric of vanishment, either metaphorically (as the dew vanishes in the rising sun; as the night yields to day; as the primeval forest gives way to the cultivated field, and so on) or by means of an appeal to presumptively empirical science (their brains are small; their languages have only nouns; their religions are crude superstitions, and so on). Whereas in the seventeenth and at least part of the eighteenth century, writers who believed Indians would have to vanish typically assigned their sad fate to the will of God, in the nineteenth century it was assigned to the laws of nature — laws that no act of man could alter or impede. Even on those few occasions when nineteenth-century writers managed to recognize that there were indeed living, breathing, intelligent, and quite able Native persons before them,[9] they nonetheless spoke of them as odd relics or remnants of a once-proud race whose fate, however sad, was simply to vanish. This belief, as Horsman notes, is a convenient "intellectual rationale for the realities of power."[10] If Indians are simply unfortunate victims of fate in the form of natural, social-evolutionary law, soon to be known only by their absence, then their story is indeed a tragic one.

When tragic narratives are used nationally, they have, as Edward Said notes, "the capacity to authorize and embody certain sequences of cause and effect, while at the same time preventing the emergence of counter-narratives."[11] Thus to narrate Native decline in something other than the tragic mode would require, as the historian Francis Jennings writes, "painful revision of the pleasant myths we all learned in grade school" about the "winning of the west," a story of decent Euro-Americans "bravely setting out with their families to conquer the wilderness and create civilization . . . [as] these sturdy, God-fearing folk endure all the hazards and toil of their mission, standing constantly at arms to fend off attacks by savage denizens of the wilderness."[12] Jennings minces no words; for him "the myth is nationalist and racist propaganda to justify conquest of *persons* who happen to be Indians, and their dispossession."[13] Insofar as this accusation is accurate — and I believe it is — the myth of Indian disappearance or vanishment is itself "nationalist and racist propaganda." The tragic narrative of Indian disappearance needs correction by the instantiation of an ironic narrative that makes it clear that it is neither the law of God nor the laws of nature but only Euro-American violence that produces Indian victimry. Such an ironic narrative must function by insisting that Indians are not merely victims but rather active and capable of full agency and that they have not vanished nor are they absent but palpably present. As Vizenor has written, "Native survivance is more than survival, more than endurance or mere response; the stories of survivance are an active presence."[14] This presence is one that can "undermine the literature of dominance."[15] Here we can turn to two texts by Apess that can, it seems to me, accurately be called "stories of survivance."

Perhaps because he is well aware that Indian peoples in his time are regularly being consigned to passivity (because they are racially inferior to the ever-active whites) and the past (they are a last remnant, a doomed and dying race), Apess opens "An Indian's Looking-Glass" with a sentence that insists upon the presence, agency, and equality of at least one Indian person, the author himself. "*Having* a desire to place a few things before my fellow creatures . . . ," Apess begins, asserting, with the participial "having" and the characterization of his audience as his "fellow creatures," the activity, contemporaneity, and equality of the Indian writer. This assertion is reinforced by his second sentence: "*Now* I ask if degradation has not been heaped long enough upon the Indians?"[16]

In his third paragraph Apess describes the neighbors of the Indians as people "who have no principle," while the second sentence of his fourth paragraph asks whether Indians are not "said to be men of talents."[17] Principles and talents are, of course, moral and intellectual qualities. But both these words also reference the economic and financial: *principle* and *interest*, that is to say, are words that have to do with money; "talents" appear in the Bible as monetary units. Apess will ironically develop the notion that the materially well-off whites are not at all superior to the Indians from a religious and moral perspective because the former are unprincipled — bankrupt — when it comes to dealing with those of a different skin color.[18] His fourth paragraph, for example, has five uses of "principle" or a variant, and in every case this usage is to establish the *un*principled actions of white in regard to red.[19]

Apess uses "black" as an adjective metaphorically to describe morals — principles — that have become corrupted by a literal aversion to "black" or colored *skin*. Apess speaks of "the impure black principle . . . as corrupt and unholy as it can be" of color prejudice, leading to his notation of the "black inconsistency that you place before me," the extremely bad "principle" of considering "skins of color — more disgraceful than all the skins that Jehovah ever made."[20] Not only is this action bad, but it is also absurd and ludicrous — ironic? — inasmuch as God "has made fifteen colored people to one white."[21] Thus in his seventh paragraph Apess writes, "But, reader, I acknowledge that this is a confused world, and I am not seeking for office, but merely [!] placing before you the *black* inconsistency that you place before me — which is ten times *blacker* than any skin that you will find in the universe."[22] Apess's rhetorical manner is a good example of what Vizenor called "trickster hermeneutics."[23] Apess is not quite a trickster, but his strategies are certainly tricky in Vizenor's sense of the word.

It is in the eighth paragraph that Apess launches his bitter and powerful indictment of the white man's crimes, a strong challenge to the latter's presumptive racial and moral superiority. Echoing the strategy with which he began, Apess poses another rhetorical question, offering a truly horrifying possibility: "Now let me ask you, white man, [if all the world's] different skins were put together, and each skin had its national crimes written upon it — which skin do you think would have the greatest?"[24]

The penultimate paragraph repeats what has been central to Apess's argument thus far as the author again addresses the reader directly: "By what you read, you may learn how deep your principles are. I should say they were skin deep."[25] He assures the reader that many "men of fame" advocate the cause of the Indians.[26] Further, he takes pains to conclude on a positive note, exhorting his readers to be hopeful: "Do not get tired, ye noble-hearted — only think how many poor Indians want their wounds done up daily; the Lord will reward you, and pray you stop not till this tree of distinction be leveled, and the mantle of prejudice torn from every American heart — then shall peace pervade the Union."[27] The "stories of liberation and survivance," Vizenor has written, conclude "without the dominance of closure."[28] So too in a manner not so very different perhaps from the conclusion of Vizenor's novel *The Heirs of Columbus* (1991) does Apess conclude with an open, hopeful vision of a different and better future.

Apess's *Eulogy on King Philip* was orally presented twice in abbreviated form in Boston, first on January 8, 1836, and again on January 26 of the same year. The January 8 was the anniversary of President Andrew Jackson's defeat of the British at the Battle of New Orleans in 1815 and thus, as Maureen Konkle has noted, Apess spoke "on the day most identified with Jackson."[29] Jackson, who had been elected president in 1828, was actively involved in the promotion of Indian removal, the relocation of the southeastern tribes to lands west of the Mississippi. Congress had passed the Indian Removal Act in 1830 giving the president the authority to negotiate treaties with the tribes to provide for their removal. As is fairly well known, most immediately threatened were the Cherokees of Georgia. Although the majority of Cherokees, led by principal chief John Ross, continued to reject the appeals to leave their traditional homelands, a small group of Cherokee progressives — wealthy landowners and slaveholders — led by John Ridge and his family, had signed the Treaty of New Echota with the government in 1835, thus giving Jackson the means legally to remove the eastern Cherokees to lands west of the Mississippi. The actual removal, sending the Cherokees on what has become known as The Trail of Tears, finally was carried out from the fall of 1838 to March 1839.

Speaking on a day identified with Jackson, Apess will use his *Eulogy*, as Konkle further notes, to tell "the story of how one gets from the Puritans to New Echota."[30] Apess's attention to Philip offers a revisionary narrative of the past that importantly bears on his present. Apess will invoke Philip as someone who is not absent but still present and relevant to Native resistance to Jackson's determination to remove the eastern Cherokees as well as to abrogate more generally Native sovereignty.

The address Apess's Boston audience heard further developed the argument of "An Indian's Looking-Glass," insisting passionately on the equal value of all in the eyes of God regardless of the color of their skin. But Apess's *Eulogy* has something much larger in mind: it endeavors nothing less than to replace the American master narrative of progress and dominance with a narrative of continuance and survivance. Apess will reject the story of Indian decline told as a tragedy, making a strong case that an ironic narrative that details the triumph of greed and injustice must take its place. Apess's story subverts and replaces the narratives of dominance that produce Indians as inevitable victims; he rejects Indian victimry and foregrounds Native presence over absence, substituting what Vizenor has called *continuance* for any Euro-American notions of progress.

Apess had himself twice been an autobiographer, and his first approach to Philip is biographical. "The first inquiry," he proclaims on the second page of his text (this is the text of an oral performance), "is: Who *is* Philip?"[31] He begins to answer this question by noting that Philip "*was* the descendant of one of the most celebrated chiefs in the known world."[32] But the present tense of the question is crucial. For Apess had insisted in his second paragraph that just as "the immortal Washington lives endeared and engraven on the hearts of every white in America, never to be forgotten in time—even such is the immortal Philip honored, as held in memory by the degraded but yet grateful descendants who appreciate his character."[33] In equating Washington and Philip, Apess, consistent with his earlier work, emphasizes the equality so far as their common humanity is concerned of whites, Indians, and all persons of color. As Washington presently lives in the hearts of white America, so too does Philip presently live in the hearts of red America. The latter is not an absence but an ongoing presence; he has not tragically vanished, nor—however "degraded" by the depredations of the settlers—have the Natives.

Let me offer some merely factual response to Apess's question of who was King Philip. Philip's name was not Philip, but Metacom or Metacomet, and his position was in no way parallel to that of a European king. Rather, he was a principal leader of the Pokanokets of Rhode Island, generally considered a branch of the Wampanoag nation of Massachusetts. The Wampanoags were attacked in 1675 by New Plymouth, Massachusetts Bay Colony, and Connecticut, leading to a war frowned upon by England, still the mother country of the American colonists. It was the colonists who named Philip, bestowed upon him his rank, and called the war that they had instigated his, implying thereby that the aggrieved party had been the aggressor. Philip and his allies inflicted substantial casualties on the English, despite the English and their Indian allies ultimately defeating Philip, killing and dismembering him, and selling many of his people (including his wife and son) into Caribbean slavery.[34] De-monized by an abundance of seventeenth-century Puritan texts, King Philip and King Philip's War were frequently topics of nineteenth-century poetry, fiction, and historiographic writing far more sympathetic to Philip. Whereas Puritan authors had uniformly been contemptuous of Philip, a considerable number of Apess's white contemporaries represented him as a sympathetic, if inevitably doomed, patriot and protector of his people and his lands and as a tragic hero, whose fate was ordained if not by God (as the Puritans and some later writers would have it), then by the laws of nature.[35]

To give some sense of what this writing was like, I'll briefly cite Washington Irving's essay "Philip of Pokanoket," first published in 1814 and reprint-ed in Irving's *The Sketch Book of Geoffrey Crayon, gent.* (1819–20). A writer far more important in his own time than we currently consider him now, Irving wrote of Philip that "he was an evil that walked in darkness, whose coming none could foresee, and against which none knew when to be on the alert."[36] Yet he also deems Philip and his people "worthy of an age of poetry, and fit subjects for local story and romantic fiction."[37] For Irving the defeat of Phil-ip and his people, like the destined vanishing of the other tribes, is a tragic story, sad—but just. Irving writes that Philip had "heroic qualities and bold achievements that would have graced a civilized warrior, and have rendered him the theme of the poet and historian."[38] He concludes his essay by ob-serving that "he lived a wanderer and a fugitive in his native land, and went down, like a lonely bark foundering amid darkness and tempest—without a pitying eye to weep his fall, or a friendly hand to record his struggle."[39] Irving pities Philip's victimry, weeps, and offers an ambiguously "friendly hand" in recording his struggle, but he never doubts that Philip's demise and that of his people was anything but just and necessary.

As we shall see, this position is also that of Edward Everett, who has the problem of how it is possible on the one hand to disapprove of Jackson's re-moval of the Cherokees while on the other defending his Puritan forefathers' "removal" and near extermination of Philip and the eastern Indians. I believe that Apess in his *Eulogy* wishes very specifically to contest the narrative of dominance contained in Everett's Address that he delivered at Bloody Brook, in South Deerfield, on September 30, 1835.

Everett's address is called "In Commemoration of the fall of the 'Flower of

Essex,' at that spot, in King Philip's War, September 18, (O[ld] S[tyle]) 1675."
The Flower of Essex consists of "her hopeful young men" who perished in
battle against Philip and his forces.[40] Everett's lengthy speech on the occasion of the dedication of a monument to these Puritan warriors tells the story of the colonists' struggle against Philip and his people in the comic mode,
as had the Puritans themselves. Thus a representative quotation from Everett's address states, "If we turn our thoughts to the grand design with which
America was *colonized*, to the *success* with which, under *Providence*, that design
has been *crowned*, I own I find it difficult to express myself in terms of moder-
ation."[41] The triumphal comedy of the Puritans' victory, as Everett narrates
it, must, of course, be a tragic story for Philip and his people, the Puritans'
victims. Another representative quotation from Everett has him imagining
"the *ill-starred* chieftain, who, hunted to his last retreat, . . . seized his gun," at
which point, after an Englishman fires and misses, an "Indian fires and shoots
the fallen chief through the heart. . . . Such was the *fate* of Philip."[42]

Apess will have none of this. Translating Philip's history into a story of survivance, he insists that Philip's defeat and the subsequent dispossession and
degradation of the Native population is neither comic, as Everett and the Puritans tell it, nor for Philip and his descendants, as Everett and a great many
writers more sympathetic to Philip and his people tell it, tragic. Rather, Apess
will insist that the defeat of Philip and that defeat's consequences for America constitute a narrative that is ironic in the extreme (violence, greed, and
treachery are unjustly rewarded).

Thus Apess offers a revisionist history of the Puritan invasion of America.
He documents the Puritans' many "inhuman" acts and rhetorically asks his audience, "And who, my dear sirs, were wanting of the name of savages — whites
or Indians? Let justice answer."[43] He develops this line of argument by describing further savage acts on the part of the "lewd Pilgrims," in particular "one
Standish, a vile and malicious fellow!"[44] Apess then asks, "And do you believe
that Indians cannot feel and see, as well as white people? If you think so, you
are mistaken. Their power of feeling and knowing is as quick as yours. . . . But
if the real sufferers say one word, they are denounced as being wild and *savage* beasts."[45] Considering the treatment of Native people at the hands of the
Puritan colonizers, Apess says, "To the sons of the Pilgrims (as Job said about
the day of his birth) let the day be dark, the 22d day of December 1622; let

it be forgotten in your celebration, in your speeches, and by the burying of the rock that your fathers first put their foot upon."[46]

Apess's vehemence here seems very much a response to what he would surely have taken as outrageously insulting remarks made by Everett, for example Everett's claim that "the settlers made as near an approach to the spirit of the gospel, in their dealings with the Indians, as the frailty of our natures admits, under the circumstances under which they were placed [sic], is clear."[47] Thus as Apess continues his narration of Philip's life, he insists that we see clearly the ways in which Philip was *not* treated in "the spirit of the gospel" but to the contrary was insulted and abused by the putatively God-fearing Puritan invaders.

When Apess comes to an account of the war that finally broke out between the settlers and the Indians, he highlights Philip's military prowess, despite his not prevailing. Speaking of Philip's death, Apess is at pains to insist that Philip was "fired upon by an *Indian* and killed dead upon the spot" so that "the Pilgrims did not have the pleasure of tormenting him."[48] The Pilgrims do, however, have the grim pleasure of quartering Philip's body then giving his head and one hand "to the Indian who shot him," later displaying the head for twenty years "upon a gibbet" in Plymouth while the hand goes to Boston, "where it was exhibited in *savage* triumph."[49]

Everett makes no mention whatever of this Puritan butchery, although he does bemoan the fate of Philip's wife and son "sold into slavery; West Indian slavery! — an Indian princess and her child, sold from the cool breezes of Mount Hope, from the wild freedom of a New England forest, to gasp under the lash, beneath the blazing sun of the tropics!"[50] Yet Everett's lament does not extend itself to criticize the noble Puritans who effected this sale.

Apess relentlessly develops the subversive idea that the degradation of the Indians in the past and the continued assault upon them in his present Jacksonian era derive from the Puritan founders. He asserts that "through the prayers, preaching, and example of those pretended pious has been the foundation of all the slavery and degradation in the American colonies toward colored people. Experience has taught me that this has been a most sorry and wretched doctrine to us poor ignorant Indians."[51] The irony of this last self-description is intensified — the speaker is in no way a "poor ignorant" Indian — as Apess tells his audience that he will mention "two or three things to amuse you a little."

Returning to the autobiographical mode for a moment, he narrates personal anecdotes that are bitter and full of a dark ironic humor. Apess recalls a time "about 15 years ago" when he was passing through Connecticut, "where they are so pious that they kill the cats for killing rats, and whip the beer barrels for working upon the Sabbath."[52] It happened that he called upon a rich man, "very pious," a member of his own church, to ask if he could stay the night. The man did not refuse outright but allowed Apess on "a severe cold night" only "a little wood but no bed, because I was an Indian."[53] "Another Christian," Apess says, was so very Christian as to ask him "to dine with him and put my dinner behind the door; I thought this a queer compliment indeed."[54] A third anecdote involves a man at an inn in Lexington, who, unaware that Apess was himself an Indian, "began to say they ought to be exterminated." Apess "took it up in our defense, though not boisterous but coolly; and when we came to retire, finding that I was an Indian, he was unwilling to sleep opposite my room for fear of being murdered before morning."[55] "These things I mention," Apess says, not boisterously but with cool irony, "to show that the doctrines of the Pilgrims has [sic] grown up with the people."[56] As ye have sown so shall ye reap: the racialist legacy of Puritanism, and the narrative of American progress and dominance, must be rejected before justice can prevail.

Apess then returns to Philip's history in a manner that will acutely demonstrate its present relevance to Andrew Jackson and his "legal" assault on the Georgia Cherokees. Philip is *not* merely a victim nor is he *absent*. Apess invites his audience to imagine the "deep . . . thought of Philip, when he could look from Maine to *Georgia*, and from the ocean to the lakes, and view with one look all his brethren withering before the *more enlightened* to come; and how true his prophecy; that the white people would not only cut down their groves but would enslave them."[57] It is surely no accident that Apess describes the trajectory of Philip's gaze as extending beyond his own lands to the south, specifically to Georgia — at that very moment working actively in its great "enlightenment" to "enslave" the Cherokees within its borders by bringing them under Georgia law. Apess indirectly refers to this just a few sentences later, writing, "Look at the deep-rooted plans laid, when a territory becomes a state, that after so many years the laws shall be extended over the Indians that live within their boundaries."[58]

But here too Apess seems quite specifically to be rewriting parts of Everett's address. Consider, for example, the moment when Everett seeks to bolster the view of Philip's story as a tragedy by inviting his audience to "think of the country for which the Indians fought! Who can blame them?"[59] Everett then offers the following imaginary tableau: "As Philip looked down from his seat on Mount Hope, that glorious eminence . . . and beheld the lovely scene which spread below . . . could he be blamed, if his heart burned within him, as he beheld it all passing, by no tardy process, from beneath his control into the hands of the stranger?"[60] Earlier Everett had also indirectly and somewhat elliptically *denied* any linkage between the treatment of the New England Indians in Philip's time (and by implication at least, in his own) and the treatment of the Cherokees in Georgia. In a note on the migration "farther west and north" of the New England tribes defeated by the colonists and their "advancing settlements," Everett says that "it can be scarcely necessary to state that considerations of this kind *have no applicability* to the questions recently agitated in the United States, relative to the rights acquired by Indian tribes under solemn compacts, voluntarily entered into by the United States, at the instance and for the benefit of an individual state."[61]

This justification Apess also forcefully rejects. In the paragraph we have been examining, he continues his attack on the treatment of the Cherokees, remarking that "even the president of the United States tells the Indians they cannot live among civilized people, and we want your lands and must have them and will have them."[62] He then turns the tables, doing to President Jackson what had so often been done to Indian people, ventriloquizing him and putting words into his mouth. Apess has the (unnamed) president say, "We want your land for our use to speculate upon, it aids us in paying off our national debt and supporting us in Congress to drive you off."[63] Consistent with his firm belief that the treatment of the Indians of his own day descends in a direct line from Puritan treatment of Indians in an earlier day, Apess has the president conclude, "This has been the way our fathers first brought us up, and it is hard to depart from it; therefore, you shall have no protection from us."[64] Georgian and Jacksonian rapaciousness are only the most recent version of Puritan greed.

Apess's conclusion in some measure echoes the conclusion of "An Indian's Looking-Glass," but I think, with some significant differences. In the earlier text he uses the phrase "poor Indians" and invokes the hope that when "this tree of distinction," color prejudice, "be leveled to the earth . . . then shall peace pervade the Union."[65] In the final paragraph of the *Eulogy*, he inscribes himself "a poor Indian" and again offers the hope that "peace and righteousness" may one day "be written upon our hearts and hands together."[66] But the general exhortation to do better so that "the Lord will reward you" that concludes "An Indian's Looking-Glass" becomes in the *Eulogy* a more specifically historical exhortation.[67] Apess encourages his audience to "rejoice that we have not to answer for our fathers' crimes; neither shall we do right to charge them to one another." Instead "we can only regret it [*sic*], and flee from it," choosing indeed to embrace "peace and righteousness."[68] We must all, whites, Natives, all peoples, as I understand this conclusion, work toward a different and better future. To help in that work, Apess offers us narratives of continuance and survivance rather than stories of progress and dominance.

Notes

Some of the material that follows has been used in somewhat different form in chapters 2 and 3 of my book *All that Remains*. This essay appears here for the first time.

1. Vizenor and Lee, *Postindian Conversations*, 93.
2. Vizenor, *Fugitive Poses*, 15.
3. Vizenor, *Manifest Manners*, 76, 14.
4. The second and shorter version was published the following year, 1837. The first publication of the *Eulogy* had the author's name spelled Apes, as indeed, did other of his publications. Barry O'Connell's edition of Apess's complete works makes the case for spelling his name Apess, which with some few objections, has become standard.
5. From the obituary in the *New Bedford Gazette and Mercury*, May 7, 1839: Dr. A. Atkinson "gave him [Apess] 30 grains of lobelia, in two doses of 15 grains each. . . . The same doctor then gave him a dose of medicine in powder, to act cathartically, consisting of charcoal, mandrake, and white wood, and dogwood bark. Some drops were then given him, he ate some toast, and in five minutes thereafter, sunk and died!" Nonetheless, after a postmortem examination, "the jury arrived at the conclusion, that the deceased died of apoplexy." This piece contains materials reprinted from the *New York Observer*'s obituary, which I have not managed to obtain.
6. And also African Americans, along with all people of color.
7. As we shall see further, the narrative of Euro-American progress was emplotted—structured—as *comedy* while the narrative of Native American decline was

emplotted as *tragedy*. Comic plots are stories that have "happy" endings that have the protagonist—in the instances we are considering, a collective protagonist (that is, a race, a nation, a people) —overcoming coarse, brutish, or evil obstacles to achieve ends that the audience understands to be good, right, and just. By contrast, tragic plots are stories that have "unhappy" endings. These unhappy endings come about because individuals—or, again, in the instances we are considering, races, nations, peoples—have some basic and (in the view of "scientific racists," irremediable) flaw or defect, leading to their downfall or demise. This downfall or demise for all its sadness is nonetheless also and importantly felt to be just. *Ironic* emplotments may be considered a form of what Vizenor has called "narrative chance." Thematically and ideologically they suggest that things simply happen as they happen, for good or ill, and that results are often the reverse of intentions, with the corollary that justice, good, and right do not necessarily prevail. I take my sense of tragedy, comedy, and irony predominantly from Frye's *Anatomy of Criticism* and White's *Metahistory*.

8. See Pearce, *Savagism and Civilization*. Berkhofer's classic study *White Man's Indian* should also be consulted.

9. Lydia Maria Child is foremost among these few with her 1824 novel *Hobomok*, her 1828 history *The First Settlers of New England*, and her 1868 *An Appeal for the Indians*.

10. Horsman, "Scientific Racism," 153.

11. Said, "Identity, Negation, and Violence," 58.

12. Jennings, *Founders of America*, 312.

13. Jennings, *Founders of America*, 312.

14. Vizenor, *Fugitive Poses*, 14.

15. Vizenor, *Manifest Manners*, 12.

16. Apess, "Indian's Looking-Glass," 155; emphasis added.

17. Apess, "Indian's Looking-Glass," 156.

18. Apess's irony is rhetorical rather than structural, operating at the semantic level of the sentence, while ironic emplotments operate at the level of overall structure. Thus irony exists at both the semantic/rhetorical and the structural levels whereas comedy and tragedy do not operate rhetorically at the level of the sentence. One can't really speak of a tragic or comic sentence or phrase.

19. Apess, "Indian's Looking-Glass," 156.

20. Apess, "Indian's Looking-Glass," 156–57.

21. Apess, "Indian's Looking-Glass," 157.

22. Apess, "Indian's Looking-Glass," 157; emphasis added.

23. Vizenor, *Manifest Manners*, 14.

24. Apess, "Indian's Looking-Glass," 157.

25. Apess, "Indian's Looking-Glass," 160.

26. He mentions here William Wirt, Daniel Webster, and Edward Everett. Wirt had served as attorney general under President James Monroe and then been the Whig Party's candidate for president. Webster had been senator from Massachusetts and

secretary of state under President William Henry Harrison. Everett had been a Harvard professor of Greek and the editor of the influential *North American Review*. He became governor of Massachusetts in 1836. Although Apess here, in 1833, refers to Everett as an ally to the Indians on the basis of a speech to the House of Representatives on May 19, 1830, that opposed removal of the eastern Cherokees, Everett's 1835 Address Delivered at Bloody Brook, as I will try to show, offered a view of history that Apess very specifically contests in his *Eulogy on King Philip*.

27. Apess, "Indian's Looking-Glass," 160–61.

28. Vizenor, *Manifest Manners*, 14.

29. Konkle, *Writing Indian Nations*, 131.

30. Konkle, *Writing Indian Nations*, 133.

31. Apess, *Eulogy*, 278; emphasis added.

32. Apess, *Eulogy*, 278; emphasis added.

33. Apess, *Eulogy*, 277.

34. Jill Lepore notes that in proportion to population, King Philip's War "inflicted greater casualties than any other war in American history" (*Name of War*, xi). At its conclusion "more than half of all the colonists' settlements in New England had been ruined and the line of English habitation had been pushed back almost to the coast" (*Name of War*, xii).

35. O'Connell had noted Washington Irving's "Philip of Pokanoket," published in *The Sketch Book* (1819), along with J. W. Eastburn and R. C. Sands's long poem *Yamoyden* (1820), commenting that "both works' sympathies are entirely with the Indians and critical of the Puritans" (Apess, *On Our Own Ground*, xixn9). He also mentions John Augustus Stone's play *Metamora, or, The Last of the Wampanoags*, first performed in 1830; all three of these titles are referenced by Cheryl Walker in *Indian Nation* (1997). Apess may also have read or known of Lydia Maria Child's *Hobomok* (1824), Catharine Maria Sedgwick's *Hope Leslie* (1828), and James Fenimore Cooper's *The Wept of Wish-ton-Wish* (1829), all texts set roughly in the time of King Philip. Child's *First Settlers of New England*, cited above, also presents Philip sympathetically. Sarah Savage's *Life of Philip the Indian Chief* (1827) treats Philip as tragic hero. Walker suggests that Apess may have known Jedediah Morse and Elijah Parish's *A Compendious History of New England Designed for Schools and Private Families* (1804), in which Philip is presented sympathetically and cast "as a tragic hero" (*Indian Nation*, 168). My claim is that Apess is rewriting all of these "tragic" narratives of Philip in the ironic mode.

36. Irving, "Philip of Pokanoket," 258.

37. Irving, "Philip of Pokanoket," 251.

38. Irving, "Philip of Pokanoket," 264.

39. Irving, "Philip of Pokanoket," 264.

40. Everett, Address, 24.

41. Everett, Address, 35; emphasis added.

42. Everett, Address, 27; emphasis added.

43. Apess, *Eulogy*, 282–83.
44. Apess, *Eulogy*, 284.
45. Apess, *Eulogy*, 285; emphasis added.
46. Apess, *Eulogy*, 286.
47. Everett, Address, 32.
48. Apess, *Eulogy*, 302; emphasis added.
49. Apess, *Eulogy*, 302; emphasis added.
50. Everett, Address, 28–29.
51. Apess, *Eulogy*, 304.
52. Apess, *Eulogy*, 304.
53. Apess, *Eulogy*, 305.
54. Apess, *Eulogy*, 305.
55. Apess, *Eulogy*, 305.
56. Apess, *Eulogy*, 305.
57. Apess, *Eulogy*, 306; emphasis added.
58. Apess, *Eulogy*, 306.
59. Everett, Address, 29.
60. Everett, Address, 29.
61. Everett, Address, 10; emphasis added.
62. Apess, *Eulogy*, 307.
63. Apess, *Eulogy*, 307.
64. Apess, *Eulogy*, 307.
65. Apess, "Indian's Looking-Glass," 160–61.
66. Apess, *Eulogy*, 310.
67. Apess, "Indian's Looking-Glass," 160.
68. Apess, *Eulogy*, 310.

Bibliography

Apess, William. *Eulogy on King Philip*. In *On Our Own Ground: The Complete Writings of William Apess, a Pequot*, edited by Barry O'Connell, 277–310. Amherst MA: University of Massachusetts Press, 1992.

———. *The Experiences of Five Christian Indians of the Pequ'd Tribe*. In *On Our Own Ground: The Complete Writings of William Apess, a Pequot*, edited by Barry O'Connell, 119–62. Amherst MA: University of Massachusetts Press, 1992.

———. *Indian Nullification of the Unconstitutional Laws of Massachusetts Relative to the Marshpee Tribe, or, The Pretended Riot Explained*. In *On Our Own Ground: The Complete Writings of William Apess, a Pequot*, edited by Barry O'Connell, 166–274. Amherst MA: University of Massachusetts Press, 1992.

———. "An Indian's Looking-Glass for the White Man." In *On Our Own Ground: The Complete Writings of William Apess, a Pequot*, edited by Barry O'Connell, 155–61. Amherst MA: University of Massachusetts Press, 1992.

————. *On Our Own Ground: The Complete Writings of William Apess, a Pequot*. Edited by Barry O'Connell. Amherst MA: University of Massachusetts Press, 1992.

————. *A Son of the Forest: The Experience of William Apes, a Native of the Forest*. In *On Our Own Ground: The Complete Writings of William Apess, a Pequot*, edited by Barry O'Connell, 3–97. Amherst MA: University of Massachusetts Press, 1992.

Berkhofer, Robert. *The White Man's Indian: Images of the American Indian from Columbus to the Present*. New York: Knopf, 1978.

Child, Lydia Maria. *An Appeal for the Indians*. In *Hobomok and Other Writings on Indians*, edited by Carolyn Karcher, 216–32. New Brunswick NJ: Rutgers University Press, 1986.

————. *The First Settlers of New England, or, Conquest of the Pequods, the Naragansetts, and the Pokanokets, as Related by a Mother to Her Children, and Designed for the Instruction of Youth*. Boston: n.p., 1828.

————. *Hobomok and Other Writings on Indians*. Edited by Carolyn Karcher. New Brunswick NJ: Rutgers University Press, 1986.

Cooper, James Fenimore. *The Wept of Wish-ton Wish*. Philadelphia: n.p., 1827.

Eastburn, J. W., and R. C. Sands. *Yamoyden, A Tale of the Wars of King Philip: in Six Cantos*. New York: n.p., 1820.

Everett, Edward. Address delivered at Bloody Brook, in South Deerfield, Boston, September 30, 1835.

Frye, Northrop. *Anatomy of Criticism*. 1957. Reprint, New York: Atheneum, 1967.

Horsman, Reginald. "Scientific Racism and the American Indian in the Mid-Nineteenth Century." *American Quarterly* 27 (May 1975): 152–68.

Irving, Washington. "Philip of Pokanoket." In *The Sketch-book of Geoffrey Crayon, Gent.*, edited by Susan Manning, 250–64. New York: Oxford University Press, 1996.

Jennings, Francis. *The Founders of America: From the Earliest Migrations to the Present*. New York: Norton, 1993.

Konkle, Maureen. *Writing Indian Nations: Native Intellectuals and the Politics of Historiography, 1827–1863*. Chapel Hill: University of North Carolina Press, 2004.

Krupat, Arnold. *All That Remains: Literary Criticism in the Twenty-First Century*. Lincoln: University of Nebraska Press, forthcoming.

Lepore, Jill. *The Name of War: King Philip's War and the Origins of American Identity*. New York: Knopf, 1998.

Morse, Jedediah, and Elijah Parish. *A Compendious History of New England Designed for Schools and Private Families*. Charlestown: n.p., 1804.

Pearce, Roy Harvey. *Savagism and Civilization: A Study of the Indian and the American Mind*. 1953. Reprint, Berkeley: University of California Press, 1988.

Said, Edward. "Identity, Negation, and Violence." *New Left Review* 171 (1988): 226–47.

Savage, Sarah. *Life of Philip the Indian Chief.* Salem: n.p., 1827.

Sedgwick, Catherine Maria. *Hope Leslie.* 1827. Reprint, New York: Garrett, 1969.

Stone, John Augustus. *Metamora, or, The Last of the Wampanoags.* In *Favorite American Plays of the Nineteenth Century,* edited by N. Barrett Clark. Princeton NJ: Princeton University Press, 1943.

Vizenor, Gerald. *Fugitive Poses: Native American Scenes of Absence and Presence.* Lincoln: University of Nebraska Press, 1998.

———. *The Heirs of Columbus.* Hanover NH: Wesleyan University Press, 1991.

———. *Manifest Manners: Post-Indian Warriors of Survivance.* Hanover NH: University Press of New England, 1994.

———, ed. *Narrative Chance: Postmodern Essays on Native American Indian Literature.* Albuquerque: University of New Mexico Press, 1989.

Vizenor, Gerald, and A. Robert Lee. *Postindian Conversations.* Lincoln: University of Nebraska Press, 1999.

Walker, Cheryl. *Indian Nation: Native American Literature and Nineteenth-Century Nationalisms.* Durham NC: Duke University Press, 1997.

White, Hayden. *Metahistory: The Historical Imagination in Nineteenth-Century Europe.* Baltimore: Johns Hopkins University Press, 1973.

7. AS LONG AS THE HAIR SHALL GROW

Survivance in Eric Gansworth's Reservation Fictions

SUSAN BERNARDIN

Hair matters, as that iconic countercultural musical *Hair* proclaims, whether

> *long, straight, curly, fuzzy*
> *Snaggy, shaggy, ratty, matty*
> *Oily, greasy, fleecy*
> *Shining, gleaming, streaming*
> *Flaxen, waxen*
> *Knotted, polka-dotted*
> *Twisted, beaded, braided.*[1]

The ways we wear our hair—permed, cropped, buzzcut, mohawked, mulleted, bobbed, bearded, or dreadlocked—announce our allegiances. Hairstyle can signal membership in specific groups—the Marine Corps, Rasta, or Hasidic Judaism—or signify resistance to group identifications. It can validate or disrupt assumptions, invite or exclude, and appropriate or reclaim. Hair then works as a signpost—albeit a notoriously unreliable one—for cultural, social, and political identifications and is capable of eliciting a host of conflicting responses. In U.S. popular culture there is arguably no more recognizable, no more over-determined hairstyle than that of the "Indian braid." Simulated in a weary procession of TV and film Westerns, coined in nickels, and donned in elementary school "cultural" activities, braids have long served as visual shorthand for "Indianness." Consider, for example, a website devoted to "Indians" that proclaims, "Thanks to the Native American, how to braid hair is an important part of every little girl's repertoire of hair styling."[2] Indian braids thus function metonymically, calling forth the body of assumptions, stereotypes, and inventions that oddly *still* define Native peoples in mainstream American imaginations. All that's missing is the feather.

Banking on the ways hair gets wrapped up in socioeconomic, cultural, and personal significations, Eric Gansworth engages the movable border between story and stereotype. He scrambles worn patterns of telling an "Indian story" through the stories of his characters who live on and off the Tuscarora reservation, home to "a thousand people, all sharing the ins and outs of their lives with each other, either willing or unwilling."[3] An enrolled member of the Onondaga Nation, Gansworth grew up on the Tuscarora Reservation in western New York and now lives a few miles down the road in Niagara Falls — close in physical distance but another "territory" altogether.[4] Comprising one large story, Gansworth's works to date, including paintings, a volume of poetry and paintings, and three published novels, explore how "the weird lives of my characters play out in this landscape of diminishing land and an immovable wall of water."[5]

His work explicitly grounds itself in the generational aftereffects of land loss: New York State Power Authority's efforts to expropriate a sizeable land base of an already-hemmed in reservation in 1957. The Tuscarora Nation fought this expropriation to the U.S. Supreme Court, whose 1960 ruling in favor of the New York Power Authority granted that organization the right to take 550 acres to create the Lewiston Reservoir for the massive Robert Moses Power Generating Station.[6] This traumatic, tangible loss explicitly initiates the narrative action in both his first and third novels, and the reservoir itself (or "dike" as the characters typically call it) figures as a narrative locus in both texts.[7] Against this story of "losing things again and again," of losing land promised "in perpetuity," Gansworth's characters, especially in his third novel *Mending Skins*, actively rearrange the patterns of their lives.[8] The novel's multiple scenes involving the cutting, keeping, and growing of hair beckon us to its own intricate braided design. Through its ensemble cast and woven composition, *Mending Skins* suggests how Native peoples reimagine patterns of loss into new stories, especially through humored stories of survivance. In doing so, this novel generates broader meditations on loss and forgetting and on memory and continuance.

Part 1: Hairtraps
In his essay "Identification Pleas" Gansworth ponders the messy politics of identities imposed by outsiders and confronted by insiders when he experiences

a "delay" at the U.S.-Mexico border. Having pulled out his wallet only to discover that his driver's license is not in it, Gansworth tries his luck with a Tribal ID card. The border officer's smirk accompanies his dismissive question: "Do you have any real ID?"[9] In comic turns Gansworth considers America's ongoing fixation with visual markers of Native identity. Why, his essay wonders, do Native people still have to negotiate others' demands for "proof," for visual badges of authenticity? After calling himself "ethnically ambiguous," a "walking, breathing Rorschach test," mistaken for Latinos, Russians, Italians, and everyone in between, he turns to the one foolproof signifier of "Indianness": the braid.[10] His own shaggy, unruly hair, which his brothers once deemed a cross between Jerry Garcia and *Saturday Night Live*'s legendary character Roseanne Rosannadanna, is offered up as a case study for the politics of hair on and off reservations. After Gansworth began growing out his job interview haircut, he received in the mail a photograph from an archivist working on Carlisle Indian School materials. The boarding school photograph displays his grandfather at the age of twelve, "look[ing] out onto the future" with hair "short, clipped, blunt."[11] Gansworth pairs this image with the only other photograph he has ever seen of his grandfather, one of a five-year-old boy with hair "that streamed wavy and thick from his head, past his shoulders."[12]

From seventeenth-century Puritan conversion efforts in Massachusetts through the long era of boarding schools, punitive rituals of cutting Native children's hair survive in memories and stories.[13] The exhaustive archive of before and after photographs taken at boarding schools simulated students' transformation into domesticated subjects. Defined as an "excess" of threatening difference, long uncut hair presented school administrators with one of their most dramatic opportunities for visual "uplift." As a rite of passage at the schools, the cutting of students' hair comprised an originary scene of "instruction" in boarding school histories. That some schools punished runaways by shaving their heads underscores how hair served as a favored colonial tool for humiliating and controlling indigenous children.[14] Gansworth's description of his hair, its texture, growth, and changing style, resides within and against narratives of loss, resistance, and affirmation dictated by histories of dominance. The act of growing out one's hair or of tying it in a long braid thereby can signal cultural defiance, resistance, and affirmation. Gansworth's brother, for example, whose AIM shirts vie in number with his Grateful Dead ones, "has kept his long hair forever, for him this is a way of life."[15]

But that long hair can also be a trap. "Ceci n'est pas un indien" Gansworth seems to have realized from his early encounters in the "Indian academic community."[16] At a Native American poetry reading he recounts that "the more I looked around, the politics of hair seemed to have grown into some absurd hierarchy, people trying to out-Indian one another with all sorts of visual landmarks, secretly eyeing the braids of others, comparing, calculating whose was longer, thicker, more impressive, who had more ribbon shirts, more turquoise, accumulating identity in acquisition."[17] Heir apparent to an authenticity contest that he refuses to participate in, Gansworth cuts off his braid but concedes that he still keeps it in his office desk drawer "to remind me of where I have been."[18]

Yet back at that zealously policed border, he notes that the braid is seventeen hundred miles away and, "braidless and hairy, I am not legitimate enough for my ID."[19] When his faded gym card succeeds where his tribal ID could not, Gansworth is allowed to cross the border into the United States, permission that offers him small consolation. That his appearance fails to "signify" to that border agent and that his membership at a gym trumps his membership within a Native nation confirms what he already knew: identifying as Native in or against "our America" also means inhabiting the relentless ironies of a postcontact world.

Gansworth's fictional characters also inhabit these ironies as some alternately (and inadvertently) pose for the expectations of others, while other characters more readily refuse to be thus framed. From the beginning of Gansworth's novel *Mending Skins*, for instance, we learn that image is everything.

The novel opens at the Seventh Annual Conference of the Society for the Protection and Reclamation of Indian Images, or SPRY, "an organization dedicated to the eradication of clichéd and stereotypical images of Indians in whatever mass-market ways that have crept into the national psyche, by exposing these images for what they are, and by then providing positive alternatives."[20] These opening words come courtesy of T. J. Howkowski, the "son" of a central character in Gansworth's novels — Fred Howkowski, also known as Plastic Fred or Frederick Eagle Cry.[21] Looking like he had "fallen straight off a nickel," T. J. works as a theatre professor and as an actor, stuck endlessly replaying the role of Chief Broom from *One Flew Over the Cuckoo's Nest*.[22] He applauds his friend and keynote speaker Dr. Anne Boans for having the "keen eye of a cultural observer who is able to see the idiosyncrasies within a group identity and yet be distanced enough from it to offer sharp, pointed, accurate, and often hilarious commentary on the marginalized viewpoints of modern Native America."[23]

Yet Annie, as her mother Shirley Mounter calls her, is hardly hilarious. In jargon-laced academic discourse, Boans delivers a humorless lecture titled "Threads: The Hair-Ties that Bind" complete with slides drawn from "my personal collection, of our visual national obsession with stereotypical images of Native America, particularly as manifested in images of braids, as somehow representing the pinnacle of Native identity."[24] In her indignant recitation of cheesy commodities and indian hair kitsch, Boans is quick to point out the ironies of stereotypical art and equally quick to chastise Native artists for their complicity in perpetuating it.

For example, she chides the indigenous maker of a black velvet painting featuring a braided Jesus at the Calvary, trudging with the cross on his back alongside a braided indian on horseback. Titled *Jesus and the End of the Calvary Trail*, the painting twins the two figures with their braids but also twins iconic religious and popular cultural images. Noting that she "did not dare ask him [the painter] for further clarification" and "fear[ing] any dialogue," Annie upbraids the artist while refusing to consider the painting's own tricky humor and multivalent points of view.[25]

Notably, Annie's lecture ends here for the readers: her mother Shirley Mounter, the novel's most prominent narrator, cuts in on the lecture three years later, revising her daughter's version of the story. By claiming, for instance, that her daughter had strong-armed the artist into reducing the price of the painting, Shirley alerts us to the multiple strands of perspective required for a telling of the full story. And it is telling that Shirley chooses to point out Annie's inability to imagine different ways of telling the story of this image. The painting pairs an iconic Judeo-Christian image from one of the Stations of the Cross with James Earle Fraser's monumental sculpture *The End of the Trail*, first exhibited at the 1915 Panama-Pacific Exposition in San Francisco. The sculpture quickly inspired an industry of mass-produced images and products, from postcards and paintings to knock-off sculptures of the noble but doomed indian. A sculptural analogue to Edward Curtis's photographs, *The End of the Trail* enshrined nostalgia toward Native defeat and disappearance as the preferred tropes for signifying "Indianness." Even today, "The End of the Trail" remains a fixture in the American popular cultural landscape. Annie interprets the painting as particularly troubling in its unthinking participation in this representational "romance" of Native extinction.

Yet the narrative encourages us to consider how this painting instead might resurrect other points of view and interpretations. For example, what if Annie considered the irreverent humor of recasting Jesus as at the end of *his* trail or of "Indianizing" Jesus with those braids? What if the artist were commenting on the entwined histories of missionizing and colonization? Of the play between "Calvary" and the U.S. Cavalry? What if the black velvet was a tip-off that the painting trafficked in parody?

A painting, albeit not in black velvet, yet also entitled *End of the Calvary Trail* occupies the bottom left panel of a triptych printed on the page before the prologue. Gansworth's triptych, titled *Patchwork Life*, acts as the novel's narrative frame, its visual commentator, and its driving metaphor. Comprised of nine separate but interrelated panels, the painting invites readers to imagine the stories suggested by the provocative, at times puzzling, images. Like a game of tic-tac-toe, the panels can be "read" through differing sequences of three stories, with each sequence testing out possible strands of meanings in the novel. As its title suggests, the triptych's design mimics that of a patchwork quilt design: each panel offers up its own story while also contributing to the meaning of the panels adjoining it and to the work as a whole.

In doing so, each panel elicits a "both/and" interpretive approach, refusing binary readings in favor of rich, often contradictory, responses. For instance, the rightmost center panel presents an object that circulates in the narrative's action: a bottle opener that Annie's husband Doug had added to her ironic collection of indian kitsch. In her slide show she describes the bottle opener as a "Lakota in war bonnet, mouth wide open, presumably in full war cry, thick braids trailing out from beneath this explosion of feathers surrounding his face."[26] The bottle opener is an artifact, a commodity, but also a practical item used by characters in the narrative. Annie's description seemingly fits this image of a hand holding the "indian head" while the other hand inserts a bottle into his "mouth."

Yet the panel's associations are also shaped by the panel directly below it, which shows a hand, palm open, offering up a cut braid to the full moon.

While these two panels invite comparison because of their similar composi-
tional arrangement, the bottle opener panel conceptually interacts with the
panel adjoining it, the centerpiece panel of the triptych, featuring the lower
half of a man's face, his mouth stretched wide to accommodate the gun awkwardly grasped by his hand. Visually these three panels are unified by the
full moon in the background of each, with the latter two most particularly by
the shared language of hands and in the echoing, similar shapes of the gun
and bottle opener. Together, these three panels create a constellation circling around identity, loss, violations, and violence.

The presence of a full moon in each of the nine panels gives the nod to the
central image of Gansworth's volume of poetry and paintings *Nickel Eclipse:
Iroquois Moon* (2000). His paintings for *Nickel Eclipse* map the progression of
a lunar eclipse through its superimposed image of a vintage indian-head nickel. Predictably designed by James Earl Fraser, the sculptor of *End of the Trail*
fame, the nickel features on one side the classic profile of an Indian chief, the
word "liberty" hovering above his head; the reverse side is its partner in extinction — the bison. The titles of the thirteen ink-and-watercolor paintings
work in concert with images drawn from the Haudenosaunee calendar that
surround, frame, or overshadow the nickel moon. The Haudenosaunee cyclical lunar calendar provides a frame of reference to its longevity as measured
against a traumatic but passing era of catastrophic events. In each painting multiple referents edge against and across each other to underscore the
struggles but also the tenacity of Haudenosaunee people coming out from
under the shadow of an overbearing outside culture.

Gansworth's triptych also carries another signature feature of his paintings. Although not discernible in its reproduction in the book, *Patchwork
Life* is painted in purple and white, the two colors that dominate his palette.
Purple and white are the colors of wampum — the language of shells woven
into the belts that carry in them Haudenosaunee world view, history, and
epistemology.

As visual texts whose stories must be known in order to be told or read,
wampum provides Gansworth with the primary structural device of his work.
The painting's colors, in concert with the stylized wampum designs border-
ing the triptych's panels, forecast the storied interaction of text and image
in *Mending Skins*. The contrasting bead colors of dark and light suggest how

the novel and the painting work to tell the same story from alternate, or alternating, perspectives. For example, the novel's narrative design elaborates on
the visual template offered by *Patchwork Life*. Organized into thirds, the novel unfolds in three major sections individually framed by one third (or three
panels) of the triptych. Each of the three sections contains three chapters,
and many of the chapters are dated by the passage of three or nine years. In
its visual and narrative composition, *Mending Skins* announces to those who
know its Haudenosaunee frame of reference. These formal patterns of threes
and nines allude to Haudenosaunee clan divisions and primary cultural values as signified, for instance, by the Three Sisters. The power of "three" is
amplified by the novel's strategic braided design. Braiding, "the interweaving
of three or more strands, strips, or lengths in a diagonally overlapping pattern," serves as both technique and metaphor in the triptych and, by extension, in the novel's entire design. The triptych's refusal to "fix" its meanings
within a single panel, reinforced by the novel's multivalent chapter titles and
entwining storylines, launches a narrative that is always in motion. Haudenosaunee principles and American popular culture and stories of survivance
and victimry entwine and separate, entangle and unknot.

Patchwork Life includes wampum belts as the outer and inner borders separating each individual panel. Yet those borders are not firm but rather are involved in making connections and braiding stories. Their narrative analogues
are two designated "border" stories, separating parts 1 and 2 and parts 2 and
3 of the novel. As border texts they offer up an excess of stories: in the first
case the dead voice of Fred Howkowksi, narrating his burial on the reservation; in the second diverse voices from Gansworth's fictionalized Tuscarora
reservation describe their reactions to the fire consuming the home of character Martha Boans. Both stories serve as textual counterparts to the visual border design of *Patchwork Life* through their meditation on acts of collective forgetting and memory.

The first border story offers a voice submerged but significant to the entire novel: the story of Fred, who "survived" the Vietnam War but couldn't
survive the peace, especially in Hollywood, where he had moved to become
a movie star.[27] A reservation celebrity whose absent presence is shown in the
proliferation of the peach-colored Plastic Fred "braves" so popular among
the children, Fred commits suicide far from home. This story occupies the

centermost panel of the triptych. Titled *Last Supper*, the panel grimly references the excessive ugliness of suicide—a gun in the mouth. It also references one of da Vinci's most famous paintings and the event that it represents: the last gathering of Jesus and his disciples the evening before Judas's
betrayal. Connections between Fred's suicide and themes of loyalty and betrayal among his friends are spun out much more explicitly in Gansworth's
fourth and still unpublished novel *Extra Indians*.

However, the cross-references linking this panel and *End of the Calvary
Trail*, as well as the panel directly above it, *Plastic Fred*, gesture toward other
elements of this unassimilable story. *Plastic Fred* presents Fred's plastic cine-
matic alter ego marching in mechanical fashion across the panel. Circling behind him is an image of a full moon overlapping a circular chamber of a gun
that highlights the symmetries of their composition. Out of step with Hollywood's cyclical disinterest in "Indian" movies in the 1970s, Fred had changed
his name to Frederick Eagle Cry in a last ditch effort to get a speaking part.
These three panels raise questions about the relationship between representational and psychic violence, between self-sacrifice and self-destruction,
and between the myths people are willing to live and die by.

Taken together, the two border stories "tell" us what's most at stake in this
narrative: the presence of loss and the threat of forgetting but also the presence of shared humor, hard-earned wisdom, and adaptiveness. The first line
of "Burying Voices" is forgetting. In this narrative Fred speaks of the ways in
which his family, friends, and acquaintances will go about forgetting and remembering him. Fred's story, its pain and despair, cannot be fully recovered.
He candidly addresses how those who have outlived him will engage in survival strategies of their own, strategies of protective memory loss. In "Burning Memories" the fire wipes out Martha's "family pictures, furniture, and a
hundred years' worth of stuff that made up her family's history."[28] Yet the
community's response to the sight, sounds, and smells of the fire not only
speaks to the ubiquity of house fires on the reservation but to its sense of
shared history. For example, Fiction Tunny immediately turns to her bead-
work "to see what I might be able to raffle off to benefit whoever it is, if need
be."[29] Martha's house fire is braided into the stories of other house fires and
of all the versions that will be told of this and future fires. Like the stories of
"police evicting us from lands that were supposed to be ours forever," these

burning stories will be stitched together to create the patchwork story of the People.[30]

Fred's fate, like those of the characters he had tried to play in Hollywood, dances at the edge of the tragic endings still assigned to Native peoples in American popular culture. It is perhaps fitting then that Annie has dedicated her research to Fred's "career," beginning with a dissertation titled "Silent Screams: The Indian Actor as Angry Landscape in the American Western." Annie herself is trapped by such emplotments: her repeated dismissals of anything she deems stereotypical are belied by her own fixation with limiting ideas about Native identity. Annie's story is mostly spun by her mother, whose narration shapes parts 1 and 3. Throughout the novel Annie's lack of self-awareness reveals itself in her shifting, contradictory attitudes toward "Indian hair." Having inherited her mother's flaming red hair, Annie complains that it "screamed 'white people' as far as she was concerned. Every time she looked into a mirror, she saw the way I've made my career as a 'professional Indian' just that much harder."[31] In high school Annie permed her hair, saying she "hated how long and straight her hair was, that it was too 'Land O'Lakes Indian girl,' whatever that meant," subsequently dying it black.[32] Later she grew out her hair and "kept it in a thick braid coiling down to the small of her back, heavy and rusty, like copper cable."[33]

In the paired chapters charting Annie and Doug's perspectives on their crumbling marriage, she scoffs at the story of how her mother and friends had cut their hair in mourning and protest over the coerced loss of their homes during the seizure of Tuscarora land for the reservoir: "Well, I would never cut off my braid for something as stupid as that. All that hokey Indian romanticism bullshit."[34] Annie's outburst startles, not only because of her single-minded reading of braids but also because of her dismissal of her mother's generation's efforts to save Tuscarora land. As she "smoothes her braid" and speaks to friends and family members gathered at the reservoir, Annie insists that her family's submerged land "doesn't mean anything to me. I wasn't even born then."[35] Yet her brother Royal's memory that their father "tried real hard to get my ma not to do it" points to other readings absent from Annie's perspective.[36] Shirley's abusive, alcoholic husband always said how he loved her hair "when what he really loved was grabbing it and hanging onto me by it."[37] Royal's added comment that "it [cutting her hair] was

the only way she could get on with things" is best understood by its reference to the story that launches the novel, the loss of Shirley's home on the
reservation.[38] In the midst of the land expropriation fight, Shirley's husband
had sold the family house one night to his friend Barry Boans. The loss of
the house — the "first pulled thread" in the novel — and their ensuing move
to the city away from the reservation richly contextualize Shirley's decision
to cut her hair.[39]

Part 2: Shearing Histories

Stuck in a pattern whose broader ironies and lessons she neither discerns nor
understands, Annie offers a cautionary tale for characters in *Mending Skins*,
most notably her mother and soon-to-be-ex-husband Doug. Her adherence
to a script of "either/or" rather than "both/and" leaves her with an inflexi-
ble, humorless outlook on herself, the reservation community, and the "outside" world. In contrast, Shirley offers a capacious, dynamic narrative of personal, familial, and community events on the reservation from 1957 to 2002.
Her efforts to identify the many threads comprising her family and community's story begin with explicit reading instructions: "These stories fold, cross
over, split, and reassemble themselves."[40] Most particularly, Shirley's stance
toward fashioning stories, acknowledging their partiality while urgently bearing witness to her world, enacts the visual soundtrack of *Patchwork Life*. In recognizing but ultimately resisting predictable plotlines of an "indian story,"
she carries out most explicitly the novel's design. One of the panel paintings informing her opening story about displacement to the city is "Needle's
Eye." In it a giant human eye stares at a needle whose thread is showing the
first signs of unraveling. The placement of the needle and its eye in the panel sharpens its references to Shirley's broken marriage and traumatic separation from her reservation home. Its jarring, unsettling resonances also call
to mind Margaret Atwood's pithy poem:

> You fit into me
> like a hook into an eye
> A fishhook
> an open eye.

Yet amid stories of loss, longing, and mourning, Shirley refuses the posture of victimry. "No matter the miseries," to paraphrase Gerald Vizenor, she

"takes on the world with wit, wisdom, and tricky poses." After Martha loses her home to that fire, Shirley takes her in. The only possession remaining to Martha is a "piece of sewing she'd been working on, but it was only the front of the blouse she'd been making."[41] In her efforts to rescue Martha and to help her reclaim the lost fragments of her life, Shirley remembers her own strategies for working through distance, loss, and separation. After Tommy Jack, Fred's army buddy and best friend and also Shirley's lover (and possible unwitting father to Annie), returns to Texas following Fred's funeral, Shirley takes the clothes that he had left with her and transforms them. Claiming that it "was the first time I consciously destroyed something to preserve it," she "cut and rearranged and sewed" his socks, boxers, and jeans "into their new life."[42] In a narrative replete with unkind cuttings — of land, of relationships, and of hair — Shirley instead envisions the creative possibilities: "The patterns I chose were complicated for such a small piece of work, but that was the way of things in our lives. His jeans now overlapped his boxer shorts in small, folded blue diamonds surrounding white centers."[43] Taking her scissors, Shirley cuts up the parts of her past most in need of reimagination, rearranging them into new, healing patterns of memory: "I had become a whiz at transforming one useless thing into something that would live on."[44]

Shirley's creativity with scissors grows over time, complementing her growing unwillingness to participate in dead-end rituals unworthy of remembrance. After practice in cutting up old patterns of her life with Tommy Jack and patching them together in more resilient ways, Shirley embarks on her most ambitious sewing project: her absent husband's closet of clothes. His decades-long disappearing act had long seemed to trap her in tired, tragic patterns of victimry, abandonment, and bitterness. So she grabs up those scissors: "I just made sure he couldn't wear them anymore if he ever came calling for them, and I started hacking away with scissors, and not only the seams, mind you, but anywhere, randomly, so, even if he thought he was going to find some woman he'd been shacked up with to sew them for him, there wouldn't be much left for her to work with."[45]

As both weapon and tool scissors achieve the paradox of destroying in order to mend and ultimately to heal: "My scissors worked their magic on his clothes but also on me that day. The fragments falling randomly to my floor began to take on new shapes, relate to one another in different ways."[46] The scattered fragments of clothes unlock for her alternative memories and stories of shared family life. Like the patchwork painting, Shirley refuses to be stuck in one pattern, instead opting for the unfolding of imaginative possibilities. Out of those fragments she forges new destinies, not just for the clothes, remade into quilts for her children, but for herself. With newfound confidence from her creative acts, Shirley states, "My passions grew for fabric that would wrestle my dreams into tight-woven reality."[47]

Recalling that over the years she and Martha had "really stitched our friendship together in the years of continually waiting for our men to return," Shirley offers Martha this same gift of creative self-reconstruction.[48] In the face of Martha's unremitting grief following the fire, mourning for what she has lost, Shirley tells her that "this blouse don't have to be lost forever." Grabbing the blouse front out of Martha's hands, Shirley recounts that "I grabbed my scissors and sliced straight into it [the blouse front].[49] Shirley then gets out her own box of cloth scraps because "there were some remnants in there that would complement this piece and hers. I threaded the eye with a good strong line, knotted it, held it to her, and invited her into the box. She picked it up and began reconstructing her life in the way only a woman who has lost nearly everything can."[50] The novel's title, with its multiple word plays, motions to this moment: Martha's new blouse will be stitched together out of bolts of slightly mismatched fabric. Observant eyes will discern the patchwork shirt and trace the seams that have put Martha back together. Sewing as survivance? Shirley's hard-won wisdom is rooted in her adaptativeness, wry humor, resilience, and above all, in her sense that "family extends out in all directions to and from you out here." Extending the novel's metaphors a bit more, Shirley recognizes that part of being alive entails the "gradual process of tanning your own hide . . . taking all the scraps and stitching them back together into some recognizable form and throwing out the parts that aren't too useful."[51]

Whether "Tanning Hides," "Mending Skins," or "Cutting Patterns," as Gansworth's chapter and section headings remind, the characters in *Mending Skins* are given the task of refashioning the damaged pieces of their lives, histories, and stories into stronger material. Those most adept at adapting include Martha's son Doug Boans, who narrates the unraveling of his marriage to Annie through the language of hair. Annie had been attracted to his "killer braiding skills."[52] However, later she wishes to replace him with T. J. Howkowski, who, according to Shirley, "*kept* a shiny black braid in the way my daughter claimed to hate on her husband these days, not a hair out of place, nothing coming untucked."[53] In Shirley's account, "One day she [Annie] had just come home without the braid during their marriage and everything was just gone."[54] Her hair then "hung crooked and short in a cut."[55] Later he discovers that she had stashed her braid in a "pool cue sheath."[56] Her decision both to hold and hide her cut braid and to preserve it but also to shield it from her husband's scrutiny encapsulates her conflicted allegiance to remembrance and forgetting, to her unresolved stance on identity and authenticity.

Out of sight but never out of her mind, the braid travels with Annie as she drives to the reservoir intent on jettisoning both her marriage and her collection of artifacts. Doug catches up with her there, confronting her and T. J. among the crowd of regulars partying at the reservoir. Everyone watches as she methodically lines up her army of kitschy indian figurines and shoots each one into tiny fragments that rain down into the water. When Annie had first brandished the revolver, hidden in with the braid in her pool cue sheath, a spectator had called out, "Yo, Annie get your gun."[57] This quick-witted reference to the musical and the person who inspired it—Annie Oakley, sharpshooter and regular in Buffalo Bill's *Wild West* show—perfectly complements Annie Boan's paradoxical investment in the images she abhors. Doug also recasts her "performance" at the reservoir after she derides him for his apparent lack of irony toward indian stereotypes. When Annie complains, "You don't even know I kept this junk around for its ironic qualities," he retorts, "No images? What would you have to study then? Save the lecture for your students and multicultural sensitivity seminars."[58]

Though Annie had shared a laugh with the crowd when she first heard the line "Annie, get your gun," she sets herself apart from the community assembled in this scene. As Doug considers how the story of Annie with her revolver will make its rounds on the reservation, he imagines his customers asking him if "Annie got his gun, and they might have a laugh about it, because that was what true Indian survival was about."[59] Later he imagines the many future tellings of the "Annie get your gun story." He knows, however, that Annie "wouldn't see the humor in it, though she'd published a little book on Indian humor in contemporary Native American art just last year."[60] Rez-raised

Doug had been so intent on "teaching her the language of home" and of "giving her a place among her people" that her annual anniversary gift had included not only an object d'indian art but also a payment toward a trailer on the reservation.[61] But he can't teach her how to develop a sharper sense of survival humor, the kind that connects rather than separates and that makes one feel at home rather than displaced.

In an earlier reservoir scene that had forecast this very public entanglement, Doug silently noted Annie's unsuccessful efforts to engage in reservation humor: "Even when she got reservation humor and snapped off a good one that cut sharp, she usually apologized somehow, canceling out the effect."[62] In the moment following her foray into reservation humor, Doug tells her, "Your braid's coming a little frayed."[63] Doug knows what Annie might someday learn that "comedy is worth more than tragedy any time where survival is at stake."[64] Like the crowd at the reservoir, he also knows the truth of Vine Deloria's words: "When a people can laugh at themselves and laugh at others and hold all aspects of life together without letting anybody drive them to extremes, then it seems to me that people can survive."[65]

Despite her cutting words in the second reservoir scene, Annie also has not yet learned the lessons offered by Shirley, or even Martha, who had infuriated her daughter-in-law by cutting up her stash of ancient, out-of-date clothes in order to make a quilt. Shirley reminds us that "Martha and me, we were always sharp women."[66] As Annie begins to drive off, speeding into an uncertain future off the reservation, Doug reassures her, "I'll still be here, your home will still be here."[67] Despite her urgent pleas for autonomy, he again voices the implicit refrain of Mending Skins: "Well, we're still here."[68] And he grabs the pool cue bag.

In a pivotal bus scene from the film Smoke Signals, Victor Joseph instructs his traveling companion Thomas Builds-the-Fire on how to be "Indian" — no smiling and definitely no braids. He exclaims, "You gotta free it. An Indian man ain't nothing without his hair."[69] Not much later, however, Victor cuts off his own long hair, acknowledging and mourning the death of his father and the long stretch of separation between them. After his confrontation with Annie and T. J., Doug "grabbed his braid and cut through it, one stroke at a time, feeling the pull and then the release as it let go. If she could have seen this, Annie would have called him a stereotype, cutting his hair in loss like that.

She would forget that she had done it first. When she came home with her trendy haircut that first time, she claimed the braid was not what a woman in her position should be wearing, and yet she had kept it all those years, like the clothes, unable to let go of their other life."[70] The pull of letting go and hanging on, of forgetting and remembering, plays out in this scene as Doug takes out her braid from the bag and joins it to his own:

> He tried unweaving the two braids and reweaving them together as one, coils of his black braid layered into her beautiful coppery lengths, but the wind strengthened, blowing strand after strand away as he worked, until all he held were a few lengths shining in the setting sun, some from each of their heads. All the while, he wondered if there would be any fry bread left for his lunch the next day and if anyone had any good jokes at his table that night, telling them even in his absence. He opened his palm and let the wind take most of the remaining threads of their lives together out across the water, toward the city.[71]

At the most tangible site of land loss and broken promises on the Tuscarora Reservation, Doug motions toward survivance. In response to her question posed years earlier about why they always had to come to the reservoir on their anniversary, Doug had replied that it "is the place where you come to remember all the things you cherish and how easy you can lose them."[72] As the locus for the power of collective memory and the perils of forgetting, the reservoir embodies what Doug's act entails. The reservoir occupies tricky terrain in Gansworth's fiction: a place seemingly defined by loss and displacement *and* a place to swim and hang out for Gansworth's postreservoir generation. Doug's act asks us to consider what is worth holding onto and what is worth letting go. What do we need to remember? And what props do we need to do so? Echoing "Fraying Threads," the bottommost right panel in the triptych, Doug's gesture tugs at conflicting motions of presence and absence. After his efforts to conjoin and preserve these two full braids fail, he opens his palm to let them go. That he does so right after wondering about the jokes he's missing that night at the dinner table and the availability of leftover fry bread for his next day's lunch directs us to his own great "sewing" abilities. His adaptive resilience ensures survivance.

Gansworth's first novel, *Indian Summers*, concludes in part with its main character, Floyd Page, engaged in a ritual of burning a pile of notebooks at the reservoir's edge. He had tried writing down the stories of his family, home, and community after a bout with memory loss, notably caused by hitting his head on one of the rocks marking his family's submerged home under the reservoir. Like Floyd, Doug has to let go in order to hold on. As Floyd declares about the rocks he had dredged up from the reservoir bottom, "We don't need them to keep our pasts. We're the only connections we need to get on in this world."[73] A dance of unburdening and remembrance, Doug's braiding ritual is echoed by the "final" commemorative act of the novel: Doug gives Shirley the remaining hair strands once he completes the story we have just heard. In turn, Shirley "crisscrossed them" in her Bible, placing them for safekeeping on the color plate of Jesus bleeding at the crucifixion. She inscribes "Annie's hair, May 21, 2002. Just in case someone ever needed to know."[74] Back on that Calvary Trail, anything can happen.

Coda: Here and Beyond

In his recently released mixed-genre work *Breathing the Monster Alive*, Gansworth extends the semiotics of hair woven throughout his reservation fictions into broader cultural imaginations. An interrelated exploration in painting, poetry, and essay, *Breathing* meditates on childhood fears writ large in the American landscape. As a young boy on the Tuscarora Reservation, Gansworth had conflated the setting and storyline of an early 1970s docudrama, *The Legend of Boggy Creek*, set in rural Fouke, Arkansas, with his own densely forested reservation home. That rooted terror, long dormant but raised to the surface upon watching the film as an adult, compelled Gansworth to treat seriously what at first glance seems laughable. In other words, he pushes past readers' grinning skepticism to tackle the "hairiest" subject of all: Bigfoot, that is, Sasquatch or the Fouke Monster. Noting the presence of this figure in indigenous stories as well as its more recent incarnations, not just in North America but elsewhere in the world, Gansworth pursues the permeable lines dividing dream and waking life, childhood and adulthood, religion and myth.

For example, in one of his "persona poems" inspired by a teenage boy featured in the actual film, Gansworth draws attention to generational, gendered, and cultural lessons learned through ritual acts of grooming. In "Jasper Applebee Shaves for the First Time," we learn that the father shaves twice a day,

sometimes three if circumstances
warranted.[75]

Turning to his son, the father intones,

Boy . . . it's time
rubbing thick soap from brush and mug
onto me, pushing my chin back
until I can barely see
myself in the mirror, this is
what separates us from the beasts.[76]

While the father shaves, "nodding at the removal / of hair I had not yet noticed," he motions to his son:

[He] hands the blade to me and says
it is my turn, so I imitate
his strokes on the left side and after
I have completed the ritual and rinsed
my tingling face, he digs back in the drawer
pulls a small vial of sharp alcohol scented
with musk, splashes some into his rough
calluses, slams his open palms onto my face
and finishes me, exclaiming: You will never feel
more like a man than you do at this moment,
and I wait for it to pass.[77]

In a scene of hovering violence, the blade scraping the barely discernible hair on the face, the son silently resists his father's scene of instruction. Gansworth contemplates here a rite of passage for boys, a moment in which cultural codes of masculinity are reinstated by the consummative act of shaving. This transition from one category to another — from boy to man — is firmly drawn by the father, who teaches his son that shaving "separates us from the beasts." As he "finishes" off his son, the father reminds him what he should have learned that day: pride and confidence in that "moment" of becoming a man. Yet what the speaker remembers is that roughness of the "open palm" and that sting of "musk" on his face. In Gansworth's hands shaving is defamiliarized to suggest its monstrous contours. In doing so, he calls to mind

similar acts of cultural self-scrutiny, such as Horace Miner's classic parody of
ethnographic discourse. In "Body Ritual among the Nacirema," Miner recasts
this "daily body ritual which is performed only by men" as "scraping and lac-
erating the surface of the face with a sharp instrument."[78]

The painting that accompanies this poem not only shares the poem's title but shares the poem's play on the permeable borders between boy and
man and between man and beast. The dominant right-hand panel reveals half
of a young man's well-shaved face staring ahead into his future. In the narrow panel adjoining this one, the hairy presence of the "monster" is barely
discernible behind an imposing, unsheathed razor that dominates the panel and with its long blade gleaming. The dark background and shadows cast
over the young man's face suggest just how permeable are the borders that
so many humans zealously maintain. In the three-paneled painting *Between
Fear and Faith*, Gansworth makes his point more explicit. The lower left panel adjoins panels featuring the "boggy creek" and a house whose TV anten-
na brings in the scary movies that will make the frame of window light indispensable against the outer darkness of the night. In an ironic visual nod to
one of Michelangelo's masterpieces, *The Creation of Adam*, the diagonal composition of the panel spotlights two hands reaching out to the other. While
the lower left corner shows a hand not unlike Adam's, the upper right corner, where God's hand should be, instead proffers a hairy hand whose index
finger reaches down to touch the "human" one. The symmetry of the two
hands underscores their similitude, despite the excess of hair on the one. In
its sly irreverence and tricky humor, the panel does more than reimagine one
of the most iconic artistic works in Judeo-Christian culture. It unbraids stories that tie meaning together in only one way, that offer only fixed perspectives and single points of view. Throughout *Breathing the Monster Alive*, Gansworth enlarges the focus of his previous works, challenging us to heed the
questions and transform the patterns of faith and fear, belief and invention,
and us and them.

A Gansworth painting entitled *The Very Cold Moon* refers to the very last
month in the Haudenosaunee lunar calendar and the last of the images accompanying the poetry of *Nickel Eclipse: Iroquois Moon*. In this image a huge
illuminated moon, its surface the "Indian" side of that early twentieth-century nickel, is cradled by antlers. The sharp points of the antlers scrape against

the indian head, that frozen emblem of a vanished people. Yet that image of the permanently braided indian gets rehung by the elements surrounding it. Strings of icy wampum beads drape the antlers in distinctly braidlike patterns. At the top right edge of the nickel moon, the word "liberty" has been supplanted by the word "survival." Recasting the nickel's original message of indian demise in the face of American freedom, Eric Gansworth asserts here the much older story of Native survivance. As his reservations fictions insist, even on the coldest winter night, the growing life of the People will be sustained.

Notes

This essay is dedicated to the memory of Bud Hirsch, whose work furthered the best instances of tricky humor and survivance. My thanks to Eric Gansworth for sharing music and conversation and for making me watch *The Legend of Boggy Creek*.

1. Lyrics from "Hair," the anthem of the rock musical *Hair*, which premiered on Broadway in 1968.

2. See "Indians.org" at http:/www.indians.org/articles/how-to-braid-hair.html (accessed August 8, 2006).

3. Eric Gansworth, *Mending Skins* (Lincoln: University of Nebraska Press, 2005), 131.

4. See Eric Gansworth's first novel, *Indian Summers* (East Lansing: Michigan State University Press, 1998), for an extended narrative consideration of the many borders demarcating reservation and off-reservation points of view and the multiple articulations of the concept of "territory."

5. Eric Gansworth, e-mail communication to author.

6. For two non-Tuscarora representations of this history, one a touristic/educational Web site, the other an official Web site of hydroelectric power in this region, see "Niagara Falls History of Power," http://www.iaw.on.ca/~falls/power.html, and New York Power Authority, "Niagara Power Project," http://www.nypa.gov/facilities/niagara.htm. While the first Web site does include a brief mention of the expropriation battle, the latter does not mention it at all. Instead, its brief history details that "in 1957, Congress passed the Niagara Redevelopment Act, which granted the Power Authority a federal license to fully develop the United States' share of the Niagara River's hydroelectric potential. Within three years—on exactly the day predicted by Robert Moses, the 'Master Builder' and then chairman of the Power Authority—the Niagara project produced first power."

7. Tuscarora artist-curator-photographer Jolene Rickard also foregrounds the immovable presence of the Lewiston Reservoir in her works, including her installation

from 2001 titled *Contact Narratives: An/Other Sacrifice*. In her artist's statement accompanying this work, Rickard notes that, while "millions of gallons of water pound over the brink [of nearby Niagara Falls] every minute" and "a five square mile reservoir sits on the western edge of our community filled with fresh water, we haul water into our homes from fire hydrants" (20). As a staging ground for collective memory, *Contact Narratives* illustrates that, "for the people of the Tuscarora nation, the reservoir is a constant reminder, like a thorn in our foot, of personal greed prevailing over communal gain. Millions of gallons of water sit behind a 100 foot thick wall on our land and our wells are dry or polluted" (20).

8. Gansworth, *Mending Skins*, 17.

9. Eric Gansworth, "Identification Pleas," in *Genocide of the Mind: New Native American Writing*, ed. MariJo Moore (New York: Thunder's Mouth Press/Nation Books, 2003), 273.

10. Gansworth, "Identification Pleas," 273.

11. Gansworth, "Identification Pleas," 275.

12. Gansworth, "Identification Pleas," 275.

13. For example, see Jon Allan Reyhner and Jeanne Eder, *American Indian Education: A History* (Norman: University of Oklahoma Press, 2004). New non-Native- and Native-authored studies of the Indian boarding schools published in recent years have added enormously to our understanding of this era. In addition, see David Wallace Adams, *Education for Extinction: American Indians and the Boarding School Experience, 1875–1928* (Lawrence: University Press of Kansas, 1995); K. Tsianina Lomawaima, *They Called It Prairie Light: The Story of Chilocco Indian School* (Lincoln: University of Nebraska Press, 1995); Brenda J. Child, *Boarding School Seasons: American Indian Families, 1900–1940* (Lincoln: University of Nebraska Press, 1998); Brenda J. Child, Margaret L. Archuleta, and K. Tsianina Lomawaima, eds., *Away from Home: American Indian Boarding School Experiences, 1875–1928* (Phoenix: Heard Museum, 2000); and Clifford E. Trafzer, *Boarding School Blues: Revisiting American Indian Educational Experiences* (Lincoln: University of Nebraska Press, 2006). Gerald Vizenor writes in *Manifest Manners: Postindian Warriors of Survivance* (Hanover NH: University Press of New England, 1994), that "English, that coercive language of federal boarding schools, has carried some of the best stories of endurance" (106). From Gertrude Bonnin to Laura Tohe and Francis LaFlesche to Leslie Silko, Native writers have articulated boarding school experiences in memoir, poetry, and fiction. Most strikingly, they have refused narratives of victimry in favor of stories of resistance and survivance. For the role of boarding schools in the development of Native literary traditions in English, see, for example, Amelia V. Katanski, *Learning to Write "Indian": The Boarding School Experience and American Indian Literature* (Norman: University of Oklahoma Press, 2005).

14. For a comparative view of hair cutting and head shaving in other colonialist "educational" settings, see the film *Rabbit Proof Fence* (2002) and the book that inspired it, *Follow the Rabbit Proof Fence* (St. Lucia: University of Queensland Press, 1996) by Doris Pilkington (also known as Nugi Garimara).

15. Gansworth, "Identification Pleas," 277.

16. Gansworth, "Identification Pleas," 276.

17. Gansworth, "Identification Pleas," 276.

18. Gansworth, "Identification Pleas," 277.

19. Gansworth, "Identification Pleas," 277.

20. Gansworth, *Mending Skins*, 3.

21. Fred is not his biological father but for several years had assumed that responsibility before giving guardianship over to his best friend and army buddy Tommy Jack McMorsey.

22. Gansworth, *Mending Skins*, 50.

23. Gansworth, *Mending Skins*, 4.

24. Gansworth, *Mending Skins*, 5.

25. Gansworth, *Mending Skins*, 9.

26. Gansworth, *Mending Skins*, 6.

27. See Jim Northrup, *Walking the Rez Road* (Stillwater MN: Voyageur Press, 1993), 8–9.

28. Gansworth, *Mending Skins*, 119.

29. Gansworth, *Mending Skins*, 109.

30. Gansworth, *Mending Skins*, 105.

31. Gansworth, *Mending Skins*, 135.

32. Gansworth, *Mending Skins*, 148.

33. Gansworth, *Mending Skins*, 148.

34. Gansworth, *Mending Skins*, 91.

35. Gansworth, *Mending Skins*, 91.

36. Gansworth, *Mending Skins*, 91.

37. Gansworth, *Mending Skins*, 20.

38. Gansworth, *Mending Skins*, 91.

39. Gansworth, *Mending Skins*, 12.

40. Gansworth, *Mending Skins*, 12.

41. Gansworth, *Mending Skins*, 119.

42. Gansworth, *Mending Skins*, 123.

43. Gansworth, *Mending Skins*, 123.

44. Gansworth, *Mending Skins*, 124.

45. Gansworth, *Mending Skins*, 125–26.

46. Gansworth, *Mending Skins*, 126.

47. Gansworth, *Mending Skins*, 127.

48. Gansworth, *Mending Skins*, 125.

49. Gansworth, *Mending Skins*, 127.

50. Gansworth, *Mending Skins*, 128.

51. Gansworth, *Mending Skins*, 50, 134.

52. Gansworth, *Mending Skins*, 88.

53. Gansworth, *Mending Skins*, 130; emphasis added.

54. Gansworth, *Mending Skins*, 149.

55. Gansworth, *Mending Skins*, 148.

56. Gansworth, *Mending Skins*, 149.

57. Gansworth, *Mending Skins*, 157.

58. Gansworth, *Mending Skins*, 157.

59. Gansworth, *Mending Skins*, 158.

60. Gansworth, *Mending Skins*, 162.

61. Gansworth, *Mending Skins*, 98–99.

62. Gansworth, *Mending Skins*, 99.

63. Gansworth, *Mending Skins*, 99.

64. Carter Revard, *Family Matters, Tribal Affairs* (Tucson: University of Arizona Press, 1998), 90.

65. Vine Deloria, "Indian Humor," in *Nothing But the Truth: An Anthology of Native American Literature*, eds. John L. Purdy and James Ruppert (Saddle River NJ: Prentice Hall, 2001), 53.

66. Gansworth, *Mending Skins*, 140.

67. Gansworth, *Mending Skins*, 159.

68. Gansworth, *Mending Skins*, 159.

69. In a recent documentary, *Half of Anything*, Sherman Alexie is one of four interviewees asked only half facetiously, "What is a real Indian?" In his ensuing comments Alexie turns to his hair — and its shift from mullet to shorn — as a way of talking about reservation identity and messing with the politics of "authenticity." This 2006 film was directed by Jonathon S. Tomhave and produced by Native Voices at the University of Washington.

70. Gansworth, *Mending Skins*, 161.

71. Gansworth, *Mending Skins*, 162.

72. Gansworth, *Mending Skins*, 87.

73. Gansworth, *Indian Summers*, 198.

74. Gansworth, *Mending Skins*, 163–64.

75. Eric Gansworth, *Breathing the Monster Alive* (Treadwell NY: Bright Hill, 2006), 27.

76. Gansworth, *Breathing*, 27.

77. Gansworth, *Breathing*, 27–28.

78. Horace Miner, "Body Ritual Among the Nacirema," *American Anthropology* 58, no. 3 (June 1956): 505.

8. THE WAR CRY OF THE TRICKSTER

The Concept of Survivance in Gerald Vizenor's
Bear Island: The War at Sugar Point

ALAN VELIE

Survivance is both an old and new word in English. The *Oxford English Diction-ary* traces it back to Sir George Buck, whose 1623 history of Richard III uses the term to mean "survival."[1] Dr. Johnson speaks of his uncertain "confidence of survivance" in a letter to Mrs. Thrale in 1773. By the twentieth century the term had become archaic, if not extinct.

Survivance means survival in French and was occasionally used by Québé-cois immigrants to the United States.[2] Gerald Vizenor, whose ancestors in-clude French Canadians as well as Anishinaabe, reintroduced the concept into English when he used it in the title of his manifesto *Manifest Manners: Postin-dian Warriors of Survivance*.[3]

As Vizenor uses the term, *survivance* is a portfolio word combining "surviv-al" and "endurance," but it is also more than that. *Survivance* connotes surviv-al with an attitude, implying activity rather than passivity, using aggressive means not only to stay alive but to flourish. Contemporary Indians achieve survivance through reinventing who they are, finding new identities through telling traditional stories, and inventing new ones. Today's Indian warriors are writers: "The postindian warriors encounter their enemies with the same courage in literature as their ancestors once evinced on horses, and they cre-ate their stories with a new sense of survivance."[4]

Among these enemies are historians, journalists, public intellectuals, and others who influence cultural attitudes, both on the right and the left. On the right are those who still cling to the idea of Manifest Destiny, a cause that Vi-zenor declares caused "the death of millions of tribal people from massacres, diseases, and the loneliness of reservations."[5] Equally dangerous, if perhaps better intentioned, are the revisionist historians and others on the left who have written what Vizenor has called "victimist history," portraying Indian history as an unbroken string of atrocities and humiliations, devoid of high-points or anything that Indians can point to with pride. Vizenor's strongest statement on this comes in an interview with Hartwig Isernhagen: "The other problem . . . is the investment in America and, I think, in most of the privileged Western world . . . in a victim . . . and 'Indians' are the simulated universal victims. Victims have no humor; they offer the world nothing but their victimization, and that makes people who invest in them feel better."[6]

Vizenor objects to people using Indians as sticks to beat white America and to offering Indians pity and condescension but no respect. He urges Indians to fight being characterized by their enemies on both flanks and to discover their identity in their own tribal traditions, especially in their tribal stories, many of which are trickster stories. One of the four "postmodern conditions" of contemporary Indian literature is "the trickster hermeneutics of liberation, the uncertain humor and shimmer of survivance that denies the obscure maneuvers of manifest manners."[7]

At this late date there is little need to rehash the characteristics of Trickster, the player and victim of tricks, perpetual underdog and survivor, a figure of unbridled appetites who transcends good and evil to serve as culture hero for diverse peoples ranging from the ancient Israelites (Jacob and David) to the Greeks (Odysseus) to the tribes of North America who still tell takes about Coyote in the Southwest, Raven in the Northwest, and Trickster's human avatars, Saynday of the Kiowa, Old Man of the Blackfeet, Wakdjunkaga of the Winnebago, or most important to a study of Vizenor, Naanabozho of the Anishinaabe.

In the introduction to his recent epic poem *Bear Island: The War at Sugar Point*, Vizenor describes Naanabozho as "an uncertain, existential shaman of creation, a healer in stories, and a comic transformation in mythic time — comic in the sense that the imagic presence of the trickster is a figurative trace of survivance, not a tragic revision of dominance or misadventure in the racial sentiments of monotheistic civilization."[8] It is Trickster as the spirit of survivance that we find in *Bear Island*, an epic account of the last military skirmish between Indians and the U.S. Army and Vizenor's return to poetry after a long period of writing in prose. In *Bear Island* Naanabozho lives in the spirit of the Anishinaabe warriors of the Pillager clan and particularly in the person of Bugonaygeshig, Hole in the Day, known derisively as Old Bug to federal agents.

Bear Island is the story of a largely forgotten incident in American history. The generally accepted end of armed warfare between whites and Indians in the United States was the massacre at Wounded Knee in 1890. The slaughter of three hundred Sioux, most of them women and children, by the Seventh Cavalry has been made famous by John Neihardt's *Black Elk Speaks*, Dee Brown's *Bury My Heart at Wounded Knee*, and the famous photo of Big Foot dead in the snow, lying on his back. The battle between the Anishinaabe and U.S. troops at Bear Island took place eight years later. It was a much fairer fight — soldiers fought warriors, not women and children — and the Indians won, but it had disappeared from collective memory until Vizenor retold the story.

Wounded Knee is a very important story in victimist Indian histories — brutal whites, outnumbered Indians, death in the snow, and pathos and guilt. Vizenor is familiar with the massacre; he mentions it in *Bear Island*, calling it "a prairie genocide," but he doesn't dwell on it.[9] To Vizenor *Bear Island* is the anti-Wounded Knee: triumphant Indians, trickster humor, underdog survivors, and a happy ending. Particularly since the Indians were Anishinaabe, this was a story waiting for Vizenor, and he tells it very well.

Bear Island is an epic in free verse. Like many other Indian novelist — Scott Momaday, James Welch, and Louise Erdrich — Vizenor began his writing career as a poet. His first eight books were collections of poems, mostly haiku, a form Vizenor discovered when in Japan as a soldier in the 1950s. But starting with the publication in 1978 of *Wordarrows*, a collection of essays and sketches, and *Darkness in Saint Louis Bearheart*, a novel, Vizenor became known primarily as a prose writer as he churned out an astonishing amount of fiction and nonfiction: novels, short stories, criticism, memoirs, and works on the culture and politics of Indian Country. *Bear Island* shows that Vizenor has not lost his touch as a poet.

Bear Island starts with an Overture:

> the anishinaabe
> natives of the miigis
> fugitive rivers

> *canoe birch*
> *white pine*
> *face the clouds*
> *and cedar boughs.*[10]

Readers, at least those of a certain age, encountering an epic of the Ojibway in their forests in what is now Minnesota will no doubt think of *The Song of Hiawatha*, with its melodious trochees:

> *By the shores of Gitche Gumee,*
> *By the shining Big-Sea-Water,*
> *Stood the wigwam of Nikomis,*
> *Daughter of the Moon, Nikomis.*
> *Dark behind it rose the forest,*
> *Rose the black and gloomy pine-trees,*
> *Rose the firs with cones upon them.*[11]

The historical Hiawatha was probably a Mohawk who lived in the late sixteenth century in what is now New York. Longfellow got the material for his poem from Henry Rowe Schoolcraft's *Algic Researches* and the trochaic meter from the Finnish epic *Kalevala*.[12] Longfellow retained nothing of the historical Hiawatha except his name, which he valued for its trochees.

Vizenor's poem is free verse, yet trochaic groupings abound:

> *worthy hunters*
> *cut the barren*
> *masks of hunger*
>
> *crafty trickster*
> *naanabozho*
>
> *tricky shamans*
> *rout the missions*
>
> *moths and menace*
> *willow catkins.*[13]

Many other examples exist, perhaps by coincidence. It is as if Vizenor is haunted by the ghost of a poem he despises, a poem he calls a "memorial to manifest manners."[14]

A far more important influence on *Bear Island* is traditional Anishinaabe song. The Anishinaabe were a particularly musical tribe. Ethnomusicologist Frances Densmore wrote of them, "Music is one of the greatest pleasures of the Chippewa. If an Indian visits another reservation one of the first questions asked on his return is, 'What new songs did you learn?'" Densmore continues, "Every phase of Chippewa life is expressed in music."[15]

Densmore records a song from Leech Lake commenting on the death of Major Wilkinson, one of the officers at the battle at Bear Island:

> *One in authority passeth wailing*
> *Thou, O chief, art by nature also a man.*[16]

Densmore explains that the Anishinaabe sang the song during what she calls the "Pillager outbreak" of 1898. She states that the "Indians honor his [Wilkinson's] bravery and speak of him with respect. The words of the song refer to the grief of his fellow officers."[17] Assuming that Densmore's translation is correct, the song seems ironic, not laudatory. It would seem that Wilkinson did the wailing, not his "fellow officers." If this is so, the second line should mean that it turns out that the major was human after all. Indians had often thought whites, who had amazing technological gadgets like rifles and Gatling guns, had extraordinary powers, but here it turns out that Wilkinson was "also a man."

The influence of Chippewa music on Vizenor is greater than the song about Wilkinson, which Vizenor undoubtedly knows, though he doesn't mention it. Chippewa songs were sung to the accompaniment of instruments like drum, rattle, and flute, but when written down, the brief, cryptic texts look remarkably like haiku, and like the Japanese poems, they had an influence on early twentieth century American poetry, especially that of the Imagists.[18] Vizenor, who lived for a while as a child with his grandmother on the White Earth Reservation, is aware of the songs as music but also as written texts. In fact he edited a volume of Chippewa songs and stories called *Summer in the Spring: Anishinaabe Lyric Poems and Stories*. The fact that he chooses the term "lyric poems" indicates that he thinks that, when the original songs are produced as texts on a page, without music, they are no longer songs but rather poems.

As poems their most noteworthy features are their short cryptic lines and vivid details, which evoke far more than they say. For example, one of the best known is:

> *A loon*
> *I thought it was*
> *But it was*
> *My love's*
> *Splashing oar.*[19]

The poem, which appears in slightly different form in Vizenor's collection, goes on to tell of the lover's departure, but the mood, the sense of loss, is vividly conveyed in the opening lines.[20] Another well-known example is the title poem of Vizenor's collection, "Summer in the Spring":

> *as my eyes*
> *look across the prairie*
> *i feel the summer*
> *in the spring.*[21]

Vizenor uses the phrase "summer in the spring" three times in *Bear Island*. More importantly, the rhythms and imagery are such that short passages from *Bear Island* look just like Chippewa songs. For instance, to cite just two of many examples:

> *midewiwin singers*
> *under cedar boughs*
> *post their colors*

and

> *wary ravens*
> *bounced on the dock*
> *at walker bay.*[22]

Enough about style: the subject of the poem is the battle between eighty U.S. infantrymen and officers and nineteen Anishinaabe warriors. The cause of the battle was the arrest of Hole in the Day, an old shaman who was arrested for refusing to testify in a trial. Hole in the Day calls for help and is rescued by Anishinaabe warriors. He flees, and General Bacon leads a detachment of the Third Infantry up Leech Lake to Hole in the Day's homestead to bring him back. When they arrive a skirmish breaks out.

Vizenor begins his account at the very beginning, creation:

> *crafty trickster*
> *naanabozho*
> *created natives.*[23]

Naanabozho creates the Anishinaabe in his own image: they are a race of
tricksters who will need all their guile to survive the spread of white civilization. Survival is the issue at Bear Island:

> *native survivance*
> *on the rise*
> *that cold*
> *october morning*
> *at sugar point.*[24]

Here Vizenor returns to the mode of his first novel *Darkness in Saint Louis
Bearheart*: Indian gothic, a variation and inversion of American gothic. British gothic novelists Monk Lewis, Anne Radcliffe, and others used medieval,
generally Catholic settings — castles, dungeons, and abbeys — to create their
frightening atmosphere. These things being in short supply in the United
States, early American novelist Charles Brockden Brown suggested substituting forests for castles and Indians for villainous noblemen. In the Preface
to *Edgar Huntly* he writes that "gothic castles and chimeras are the materials
usually employed for this end. The incidents of Indian hostility and the perils of the western wilderness are far more suitable."[25]

Whether American writers got the idea from Brown or, more likely, came
to the conclusion by themselves, they did exploit the wilderness and its Indian perils. Hawthorne's "Young Goodman Brown," Cooper's Leatherstocking series, *Tom Sawyer*, dime novels, and Hollywood horse operas all depict
the perils of entering areas of untamed nature in which wild men lurk. Leslie Fiedler explains the meaning of the adaptation of British gothic to America: "*The change of myth involves a change of meaning.* In the American gothic . . .
the heathen, unredeemed wilderness and not the decaying monuments of a
dying class, nature and not society becomes the symbol of evil. Similarly not
the aristocrat but the Indian, not the dandified courtier but the savage colored man is postulated as the embodiment of villainy."[26]

Vizenor, writing from an Indian point of view, naturally sees the situation differently. In *Bear Island*, as in *Bearheart*, the forest is the refuge for the

sympathetic characters; it is the encroachment of civilization that is dangerous. Survivance is a matter of preserving native culture from contamination by
white invaders and occupiers. The horror in *Bear Island* is thus that of the

> *hungry children*
> *bound in blankets*
> *[who] wait outside*
> *for late annuities.*[27]

The "savage colored man" is not the enemy, he is the hero

> *bugonaygeshig*
> *bear island pillager.*[28]

The enemies are the light-skinned intruders, the Anglo-Saxon snakes that
penetrate the forest Eden. The bad guys include timber barons who denude
the forests, engineers who dam the gichiziibi (Mississippi), swindling Indian
agents, soldiers, and missionaries. The timber barons

> *with empty eyes*
> *scorched the pine.*[29]

The anthropomorphized trees

> *exiled forever*
> *in millions of homes*
> *built with timber*
> *clearcut at leech lake.*[30]

The lumber industry has been very hard on the Anishinaabe, and Vizenor
has railed against "treekillers" since his first novel *Darkness in Saint Louis Bearheart*. Louise Erdrich has also decried the despoliation of the forests on Chippewa reservations in her Little No Horse series, especially in *Tracks* and *Four
Souls*.

The engineers build the dams that "flood the seasons / serve the mill masters" while

> *wild rice*
> *and native bones*
> *[are] washed away.*[31]

The engineers bringing civilization to the dark forests

> *never notice*
> *summer in the spring*
> *never hear*
> *the tease of bears*
> *ceremony of cranes*
> *never see ravens alight*
> *on the mighty rise*
> *of the white pine.*[32]

The sympathetic characters in *Bear Island*, the ones who are at home in the forest, are the Pillagers, one of the original five clans of the Anishinaabe tribe.[33] The Pillagers received their name from eighteenth-century French fur trader Alexander Henry, and like other groups saddled with a pejorative moniker—such as Yankees or Tories—they appropriated it and used it with pride. The Pillagers have achieved some notoriety in fiction: Louise Erdrich's Little No Horse Saga features several prominent Pillagers including the matriarch Fleur Pillager and Gerry Nanapush, the son of Fleur's daughter Lulu and Moses Pillager.

The Pillagers, like the other Anishinaabe, live in harmony with nature in the "sacred cedar" on the banks of Leech Lake; they are at home among the cranes, catfish, loons, bears, martens, and other totem animals. General Bacon and his men may have felt they were going into the heart of darkness as they approached Bear Island, but Vizenor sees things more like Chinua Achebe than Joseph Conrad. The Pillagers are like the Igbo in *Things Fall Apart*, a forest people threatened by the incursion of Anglo-Saxon religion and civilization.

In *Bear Island* the "dirty mirrors of civilization" reflect the

> *godly triumphalists*
> *almighty traitors*
> *crown the conquest*
> *sneaky treaties*
> *and frontier justice.*[34]

The Anishinaabe Eden is violated by

> *sweaty newcomers*
> *nervy soldiers*
> *soul savages*
> *in heavy uniforms.*[35]

These newcomers are the latest in a long line of white intruders in Indian country, "bounty savages / [on] missions of genocide," an egregious example of
which was Colonel Chivington's massacre of the Cheyenne at Sand Creek.[36]

The invasive soldiers are abetted not only by missionaries, the perpetual
curse of the Indians and other colonized indigenes, but also by writers such
as Whitman, whose

> *crucial catchwords*
> *invite no one*
> *[and who] promises nothing*
> *but memory.*[37]

The passage Vizenor has in mind is in "Starting from Paumanok":

> *And for the past I pronounce what the air holds of the red*
> *aborigines.*
>
> *The red aborigines,*
> *Leaving natural breaths, sounds of rain and winds, calls as of birds*
> *and*
> *animals in the woods, syllabled to us for names . . .*
> *Wabash, Miami, Saginaw,* Chippewa . . .
> *Leaving such to the states they melt, they depart, charging the water*
> *and the land with names.*[38]

Of course, the Chippewa had not melted or departed from their tribal homeland when Whitman wrote the passage, almost a half century before the battle
at Sugar Point; they were merely beneath his notice. Whitman claims to "sing
the song of companionship," though of course he is the greatest of solipsists,
inviting himself as he loafs, but clearly not inviting the Vanishing Americans.[39]
When Whitman sings of the Modern Man, he doesn't include the Red Man,

who exists only in the past.[40] Whitman's song is addressed to "Americanos! conquerors! . . . Libertad masses!"[41] He chants for the conquerors, not the conquered, and so his song rings hollow to Vizenor.

Vizenor's quarrel with the missionaries is their intolerance. The Anishinaabe, like other Indians, were henotheistic: they adopted elements of other religions, including Christianity, without relinquishing their own beliefs. American Christians have never understood this practice. The Ghost Dance that brought the massacre at Wounded Knee was Christian, though the army didn't know and probably wouldn't have cared. Vizenor recognizes the irony of Bigfoot dying at Christmas for practicing rituals intended to bring a second coming of Jesus, the *parousia* that the missionaries themselves had taught the Indians to expect.

Vizenor emphasizes the irony of America, the country founded on Enlightenment ideals, sending the Indians missionaries who hate natural religion, religion based on reason:

> crusades and salvation
> set by shame
> and never court
> natural reason.[42]

Vizenor recognizes the dichotomous opposition between Indian religion and its deployment of trickster stories, with their communal, comic approach, and the humorless, tragic American Christianity that sacrifices

> trickster stories
> overnight
> at the holy rails
> only to celebrate
> the lordly separatism
> of biblical names.[43]

The treatment of Hole in the Day, Old Bug to Indian agents and soldiers, exemplifies the heavy-handed and hypocritical treatment of Indians by whites in the United States in the nineteenth century, in fact until the last three decades of the twentieth. The Anglo-Saxon attitude toward natives, a combination of idealism, racism, legalism, condescension, obliviousness, and intentional and unintentional cruelty varied little from the Raj to Bear Island.

The backstory to the battle at Sugar Point begins with Hole in the Day being dragged to Duluth to stand trial as a whiskey trader. Fortunately Hole in the Day draws a good judge, who dismisses the charges. Initially it seemed as if the system—the vaunted American judicial system—has worked. However, this system, satisfied for the time being that Hole in the Day is innocent, or at least that it can't pin anything on him, simply turns him loose a hundred miles from home. Hole in the Day tries to get back to Leech Lake by train, but the conductor throws him off, and Hole in the Day can't even catch a ride in a boxcar.[44] The sixty-year-old shaman ends up walking home.

Small wonder then that, when the feds wanted Hole in the Day to testify in another case, he calls for help from Anishinaabe warriors. They secure his release, starting the fracas that leads to the battle at Bear Island. The government responds to Hole in the Day's liberation by sending two boats, the *Chief of Duluth* and the *Flora*, and a detachment of eighty officers and men of the Third Infantry to bring him back. As the soldiers move into the heart of Anishinaabe darkness, General Bacon and his troops see the naked natives on the shore, much like something in Conrad, but instead of the stifling heat of the Congo the troops are pelted with snow and sleet. Indians in red blankets watch the blue-clad soldiers, soaked through, exuding the "wooly stench of wet uniforms."[45]

Landing at Sugar Point the infantry occupies Hole in the Day's medicine lodge, take captive two of the warriors who released him, and pitch camp. Nineteen Anishinaabe warriors surround the troops. In stacking arms one careless soldier forgets to take the round out of his rifle's chamber or to engage the safety. When the stack of rifles falls, a shot goes off. The Indians, thinking that they are under attack, return fire, and the battle is on. Vizenor takes an ironic tone in describing the battle, which takes place in Hole in the Day's garden:

> lieutenant ross
> commander of the left flank
> over the turnips
> major wilkinson
> center of the war
> over cabbages . . .
> summoned

immigrant recruits
by their bravery
and frontline strategy
to scorn and dare
the ghostly enemy.[46]

There is an amusing contrast between the intrepid but foolhardy Major Wilkinson, exposing himself to enemy fire while exhorting his troops in deadly seriousness, and Boy River Water, the Anishinaabe warrior who jumps on a fence mocking and laughing at the soldiers. Wilkinson

treads . . . over cabbage shouting "give 'em hell
we've got 'em licked."[47]

He survives two bullets but dies of the third. Boy Rover Water escapes unscathed, as did all of the Anishinaabe warriors. Wilkinson is the spirit of earnest white American tragedy; Boy River Water embodies the trickster spirit of Anishinaabe comic survivance.

All in all, the Third Infantry loses five soldiers and one officer. The sole Indian casualty is an Indian policeman, a Christian, whom a sentry kills by mistake. Nineteen Indians defeat eighty soldiers and officers, who are not only routed but also deserted when Colonel Tinker, like Mark Antony at Actium, flees the battle. Commanding the *Flora* to sail back to home port, the colonel leaves the wounded soldiers to sleep in the cold without provisions. The following day the Anishinaabe slip away, leaving the Third Infantry to withdraw, licking its wounds.

The last soldier to die in the last war between the U.S. army and Indians was Private Daniel Schallenstocker, a German immigrant who is shot trying to reach some potatoes. Many of the soldiers were immigrants, having joined the army as a quick way to citizenship. The irony of the last to arrive in America dying at the hands of the first is not lost on Vizenor. In reading his account of the Italian, Norwegian, German soldiers who die at Sugar Point, one thinks of Choctaw writer LeAnne Howe's remarks about Emma Lazarus as an Indian. Howe quotes Lazarus's inscription on the Statue of Liberty ("Give me your tired, your poor . . .") and adds, "You did. Now where do we go from here?"[48]

That of course is the question that faced every Indian in America as the nineteenth century drew to a close, and the fighting ended between the Indians and whites. The end of hostilities, the losing of the West, left many Indians with the bleak prospect of trying to turn into Americans without even having citizenship.[49] Indian population was at its nadir. From a height of perhaps five million people in 1492, the number of Indians had fallen to two hundred and fifty thousand by 1890.[50] Faced with extinction as a people, they had a choice of bare survival—hanging on in despair or of survivance—survival on their own terms, maintaining their cultures and keeping their sense of humor. Gradually throughout the twentieth century, Indian population rebounded (it is now about 2.5 million), accelerating as tribal economic fortunes improved in the cultural and economic renaissance that began around 1970.

As for the Anishinaabe, Hole in the Day is a symbol of their resilience. When the army decamps, he comes back to his garden and medicine lodge, both of which are badly damaged. Undaunted, he fashions a war necklace from spent cartridges from the army's Norwegian rifles:

> *war necklace*
> *native survivance*
> *remembrance*
> *a defeated army*
> *overcome by winchesters*
> *and fierce irony.*[51]

The poem ends with a litany of the dead soldiers. The final stanza laments the

> *immigrants*
> *farmers and adventurers*
> *turned soldier*

who died over the "chance discharge of a rifle."[52] It concludes with the observation that native reason and treaty rights had been spoiled by

> *discovery*
> *cultural conceit*
> *and constitutional trickery.*[53]

In Vizenor's antigothic the whites' discovery and imposition of civilization in the northern woods turns a pastoral Eden into Minnesota, a place with an Indian name but a bad place nonetheless for Indians.

Notes

1. The *Oxford English Dictionary* also records a secondary meaning of "succession of an estate."

2. See Balenger, "*Survivance* in New England."

3. The Anishinaabe are also called "Chippewa" and "Ojibway." I use the terms interchangeably.

4. Vizenor, *Manifest Manners*, 4.

5. Vizenor, *Manifest Manners*, 4.

6. Isernhagen, *Momaday, Vizenor, Armstrong*, 85.

7. Vizenor, *Manifest Manners*, 66.

8. Vizenor, *Bear Island*, 3.

9. Vizenor, *Bear Island*, 32.

10. Vizenor, *Bear Island*, 13.

11. Longfellow, *Song of Hiawatha*.

12. Vizenor, *Manifest Manners*, 38.

13. Vizenor, *Bear Island*, 13, 15.

14. Vizenor, *Manifest Manners*, 38.

15. Densmore, *Chippewa Music*, 1.

16. Densmore, *Chippewa Music*, 2.

17. Densmore, *Chippewa Music*, 2.

18. See Day, *Sky Clears*, 32.

19. Densmore, *Chippewa Music*, 150.

20. Vizenor, *Summer in the Spring*, 58.

21. Vizenor, *Summer in the Spring*, 23.

22. Vizenor, *Bear Island*, 24, 28.

23. Vizenor, *Bear Island*, 13.

24. Vizenor, *Summer in the Spring*, 24.

25. Quoted in Fiedler, *Love and Death*, 159.

26. Fiedler, *Love and Death*, 159.

27. Vizenor, *Bear Island*, 39.

28. Vizenor, *Bear Island*, 39.

29. Vizenor, *Bear Island*, 46.

30. Vizenor, *Bear Island*, 48.

31. Vizenor, *Bear Island*, 49, 47.

32. Vizenor, *Bear Island*, 49.

33. Vizenor, *Bear Island*, 4.

34. Vizenor, *Bear Island*, 29–30.

35. Vizenor, *Bear Island*, 16.

36. Vizenor, *Bear Island*, 31.

37. Vizenor, *Bear Island*, 32.

38. Whitman, *Complete Poems*, 23; emphasis added.

39. Whitman, *Complete Poems*, 17.
40. Whitman, *Complete Poems*, 6.
41. Whitman, *Complete Poems*, 16.
42. Vizenor, *Bear Island*, 34.
43. Vizenor, *Bear Island*, 35.
44. Vizenor, *Bear Island*, 44.
45. Vizenor, *Bear Island*, 58.
46. Vizenor, *Bear Island*, 67–68.
47. Vizenor, *Bear Island*, 69.
48. Vizenor, *Bear Island*, 45.
49. Some had it. The rest received it in 1924 as a result of Congress's appreciation of their participation in World War I.
50. Thornton, *American Indian Holocaust*, 32.
51. Vizenor, *Bear Island*, 86.
52. Vizenor, *Bear Island*, 93.
53. Vizenor, *Bear Island*, 93.

Bibliography

Balenger, Claude. "*Survivance* in New England and the Flint Affair." Marianopolis College. http://www2.marianopolis.edu/quebechistory/events/flint.htm (accessed June 1, 2007).

Day, A. Grove. *The Sky Clears*. Lincoln: University of Nebraska Press, 1951.

Densmore, Frances. *Chippewa Music*. Washington DC: U.S. Government Printing Office, 1910.

Fiedler, Leslie A. *Love and Death in the American Novel*. New York: Stein and Day, 1982.

Isernhagen, Hartwig. *Momaday, Vizenor, Armstrong*. Norman: University of Oklahoma Press, 1999.

Longfellow, Henry Wadsworth. *The Song of Hiawatha*. University of Virginia Library. http://etext.lib.virginia.edu/toc/modeng/public/LonHiaw.html.

Thornton, Russell. *American Indian Holocaust and Survival*. Norman: University of Oklahoma Press, 1987.

Vizenor, Gerald. *Bear Island: The War at Sugar Point*. Minneapolis: University of Minnesota Press, 2006.

———. *Manifest Manners: Postindian Warriors of Survivance*. Norman: University of Oklahoma Press, 1994.

———, ed. *Summer in the Spring: Anishinaabe Lyric Poems and Stories*. Norman: University of Oklahoma Press, 1993.

Whitman, Walt. *Complete Poems and Selected Verse*. Boston: Houghton Mifflin, 1959.

9. Shifting the Ground

Theories of Survivance in *From Sand Creek*
and *Hiroshima Bugi: Atomu 57*

LINDA LIZUT HELSTERN

Many Americans watching the NBC *Nightly News* on the eve of the dedication
of the National Museum of the American Indian in September 2004 heard the
term *survivance* for the first time. Founding director W. Richard West chose his
words carefully when he spoke on camera. The new institution on the Washington Mall, West told the nation, signaling the importance in tribal circles
of the term coined by Gerald Vizenor, was a tribute to the survivance of the
Native peoples of the Americas, to their cultural vitality and continuance. In
a longer sound bite he might have added that the museum would not show-
case the history of Native genocide, the only Native history known to many
members of the dominant culture, but would rather contextualize that tragic
history within the long continuum of tribal life in this hemisphere. West told
the National Press Club that "buffeted though we may have been by the often cruel and destructive edge of colonialism, we are not, ultimately, the victims of that history—indeed, we retain a vigorous contemporary cultural
presence in the Americas."[1] While fifteen thousand Native American Indians
danced in the streets during the museum's joyous opening celebration, visible proof of their living presence and tribal survivance, across the Mall the
Smithsonian Museum of Natural History was engaged in changing the culture
of dominance, dismantling its freeze-frame dioramas of Indians as Stone Age
hunters and returning thousands of items in its collection, including Native
bones, to the tribes from which they came.

Striking a new balance with dominance is the very heart of survivance, as
the semantic parallelism suggests. In *Fugitive Poses: Native American Scenes of
Absence and Presence* Vizenor asserts that survivance "is more than survival,

more than endurance or mere response; the stories of survivance are an active presence . . . an active repudiation of dominance, tragedy, and victimry."[2] His words are echoed almost word for word by the Manidoo Envoy who glosses the text of the absent author Ronin Ainoko Browne in Vizenor's 2003 novel *Hiroshima Bugi: Atomu 57*. Survivance, the Manidoo Envoy tells us, "is not merely a variation of 'survival,' the act, reaction, or custom of a survivalist. By 'survivance' [Ronin] means a vision and vital condition to endure, to outwit evil and dominance, and to deny victimry."[3] Vizenor's sleight-of-hand suffix change, which keeps the action in the present moment, tacitly acknowledges the power of dominance to assume new guises even as it affirms both the power of personal agency and the Native world view in which life includes death and in which living is a process of change ongoing.

Even before Vizenor's first use of the term, survivance empowered Native writers in their work of decolonizing the mind. It grounds such texts as Simon Ortiz's major poem sequence *From Sand Creek*, first published in 1981 and reissued in 2000, the year the Sand Creek Massacre National Historic Site received Congressional authorization. It also underpins Vizenor's own fiction, most recently *Hiroshima Bugi*, the story of the return to Japan of a Japanese-Anishinaabi orphan born during the American Occupation. Significant if unexpected parallels exist between *Hiroshima Bugi* and *From Sand Creek*. Their links to history grounded in landscape (and specifically to landscapes synonymous with massive civilian death at the hands of the American military), their focus on Native veterans, their stance against separatism and racialism, and their emphasis on the importance of dream and story, especially self-conscious use of trickster story and its inherent irony as a teaching device, as well as their emphasis on changing signification and their unusual two-part form, offer a unique opportunity for comparing two rather different theories of survivance, both central to the contemporary Native oeuvre.

While the theory of survivance grounding *From Sand Creek* may be termed Deep Memory, that grounding *Hiroshima Bugi* merits the name Perfect Memory. Deep Memory in this usage does not refer to the recovery of repressed personal memory but rather to the development of a profound emotional/ psychological connection with the transpersonal traumas of Native history in order to render them a source of personal strength. Native history is traditionally encoded in landscape, and Ortiz alludes to both ideas in his title.

In 1974–75 he came to know the environs of Fort Lyon, Colorado, literally the origin site of the Sand Creek Massacre, as a patient in the drug and alcohol rehabilitation unit of Veterans Administration Hospital that operated there until 2001. In 1864 the soldiers who committed the atrocities against Black Kettle's band of Cheyennes and Arapahos rode out of the very same compound. Survivance in this text begins with an understated and almost inexplicable personal tragedy that finds its analogue in the tragedy of Sand Creek. An active participant in his own healing, Ortiz's understanding of the massacre ultimately comes through dreams and images. Black Kettle, who respected the generosity of his ancestors and welcomed the whites to share his homeland, exemplifies for Ortiz the traditional values that will ensure Native survivance, but even he turned to alcohol. Ortiz's self-decolonization and the recovery of his emotional health depends upon living these traditional tribal values, but Ortiz understands that survivance is tricky business. Step by step in *From Sand Creek*, he shifts the signifier *American* until it ceases to be a synonym for dominance and becomes the Native ground of being.

As a theory of survivance Deep Memory focuses on the human mind engaged in the difficult emotional work of rendering the unconscious conscious: dominance is not so much an external as an internal phenomenon. In contrast, Perfect Memory focuses relentlessly and unsentimentally on the body, and more specifically upon the body as social construction. If dominance begins with the ideological inscription of othered human bodies, survivance resides in the refusal to internalize or endorse these stories. In *Hiroshima Bugi* the interplay of race, disability, and gender across cultures reveals the very mechanisms of dominance, making processes intellectually comprehensible that are in fact external to the individual. To understand the workings of culture without emotional attachment fosters personal agency as individuals come to see that they have the power to perform or not to perform the roles in which they have been cast.

Perfect Memory has an analogue in Anishinaabe culture, in which traditional naming practice reflected the transitory nature of socially constructed identity. Names distilled memorable stories, and an even more memorable story led to a new name and social identity.[4] Not surprisingly in *Hiroshima Bugi* Vizenor's protagonist has two names before his traditional warrior role is acknowledged through the name Ronin. He arrives at White Earth already a Japanese warrior, equipped with his own wooden sword. Cultural continuity is central to survivance, and Vizenor, like Ortiz, builds his text on dreams, visions, compassionate openness, and a belief in life as movement and continual transformation even into death. Vizenor, however, explicitly values the importance of cultural exchange in the ongoing process of hybridity and cultural change.

"Perfect memories," Vizenor's Manidoo Envoy observes, "arise from natural reason, communal wit, experience, and native trickster stories."[5] Given Vizenor's lifelong interest in the Anishinaabe trickster, it should come as no surprise that his theory of survivance is trickster inspired. The very name *Perfect Memory*, like any trickster story, is ironic and underscores the fact that memories change in light of subsequent experiences, personal and cultural. "Facts" are displaced again and again in our memories through the very process of living, and Perfect Memory reflects this displacement, although when viewed according to the common misconception that the facts of history are unalterable, it appears closer kin to imagination than memory.

Hiroshima, where Vizenor's text begins, provides perhaps the premier example of the malleability of historical fact. What the world remembers today about the use of the atomic bomb to end World War II is American culpability for the instantaneous destruction of a city populated by civilian innocents. In *The Victim as Hero: Ideologies of Peace and National Identity in Postwar Japan*, James J. Orr argues that this image was carefully constructed and politically manipulated to erase Japanese culpability for a war grounded in nationalistic superiority. After the Occupation not shame but victimry became the foundation of Japan's national identity. Even Americans have forgotten that Japan's objective was to build a vast colonial empire in East Asia and that Hiroshima, historically a military city, housed major industries that supported the war effort.

According to the Manidoo Envoy, Perfect Memory is close kin to Theodor Adorno's "exact imagination," which is "configurational, or the compact of elements and episodes, rather than creative. The details and arrangement are endorsed by imagination, the actual configuration of material and experience that reveals the inseparable and yet tricky connection of objective and subjective activity."[6] In *Hiroshima Bugi*, as in his other fictions, Vizenor finds analogues for experience, appealing to the intellect rather than to the emotions, a practice consistent with the teaching philosophy that lies behind traditional Native storytelling. The Japanese landscape of *Hiroshima Bugi* is a landscape of displacement, a calculated move on Vizenor's part to destabilize the Indian-white binary that so effectively underwrites colonial dominance on American soil.

Here his GI mixed-blood protagonist enacts the role of cross-cultural warrior. Ronin returns to Japan, where America stood staunchly against colonialism and racialist notions of purity, as his father's son, a warrior simultaneously White Earth and American. His tribal name Ronin reminds us that he is also his mother's son, a traditional Japanese warrior as well, though one socially marginalized for lack of a samurai lord. In Hiroshima Ronin actively attacks the city's well-established identification with peace (and by extension victimry) on the site where it is most actively and most aggressively promoted, in Peace Memorial Park and the Peace Memorial Museum. He stages his raids from "home," the Atomic Bomb Dome, the one ruin in the park that survived the atomic blast. Here Ronin's story begins. Like traditional ronin when the occasion demanded, he puts his body on the line inside a sumo ring. At Ground Zero this traditional circle displaces the passive target circle with an arena for personal agency.

The history that Vizenor displaces in *Hiroshima Bugi* is variously personal, tribal, national, and global in scale, and his displacements may be creative inventions or verifiable facts. The shifts follow no predictable pattern. On the personal level Vizenor's early experience as a mixed-blood foster child certainly has affinities with young Ronin's parentless state, but Vizenor's mother was Swedish American, not Japanese, and the childhood helpers he describes in *Interior Landscapes: Autobiographical Myths and Metaphors* are Anishinaabe Little People, not Japanese Kappa. Like Ronin's father, Vizenor was stationed in Japan but after, not during, the American Occupation. At the national level Vizenor displaces the accepted facts of history with documented but little-known accounts. The first North American to visit modern Japan was not Commodore Perry, but as Vizenor tells us, an obscure mixed-blood named Ranald MacDonald, the son of a Scots fur trader and a Chinook chief's daughter, the Princess Sunday, who becomes the Princess Raven in Vizenor's telling.[7] MacDonald arrived on Hokkaido in 1848 looking for tribal ancestors and became Japan's first resident English teacher. In a displacement of a different sort, Ronin follows his father's vision of following in MacDonald's footsteps, a trip that he can only imagine. In Vizenor's text even his arrival in Japan is displaced. Ronin's experience in Hokkaido is rendered as a flashback after we see him in action in Hiroshima.

For Oritz, placing his story of survivance on the western Great Plains in the heart of America requires that he confront the Indian-white binary directly. *From Sand Creek* relates the story of dominance and survivance in a place at once present and past in all of its living complexity. Season, topography, flora, fauna, and human life are all important aspects of the whole. Ortiz demonstrates survivance through Deep Memory as he weaves all of these strands together into a complicated braid, revealing not only an alternative to canonical American history but an alternative geographically based historiography. He tells the story of a group of veterans, including himself, being treated for posttraumatic stress and other emotional disorders at the Ft. Lyon VA hospital some forty miles from Sand Creek as the crow flies. The facts of the 1864 Sand Creek Massacre stand as a preface, an open frame, for Ortiz's story: 28 men and 105 women and children died in Black Kettle's camp, with the 700 U.S. Army soldiers responsible departing from Ft. Lyon. That these facts are sandwiched between Black Kettle's formal expression of his desire for peace on two different occasions says much about the story that will follow.

It is clear almost immediately that *From Sand Creek* is not a story of Indian victimry, past or present, but of life choices and of stories left untold. The poem cycle stands as a testament to the Native will to endure and to outwit evil and dominance. Indeed, what is most remarkable about *From Sand Creek* is the vision that ultimately transforms abject weakness into power and the signifier *Indian* into the signifier *American*. Ortiz accomplishes this transformation by shifting the concept of weakness out of the Western paradigm that equates weakness and powerlessness and into the Native paradigm in which abject weakness is rather the beginning of power, the only condition out of which the warrior's personal vision ever emerges. Ortiz accepts his own weakness and in his final poem shares the vision he is given of an inclusive America, "our America,"

> *wealthy with love*
> *and compassion*
> *and knowledge.*[8]

Ortiz dedicated his book to the patients whose individual stories became part of his larger story: "Danny, Billy, Nez, Larry, the Oklahoma Boy, Bingo, Ed, Apache, W., Ruidoso, Dusty, all those warriors."[9] What they have in common beyond their various psychological disorders is not that they are Indian, though many clearly are. It is their military service. Ortiz honors this shared American warrior identity without regard to race.

In the first poem of his text Ortiz places his sequence in the Plains landscape, foreshadowing the transformational nature of his larger story. Set in bold type on the facing page, it follows the hard facts of the Sand Creek Massacre. Here the cycle of life continues: "Look now," Ortiz enjoins,

> there are flowers
> and new grass
> and a spring wind
> rising
> from Sand Creek.[10]

In a shared vision we witness nothing less than the transformation of America, knowing that for Native peoples it

> has been a burden
> of steel and mad
> death.[11]

This poem and Ortiz's concluding vision, also set in bold type, formally frame the multistranded story. The format Ortiz establishes in the main text suggests the new balance that has to be achieved against the weight of the old story. As in his opening, each pair of facing pages stands in dialogic relationship. A two- or three-line prose statement at the top of the left-hand page prefaces the poem on the right. Each statement, set in italic, typographically echoes the longer Sand Creek story, but the vertical column of the unitalicized poem on the right always carries greater visual weight, moving the story along.

The connection between the prefatory statement and the linked poem is seldom easy or obvious although the reader soon comes to trust both the gap and the connection. The statements are often factual, offering useful background information or grounding the poems in daily realities. In the first

statement, for example, Ortiz sets his scene at the VA hospital, hinting that
he may be starting a Coyote story. "Passing through," Ortiz begins, con-
juring a passing thought of the fast-moving trickster, "one gets caught into
things."[12] The facing poem has no obvious connection with the hospital or
with the trickster. It does, however, point both toward a trap and a way out
of that trap though the process of transformation. The poem begins without a personal subject, no *I*. Rather, Ortiz focuses on the emotional state
that precedes tragic wisdom:

> Grief
> *memorizes this grass.*

The poem's third line, the single word "Raw," precisely defines the quality
of this grief as it enters personal consciousness. While technically modify-
ing the noun "courage," line four, its strategic positioning between the two
abstract nouns, both also single-word lines, effectively transforms grief into
courage. "Raw / courage," however, looking very much like grief, "red-eyed
and urgent," quickly undergoes its own transformation. Line by line Ortiz returns the concept of courage to palpable materiality. Before any city or any
sword, courage, "Like stone / like steel," is made real through the coercive
power of language. Ortiz reminds us,

> *the words from then*
> *talk like that.*

"Believe it," he insists, not once but twice.[13]

   This statement/poem pairing speaks on one level to the process of change
facilitated through hospitalization, but at another level, it reveals the workings
of Deep Memory as the key to survivance. Survivance, Ortiz suggests, entails
more than knowing a few old stories. It depends upon a vital understanding
of how these stories construct the world as a place of constant change and
of connection with the coercive language that brought the old stories themselves into being. By the end of the poem cycle, readers have a catalog of examples through which to infer the meaning of Ortiz's method.

   The veterans themselves begin to emerge in the second poem of the sequence. Toby, explicitly identified as Indian, symbolizes their emotional state.
In the white town of La Junta, they are hidden even from themselves, frozen in

fear, unable to speak, but stasis is death as Ortiz emphasizes on several occasions in the sequence. To live is to move, like Coyote and the white settlers
who built their windowless sod houses on the plains, consulting "the dream
called America."[14] As the seasons change, even birds migrate, a survivance
strategy, Ortiz observes, citing as a negative example one trickster magpie

> *determined*
> *to freeze.*[15]

A recurring dream finally sets Ortiz himself in motion, but as he drives
east near Sand Creek, he senses danger. He is moving in the same direction
as the clouds, as

> *Ghosts Indian-like*
> *still driven*
> *towards Oklahoma.*[16]

Danger lies ahead but also behind. He knows the horrific cannibal end that
one Paiute chief met when "Conquest reached Nevada."[17] Westering, the
movement of dominance and Manifest Destiny, asserts itself as an oppositional force with greater and greater intensity as the cycle continues. Even
after the American dream

> *crossed*
> *rivers and burned forests*
> *and scarred futures,*

the settlers marched

> *onward,*
> *and westward.*[18]

No matter how much danger lies in movement, however, stopping always
poses the greater risk. The immigrants running from Europe were simple people, Ortiz assures us. They became dangerous only because they stopped
for lessons in Puritan ideology. The catatonic Oklahoma Boy, without the
will to move, stands as a final warning of what it means to be frozen by fear.
Survivance is contingent upon the ability not only to keep moving but to
change direction whenever necessary. All Billy ever talked about, Ortiz tells

us when he introduces him for the first time, "was going to Kansas City and freedom."[19] This seems reasonable until Billy confides his secret plan for securing freedom:

> head east for Kansas, make arrows.
> Send for the IRA.

Unwilling to change his focus, Billy loses all sense of direction. In his attempt to counter dominance directly, he ultimately vanishes,

> a swirl of America
> in his brain.[20]

Ortiz is still looking for Billy at the end of the text when, instead of Billy, he finds the Oklahoma Boy.

In this affirmation of movement and survivance, Ortiz denies victimry, whether collective or personal, at every turn. Sometimes he accomplishes this denial through bitter irony, as when he asserts early in the text,

> In 1864,
> there were no Indians killed.[21]

Sometimes he does it through a reversal of expectations. When he reaches his most profound emotional connection with the events at Sand Creek, what he sees is not the blood of death but the blood of life, brilliant red, literally uncontainable:

> Spurting,
> sparkling,
> splashing, bubbling.[22]

The tragedy for those who would use this fountain of life to replenish their own lives lay in finding that

> Their helpless hands
> were like sieves.[23]

Most often, however, Ortiz denies victimry through his emphasis on personal agency, which he demonstrates through his respect for each veteran as an individual, through his sparing use of the first-person pronoun, and through his ironic humor. Ortiz's compassion is his greatest emotional strength. He sees in every individual the capacity for agency, from Toby, the Indian separated from his shadow in the second poem, to the Oklahoma Boy in the last. Though mute, Toby is alert to danger, even if he does not recognize that the only threat comes from the sight of his mirror self, his own wounded soul. The Oklahoma Boy is no more conscious than the couch on which he is sitting, yet Ortiz honors him for living "the life he now matters by."[24] The individual who hits his shoe with the janitor's broom demonstrates no such respect.

No individual, no matter how divorced from day-to-day reality, is ever reduced to an object of Ortiz's or our anger or pity. Each has the potential for agency despite all odds, though the odds should never be underestimated. Ortiz's Casino Night story, which occurs about three-quarters of the way through the text, reveals much in this regard, both about Ortiz's sense of respect and his sense of humor. This is a story, indeed, from which he initially wants to exclude himself, embarrassed perhaps that he has not yet mastered the first lesson of gambling with the Evil Gambler: without help no one can beat the odds. Ortiz and three buddies, all convinced they

> might be winners
> at any moment,

pick up a much older vet on their way to the gaming hall, a man so out of touch with reality that even the door "was not a door for him." Danny and Larry help him out and cheer him on. Ortiz, however, sees this vet's power rather than his weakness: he embodies the knowledge Ortiz and his buddies lack. Ortiz wryly reports,

> The old man knew he would not win.
> He was as fortunate as all of us.[25]

How Ortiz uses *I* in this text reveals much about the sense of agency that enables him to show us his deepest vulnerability and thereby turn the weakness that brought him to the VA hospital into the power of vision. Ortiz uses *I* to mark four phases of healing. Through these stages we gauge his progress toward self-decolonization as we witness growing strength of traditional Native values, often explicitly labeled American, in his personal interactions. The first phase of the healing lays out the parameters of the problem.

In the first quarter of the text, anger and grief are depersonalized. There is no *I* to be found. Instead, Toby, the only veteran in this text explicitly identified as Indian, stands before us as a symbol of the problem that does not yet recognize itself. The second phase of Ortiz's healing involves taking personal responsibility in the second quarter of the text. The third phase tests the strength of his self-decolonization in the face of real world dominance. Two such tests occur in the third quarter of the text. Finally comes the hard-won consciousness of strengths and limitations and the recognition that power comes only in the conscious acceptance of one's utter weakness. Only then does vision emerge.

Ortiz uses the first person singular pronoun sparingly, but whenever he introduces *I* into the text, he uses it to assert agency and responsibility — or irresponsibility — as the case may be. This assertion happens for the first time when he boasts,

> *In Denver,*
> *I could drink them under*
> *the table anytime.*

In the only allusion to the problem that sent him to the hospital, there is no hint of victimry. Rather Ortiz casts himself as prototypically American. In a paradoxical echo of Manifest Destiny, he insists,

> *Me.*
> *I think as far as California,*
> *I do.*

This tricky assertion of a vision on the move, however, also suggests the breadth of Native understanding of the American continent. On the other hand, Ortiz's Denver drinking buddies, disenfranchised white farmers, seem like Indian stereotypes, living in the past and cultivating their memories of "open plain and mountains."[26]

Four poems later, when Ortiz reintroduces the first person singular, the *I* separates him from the hospital group of which he does not want to be part. Repeated at the end of the poem, *I* claims full, if distasteful, partnership in the group. This act represents progress.

Ortiz's first vivid, though veiled, image of the violence at Sand Creek follows:

> *One, or two, several soldiers*
> *swiftly*
> *expertly*
> *at her*
> > *self her generations.*[27]

His language hints at the truth that psychologists have observed: genocidal violence continues as a living and deeply painful presence in the lives of subsequent generations of survivors.[28] By the time Ortiz introduces *I* again two poems later, he is fully engaged in the therapeutic process, persuading a buddy of the value of telling his dreams, stories "reliable as those river stones," and commending his courage in the face of his fear. Ortiz has become a reliable guide because he knows this territory, the river's "sorrowful blood" and the "blades glistening."[29]

The first real world test of Ortiz's self-decolonization marks the midpoint of the text. The results are mixed. When Ortiz finds himself under assault at the Salvation Army, fulfilling the clerk's stereotype of the thieving Indian, he feels impelled to counter the stereotype head on by making an honest purchase. Only in retrospect can he accept the negatives attributed to Indian identity. Ortiz asserts, not once but twice as he replays the scene in his memory,

> *I should have stolen.*
> *My life. My life.*[30]

Although it satisfies the ego, direct action against evil and dominance seldom achieves the desired result. Ortiz's irony here is subtle. The statement that prefaces the poem implicates both the Reverend Colonel Chivington, who orchestrated the Sand Creek massacre with his own salvation army, and Kit Carson in theft and murder. Ortiz, who has demonstrated his moral strength and personal responsibility, leaves it for the reader to infer that any claim to power through revenge would situate him in the same camp as Chivington and Carson.

This was the camp, indeed, with which armed revolutionaries worldwide, notably in Africa, had affiliated themselves, and Ortiz wakens one night with the startling realization that the madness he is witnessing at the VA hospital, the scream he hears, is directly connected with the worldwide colonial enterprise present and past:

> *the basement speaks*
> *for Africa, Saigon, Sand Creek.*

He is quick to imagine that his Indian buddies have enlisted in the fight. It is the obvious way to counter his own unvoiced pain and his fear, proactive rather than reactive. Warriors are not victims. More importantly, however, Ortiz here denies victimry by asserting his presence as a speaker in the darkness. His use of *I* is linked to the act of naming: "stark, I said."[31] Whether he has named a condition or an individual is ambiguous. In either case Ortiz has opened the door to a new relationship with the fear engendered by dominance.

The second test of Ortiz's self-decolonization takes place within the hospital, where Ortiz himself is in charge of a stock of sundries. He claims power here — but indirectly and ironically — by claiming a vice president from Texas, a hint in light of American history that his power might not last long. Still the tacit association with JFK suggests the hope that the latter's New Frontier brought to minority communities. The statement prefacing this poem acknowledges the "brute persuasion and force" through which American institutions have traditionally constructed their authority.[32] The poem reveals the workings of American power but not without showing an alternative. Ortiz's own power derives from the traditional Native model of leadership grounded in the reciprocity between generosity and loyalty. Ortiz sees to it that all of the patients' modest needs are met. Though the source of his stock remains a mystery, whatever they beg for, he provides:

> *Coffee.*
> *Cigarettes.*
> *Shaving cream.*
> *Shoe laces.*[33]

In a tricky move he configures this generosity not as Indian but as typically American. Still the Texan doesn't understand. Ortiz feels so threatened by the Texan's censurious look that he admits, "I have to move away." This *I* is his Indian self,

> *the aboriginal*
> *and the savage that cringes*
> *under his murderous eyes.*

Ortiz loses his status and power, but he never loses the capacity for agency. Speaking of his own vulnerabilities for the first time in the first person, he admits ironically,

> The derelicts and I
> trade poor comfort.[34]

Moving away was Ortiz's choice, seemingly the result of personal weakness, but the measure of one's strength often depends upon acknowledging one's weaknesses. Avoiding direct confrontation is also a trick of survivance. The power of dominance asserts its full and almost incomprehensible strength as Ortiz is almost immediately called upon to witness the full impact of Sand Creek, the living blood and helpless hands. He is strong enough now to hold the image.

At this point Ortiz shifts the *I* out of the poems and into his prefatory statements, sharing some typically American facts about himself, including his unabashedly American love for movies and his youthful love for Whitman, now dead. The strength he has gained, however, allows Ortiz to make an agonized reappraisal of Whitman, to separate the ideological Whitman, the advocate of Manifest Destiny, from the human being with his own deeply felt emotions in the face of American rejection. This new emotional connection allows Ortiz in the next poem to see the America that lies before him in a new way. Here *I*, unlike Toby at the beginning of the cycle, both sees and knows. A vision of the sunlit panorama of the plains landscape, joyously peopled, opens before Ortiz, coerced into being through his repetition of "I know." This landscape is precisely balanced by the engineered landscape, the constructions of dominance, that Ortiz sees before him: fortress walls and

> a train that carries dreams
> and freedom away.[35]

Filled and then emptied by the power of the thunder, utterly humbled, Ortiz asks of the greater world to be seen within the context of the pain the hospitalized veterans share. The wrenching cry that follows in the next poem comes not from Ortiz but from an unnamed man crying for his mother, his anger

> so ferocious it rang
> and cracked

> *through the hospital*
> *walls.*[36]

This cry is nothing that Ortiz wants to hear, but refused wings by his own muscles, which deny victimry by retaining the power to act even in paralysis, Ortiz endures. "I could only cry," he admits,

> *mangled*
> *like his anger,*
> *amazed,*
> *and dismayed.*[37]

With his plea granted, we see Ortiz within the context of greater pain, but never alone, never a victim.

The strength of his emotional connection calls forth compassion deep enough to begin a national healing. Ortiz tells us,

> *Probably*
> *they didn't know,*

in an effort to excuse the behavior that has resulted in such pain: the settlers couldn't foresee the human consequences of their arrogance, which grew out of fear for their own survival. Ortiz here exposes dominance itself as weakness, reminding us that even the creators of the nation's atomic legacy

> *will have to share reports*
> *of history which now rise*
> *before us as mutant generations.*[38]

"Generations" here keeps the image of Sand Creek before our eyes. The power of colonial dominance to destroy individual lives is no less today than it has ever been. To make this point, in his next prefatory note, Ortiz introduces Apache, who is so like Billy. The paired poem, however, offers a perspective on dominance that is antithetical to the Western world view. Ortiz would not eradicate those moments of extraordinary terror with their power to destroy. Instead, balancing survivance and dominance, he views them together as a gift that calls forth our deepest appreciation of life.

The way to change the consequences of historic American arrogance, the pattern set by Andrew Jackson, however, is not through more violence and terror but through love and responsibility. Refusal to change has but one consequence: the Oklahoma Boy,

> the American,
> vengeful and a wasteland
> of fortunes, for now.[39]

Stark, but not without hope, this image grows out of Ortiz's impassioned first-person declaration of love for America, an America insistent upon "story, poetry, song, life, life."[40] In his final framing poem Ortiz changes the dream that now imprisons Americans, that has long imprisoned Indians like Toby and Apache and Billy. He brings into being the reality of "our America."[41] The settlers, who

> could have
> matched the land,

rejected the opportunity to accept love, compassion, and knowledge as gifts from the Arapahos, their children fearful even as they heard the

> wind
> speaking the Arapaho words
> for pain and beauty and generations.[42]

Now these fundamental values rise from Sand Creek as surely as the spring wind and the new grass, a testament to survivance as hard-won emotional reality.

Gerald Vizenor, in contrast, develops his theory of survivance against the backdrop of global historic events known to virtually every American. In *Hiroshima Bugi* Vizenor keeps the focus on family as he weaves an intergenerational story set in contemporary Japan. His central character Ronin Ainoko Browne is a master of the tricks of survivance who by encouragement and example helps others develop the skills necessary to outwit evil and dominance and to deny victimry. He is the mixed-blood son of a warrior who made his career in the U.S. Army, conceived in the very place and at the very moment when Occupation forces were beginning the decolonization of the collective Japanese mind.

Ronin's Anishinaabe father, we are told, served as an interpreter who learned his Japanese at Camp Savage, an ironic signal of the import of survivance strategies for tribal warriors of his generation. Nightbreaker's first stop in Japan, just days after the atomic bombing, was Hiroshima. Later in his career, he moved on to other atomic sites, but Hiroshima is where we first meet his son, who positions himself on the margins to society, taking up residence in the hulking ruin of the Atomic Bomb Dome. Claiming this space as his own, Ronin demonstrates that each generation must assert its own survivance in the face of dominance. "The Atomic Bomb Dome is my Rashomon," he proclaims in the first sentence of the novel, the reader's first clue to its theoretical grounding in the conception of survivance as Perfect Memory.[43]

The Rashomon that readers are most likely to recall is the film starring Toshiro Mifune, in which the events of a theft spawn a multiplicity of stories, each witness's account conflicting substantively with those of the others. Nothing is ever resolved because there is no way to reconcile the differences. Instead, all of the stories live on. To deny finality is the first trick of survivance according to the theory of Perfect Memory, and Vizenor's Manidoo Envoy points back further to the very origin of the film script in the instability of story. His message is reinforced in the very construction of this text. Each chapter of Hiroshima Bugi consists of two parts, two voices with different narrative styles that alternate in dialogic relationship, each visually cued by its own type style. Ronin tells his sometimes elliptical story in the first person. Then the Manidoo Envoy glosses Ronin's text, his additions often reading like footnotes as he meticulously credits his sources. Some of the material that the Manidoo Envoy adds, however, precedes rather than follows related material in Ronin's text. Through multiple disconnections and the lack of obvious order, Vizenor insists that the reader focus on the constructedness of this text, its manifold parts, rather than the perfect simulacrum of a unified whole. Like the mirror fragments in the story's paintings, each disjunction breaks the illusion of reality all over again.

The film Rashomon, the Manidoo Envoy reminds us, displaces the plot of Akutagawa's original short story by conflating two different stories. Nightbreaker, he confides, knew the original, the story of a ronin newly released from his master's service who arrives, suicidal, at Rashomon Gate and finds an old woman living by her wits, making wigs with hair she steals from the dead. Inspired by her to live, the ronin kills the old woman and occupies the gate himself, now master of his own survivance. The Manidoo Envoy never tells this story, however. Instead, Akutagawa's story of survivance in the ruins of war-torn medieval Kyoto becomes Ronin's own through a complex process of displacement: he now takes the role of teacher.

Ronin's dreams have already taken him through atomic death, as we learn when he tells his dream to his first visitor. This man also has a natural way with words and a horrific story to tell. Even before they elaborate their stories, however, Vizenor signals that their experiences should be read in parallel. When the visitor declares that "my only friends are lepers," Ronin parries with "my only friends are orphans."[44] The fact that both choose to establish their identities through relationships rather than personal claims to victimry hints at their mutual commitment to survivance.

Ronin does not tell the story of the lonely childhood that we expect. In a trick of displacement that exemplifies Perfect Memory, he focuses on his dream life. We soon learn that the most horrific event in Ronin's atomic nightmare is not his death but the subsequent museum exhibit of his bones, a story with a decidedly Native resonance. Beyond this image his dream calls forth the living presence of Hiroshima's dead in a ghost parade that passes through the Atomic Bomb Dome each morning at 8:15. Ronin's guest with the disfigured face tells a different kind of story, the horror of his sixty-year incarceration in a leper colony on the island of Oshima. Neither is the story of *hibakusha* disability that we expect to hear at Ground Zero.

Ultimately Ronin gives his new acquaintance the nickname Oshima, a trick that makes the nation's shame his public face. Ronin's Japanese shame has similarly been made public. *Ainoko*, the middle name he was given at the time of his White Earth tribal adoption, means orphan. Unable to face the shame of his racial impurity, his mother abandoned him at a progressive orphanage. Although his identity as an orphan takes precedence over his half-half racial identity, neither his name nor Oshima's leaves room for hiding. In a tricky way both names foreground embodied identities. Ronin, too, has been abandoned by his nuclear family, and both Ronin and Oshima have experienced a personal emptiness analogous to that of the nuclear ruin they occupy.

Oshima's original name was erased in order to escape any family association with the shame of his leprosy. He tells the story of profound isolation, the rejection of literally anything lepers touched, including prize chrysanthemums, which mainland Japanese even refused to buy after their origin was discovered. Sterilization did not solve the problem. It brought quick death not only to the flowers but also to the disconsolate gardeners.

Such irrational fear, indeed, kept Japanese lepers in isolation for four decades after isolation had ceased to be acceptable medical practice. They were not released from their legally mandated incarceration until 1996.[45] This is but another example of the destructive effects of the national ideology of purity that grounded modern Japanese identity and built the war machine of World War II. It lived on during the Occupation when Japan refused to accept thousands of mixed-race children like Ronin, "the untouchables of war and peace in two countries."[46]

Oshima's new name, which connects place and history, honors the tragic wisdom gleaned from his dehumanizing isolation as it restores him to the world of human relationships. This name, of course, both echoes and displaces Hiroshima in the novel as Vizenor layers analogous experiences. In his Rashomon Oshima plays the suicidal ronin who has yet to appreciate his talent for survivance until Ronin opens a new world to him, sharing such simple pleasures of daily life as communal bathing in the sento, friendship with an attractive woman, and morning tea and pastries at the local bakery. Every new role, however, requires preparation. Before Oshima enters the city proper, he hones his skills in the peace park by performing in "tricky kabuki version[s] of Rashomon" In the first he plays "a lightning chancer," in the second "a leper who stole hair from bodies abandoned at the gate."[47] Oshima is on his way to earning the warrior title Ronin conferred at their first meeting, "samurai of leprosy."[48]

The peace park is home to other displaced persons as well, and the alliances that develop here cross many boundaries. Ronin becomes a model not only for the leper, who in other circumstances might be sentimentalized as a victim, but also for a rather more controversial figure. Kitsutsuke is a World War II veteran who lost his leg in combat and his family in the bombing of Hiroshima. He hates the emperor more even than Ronin, and quickly adopts Ronin's strategy for getting revenge.

The ironic survivance strategy that Gerald Vizenor deploys here using the theory of Perfect Memory depends upon the ability to inhabit the free space between the signifier and the signified. Vizenor utilizes historical facts from

two different periods of Japanese history to offer insight into the way signification functioned to construct a Japan of rigid isolationist purity. According to the Manidoo Envoy, Ronin reinvents the nineteenth-century trampling
ritual that forced Christians to renounce their faith by treading on a sacred
image of Mary or Jesus. Some did so with a clear conscience by waiting until
the image had already been desecrated. During the Second World War, the
emperor's photo was held sacred, "a revered object more important than life
itself."[49] Ronin, therefore, institutes the "practice of stomping on pictures of
the mighty emperor [as] an original, specific resistance to the consecration
of dominance."[50] Kitsutsuke takes this idea one step further, beheading the
image with Ronin's wooden sword.[51] While one ultranationalist in the text is
so bothered by the mutilated photos that he "trie[s] to mend the creases,"
Vizenor could not be more serious in his desire to deconstruct ideologies
and the true believers who perpetrate them.[52]

Ronin's vision of survivance clearly extends beyond the personal, and he
meanwhile declares a one-man war on peace, the sacred cow that has permitted victimry to become the central feature of Hiroshima's postwar identity. For his first engagement in the gift shop of the Peace Memorial Museum,
Ronin sports a tricky T-shirt of his own design. He is, however, easily defeated, shamed when museum guards read his slogan quoting Nils Bohr's famous
question — "Is it big enough?" — as a reference to his own penis. Only Ronin
remembers the original context of the question: whether the atomic bomb
was actually big enough to ensure peace for all time.

When Ronin makes the Peace Memorial itself his battleground in his next
attempt to defeat the twin ideologies of peace and victimry, he fights fire with
fire. Trying to destroy the eternal flame in a conflagration set from the opposite side of the reflecting pool has clear trickster affinities. The fire causes
no damage but does burn "shadows, faint traces of the ghost parade" on
the concrete walls.[53] This displacement is in accord with the theory of Perfect Memory. The atomic explosion itself left just such shadows on the ruins. This attack succeeds principally in getting Ronin into hot water with local authorities bent on protecting civic pride and property, but he effectively
demonstrates his skill in wordplay in a one-on-one with his police interroga-
tor. Ronin is ultimately released from custody with a new identity: *police maniac*, henceforth his perfect cover.

In his next attack Ronin targets the etched endorsements of peace by international leaders posted on columns under a simulation of the Atomic Bomb
Dome. Although he appreciates the ironic readings given by Margarito Real,
the inflection is insufficiently caustic for Ronin. He uses chemicals against
what he calls "peace simulations" and succeeds in shutting down the Peace
Memorial Museum, at least temporarily. The police, convinced of the accu-
racy of their own signifier for Ronin, refuse to arrest him.

Real, who becomes an important cross-cultural ally with his own arsenal
of trickeries, reminds us and Ronin how powerful a tool comic irony can be.
His Spanish name disguises his English origins, offering an ironic turn on the
real when Real, a serious critic of British imperialism, parodies the royal. At
dinner he underscores the very real effects of ideologically driven behavior.
Real borrows the rubber gloves Ronin used in his chemical attack to mount
a covert action of his own. He dubs them his leprosy gloves and succeeds
in terrorizing the hotel manager, who retains a morbid fear of leprosy — or
more precisely the idea of leprosy — and refuses to touch his money when
Real tries to pay the bill.

Oshima must inevitably come face to face with the living reality of such fear,
but he is not without allies the morning the bakery clerk calls the police to
have the leper removed. Together, the attractive Miko and Ronin give Oshima
a lesson in outwitting evil and dominance through displacement, once again
divorcing the signifier leprosy from the signified. The police find no leper because Miko is holding Oshima's hands, the perfect disguise for his deformity,
while Ronin greets them with cricked fingers. Recognizing Ronin as a police
maniac, they immediately discount the clerk's report. A second clerk apolo-
gizes to Oshima, who is so touched that the clerk is moved to tears.

Vizenor will ultimately turn his focus to the ideological construction of
Ronin's own body through his erotic relationship with the lovely Miko, one of
the new generation of wasp-waisted Hiroshima women whose physical attrac-
tions Ronin's dinner partners duly note, simultaneously deconstructing Yukio
Mishima and Simon Ortiz with their punch line, "Mutant generations."[54] First
attracted to her in the bakery, Ronin comes to know Miko more intimately
through her paintings, imaginative renderings of Hiroshima's ghost children
that grew out of a sensitivity akin to his own. Sentimentality is entirely absent as the lovers establish intimacy through their mutual discovery of one
another's tattoos in the central incident of Vizenor's text.

Miko's is a recognizably contemporary tattoo, a blue morning glory, almost closed. Ronin's, however, are unique, invisible tattoos ostensibly created by a closely guarded Ainu technique. Colorless, they might better be called scars of indigenous survivance inasmuch as they bear a decided resemblance to the scars of victimry and can only be seen on red skin. On Ronin's chest "Atomu 1, Eight Fifteen," according to the Manidoo Envoy, marks the moment of the beginning of a new era of Japanese history, a "calendar that starts with *hibakusha* pain, torment, and misery."[55] What personal meaning may be encoded here along with this indelible remembrance of the fragility of the body in the face of nuclear weapons remains unspoken. Ronin explains nothing about the meaning of these tattoos when Miko asks, his only response a second arousal worthy of a tribal trickster. She is a deeply perceptive reader, however, and in the morning, she counts the minutes until 8:15 when the ghost parade begins.

Perfect Memory reveals another side to the story of the beginning of the Atomic Era, and Ronin does eventually explain the profusion of floral images on his back: horseweed in honor of the first edible plants to sprout in Hiroshima after the bombing, morning glory for nuclear survivance, and chrysanthemum to tease his mother's imperial devotion. Here in symbolism akin to the floral motifs of the Woodland tribes, the resilience and power of the life force grows out of the tragedy of pain and death. These invisible tattoos carry the intimate tragic wisdom gleaned from dark stories lodged in living bodies that have a way of getting under the skin. Survivance resides not merely in the symbols but in the very process of creating them, quite inauthentically Ainu.

When Ronin agrees to create an invisible tattoo for Miko, she chooses a chrysanthemum as a tribute to Oshima, Ronin's apprentice. The tattoo Ronin signs in the manner of a traditional Japanese tattoo artist tells a fuller version of his story. On her back he incises a chrysanthemum in the deformed hand of a leper. What Ronin tells us Miko sees in the mirror when she looks at her tattoo for the first time in the sauna, however, is a morning glory, an inexplicable displacement or perhaps a mirror trick. The Manidoo Envoy reports that he saw the leper's hand the day he massaged Miko's back, but there is no way to know for certain.

Ronin's final assault on the Peace Memorial Museum, colored, no doubt, by his erotic experiences with Miko, relies upon an entirely new strategy, changing the signifier. Ronin successfully unfurls a banner proclaiming it the "Hiroshima Mon Amour Museum" to the delight of guards and the chagrin of the museum director. Standing like a good docent in front of the "diorama of aesthetic victimry" in which miniature figures remain clothed for the tourists in the midst of simulated atomic devastation, Ronin acts his own version of the movie that inspired the name change. He speaks the first line with assurance: "You saw nothing at Hiroshima."[56] This statement is the unvarnished truth and a note of bitter irony in the text.

The Manidoo Envoy embellishes the plot of *Hiroshima Mon Amour* with the story of Ronin's uncontainable anger, anger that spills over from the museum diorama to the horrors of history it does not depict. In Ronin's version, however, the story makes a tricky transition via flashback to a personal confrontation over his Native identity. The ultranationalist literature department chairman who has invited him to dinner during his visit to Hokkaido is obsessed by Ronin's Indian authenticity, a topic Ronin brushes aside. The chairman also insists that the Ainu are extinct. Changing the subject to the atomic bomb and the Japanese constitution, key American strategies against the ideology of purity that once reigned in Japan, distracts the chairman briefly, but when he returns to his identity rant, Ronin leaps onto the dining table, strips naked, and insists on being examined for inauthentic Ainu tattoos. When Ronin ultimately moons him, the chairman flees the scene, but the rest of Ronin's small audience responds to his performance enthusiastically. Taking personal freedom to the ultimate, he simply refuses to allow his body to be categorized according to the chairman's ideological rules.

If the theory of Perfect Memory holds, even bodies can be displaced. The Manidoo Envoy, whose information is usually, though not always, accurate, tells us that Miko confesses to having sex with Oshima twice on the bench in the peace park and that the second time "he almost died by orgasm."[57] Ronin, of course, claims he was the lucky man, but he acknowledges his own slippage in a Tokyo liaison with a former shrine miko who wants an "*Amerika indian*" baby. Ronin, dressed in his father's vintage uniform, will cheerfully stand in for the preferred father, AIM warrior Dennis Banks. This mixed-blood liaison, not quite a desecration of the sacred precincts of the Yasukuni Jinja, the icon of Japanese ultranationalist purity, stands as the prelude to Ronin's greatest triumph.

Mistaken for a Japanese war veteran, Ronin co-opts a sound truck to broadcast a celebration of American cultural hybridity: spirituals, blues, and country western music. Democracy and hybridity, racial and cultural, were America's Occupation legacy to Japan, and the new Japan responds with a riot of dancing in the streets. Ronin does not leave Japan a hero though. He slips out of Matsue, an old samurai town, under an assumed identity. In the pose of the mixed-blood writer Lafcadio Hearn, who did so much to construct America's twentieth-century notions of Japan, Ronin vanishes like the Anishinaabe Little People into the face of a rock cliff by the water.

Out of two very different theories of survivance, Simon Ortiz and Gerald Vizenor create stories of courage and tragic wisdom in the face of dominance, old stories that live in the landscape and live anew in every generation. Survivance is the heart of Native communities across America. Dominance, according to the Manidoo Envoy, is "a dead voice pursued by trickster stories."[58]

Notes

1. W. Richard West Jr., "The National Museum of the American Indian: A Historical Reckoning" (speech, National Press Club, Washington DC, September 9, 2004). Available from the National Museum of the American Indian Press Archive at http://www.nmai.si.edu/subpage.cfm?subpage=press&second=aboutnmai (accessed September 3, 2006).

2. Gerald Vizenor, *Fugitive Poses: Native American Scenes of Absence and Presence* (Lincoln: University of Nebraska Press, 1998), 15.

3. Gerald Vizenor, *Hiroshima Bugi: Atomu 57* (Lincoln: University of Nebraska Press, 2003), 36.

4. Gerald Vizenor, *The People Named Chippewa: Narrative Histories* (Minneapolis: University of Minnesota Press, 1984), 13.

5. Vizenor, *Hiroshima Bugi*, 36.

6. Vizenor, *Hiroshima Bugi*, 36.

7. Herb Gowen, *Five Foreigners in Japan* (1936; repr., Freeport NY: Books for Libraries Press, 1967), 36; Vizenor, *Hiroshima Bugi*, 139.

8. Simon Ortiz, *From Sand Creek* (1981; repr., Tucson: University of Arizona Press, 2000), 95.

9. Ortiz, *From Sand Creek*, 5.

10. Ortiz, *From Sand Creek*, 9.

11. Ortiz, *From Sand Creek*, 9.

12. Ortiz, *From Sand Creek*, 10.

13. Ortiz, *From Sand Creek*, 11.

14. Ortiz, *From Sand Creek*, 17.

15. Ortiz, *From Sand Creek*, 19.

16. Ortiz, *From Sand Creek*, 25.

17. Ortiz, *From Sand Creek*, 28.

18. Ortiz, *From Sand Creek*, 75, 77.

19. Ortiz, *From Sand Creek*, 44.

20. Ortiz, *From Sand Creek*, 45.

21. Ortiz, *From Sand Creek*, 15.

22. Ortiz, *From Sand Creek*, 67.

23. Ortiz, *From Sand Creek*, 67.

24. Ortiz, *From Sand Creek*, 93.

25. Ortiz, *From Sand Creek*, 73.

26. Ortiz, *From Sand Creek*, 31.

27. Ortiz, *From Sand Creek*, 41.

28. Eduardo and Bonnie Duran connect the unresolved rage and grief of intergenerational posttraumatic stress with alcoholism and other self-destructive behaviors among tribal peoples. See Eduardo Duran and Bonnie Duran, *Native American Postcolonial Psychology* (Albany NY: SUNY Press, 1995).

29. Ortiz, *From Sand Creek*, 45.

30. Ortiz, *From Sand Creek*, 53.

31. Ortiz, *From Sand Creek*, 55.

32. Ortiz, *From Sand Creek*, 62.

33. Ortiz, *From Sand Creek*, 63.

34. Ortiz, *From Sand Creek*, 63.

35. Ortiz, *From Sand Creek*, 83.

36. Ortiz, *From Sand Creek*, 85.

37. Ortiz, *From Sand Creek*, 85.

38. Ortiz, *From Sand Creek*, 87.

39. Ortiz, *From Sand Creek*, 93.

40. Ortiz, *From Sand Creek*, 92.

41. Ortiz, *From Sand Creek*, 95.

42. Ortiz, *From Sand Creek*, 47, 35.

43. Vizenor, *Hiroshima Bugi*, 1.

44. Vizenor, *Hiroshima Bugi*, 2.

45. In 2001 Japanese lepers won a class action suit against the government and were awarded damages for their forced incarceration. A similar case brought by lepers in former Japanese colonies is now pending. See "Japan's Leprosy Victims to Get Paid," *Guardian (London)*, November 8, 2005. Available from *Taipei Times* at http://www.taipeitimes.com/News/taiwan/archives/005/11/08/2003279218 (accessed April 9, 2006).

Prior to adoption of a 1953 amendment to the 1907 Japanese Leprosy Prevention

Law, isolation of lepers had been voluntary in Japan. The new policy remained in effect even though the Seventh International Congress of Leprology, which met in Tokyo in 1957, formally recommended the abolishment of isolation policies. See Michio Miyasaka, "A Historical and Ethical Analysis of Leprosy Control Policy in Japan" (unpublished paper, read at the eighth Tsukuba International Bioethics Roundtable, Tsukuba, Japan, 2003). Available at http://www.clg.niigata-u.ac.jp/~miyasaka/hansen/leprosypolicy.html (accessed April 9, 2006).

46. Vizenor, *Hiroshima Bugi*, 22.

47. Vizenor, *Hiroshima Bugi*, 46.

48. Vizenor, *Hiroshima Bugi*, 4.

49. Kiyosawa Kiyoshi, *A Diary of Darkness*, in Vizenor, *Hiroshima Bugi*, 66.

50. Vizenor, *Hiroshima Bugi*, 53.

51. Vizenor, *Hiroshima Bugi*, 53.

52. Vizenor, *Hiroshima Bugi*, 128.

53. Vizenor, *Hiroshima Bugi*, 39.

54. Vizenor, *Hiroshima Bugi*, 92.

55. Vizenor, *Hiroshima Bugi*, 103.

56. Vizenor, *Hiroshima Bugi*, 119.

57. Vizenor, *Hiroshima Bugi*, 113.

58. Vizenor, *Hiroshima Bugi*, 36.

10. TOTAL APOCALYPSE, TOTAL SURVIVANCE

Nuclear Literature and/or
Literary Nucleus — Melville, Salinger, Vizenor

TAKAYUKI TATSUMI

Whenever and wherever war breaks out, we often find ourselves thinking of Herman Melville's *Moby-Dick* (1851). In the wake of the September 11 terrorist attacks, for example, contemporary intellectual Edward Said compared President George W. Bush to Captain Ahab in his obsessed drive to pursue the white whale that once harmed him. By the same token, however, we should not forget a shocking message in J. D. Salinger's *The Catcher in the Rye* (1951), published during the centennial of *Moby-Dick*: "Anyway, I'm sort of glad they've got the atomic bomb invented. If there's ever another war, I'm going to sit right the hell on top of it. I'll volunteer for it, I swear to God I will."[1] Plausibly enough, this dangerous vision appealed to the distinguished director Stanley Kubrick, whose black-humor masterpiece *Dr. Strangelove* (1964) featured Major King Kong progressing from reading *Playboy* to arming the bombs to the orgasmic launch and ride on one bomb to the death. This genealogy of total apocalyptic narratives that I am tracing, from Melville to Salinger to Kubrick, offers us insight into historical transpacific transitions from the mid-nineteenth century through the Cold War years of McCarthyism in the 1950s and right down to the Cuban Missile Crisis in the 1960s. Is it possible to push the limits of the nuclear imagination in order to discover its literary nucleus? To begin tackling this problem, I would like to start by outlining transpacific literary and cultural history.

The Paradox of Happiness

One huge whale dashes himself against a whaler and mortally staves in its hull. This primal scene allows us to reconsider the significance of revenge in the text of *Moby-Dick*. Although Captain Ahab obviously attempts to revenge himself on the white whale for the leg the beast had bitten off a long time ago, he also believes that it is the whale itself that wants to strike back: "*Retribution, swift vengeance, eternal malice were in his whole aspect*, and spite of all that mortal man could do, the solid white buttress of his forehead smote the ship's starboard bow, till men and timbers reeled. Some fell flat upon their faces. Like dislodged trucks, the heads of the harpooners aloft shook on their bull-like necks. Through the breach, they heard the waters pour, as mountain torrents down a flume."[2]

It is well known that in describing the climatic shipwreck of this narrative, Herman Melville had been inspired by Owen Chase's book *Narrative of the Most Extraordinary and Distressing Shipwreck of the Whaleship Essex, of Nantucket; Which was attacked and Finally Destroyed by a Large Spermaceti-Whale in the Pacific Ocean*, which was based on the author's own experience on November 20, 1820, and which was published and widely read in 1821. If one reads Owen Chase's narrative, one will have little trouble recognizing the passage that must have inspired Melville: "The words were scarcely out of my mouth, before he came down upon us with full speed, and struck the ship with his head, just forward of the fore-chains; . . . and I could distinctly see him smite his jaws together, as if distracted with rage and fury . . . and to me at that moment, *it appeared with tenfold fury and vengeance in his aspect*."[3] A comparative glance at Chase's and Melville's passages, particularly those sections that I have underlined, reveals that it is the whale that is full of fury and vengeance against human beings. Chase and Melville both depict the violent whale not simply as representative of natural disaster but also as a sort of terrorist charged with its own inevitable, malicious will.

Although Edward Said reminds us of how to interpret the 9/11 terrorist attacks in terms of *Moby-Dick*, his analogy does not go far enough. Chase's and Melville's description of the huge whale as a malicious avenger even before men such as Ahab have a reason to seek retaliatory revenge very naturally leads us to question a fearful ambivalence: a United States as a democratic republic in pursuit of happiness and a United States as an empire in pursuit of vengeance even before it has been wronged. It is somewhat ironic that the first democratic nation in world history, the United States, now legitimates the discourses of unilateralism and preemptive warfare that are so radically incompatible with the ideals of democracy. Seeing this ambivalent face of the United States may help us to understand its logic of retaliation in the face of its contemporary great white whale; it is an ambivalence and logic that threatens the whole world.

The scene of a whale attacking and sinking a ship in Victorian America has persistently attracted and even obsessed me, for it reveals what is at stake in the Globalist Age. The logic of retaliation imprinted deep in the face of Moby-Dick gets revived in postmodern literature, particularly in the last sequence of Thomas Pynchon's *Gravity's Rainbow* (1973), in which a v-2 rocket plummets straight down to explode the Orpheus Theatre on Melrose managed by Richard M. Zhlubb, a caricature of President Richard Nixon: "This ascent will eventually be betrayed to Gravity. . . . And it is here, just at this dark and silent frame, that the pointed tip of the Rocket, falling nearly a mile per second, absolutely and forever without sound, reaches its last immeasurable gap above the roof of this old theatre, the last delta-t."[4] Here we see Pynchon attempting to recreate Melville. Melville rightly grasped the significance of the whole Victorian era's dependence upon whale oil, which attracted a number of international whalers to the "Japan Ground," the whaling ground surrounding the Ogasawara Islands and the Japanese Archipelago. Pynchon likewise grasped the zeitgeist of the twentieth-century's dependence upon oil found in such abundance around the Persian Gulf.

This paradigm shift from whale to fossil fuel oil between the two centuries clarifies the transition from steam engine to nuclear energy. Insofar as the pursuit of happiness always requires revival of a gold rush ethos, the pursuit of happiness is inextricable from the pursuit of vengeance against those who are believed to impede that quest. It is this paradox that has promoted and complicated the American national narrative. Our meditation upon nuclear literature is leading us toward its literary nucleus.

From Whales to Missiles

The whale throwing itself at a ship generates a fear that is revived in the Cuban Missile Crisis of October 1962 during John F. Kennedy's presidency. According to Lloyd Etheredge, an authority on the psychology of politics, soon after the Castro government came to power in 1959, it turned away from its previous promises, permitted communist influence to grow, attacked and persecuted its own supporters in Cuba who expressed opposition to communism, arbitrarily seized U.S. properties, and made a series of baseless charges against the United States. At the same time, however, it was also true that the early 1960s saw the CIA's secret project to assassinate Castro.

In 1960 Cuba came to establish close political, economic, and military relations with the Sino-Soviet bloc, with whose help Cuba armed itself with Medium Range Ballistic Missiles (MRBM). Such missiles could reach the United States in only five minutes, and each one could kill more than eighty million Americans. The American government very naturally regarded this military buildup as a preemptive strike against the United States on the part of the USSR.

The brinkmanship of the Cuban Missile Crisis terrified Americans and highlighted the potential for nuclear catastrophe. Hence Scott Zeman and Michael Amundson call this period the "legacy of the hot days of the Cold War and an arms race that had spiraled out of control."[5] Of course, history tells us that, during the thirteen days of the crisis between October 14 and 28, 1962, President Kennedy made every effort to negotiate with General Secretary Khrushchev and finally succeeded in avoiding a nuclear war that could have exterminated everyone on the planet.

What essentially complicates the Cuban Missile Crisis, however, is that while President Kennedy made a highly political and deeply intellectual decision to negotiate, the military authorities were eager instead to wage another war. Thus it is widely believed that the discord between politicians and militarists ended up in the assassination of the U.S. president on November 22, 1963. According to Zeman and Amundson, it was during this dramatic upheaval that High Atomic Culture (1949–63) was replaced by Late Atomic Culture as Americans became more openly critical of nuclear weapons.[6] This transition is aptly symbolized by Stanley Kubrick's *Dr. Strangelove or: How I Learned to Stop Worrying and Love the Bomb* (1964), which apparently reflects the political context of the Cuban Missile Crisis. Interestingly enough, although this movie was scheduled for release in 1963, the Kennedy assassination suspended its road show until the following year.

When Kubrick started writing the screenplay for *Dr. Strangelove*, he only wanted to produce a serious adaptation of Peter George's original novel *Two Hours to Doom* (1958). Nevertheless, he gradually changed his mind, choosing instead the concept of "nightmarish comedy." Kubrick decided to cowrite the screenplay not only with Peter George but also with Terry Southern, letting George publish the novel version.

The concept of *Dr. Strangelove* is very simple, partly coinciding with Kurt Vonnegut's *Cat's Cradle* published in the same year. Kubrick was so deeply motivated by the rift between the politicians and the militarists that the Cuban Missile Crisis opened up that he wanted to dramatize the process of out-of-control decision making by creating General Ripper as a caricature of the cigar-chomping Curtis LeMay, a general in the United States Air Force. LeMay (1906–90) was notorious for his aggressive and systematic strategic bombing campaigns in the Pacific Theatre of World War II and also for his role in the later Cuban Missile Crisis.

Although *Dr. Strangelove* does not refer to Japan at all, this film nonetheless shows the power and aggression of its representative militarist, a power and aggression that the real General LeMay exercised in the transpacific and transatlantic arenas from World War II through the Cold War. During World War II General LeMay commanded B-29 operations against Japan, including massive incendiary attacks on sixty-four Japanese cities. These raids included the firebombing of Tokyo in early 1945. For this attack LeMay removed the standard bombs on 325 B-29s, loaded each plane with firebomb clusters, and ordered the bombers out to fly at 5,000 to 9,000 feet over Tokyo. The first planes arrived over Tokyo just after midnight on March 10. In a three-hour period the attackers dropped 1,665 tons of incendiary bombs that killed more than one hundred thousand civilians and incinerating sixteen square miles of the city.

Seventeen years later, during the Cuban Missile Crisis, LeMay clashed with President John F. Kennedy and Defense Secretary McNamara, opposing the naval blockade and arguing that he should be allowed to bomb nuclear sites in Cuba. Even after the end of the crisis, he wanted to invade Cuba anyway, even after the Russians agreed to withdraw.

With this historical warmonger in mind, it is easier for us to comprehend the way in which Kubrick's movie's depiction of the loss of communication only emphasizes the helplessness of the human agents, resulting in an "accidental" total nuclear war. One of this film's most unforgettable scenes is when Major King Kong flails at the bomb with his ten-gallon hat like a rodeo cowboy atop a bucking bronco, howling wildly as he rushes toward oblivion, "YAHOO!! YAHOO!!" The bomb plummets toward its target and detonates in a white, climactic flash on the ground.

Yes, here the tragic but happy end of the world is only made possible by the genius of Kubrick. What is more, as David Seed has suggested, the mismatch between sound track and image strengthens this irony by playing Vera Lynn's very elegant and even romantic tune "We'll Meet Again" over repeated nuclear explosions and mushrooming clouds. The whole point of this black humor, of course, is that there will be no "again."[7] More importantly, however, it dramatizes the willful disbelief in the end of war or losing as the result of nuclear weapons ("we'll meet again"), a willful disbelief that sustains the comical "logic" of nuclear retaliation. Let us read how Peter George represents in the novel the blackest and most humorous scene in American literary and cultural history:

> [Major] King [Kong] descended into the bomb bay for the second time. . . . He patted Hi-There affectionately, then climbed onto Lolita. It was a difficult climb. He stood on Lolita and reached for the broken wires, connected them, then sat down on Lolita to throw the emergency switches on the side of the bomber. Lothar Zogg looked down at him anxiously. He said, "You all right, King?" "Sure," King said, "I'm awright." He was sitting astride Lolita, ready to throw the final switch. He looked carefully at his watch. He estimated they were over their target. He reached across and threw the switch. Nobody would ever know what passed through King's mind in the next few seconds. The bomb doors began to open and King was illuminated by the light from below. Lolita began to fall and King fell with her. Perhaps he thought in this ultimate moment that he could accelerate the bomb's fall, or maybe even give it guidance. Nobody knows. King dropped with the bomb from Leper Colony. What happened after that is anybody's guess. What is certain is that three minutes later Lolita detonated in a twenty-megaton explosion.[8]

We should note that, while the film version features a couple of hydrogen bombs nicknamed "Hi, There!" and "Dear John" respectively, George's novel cleverly replaces "Dear John" with "Lolita," which cannot but recall Kubrick's own movie version of Vladimir Nabokov's 1955 novel that was released in 1962, just two years before *Dr. Strangelove*. Insofar as the bomb's nickname is concerned, I prefer George's choice to Kubrick's because the sexual nuance of Major "King Kong" riding astride a missile called "Lolita" is a far more devastating critique of Bomb worship. For while Major King Kong adopts the name of the notorious post-Moby-Dick and pre-Godzilla monster, the bomb "Lolita" signifies the famous nymphet who was the object of pedophilia. Thus at the climax of the black humor narrative of *Dr. Strangelove*, George both revives the quasipagan myth of "Beauty and the Beast" to laugh at human progress and also eroticizes the man-machine interface so characteristic of High Atomic Culture.

Holden as an Atomic Picaro

The black humor of *Dr. Strangelove* coincides with the comic apocalypse as represented by Vonnegut's *Cat's Cradle* and it prefigures Thomas Pynchon's *Gravity's Rainbow*. *Dr. Strangelove* is doubtless the archetype of all postmodern apocalyptic narratives. Nonetheless, here we should be aware that in producing this movie Stanley Kubrick must have received much inspiration from the postwar canon of American literature that included Salinger's *Catcher in the Rye*, which features sixteen-year-old Holden Caulfield who challenges at every turn his "phony" society. He protests by dropping out of prep school and leaving his dorm in the middle of the night. Too afraid to confront his parents with his failure, he spends three days wandering through the hotels, bars, and parks of Manhattan. The author astonishes us most radically by disclosing at the end of the novel that this antihero has narrated the whole story from a mental hospital, where he sees a psychoanalyst who asks him if he will apply himself when he returns to school in the fall. Just as the major New Americanist critic Alan Nadel has pointed out, *Catcher in the Rye* represents the logic of McCarthyism, repressing dissidents and radicals, and thereby appealing to a wider audience. Alan Nadel never expresses sympathy for Holden as an outsider but recasts this character as a typical reactionary hero embodying the political unconscious of Containment and Pax Americana: "Donning his red hunting hat, he attempts to become the good Red-hunter, ferreting out the phonies and subversives, but in so doing he emulates the bad Red-hunters, those who have corrupted the conditions of utterance such that speech

itself is corrupt."[9] While I very much like Nadel's recharacterization of Hold-
en as a homophobic McCarthyist, I also want to call attention to Holden as
a suicide bomber or terrorist.

To better see Holden's terrorist tendencies, let's reread a couple of passages in chapters 13 and 14. Explaining his theory of fighting, he states, "If
you're supposed to sock somebody in the jaw, and you sort of feel like doing it, you should do it. I'm just no good at it, though. I'd rather push a guy
out the window or chop his head off with an ax than sock him in the jaw. I
hate fist fights."[10] After he finds himself cheated by a prostitute and an elevator man who is a pimp, Holden makes up his mind: "But I'd plug him [the
elevator man] anyway. Six shots right through his fat hairy belly. Then I'd
throw my automatic down the elevator shaft—after I'd wiped off all the finger prints and all."[11]

However, it has to be the following portrait of Holden as a suicide terrorist,
one that does not contradict Alan Nadel's image of Holden as a homophobic
McCarthyist, that inspired George's and Kubrick's works:

> What gets me about D. B., though, he hated the war so much, and yet
> he got me to read this book A Farewell to Arms last summer. He said
> it was so terrific. That's what I can't understand. It had this guy in it
> named Lieutenant Henry that was supposed to be a nice guy and all. I
> don't see how D. B. could hate the Army and war and all so much and
> still like a phony like that. I mean, for instance, I don't see how he
> could like a phony book like that and still like that one by Ring Lard-
> ner, or that other one he's so crazy about The Great Gatsby. D. B.
> got sore when I said that, and said I was too young and all to appre-
> ciate it, but I don't think so. I told him I liked Ring Lardner and The
> Great Gatsby and all. I was crazy about The Great Gatsby. Old
> Gatsby. Old sport. That killed me. Anyway, I'm sort of glad they've
> got the atomic bomb invented. If there's ever another war, I'm
> going to sit right the hell on top of it. I'll volunteer for it, I swear
> to God I will.[12]

Readers of Salinger have long had difficulty reading the last part of this
passage, which not only justifies but also looks forward to repeating Hiroshima and Nagasaki. Holden's terrorist mentality, it seems, here overtakes

the pacifist ideology of Salinger himself. Indeed, it is Holden as a terrorist that captured the imagination of a couple of famous assassins who were obsessed with *Catcher in the Rye*: Mark Chapman, who assassinated ex-Beatle John Lennon on December 8, 1980, and John Hinkley, who attempted to assassinate President Ronald Reagan on March 30, 1981. What makes the latter's terrorism so ironical is that in 1983, two years after Hinckley's failed attempt, President Reagan announced the Strategic Defense Initiative (SDI), the so-called Star Wars program. SDI revised the strategic offence doctrine of MAD (Mutual Assured Destruction), conceived back in the 1960s as another name for deterrence, and rationalized the strategy of destroying incoming missiles as a means of national self-defense. One cannot help but wonder to what extent it was John Hinckley's attack that inspired Reagan with the urgency of this "self-defense" idea. By the same token, however, we should not forget such Golden Age Hollywood films as *Murder in the Air* (1940), which features minor Hollywood actor Ronald Reagan as a secret agent disrupting the enemy's technology. In short, retaliation and preemptive attacks often go hand in hand.

The logic of SDI was first nurtured neither in World War II nor in Cold War but rather in the early republic. Robert Fulton, an early genius of technology, invented not only super weapons but also the logic of the prenuclear imagination. Biographer Kirkpatrick Sale states that "his [Robert Fulton's] interest was fixed on a new contrivance, something he described as 'a curious machine for mending the system of politics,' indeed for annihilating the British navy and establishing 'the liberty of the seas' and 'a guarantee of perpetual peace to all maritime nations': a submarine, armed with 'torpedoes.'"[13] This Fultonian logic very naturally makes it difficult for us to distinguish between strategic defense and strategic offence. We have to survive the contemporary ambivalence between the United States as the world's policeman and the United States as the world's most feared terrorist.

Origins of the Nuclear Imagination
Just as one huge whale dashes himself against a whaler, one huge missile plunges into the enemy and mortally destroys that enemy. Since pre-Civil War, or antebellum, times in the United States the logic of retaliation has powerfully motivated the United States. In order to fully understand the theory of

revenge, it is helpful to listen to what Captain Ahab said in response to his first mate Starbuck, whose sense of capitalism radically conflicts with Ahab's paranoiac project. Starbuck says, "Vengeance on a dumb brute . . . that simply smote thee from blindest instinct! Madness! To be enraged with a dumb thing, Captain Ahab, seems blasphemous."[14] Ahab replies, "Talk not to me of blasphemy, man; I'd strike the sun if it insulted me. For could the sun do that, then could I do the other; *since there is ever a sort of fair play herein, jealousy presiding over all creations*. But not my master, man, is even that fair play. Who's over me? Truth hath no confines."[15]

Now it is ironic that Captain Ahab challenges his own God by appropriating the sacred logic expressed in the Old Testament. In my underlined passage above, one can see how Ahab's thought reflects the concept of a jealous and zealous God who does not allow for idolatry and impiety: "Thou shalt not bow down thyself to them, not serve them: for *I the Lord thy God am a jealous God*, visiting the iniquity of the fathers upon the children unto the third and fourth generation of them that hate me; And shewing mercy unto thousands of them that love me, and keep my commandments" (Exodus 20:5–6; emphasis added). Thus Captain Ahab takes the place of God and prefigures what Nietzsche calls the "Anti-Christ" at the turn of the century. In short, it is the jealous God of Exodus that inspires Captain Ahab to justify his own personal vengeance and to unwittingly support the national cause of retaliation. Captain Ahab simultaneously rejects and legitimizes the Judeo-Christian jealous God, risking the danger of total apocalypse as the cost of a display of Godlike, vengeful power.

Is it possible to avoid the logic of retaliation and the advent of Doomsday? To answer that, let me introduce the cutting-edge postnuclear and avant-pop narrative *Hiroshima Bugi: Atomu 57* (2003), written by the self-proclaimed postindian writer Gerald Vizenor. Partly recreating the black humor of Kurt Vonnegut and Joseph Heller, this novel features an atomic kabuki designed by Ronin Browne, the hybrid orphan son of Okichi, a Japanese boogie-woogie dancer, and Nightbreaker, an Anishinaabe from the White Earth Reservation who served as an interpreter for General MacArthur during the first year of the American occupation in Japan. Resembling the famous actor Mifune Toshiro in the 1950 Akira Kurosawa movie *Rashomon*, whose story was based on Ryunosuke Akutagawa's 1915 short story "In a Grove" as well as on

Rashomon, Vizenor's antihero Ronin survives the postwar decades and comes to love the Atomic Bomb Dome in Hiroshima as "my Rashomon." Ronin is "a dreamer, a mind roamer, a teaser of peace, and a master of irony" and "a visionary, an aesthetic warrior of eternal survivance, a hafu samurai, but never a fanatical romancer of nationalism or the emperor."[16] Wearing goggles and rubber gloves, Ronin is a homeless park roamer and very often questioned by the police. Yet he never gives up the dream of performing atomic kabuki, together with his fellow roamers Oshima, Kitsutsuki, and Osaka.

Let us note that it is antebellum biracial Native American Ranald MacDonald who inspired Vizenor to create this biracial personality of Ronin Browne. Vizenor first introduces Ranald as the author of a Japanese captivity narrative, one who taught English in Japan before the arrival of the naval officer and diplomat Commodore Matthew Perry in 1853 and whose writings revealed that "the Ainu [the indigenous natives of the islands of northern Japan] and the Anishinaabe told similar stories about natural reason, their creation, animal totems, and survivance."[17]

Born in 1824 to a Scottish father and Native American mother in Astoria, Oregon, the historical Ranald MacDonald believed that the ancestors of Native Americans came from Japan. Oppressed by racism and dying for the freedom he dreamed existed in the Far East, he shipped out on December 2, 1845, at Sag Harbor onboard the whale ship *Plymouth*. "Being off the island of Japan, I left the ship at my own desire, agreeably to a previous understanding with the captain. He was to furnish me with a boat, etc., and drop me off the coast of Japan, under favorable circumstances for reaching the shore."[18] Near Rishiri Island, he capsized the boat on purpose so as to stage a state of distress at sea. On July 2, 1849, he saw smoke on the island and was rescued by the Ainu and turned over to the Japanese on Hokkaido. He was forced to stay in Matsumae close to Hakodate for a time, and then he moved to Nagasaki in Kyushu. In the end MacDonald pioneered English education and trained a number of translators, such as Moriyama Einosuke, who undertook many foreign negotiations in Meiji Japan.

What matters for our purposes here is that Vizenor's hero Ronin Browne notices a coincidence between his life and MacDonald's. Just as the latter's boat was overturned by a sudden wind in the same month more than a 150 years before, so was the former's in Atomu 53, that is, 1997 AD: "I washed ashore, abandoned my makeshift sailboat, and slowly made my way south, a route of spas that my father might have taken, first to the Toyotomi onsen near Horonobe, Hokkaido. My backpack was light, only a change of clothes, scant toiletries, and three wet books, *Narrow Road to the Far North*, a haiku journey by Matsuo Basho, *Glimpses of Unfamiliar Japan* by Lafcadio Hearn, and *Japan: Story of Adventure* by Ranald MacDonald."[19]

With Ranald MacDonald as the prototype of Ronin and the literary precursor of Vizenor himself, it becomes easier for us to set up a cogent analogy between antebellum pacific and postmodern transpacific. For it is highly plausible that MacDonald's narrative provided his contemporary Herman Melville with information. If one reopens *Moby-Dick* and looks at the second paragraph of chapter 109, "Ahab and Starbuck in the Cabin," one will immediately find a reference to Japan: "And so Starbuck found Ahab with a general chart of the oriental archipelagoes spread before him; and another separate one representing the long eastern coasts of the Japanese islands—Niphon, *Matsmai*, and Shikoke."[20] In writing his meganovel, Melville apparently read an article on the life of Ranald MacDonald, "A Sailor's Attempt to Penetrate Japan," which was published in the December 1, 1848, issue of the *Friend*, a Hawaiian newspaper, and which reports the way Ranald was accepted by the Japanese: "After being on shore eight days he was taken under the charge of four *Matsmai* officers. At Matsmai he was imprisoned from the 6th of September until about the first of October."[21] What is more, MacDonald starts his own narrative *Japan* with the following sentence: "About noon of the fifteenth day of our voyage (September 7th) we entered the port of *Matsmai*."[22]

Though unfamiliar to most postmodern Japanese, the signifier of "Matsmai" is everywhere in narratives of and by Ranald MacDonald, whose work must have had a tremendous impact upon Melville. Of course, in today's transliteration this proper noun "Matsmai" would be spelled "Matsumae." Likewise, "Niphon" would be "Nippon" and "Shikoke" rendered as "Shikoku." What matters here, however, is that back in the mid-nineteenth century Matsumae was well known as one of the best ports for American whalers active in the north Pacific. Therefore, it was only natural that in March 1854 Commodore Perry required Japan to open not only Hakodate but also Matsumae to foreign trade. While Ranald MacDonald himself adventured into Japan out of curiosity about the origin of his own tribes, the series of accidents he survived were some of the most critical points in modern history; he witnessed the forced opening and subsequent modernization of Japan.

At this point, I do not hesitate to consider Ranald MacDonald as endowed with what another biracial postindian writer Steve Erickson (son of a Swedish father and Franco-Potawatomi mother) designates "nuclear imagination." Of course, this term may sound strange and simply anachronistic to our ears at first; after all, Ranald MacDonald was the son of a steam engine civilization not an heir of the atomic age. Nonetheless, if one recalls Erickson's anachronistic redefinition of Thomas Jefferson as the inventor of rock and roll, then the idea of nuclear imagination applying even to people of the prenuclear age is not so surprising:

> The nuclear imagination isn't simply the heightened awareness of the doom, it's the relationship one establishes with doom. Billy Holiday had nuclear imagination but Judy Garland didn't: doom raped Judy while Billie managed to get on top, humping doom to the last orgasmic throe. . . . Gandhi had it, but so did Hitler, who never even lived to see the first nuclear bomb. . . . In the realm of politics not many major figures have nuclear imagination, because to a large extent their political fates depend on the perpetuation of what the conventional imagination is comfortable with; and those with nuclear imagination remain fated to the oblivion which is integral to the vision they're trying to define.[23]

Is it not possible to reconsider Commodore Perry's black ships as a metonym of apocalypse and recharacterize Ranald MacDonald as the genius of prenuclear imagination? Only in adopting this new perspective as a plausible one are we able to reinvestigate the nuclear imagination as a strategy for postindian survivance. Certainly, colonial America produced a number of Indian captivity narratives — the premodern version of contemporary abduction narratives — but it was an antebellum biracial Native American who authored a Japanese captivity narrative and premodern survivance narrative, one which came to inspire another biracial writer, Gerald Vizenor, to create the postindian picaro Ronin Browne.

Ishmael Ashore in Hiroshima: We Are All Ranald's Children

What makes *Hiroshima Bugi* so very radical is the romance between Ronin and his girlfriend Miko, another trickster and shamaness nicknamed the "atomu bugi dancer."[24] They start making love on a shrouded bench close to the peace bell of the Peace Memorial Park, their erotic moans and wild, native shouts arousing fellow park roamers: "They sounded the peace bell to celebrate our lusty moment on the bench. The park ravens croaked their consent from the trees and monuments."[25] Likewise, Ronin also makes love to another shamaness on the bench at the notorious national shrine Yasukuni Jinja in Tokyo: "Every motion on the bench, every sound, touch, and rush was ecstatic. Truly, she was a kami spirit, inspired by wild lust, and the heat of her passion shook the foundation of the booth."[26] By closely describing these mostly blasphemous and extremely pornographic scenes, Vizenor succeeds in exhibiting a new sense of black humor only possible in the nuclear and postcolonial present.

Moreover, this story reaches its climax when Ronin, driving around the Ginza district and playing at top volume the music of Mahalia Jackson, Chuck Berry, Roy Orbison, and Johnny Cash, attracts a crowd of Japanese people: "By chance the black van became a kami shrine, the natural center of a gospel occupation, a new blue bugi on the Ginza."[27] Here Vizenor does not criticize the aftereffects of World War II but looks for a festive space in which a number of tricksters, whether Japanese, Ainu, or Anishinaabe, can join forces to create what Vizenor calls a postmongoloid narrative.

Vizenor's multicultural vision revives nineteenth-century Native American whaler Ranald MacDonald in Ronin Browne. Moreover, it explores the Japanese frontier in which bears survive, bears cherished by both the Ainu and the Anishinaabe as "original totems in their creation stories."[28] Being a postindian endowed with a transpacific imagination, Vizenor is keenly conscious of North American castaways like Ranald MacDonald and Herman Melville, as evidenced in a lecture he gave called "Ishmael Ashore in Hiroshima: The Pequots, Moby Dick and the *Pequod*, Ranald MacDonald, Little Boy, and Ronin Browne in *Hiroshima Bugi*" at Keio University on October 26, 2004. As part of its postmodern and postcontemporary outlook, this novel skillfully interweaves transpacific traditions and American literary history.

In antebellum America Herman Melville anticipated the end of the world by writing the shipwreck narrative *Moby-Dick* in 1851, whereas its centenary saw the publication of J. D. Salinger's *Catcher in the Rye* (1951) with a suicide terrorist as its protagonist, whose impact upon subsequent total nuclear war narratives such as Stanley Kubrick's *Dr. Strangelove* (1964) was tremendous.

This literary and cultural passage from Melville to Salinger and Kubrick amplifies the cause of preemptive and retaliation attacks justified by the jealous God of the Old Testament. However, in his novel *Hiroshima Bugi* Gerald Vizenor speculates on how to avoid terrorist attacks and revenge and how to create an alternative to existing conservative strategies from the perspective of postindian survivance.

Unlike Native American writers such as Louis Owens, whose cross-cultural dialogic approach he seems to share, Vizenor radically critiques Western authorities from Columbus to Levi-Strauss, revealing their simulations of "manifest manners" to be treacherous and elusive.[29] Keenly aware of what Umberto Eco has called the age of hyperreality, he further transgresses the limits of postcolonial hybridity and redefines Indians as "the simulations of the 'absolute fakes' in the ruins of representation, or the victims in literary annihilation."[30] The Atomic Bomb Dome in Hiroshima is able to substitute for that perfect metaphor, Rashomon, a place where postwar Japanese outlaws nicknamed Japanese Apache inhabit a postwar junkyard that serves as the ruins of representation, or in Jean Baudrillard's terms the "desert of the real." While Ranald MacDonald looked for the origins of Native Americans in Japan in the mid-nineteenth century, some post-Hiroshima Japanese came to enjoy the designation of Japanese Apache and simulated a Native life style, as seen in Ken Kaiko's *Nippon Sanmon Opera* (The Japanese Three Penny Opera) (1959) and Sakyo Komatsu's *Nippon Apatchi Zoku* (The Japanese Apache) (1964). Yes, as I spelled out in chapter 11 of *Full Metal Apache: Transactions between Cyberpunk Japan and Avant-Pop America* (2006), postwar history has shown us the ways in which non-Native Americans have come to simulate Native Americans and survive the predicaments of the postwar years, also disclosing thereby the fate of "American Indian" as a floating signifier. Against this literary and cultural background, Vizenor's novel mocks the simulations of peace represented both by advocates of nuclear victimhood and by advocates of nuclear deterrent, undertaking instead to redefine the Atomic Bomb Dome. In doing so, the author opens up the possibility of postmodern survivance in a nuclear world in which the opening of Pandora's Box (such as "Lolita" for Peter George) cannot be undone. It is from this angle that I find Gerald Vizenor's version of Rashomon at the literary nucleus, or ground zero, in our understanding of nuclear literature from a transpacific perspective.

Notes

The early version of this article was delivered at a special forum "Trans-pacific Traces in American Literature" at the 52nd Annual Conference of the Kyushu American Literary Society, Kyushu University, May 13, 2006. The forum was chaired by Chris S. Schreiner, University of Guam, with panelists Scott Pugh, Fukuoka Women's University, and Takayuki Tatsumi, Keio University.

1. Salinger, *Catcher in the Rye*, 127.
2. Melville, *Moby-Dick*, 425.
3. Quoted in Melville, *Moby-Dick*, 566–67; emphasis added.
4. Pynchon, *Gravity's Rainbow*, 887.
5. Zeman and Amundso, *Atomic Culture*, 4.
6. Zeman and Amundso, *Atomic Culture*, 4.
7. Seed, *American Science Fiction*, 150.
8. George, *Dr. Strangelove*, 152.
9. Nadel, *Containment Culture*, 71
10. Salinger, *Catcher in the Rye*, 81.
11. Salinger, *Catcher in the Rye*, 94.
12. Salinger, *Catcher in the Rye*, 127; emphasis added.
13. Sale, *Fire of His Genius*, 63.
14. Melville, *Moby-Dick*, 139.
15. Melville, *Moby-Dick*, 140; emphasis added.
16. Vizenor, *Hiroshima Bugi*, 69, 71.
17. Vizenor, *Hiroshima Bugi*, 51.
18. MacDonald, Report, 126.
19. Vizenor, *Hiroshima Bugi*, 123.
20. Melville, *Moby-Dick*, 361; emphasis added.
21. Kawasumi, *Shiryo*, 123, 125.
22. MacDonald, *Japan*, 130.
23. Erickson, *Leap Year*, 42–44.
24. Vizenor, *Hiroshima Bugi*, 86.
25. Vizenor, *Hiroshima Bugi*, 98.
26. Vizenor, *Hiroshima Bugi*, 153.
27. Vizenor, *Hiroshima Bugi*, 172.
28. Vizenor, *Hiroshima Bugi*, 125.
29. Vizenor, *Manifest Manners*, 8.
30. Vizenor, *Manifest Manners*, 9.

Bibliography

E. P. F. "A Sailor's Attempt to Penetrate Japan." In *Shiryo: Nippon Eigakushi* [A History of English Studies in Japan: Texts and Contexts], edited by Tetsuo Kawasumi, 2:120–26. Tokyo: Taishukan Publishers, 1998.

Erickson, Steve. *Leap Year.* New York: Avon, 1989.

Fitzgerald, Frances. *Way Out There in the Blue: Reagan, Star Wars and the End of the Cold War.* New York: Touchstone, 2000.

Franklin, Bruce. *War Stars.* New York: Oxford University Press, 1988.

George, Peter. *Dr. Strangelove, or: How I Learned to Stop Worrying and Love the Bomb.* New York: Bantam, 1963.

Jones, Jack. *Let Me Take You Down: Inside the Mind of Mark David Chapman, the Man Who Killed John Lennon.* New York: Villard, 1992.

Kawasumi, Tetsuo, ed. *Shiryo: Nippon Eigakushi* [A History of English Studies in Japan: Texts and Contexts]. Vol. 2. Tokyo: Taishukan Publishers, 1998.

MacDonald, Ranald. *Japan: Story of Adventures of Ranald MacDonald, First Teacher of English in Japan AD 1848–1849.* In *Shiryo: Nippon Eigakushi* [A History of English Studies in Japan: Texts and Contexts], edited by Tetsuo Kawasumi, 2:130–34. Tokyo: Taishukan Publishers, 1998.

——. Report. Senate Executive Document. 32nd Cong., 1st sess., April 30, 1849. Vol. 9, Doc. 59. In *Shiryo: Nippon Eigakushi* [A History of English Studies in Japan: Texts and Contexts], edited by Tetsuo Kawasumi, 2:126–30. Tokyo: Taishukan Publishers, 1998.

McCaffery, Larry. *After Yesterday's Crash: The Avant-Pop Anthology.* New York: Penguin, 1995.

Melville, Herman. *Moby-Dick.* 1851. Reprint edited by Hershel Parker and Harrison Hayford. New York: Norton, 2002.

Morris, Edmund. *Dutch: A Memoir of Ronald Reagan.* New York: Modern Library, 1999.

Nadel, Allan. *The Containment Culture.* Durham NC: Duke University Press, 1995.

Newman, Kim. *Apocalypse Movies: End of the World Cinema.* New York: St. Martin's Griffin, 2000.

Pulitano, Elvira. *Toward a Native American Critical Theory.* Lincoln: University of Nebraska Press, 2003.

Pynchon, Thomas. *Gravity's Rainbow.* New York: Bantam, 1973.

Said, Edward. Interview. By David Barsamian. *Progressive,* November 2001.

Sale, Kirkpatrick. *The Fire of His Genius: Robert Fulton and the American Dream.* New York: Simon and Schuster, 2001.

Salinger, J. D. *The Catcher in the Rye.* 1951. Reprint, New York: Penguin, 1994.

Seed, David. *American Science Fiction and the Cold War: Literature and Film.* Edinburgh: Edinburgh University Press, 1999.

Tatsumi, Takayuki. *Full Metal Apache: Transactions between Cyberpunk Japan and Avant-Pop America.* Durham NC: Duke University Press, 2006.

Vizenor, Gerald. *Hiroshima Bugi: Atomu 57.* Lincoln: University of Nebraska Press, 2003.

——. *Manifest Manners: Narratives on Postindian Survivance.* Lincoln: University of Nebraska Press, 1994.

——. *Shadow Distance: A Gerald Vizenor Reader.* Hanover NH: Wesleyan University Press, 1994.

Zeman, Scott, and Michael A. Amundso, eds. *Atomic Culture: How We Learned to Stop Worrying and Love the Bomb.* Boulder: University of Colorado Press, 2004.

11. FACING THE WIINDIGOO

Gerald Vizenor and Primo Levi

JOE LOCKARD

There is a monster with a heart of ice, the unseen ghost who trails behind and appears in order to eat the human soul. This is the mythic creature of Anishinaabe legend, one used and transfigured in the fiction of Gerald Vizenor. "The *wiindigoo* monster lures those who have been weakened by contradictions" and devours its victims with authentic stories.[1] The wiindigoo, Vizenor argues, feeds off claims of cultural dominance and scapegoating. In the ethic that Vizenor constructs across the body of his fiction, the wiindigoo spirit travels together with violent monoculturalism, that originating force in U.S. society.

The concept of survivance — survival through resistance — entails defining what it is that has been survived: for Native America that destructive cannibalistic force has been the colonial Euro-wiindigoo emerging from cold seas and forests. Colonial violence sought to negate native consciousness in all its continental variety as well as ensuring submission to displacement, exile, and extermination. To define survivance is to refuse negation, to refuse an identity based on social eradication. As Zubeda Jalazai pointed out, "Survivance takes into account the mediation of identity but still illustrates identity's 'presence' in the world."[2] In other words, survivance incorporates a consciousness with which one lives with terms of self-reference imposed by a dominant culture: it places quotation marks around identity references. Ethnic or tribal identity encompasses responsibility for its guardianship, and narrative agency comes together with that responsibility. Sonya Atalay writes that "the concept of survivance is not about avoiding or minimizing the horrors and tragedy of colonization. It includes agency and Native presence but does not refuse stories of struggle, particularly those that create a context for understanding and appreciating the creative methods of resistance and survival in the face of such unimaginable turmoil."[3] This is storytelling that identifies the wiindigoo together with the stories of resistance, survival, and autonomy.

The ethical content emerging from anatomization of such monsters manifest lies in the multidirectional struggle between blind particularism and pseudouniversalism. How do we create a society that rejects the false dichotomy of these paradigms, one that synthesizes an ethical confrontation with both? Vizenor's concept of a social and mythic wiindigoo is of an invisible beast that feeds off those who fall under the spell of such enticing purist deliriums of identity. How shall we learn to avoid the beast of purism, the ice-hearted monster?

There is another ethical question that inhabits Vizenor's storytelling: how does narrative act to resolve the contradictions of competing identity-stories? Can the story through its diagetic memory merge old and new cultural approaches so as to foster survivance? In Vizenor's vocabulary survivance is the condition of self-reliant or communal survival without the social or personal indulgence of victimization. The wiindigoo feeds off victim-survivors, those who place their faith in concrete fantasies of their own heroic identity and privileged trauma. Survivance, the arch-opponent of victimization, speaks from a powerful social position that recognizes a common human condition and responses to violence. Whether the malevolent wiindigoo is Euro-American colonialism and racism or whether it is militant modern fascism, the survivance story opens itself to both particularisms and universalism in order to reconcile them into a shared defense of humanity through storytelling. It turns violence back on itself, rejecting the varieties of sadism by reformulating them in storytelling that counters aggression. The wiindigoo of the hour has been seen before: survivance stories are the history of its previous appearances.

A survivance story is not a neat social morality play geared to the defense of cultural preconceptions and stereotypes, nor is it an angry rant shouted out through careless mix-and-match Manicheanism in which identifying enemies for historical anger — any enemy will do — is more important than careful, calm understanding. When Coke de Fountain, the pseudowarrior of *The Trickster of Liberty*, stands to rant against racism and genocide, he embodies

the use of victimry as professional opportunity and as a call for a new eth-
nopurism.⁴ Vizenor rejects such oppositional purities as being erroneous as
any alleged purity of blood or truth. Rather, survivance emerges from hybrid,
syncretic mixed-blood stories whose conscious cultural borrowings assem-
ble strength from a multiplicity of sources.

Survivance stories may begin within an indigenous narrative tradition, but
they do not stop at cultural barriers proclaimed by the guardians of narrative authenticity. The ice-spirit of the wiindigoo lives in these attempted but
impossible fencings of "authentic" culture as much as it does in violent incur-
sions against native cultures. Hallmarks of this narrative ethos of resistance
include an embrace of syncretic openness and ironic welcome to all compatriot storytellers, whatever their culture, who face the imminence of human
death with self-knowledge and even a smile.

A wiindigoo is recognizable through social self-knowledge; it is part of the
known world, not an unknown source of terror. It terrifies only those storytellers of ignorance who remain deliberately unaware of evil, who refuse to
witness social cannibalism, and who remain selfishly placid as the wiindigoo
transforms then consumes their neighbors. Wiindigoos know no provincial or
national borders; all human cultures have been visited by shape-shifting wiindigoos. Their global visitations speak to the inseparability of human experiences. As Vizenor observes concerning the shape-shifting horror-creature whose
appearance has punctuated U.S. history, "The Vietnam War, and the horrors
of racialism recounted in the literature of survivance, aroused the nation to
remember the inseparable narratives at My Lai, Sand Creek, and Wounded
Knee."⁵ Richard Drinnon makes the same historical linkages and suggests that
this pattern of atrocities reveals a history that "lawmakers, generals, and so
many of their compatriots were eager to forget."⁶ The wiindigoo spirit, arriving in diverse locales through such diverse figurations as Lieutenant William
Laws Calley Jr.; Colonel John Milton Chivington; and Obersturmbahnführer
Rudolf Franz Ferdinand Hoess, overcomes human persona and social histories. National identity is irrelevant to this borderless horror.

A survivance storyteller is one who has faced the wiindigoo and lived to tell
the tale or, rather, who has told the tale and so lived. In Anishinaabe tradition, the wiindigoo is a once-human who has become a cannibal, a destroyer
of humanity; the survivance storyteller is a human who has refused either to

join cannibalism or to be consumed by cannibals.[7] It is that refusal and resistance toward transformation into the nonhuman that marks out survivance literature. Yet we have difficulty recognizing the wiindigoo, just as did Father J. Emile Saindon, a missionary in Canada during the 1920s and early 1930s.[8]

Saindon, who served with the Missionary Oblates of Mary Immaculate, published a 1933 essay touching on "Windigo psychosis." It appeared in *Primitive Man*, the journal of the long-defunct Catholic Anthropological Conference. This was a missionary-oriented journal established and edited by the profoundly reactionary sexophobe, Rev. John Montgomery Cooper, an anti-contraception advocate who was to become president of the American Anthropology Association.[9] *Primitive Man* was a forum in which Saindon could comfortably employ the most discreditable forms of cultural patronization and pseudoscientific racism.[10] He encountered and reported on wiindigoo fear in the same patronizing language:

> *F. had the Windigo malady. She did not want to see anybody but her husband and her children, because strangers became metamorphosed in her eyes into wild animals, — wolves, bears, lynxes. These animals are dangerous to life. To protect herself she was driven by the desire to kill them. But this was repugnant to her because these animals are human beings.*
>
> *She fought against the obsessing idea that found lodgement in her consciousness. She wished to kill and she didn't wish. . . . As a solution of her conflict, she fled from reality and took the stand of not wishing to see anyone or speak to anyone.*[11]

In this anthropological report F. remains in her tent, preferring not to risk harm to her neighbors. Saindon "cures" F. by suggesting that she go to confession, receive communion, and then go about daily life. He reports that "the suggestion succeeded perfectly. These simple people are easily influenced by suggestion."[12]

A culture of racial superiority blinds his eyes to other possibilities, including that F's fears came true because Saindon and his carnivorous and soul-snaring missionary culture were the wiindigoo. A belief in the native as potential cannibal is one of the persistent markers of cultural imperialism. As did Melville much earlier in *Typee*, Carolyn Podruchny observes that "cannibalism and western imperialism have been inextricably linked in western writing, as cannibalism became a defining characteristic of non-European, supposedly uncivilized peoples, and a lens through which to view indigenous peoples."[13] A fear of native cannibalism, of being consumed by the subordinate, precisely reverses the actions of colonialism, imperialism, and corporatist fascism. The apparition of cannibalism is more a projector than an ethnographic lens. What F. manifested was a fear of being consumed and of being transformed by and into that foreign culture that was consuming native life around her. The phantasm that Saindon could not see was his own self, the putative humanitarian-as-wiindigoo, the missionary cannibal.

Such tangible phantasms stand at the threatening edges of Vizenor's fictions of survivance. Little but the heroic trickster-storyteller stands between the evil and the destruction of peoples; individual and collective survival are an achievement against improbable odds. It is this improbability rather than attempts to guarantee against fate that intervenes. In *The People Named the Chippewa*, for instance, the trickster's good fortune at gambling prevents the advent of apocalypse:

> The destinies of the trickster and tribal people of the woodland depended upon the one chance remaining, the last throw of the dish. Should the figures of the four ages of man come down in the standing position then the trickster would lose and the spirit of tribal people would be consigned to the wiindigoo, the flesh eaters in the land of darkness.
>
> When the gambler prepared to make the final shake of the game, the woodland trickster drew near and when the dish came down to the ground he made a teasing whistle on the wind and all four figures of the ages of man fell in the darkness of the dish. The great gambler shivered, his flesh seemed to harden and break into small pieces when he looked up toward the trickster.
>
> Naanabozho smiled at the great gambler. The woodland tribes had not lost their spirit to the land of darkness. The trickster had stopped evil for a moment in a game.[14]

"The land of darkness," the death of humane and civilized values, is postponed rather than permanently avoided. One does not know how long the postponement lasts, only that the "darkness of the dish," whichever gambling dish of the day that holds the emblems of life, can turn either way. There are no guarantees against the wiindigoo. Naanabozho the trickster is a contrarian, one who escapes the odds today but whose luck is finite. If civilization itself hangs on the fate of Naanabozho, it will rise or fall on his ability to make "a teasing whistle on the wind," to tell a story as a means of self-defense. For Vizenor the kind deceits of storytelling are crucial to the preservation of humanity; when the story ends, unending night begins.

Naanabozho in Auschwitz

In his poem "Journeys" Irish-born poet Fergus Allen tells of sitting in the park reading Primo Levi and imagining a punctuation period floating off the page. This escapee full stop hovers in the sky, struck by the anticivilizational threats it encounters:

> A striped gunship circled overhead
> And filled the sky, chemical weapons
> Visible, protruding from tail-end port.[15]

Primo Levi, particularly in his *Survival in Auschwitz* memoir, serves as an iconic reference to the worst of twentieth-century history. The connection between Levi's text and an exterminatory vision that Allen makes is a measure of the negative power of Levi's story, a power that maintains a strong international readership for his writing. Over 250 translation editions of his work manifest the cross-cultural appeal of Levi's writing.[16] As with the malignant hovering helicopter-wiindigoo invoked in Allen's poem, the text is popular because it provokes imaginative engagement with mass murder, industrial cannibalism, and human abomination.

While separated by culture and geography, Levi and Vizenor share many questions of survivance.[17] This comparison does not indulge the minor literature of Indians-Jews comparatism that sometimes seems a forced exercise pursued for academic amusement or dubious rationales. Levi and Vizenor are not comparable in terms of personal biography; they have lived through quite different histories. What they do share especially is a fascination with the psychological states associated with survival as well as stories demonstrating eventual mastery of survivance. Whatever its local name, how do we confront the wiindigoo and live? Where survival comes out of the gambling bowl as happenstance and chance, how do we discover social and personal meaning in our survival? How do we oppose victimization overcoming individual personalities and entire cultures and creating ceaseless preoccupation with their victim status? How does a particular communal experience speak across cultures through the melding of survival and resistance?

There was much of the trickster's fascination with transfiguration in Primo Levi. Naanabozho/Nanabush the rabbit-trickster storyteller arrived in Auschwitz in the form of a young Italian chemist-alchemist preoccupied with transmutation of the physical world and the empiricism of shape-shifting. His formal education and self-education in 1930s fascist Italy, which he describes in his memoir *The Periodic Table*, centered on the transformation of raw into refined substance, of nature into artifice.[18] Levi-Naanabozho finds fundamental natural forces both in chemical transformation and in impurities: "In order for the wheel to be turned, for life to be lived, impurities are needed, and the impurities of impurities in the soil, too, as is known, if it is to be fertile. Dissension, diversity, the grain of salt and mustard are needed: Fascism does not want them, forbids them."[19] As a mining chemist occupied with experiments on extraction and magnetic enrichment of nickel, he lives in a magic world: "The entrails of the earth swarm with gnomes, kobalds (cobalt!), *nickel*, German 'little demon' or 'sprite' . . . many are the minerals whose names have roots that signify 'deception, fraud, bedazzlement.' "[20] In this magic world he has joined the "chemists, that is, hunters," who pursue the possibilities of transforming minerals in order to feed the all-consuming appetite of the fascist wiindigoo.[21]

The fascist militia's dispersal of a small resistance group that Levi joined and his capture in the local mountains results in deportation. When Levi and his compatriot deportees encounter fully the monster that consumes lives, they do so with foreknowledge of their probable fates: "Everybody said farewell to life through his neighbor. We had no more fear."[22] They face death and the question becomes how to comport oneself so as to comfort each other. Metamorphosis draws near, whether they are to live or die: the shadowland begins and their future grows dim, palpably short. Levi emphasizes metamorphosis as both normative and horrendous, as a function of nature, and as a malfunction of humanity. Despite the immediacy of threats once they reach the extermination camp, "we are not dead."[23] This contradiction between the present continuation of life and the apparent certainty of death in this hell—that dark moment of contradiction as Naanabozho and the woodland tribes watch the dice-figures fall—shapes their consciousness. We are dead, but we are not dead today. We know that we shall die, but we live now. We hope to find another trick; we hope to persist in life. How long can we live as the dice-figures fall toward inevitable loss in the cold darkness of this gambling dish?

The metamorphosis to death continues step after step toward a fundamental alteration of the human condition, all in preparation for industrial cannibalism. A systematic transformation occurs in order to create "a hollow man, reduced to suffering and needs, forgetful of dignity and restraint."[24] Separation from clothes, from the most minute of possessions, and from a sense of individuated self creates a daily netherworld. Paradoxically, it is this same reduction that creates survivance: "Precisely because the Lager was a great machine to reduce us to beasts, we must not become beasts; that even in this place one can survive, to tell the story, to bear witness; and that to survive we must force ourselves to save at least the skeleton, the scaffolding, the form of civilization."[25] The wiindigoo relies on precisely this stripping of humanity in order to create its malevolence as the monster first consumes humanity and then the human.

It is in their recognition of this process that Levi and Vizenor bear special comparison. Both recognize but reject terror as a response to such consumption of humanity and humans; consequently both emphasize introspective self-respect as a response to terror and indeed as fundamental to humane civilization. Forcible theft of that self-respect enables complete destruction of humanity within humans and the creation of hollowed-out *Muselmänner* barely human in form and robbed of spirit. As Levi observed in his famous "The Drowned and the Saved" chapter, this crushing of spirit was the primordial function of the Lager.[26] Such eradication created "an anonymous mass, continually renewed and always identical, of non-men who march and labor in silence, the divine spark dead within them. . . . One hesitates to call them living: one hesitates to call their death death."[27] It is these who will be consumed first by the wiindigoo-Nazi. Mere physical survival alone does not enable prisoners to prevail against death, but it is the maintenance of that spark, survivance, and most critically of memory, that prevents them from becoming spiritual *häftlings* (prisoners). It is the story and its telling, as Levi and Vizenor argue, that save us from being among the Drowned.

When Naanabozho-Levi discovers himself among the diminished population of the Saved at Auschwitz, he finds no real cause for his survival beyond simple persistence and occasional good luck. The Lager has no explanations for such questions; indeed, questions about the reasons for survival remain little asked. Rather, Levi's questions and memories center on the acts of resistance that he witnessed. After watching the hanging of a *Sonderkommando* (crematoria worker) rebel who cries, "Kamaraden, ich bin der Letzte!" (Comrades, I am the last one!), Levi feels shame that he too has not been a rebel.[28] His sentence "to destroy a man is difficult . . . but you Germans have succeeded. Here we are, docile under your gaze" belies itself, for by writing these lines he has carried forward the rebellion of that death cry.[29] By living on as the storyteller, although Levi continually evidences guilt that he is a survivor, he is the guarantee that those final words will echo.

Naanabozho in the Anishinaabe tradition is intrinsically a resistance figure, one able to absorb existential threats and transform them into a cultural resource that reinforces indigenous civilization. He is the one who can look the wiindigoo in the face and live to tell stories that defeat their cannibalism. As Naanabozho at Auschwitz Primo Levi refuses the roles of victim or victim-survivor, instead becoming the storyteller-survivor. Levi does not dwell on survival as its own value; he frames stories for the future, for remembrance. Crucially this framing comes in the context of an absolute refusal to celebrate victimhood. In an article written in 1955 on the tenth anniversary of the liberation of the camps, Levi wrote that "it is absurd to proclaim as glorious the deaths of countless victims in the extermination camps. It was not glorious: it was a defenseless and naked death, ignominious and vile."[30] Ignobility and degradation in the face of viciousness are not a cause for celebration, let alone latter-day festive competition over claims of greater oppression between historically oppressed peoples. Rather, as the works of Vizenor and Levi testify, survivance and the work to restore self, family, and community are the center of an ethical response to these histories.

Notes

1. Gerald Vizenor, *Chancers* (Norman: University of Oklahoma Press, 2000), 57.

2. Zubeda Jalazai, "Tricksters, Captives, and Conjurers: The 'Roots' of Liminality and Gerald Vizenor's 'Bearheart,'" *American Indian Quarterly* 23, no. 1 (1999): 28.

3. Sonya Atalay, "No Sense of the Struggle: Creating a Context for Survivance at the NMAI," *American Indian Quarterly* 30, nos. 3–4 (2006): 609.

4. Gerald Vizenor, *The Trickster of Liberty* (Minneapolis: University of Minnesota Press, 1988), 111–14. For a recent polemical use of the term *wiindigoo* in reference to American Indian Movement leader Clyde Bellecourt, see Vincent Hill, Editorial Comment, *Ojibwe News (St. Paul MN)*, June 9, 2006.

5. Gerald Vizenor, *Manifest Manners: Postindian Warriors of Survivance* (Hanover NH: University Press of New England, 1994), 149.

6. Richard Drinnon, *Facing West: The Metaphysics of Indian-Hating and Empire-Building* (Minneapolis: University of Minnesota Press, 1980), 457.

7. The major anthropological survey of wiindigoo stories is A. Irving Hallowell, *Culture and Experience* (Philadelphia: University of Pennsylvania Press, 1974). For a chapter-length review of wiindigoo literature, see David Gilmore, *Monsters: Evil Beings, Mythical Beasts, and All Manner of Imaginary Terrors* (Philadelphia: University of Pennsylvania Press, 2003), 75–90. Robert A. Brightman provides an extended and insightful discussion of wiindigoo psychology in "The Wiindigo in the Material World," *Ethnohistory* 35, no. 4 (Autumn 1988): 337–79.

8. Saindon serves here only as example, for he is part of a much longer history of Euro-American missionary accounts of encounters with the wiindigoo. One of the earlier accounts appears from Father Paul Le Jeune in 1661 and concerns the killing of a guide party for wiindigoo cannibalism—"neither lunacy, hypochondria, nor frenzy"—in the Lake St. John region of Quebec. See Reuben Gold Thwaites, ed., *The Jesuit Relations and Allied Documents, Travels and Explorations of the Jesuit Missionaries in New France, 1610–1791* (Cleveland: Burrows Brothers, 1899), 46:261.

9. Saindon (1891–1934) left no mark on anthropological literature, whereas Cooper made a significant contribution. For a more positive evaluation of Cooper, see Sharon M. Leon, "'Hopelessly Entangled in Nordic Presuppositions': Catholic Participation in the American Eugenics Society in the 1920s," *Journal of the History of Medicine and Allied Sciences* 59, no. 1 (2004): 3–49.

10. J. Emile Saindon, "Mental Disorders among the James Bay Cree," *Primitive Man* 6, no. 1 (January 1933): 1–12. For an example of Saindon's psychological racism: "The Indian is a big child, credulous, impressionable, sensitive, imaginative. While he is intelligent and is gifted with a marvelous memory, on the other hand his powers of memory are in many respects little exercised and little developed. . . . He is, in many things, weak in reasoning power" (2).

11. Saindon, "Mental Disorders," 11.

12. Saindon, "Mental Disorders," 12.

13. Carolyn Podruchny, "Werewolves and Windigos: Narratives of Cannibal Monsters in French Canadian Voyageur Oral Tradition," *Ethnohistory* 51, no. 4 (Fall 2004): 684.

14. Gerald Vizenor, *The People Named the Chippewa: Narrative Histories* (Minneapolis: University of Minnesota Press, 1984), 5–6.

15. Fergus Allen, *Who Goes There?* (London: Faber and Faber, 1997), 36, lines 17–19.

16. Based on an RLG Union search, October 1, 2006.

17. Vizenor's fictions rarely touch directly on Holocaust-related issues. For analysis of one occasion on which he does, see Chadwick Allen, "Blood (and) Memory," *American Literature* 71, no. 1 (March 1999): 106–7.

18. Primo Levi, *The Periodic Table*, trans. Raymond Rosenthal (New York: Schocken, 1984). Originally published as *Il sistema periodico* (Turin: Giulio Einaudi editore, 1975).

19. Levi, *Periodic Table*, 34.

20. Levi, *Periodic Table*, 64; also at 74–75.

21. Levi, *Periodic Table*, 75.

22. Primo Levi, *Survival in Auschwitz*, trans. Stuart Woolf (New York: Macmillan, 1961), 14. Originally published as *Se questo è un uomo* (Turin: Giulio Einaudi editore, 1958).

23. Levi, *Survival in Auschwitz*, 18.

24. Levi, *Survival in Auschwitz*, 23.

25. Levi, *Survival in Auschwitz*, 36.

26. Levi, *Survival in Auschwitz*, 79–91.

27. Levi, *Survival in Auschwitz*, 82.

28. Levi, *Survival in Auschwitz*, 135.

29. Levi, *Survival in Auschwitz*, 135–36. This shame reaction evident in Levi's *Survival in Auschwitz* does not appear in his later writing on camp resistance, such as his 1966 essay "Resistance in the Camps," in Primo Levi, *The Black Hole of Auschwitz*, ed. Marco Belpoliti, trans. Sharon Wood (Malden MA: Polity Press, 2005), 16–21. Originally published as *L'assimmetria e la vita* (Torino: Guilio Einaudi editore, 2002).

30. Levi, *Black Hole*, 4.

12. TACTICAL MOBILITY AS SURVIVANCE

Bone Game and *Dark River* by Louis Owens

JOHN GAMBER

> It's not wrong to survive. . . . We read their books and find out we're
> supposed to die. That's the story they've made up for us. Survivor's
> guilt is a terrible burden.
>
> Louis Owens, *Bone Game*

In his 1997 *Routes: Travel and Translation in the Late Twentieth Century*, James
Clifford challenges anthropological conceptions of cultural purity and static territorialities. Instead, Clifford offers a study of cultural wanderings. He
notes that "cultural centers, discrete regions and territories, do not exist pri-
or to contacts, but are sustained through them, appropriating and disciplin-
ing the restless movements of people and things."[1] He continues, asserting
that "stasis and purity are asserted—creatively and violently—*against* historical forces of movement and contamination."[2] In other words, not only are
notions of ethnic purity misguided but so are ideas that cultures and subcul-
tures are not always shaped by their interactions with others, by movements
between and among groups of people. Furthermore, these issues are central
to understanding Native cultures in the Americas; these cultures are too often defined in terms of these kinds of blood-based and geographic purities.
The reality is that Native people have always been on the move just as Native
communities (like all communities) are and have always been fluidly defined.
Native stories and storiers reflect and shape these mobilities.

Within this chapter I examine Louis Owens's concept and portrayals of "indigenous motion" within his novels *Bone Game* (1994) and *Dark River* (1999)
as a methodology of Native survivance. Owens crafts characters in these stories who succeed to varying degrees in terms of their movements between

specific Native communities. Their abilities to adapt and to show the fluidity of communal, personal, tribal, and national boundaries resist static notions of Native peoples and speak to a postindian assault on notions of tribal purity. In my examination of Native movement, I draw upon critical and autobiographical work by Owens himself in order to relate these novels as stories of Native presence rather than absence. Moreover, because Owens couches his critiques of the solitary individual through references to modernist texts that foreground individual isolation and alienation (two traits that are supposed and imposed to exist in Native people who are not placed within their specific "traditional" locations), I make use of Caren Kaplan's *Questions of Travel*, a critique of modernist literary portrayals of exile. Kaplan works to "question the modernisms of representations of movement, location, and homelessness in contemporary critical practice."[3] In other words, modernist artists failed to recognize the communities of which they were members even in their travels. Moreover, the protagonists of the novels I examine here mirror Kaplan's subjects, especially in their fascination with modernist literature.

However, Owens's texts are not so simplistic as to merely paint a neat dichotomy between alienation and community or mobility and stasis. Instead, the characters within these stories illustrate a multivalence (rather than ambivalence) of mobilities and histories. To that end I draw upon Michel de Certeau's concept of tactical mobility in order to illustrate a mode of (postmodern) survivance as a message within these stories. De Certeau discusses the positive ways people are able to "disguise or transform themselves in order to survive."[4] This survival is active, often subversive, and antiessentialist.[5]

Owens's notion of indigenous motion relates to some degree to Vizenor's concept of transmotion, a movement, though not necessarily linear, across imagined boundaries as well as to de Certeau's tactic (as we will see shortly). Vizenor notes that "the connotations of transmotion are creation stories, totemic visions, reincarnation, and sovenance; transmotion that sense of native motion and an active presence, is sui generic sovereignty," that is, these stories illustrate crossings of temporal, species, ethereal, and mental boundaries; Vizenor continues, "Native transmotion is survivance, a reciprocal use of nature, not a monotheistic, territorial sovereignty."[6]

Within *Bone Game* and *Dark River* each of the traits Vizenor names are present, but the reader particularly encounters creation stories, especially rearticulated and ever-expanding creation stories, and sovenance or remembrance. Perhaps above all else, these novels work to overcome conceptions of territorial sovereignty with their placement of Native people within tribal contexts that are not those of their distant ancestors. The protagonist's "outsider" status serves as a central and pivotal plot point in both *Bone Game* and *Dark River*; both are mixed-blood Choctaw and Irish. *Bone Game*'s Cole McCurtain is a professor at UC Santa Cruz while *Dark River*'s Jacob Nashoba is a Vietnam veteran, who upon his return marries Tali, an Apache woman on the fictional Black Mountain Reservation. Cole and Jake, respectively, become deeply enmeshed in Ohlone and Apache stories, expanding Native and tribal consciousnesses and identities in order to adapt to and to contend with the limiting and hegemonic portrayals of tragic victimry and static manners foisted upon Native peoples.

Owens's novels focus not only on what happens to characters who move but on characters who, having moved, stay in their new locations. Such stories are particularly necessary because, as Owens points out, Native people because of "many generations of displacement and orchestrated ethnocide are often far from their traditional homelands and cultural communities. Such a frontier/transcultural location is an inherently unstable position, from which it is difficult and undoubtedly erroneous to assume any kind of essential stance or strategy, despite many temptations to do so."[7]

Owens's use of the term "strategy" invokes the work of Michel de Certeau, whose concepts of strategy, tactics, space, and place mirror and illuminate issues present in these novels. Indeed, a number of characters embody mobility in ethical as well as physical terms. I relate their contradictory movements to what de Certeau calls a tactic, which he opposes to a strategy. De Certeau describes a tactic as "a calculus which cannot count on a 'proper' (a spatial or institutional localization), nor thus on a borderline distinguishing the other as a visible totality. The place of a tactic belongs to the other. A tactic insinuates itself into the other's place."[8]

Owens's work on mixed-blood identities and stories likewise challenge assertions of the proper and the borderlines between people and peoples. In their stead Owens offers the concept of the frontier as a zone rather than a discrete line or singular space. De Certeau reinforces such a reading in his concept of a region, "the space created by an interaction."[9] In *Mixedblood*

Messages Owens discusses the "'frontier' space, wherein discourse is multidirectional and hybridized."[10] For Owens the frontier exists everywhere in the Americas because colonizers and colonized are always meeting here and always interacting. Thus the Americas become a mixed-blood space. But Owens also focuses on people's "'place' within the landscape" and on human relationships to the land and the other species with whom we share it.[11] Along these lines he asserts that "to survive on this globe, it has become clear that we must achieve a transition from egocentrism to ecocentrism."[12] This unacceptable egocentrism is not only of the individual self but also of collective human delusions of superiority. De Certeau further suggests that this tactical mobility and flexibility may trace its roots to "the age-old ruses of fishes and insects that disguise or transform themselves in order to survive."[13] He continues, "The 'proper' is a victory of space over time. On the contrary, because it does not have a place, a tactic depends on time — it is always on the watch for opportunities that must be seized 'on the wing.' Whatever it wins, it does not keep."[14]

Ultimately essentialism rests on the proper, on the strategic, and on the place. Fixed essentialisms (in these novels, essentialisms of race, place, culture, and history) come from places of power and attempt to control existence by naming and describing something and the borders, boundaries, and frontiers delimiting that something from everything else.

In order to understand some of the nuances of de Certeau's argument, it becomes necessary to further examine his definitions of the terms "space" and "place" and their relationships to those of "tactic" and "strategy" respectively. He writes, "I shall make a distinction between space (*espace*) and place (*lieu*) that delimits a field. A place (*lieu*) is the order (of whatever kind) in accord with which elements are distributed in relationships of coexistence. It thus excludes the possibility of two things being in the same location (*place*). The law of the 'proper' rules in the place. . . . A *space* exists when one takes into consideration vectors of direction, velocities, and time variables. Thus space is composed of intersections of mobile elements."[15] So place equates to structure, stasis, power, strategy, and a conceived, but unlived, unlivable theory and panoptic mandate. On the other hand, space corresponds to movement, intersection, interaction, subversion, tactic, transmotion, and in short, the real way that humans experience and shape the shifting locations in which they live. Moreover, we note that de Certeau rightly combines the concepts of time and space as foundational for one another, recognizing that spaces are always in flux, shaped by our presence and motion, and always in motion themselves. In *Dark River* Owens likens this mobility to "situational ethics."[16] We also note a connection between people and our environment. De Certeau notes, "I call a 'strategy' the calculus of force-relationships which becomes possible when a subject of will and power . . . can be isolated from an 'environment.' "[17] But, as we will see—and as de Certeau implies—such isolation is always illusory.

Elsewhere, Owens observes that, since the majority of "American Indians [have been and are] displaced far from traditional cultural centers [, those] stories, too, must be told. For stories are what we carry with us through time and across distance."[18] Moreover, one of the foci of Owens's stories is the role of mixed-bloods. As such, these stories further push the issues of Native identities away from conceptions of purity. Owens asserts that "mixedbloods are recorded and erased, having no place in the metanarrative of fixed colonial others."[19] What's more, Susan Bernardin illustrates how Owens's emphasis on mobility and intertribal communities counters the calls for tribal nationalism in the work of Elizabeth Cook-Lynn and Craig Womack.[20] Cook-Lynn writes that "the challenge today . . . is to keep the focus of the early ideas of nationalism and our connections to specific geographies," while Womack asserts, "It seems foolhardy to me to abandon a search for the affirmation of a national literary identity simply to fall in line with the latest literary trend."[21]

By contrast, Owens notes that his characters often ask, "Who am I? and How do I live in this place and time?"[22] In other words, his characters are not dealing with their own specific tribal national locales but with movement and travel. In *Bone Game* protagonist Cole McCurtain has left New Mexico for California, a return to the region of his youth. Thus he begins in Choctaw country in Mississippi, moves to central California, moves again to New Mexico, returns to California, and finally returns to New Mexico, a location he refers to as "home." In *Dark River* Jacob Nashoba moves from Mississippi to California, goes to Vietnam, and then returns to the States (bodily, at least) to settle in Arizona. These characters' varying and changing (in)abilities to be at home where they are serve to engage the readers in their own conceptions of home, challenging static, nationalistic, and monolithic territorialities.

What then happens to our understanding of not only Native life but more pressingly to this discussion of Native stories in light of this reemphasis on motion? Along these lines, Owens offers his own term: "indigenous motion." He argues that "tribal people have deep bonds with the earth, with sacred places that bear the bones and stories that tell them who they are, where they came from, and how to live in the world they see around them. But of course almost all tribal people also have migration stories that say we came from someplace else before finding home."[23] Similarly de Certeau avers that "stories . . . organize places through the displacements they 'describe' (as a mobile point describes a curve)."[24] In other words, these stories show, create, and define trajectories, which, even if they are used to delimit place as a static construct, have at their very core the seeds and fruits of motion. Throughout *Dark River* characters refer to the ways Apache identities are created and sustained through the movements back and forth between Mexico and interactions with Anglo, Mexican, Spanish, Hopi, Navajo, and now Choctaw neighbors. Owens creates a further cross-tribal flow by placing the narrative of another mixed-blood Choctaw protagonist within a distant tribal context (this time Ohlone) in *Bone Game*.[25] This intertribal story is somewhat akin to what Owens notes about *House Made of Dawn*: that it is a novel about "Jemez Pueblo in New Mexico [from] an outsider . . . assuming insider privilege."[26] Again, such a multi- or intertribal focus continues its challenges to literary tribal nationalism in favor of a flexibility of community. Owens rhetorically wonders, "How in the world did tribal people survive . . . unless we know how to pick up and carry our selves, our histories, our stories, our self-knowledge?"[27] Indeed, as this quote's reference to history suggests, we must remember that transit is never only spatial; it is also temporal.

Within Owens's novels, and especially within *Bone Game*, this movement within time is certainly as critical and central as that of movement within space. Ultimately our stories and memories unify past and present, thereby linking all time, all space, and all elements into a dynamic, ever-expanding whole. Moreover, Owens asserts that "people who do not live in reservation communities [,] if they are artists, may create art about urban or rural mixedblood experience at a distance from their tribal communities."[28] In other words, the storiers will create stories that not only reflect but also expand for their experiences of mobility as stories of survivance.[29] De Certeau further notes that "every story is a travel story—a spatial practice."[30] Owens's texts nonetheless show that, while interspecies communities are vital, they must not be fostered at the expense or to the exclusion of human communities.

Cole's and Jake's initial refusal to recognize the importance of human communities relates in large part to their choice of reading, the fact that both are drawn to modernist texts. Throughout *Dark River* Jake is reading *The Sun Also Rises*.[31] He claims to like Hemingway's work because "it doesn't require some kind of action[;] there's this sense that he's not trying to hide anything, that nothing's going to change."[32] Jake is drawn to inaction and complacence, and this inaction has serious social implications. If survivance is "more than survival, more than endurance or mere response" but instead is "an active presence," as Vizenor defines it in *Fugitive Poses*, then Jake doesn't seem to fit the bill.[33] Jake is merely surviving, but he fails to take an active part in anything. For Jake the fixation on the river leads to isolation from his community, including his wife. Jake realizes that "the more he learned about the land the less he knew about the people. In fact, he had unthinkingly willed himself not to learn about Tali's people, feeling every bit an outsider without the right to know such things."[34] Bernardin observes that "Nashoba insists on 'going it alone'; in doing so, he offends the community and reinforces his marginal status."[35] However, it is important to note that, despite the fact that Jake knows this landscape better than anyone else, that knowledge does not save his life.

Like Jake, Cole is drawn to modernist literature. A third-person narrator notes that Cole "loved the painful sincerity of the modernists, how hard they had tried to find the questions and then answer them. Their poignant attempts to rediscover or replace God attracted him. Like they knew they had lost something precious and indispensable and they lived in a world bereft and haunted. But, they believed that what they'd lost was still there, somewhere, if they could only find the clues. The solution was just out of reach. His heart went out to them in spite of all their white, racist, empirical superiority."[36] Cole's attachment to modernism is rather condescending, a parental view of a childlike innocence. Nonetheless, Cole's appreciation of the modernist quest for meaning reflects his own search for belonging as some kind of absolute. That search is further reflected in his appreciation of certain objects as things upon which so much might depend. For example, Cole's coffee pot serves as an object, one around which a great deal of Cole's energy revolves and whose "heavy solidity was a comfort."[37] This comfort relates to Cole's love of modernism, a movement striving to find a solid base on which to stand, a movement that to a large extent firmly believed that such a base existed and could be found.

Nevertheless, Cole sees some of the inherent flaws in modernism. Similarly Vizenor comments that postmodernism treats "authors, readers, tricksters and comic world views rather than tragic themes, individualism, and modernism."[38] Elsewhere he writes that "the postindian warriors . . . contend with manifest manners . . . and the curse of racialism and modernism in the ruins of representation."[39] Vizenor's linking of modernism and individualism becomes further reinforced through Kaplan's critique of modernist exile. One level of this critique comes for Kaplan because modernists' "dislocation is expressed in singular rather than collective terms, as purely psychological or aesthetic situations rather than as a result of historical circumstances," that is, part of the problem of modernist exile or alienation is that it is *imagined* as an individual crisis.[40] Jake Nashoba's central dilemma, for instance, comes in the form of his distance from his community. Jake's isolation is in part of his own making, in part as a result of what has been done to him, and in part as the result of a xenophobia that certainly belies any multitribal constructions of community. Ultimately, though, Jake seems to revel in this sense of dislocation.

Kaplan notes of the modernist subject that "Euro-American modernisms celebrate singularity, solitude, estrangement, alienation, and aestheticized excisions of location in favor of locale."[41] De Certeau offers a similar critique, challenging the privileging of "the individual — on the basis of which groups are supposed to be formed and to which they are supposed to be always reducible."[42] Instead, he notes that "a relation (always social) determined its terms, and not the reverse, and that each individual is a locus in which an incoherent (and often contradictory) plurality of such relational determinations interact."[43] De Certeau and Kaplan recognize communal identity formation and show that the modernist emphasis on the individual misidentifies the self.

In contrast to Jake, Cole recognizes the problems in his isolation more quickly, a recognition that leads him at the end of *Bone Game* to a return home.[44] He leaves Santa Cruz, one of his boyhood homes, for New Mexico, a new home space whose hominess is predicated to a large extent on the presence of his daughter. But that sense of home also comes in his relationships to the nonhuman. While living in Santa Cruz, Cole never comes to explore the woods near his house, although "he'd never lived anywhere before where he didn't know the terrain of his existence."[45] Similarly he takes little time to invest in forming any human relationships. Abby notices that "it was as if, except for Alex Yazzie, her father had spoken to no one since he'd loaded the pickup and driven out of the Sandia Mountains."[46] Jake, on the other hand, explores the space of the river while failing to form real interpersonal or communal relationships.

Cole and Jake further illustrate modernist nostalgias for place, which again, in de Certeau's construction, are static and binaristic assertions of location. Kaplan contends that "the difference between modernist and postmodernist imaginary geographies may be a nostalgia for clear binary distinctions between 'country and city' on the one hand and an attachment to less oppositional hybrid cosmopolitanisms on the other."[47] I would rearticulate this binary distinction within Owens's modernist characters as one between home and not-home, that is, both Jake and Cole fail to recognize that their current locations can be home and that home is a mobile concept, not a static absolute, and instead they draw nostalgically on other places and other times. This combination of temporal and geographical nostalgia is especially ironic in light of both novels' insistence that all time and space are one. In these novels, then, the focus is not so much on replacing some tragic notion of place or a home that has been lost but rather on *re-placing*, or establishing ourselves where we are, of being able to *re-place* wherever we might go.[48]

Each of these novels pays particular attention to the roles of outsiders and insiders, on who counts as which, and to what degree. Ultimately Owens shows that these conditions are fluid, cultural, and tactical rather than "racial." As Vizenor argues, "Native resistance is survivance, not separatism, and many natives continue to resist the racialists and separatists."[49] While the roles of outsiders within these novels are played most clearly by the protagonists, Cole and Jake and by Avrum Goldberg, an anthropologist who has been living on the Apache reservation for years, both these novels resist the racialists and seperatists. Of these characters Jake is most clearly the outsider. Mrs. Edwards, a respected elder in *Dark River*, is the most assertive about this status, calling Jake a "mixedblood outsider."[50] When Tali asks her why she has always opposed his presence Mrs. Edwards replies, "Because Jacob Nashoba always opposed me. From the first day he came, when he could barely talk, I felt it and saw it in his eyes. He wanted you [Tali] for himself, and he wasn't one of us."[51] In other words, Jake fails to recognize the communal bond between people and instead hungers greedily for his wife. Mrs. Edwards goes on to say that he only loves the river and that his house is "like those forts the army used to build to fight Indians."[52] The problem, Mrs. Edwards argues, is that Jake "didn't care enough about [Tali] to find medicine for his anger." Again, Jake is an outsider because he fails to recognize his responsibilities to his wife and community that include taking care of himself.

Like Jake, Cole is a bit of a loner, but his outsider status is described much more ironically than Jake's. When Alex Yazzie, a Diné anthropologist, first meets Cole, he calls him "the new Indian they hired in literature, a poor mixedblood trapped between worlds and cultures if I can believe my eyes."[53] This passage has for the most part been read as sincere, a statement of mixedblood identity as a nebulous netherworld that precludes any sense of belonging. And while Cole seems to see himself to some degree as representative of such a lack of place, Alex seems much less likely to utter such a phrase as "poor mixedblood" without irony.

Later, Alex once again self-consciously points to what Cole's *indian* persona is supposed to be, lamenting, "You poor, homeless halfbreed. . . . The real lost generation, trapped between worlds. Living your liminal life. If you were a fullblood like me, you wouldn't have this identity crisis. You'd have a card from the BIA telling you exactly who you are."[54] The irony in this passage is more obvious than that of the first. The idea that the cross-dressing trickster figure would place any actual stock in the BIA's method of cataloguing Native identity by membership cards and blood quantum is just plain funny. What's more, the humor in *Bone Game* largely comes, as LaLonde notes, with "Alex in dialogue with Cole and others." We must note the communal nature of this humor as well as its empowering aspects. So while Cole might see himself as some kind of inherent outsider, the text, the story of *Bone Game*, denies such an idea as soon as it proposes it.

If Alex, an anthropologist, shows Cole the error of his tragic "lack of community," Avrum Goldberg, the anthropologist in *Dark River* occupies a much more (suitably) tenuous position. We might suspect that, being an anthropologist, he'd be forever an outsider, and he is to some degree. Most notably, Owens directly examines the static and anthropological concepts of "tradition" via discussions between and about Avrum and Shorty, a former Hollywood western extra. Tali, for example, says, "Avrum is traditional. He doesn't drink at all."[55] But Jake responds, "Traditional what? As a matter of fact, Shorty told me that your tribe used to make beer. . . . So, if Avrum was traditional, he'd be out getting zonked."[56] The idea of tradition is used in this case as a romantic vision of precontact Native peoples. Vizenor implores that we "set aside the word *tradition*, as in '*indian* traditions,' because it suggests that trickster stories, irony, and the originary deception of language, is a cultural and determined practice. . . . Tradition, as you know, is a tamer, not a liberator."[57] Similarly Kaplan notes that "part of the configuration of contradiction and ambivalence that mark . . . theories of modernity includes tensions between progress and tradition."[58]

Owens furthers this assertion about tradition as Shorty and Avrum discuss a plan that the anthropologist proposes before the tribal council. Avrum's proposal "is that the tribe give up the casino and lodge and commercial hunting and instead become a traditional tribe again, living the way everyone lived before the white men came."[59] As the people in attendance realize, there would be no way to spend the millions of dollars they would make by this plan, and so they dismiss Goldberg with an "easy laugh."[60] Of course, this plan rests on the simplistic and anthropological view of Native societies as static, and at their heart atavistic. At this point Goldberg becomes preachy and condescending. He insists, "The problem with you Indians is that you don't understand that. I try to convince you that you should live the way your ancestors did two hundred years ago, but nobody listens. I could teach you all how to do that, but nobody cares."[61] Shorty responds, "You think elders like Mrs. John Edwards are going to let you teach them how to live traditionally? You're forgetting that change is traditional, too. We were running around on foot until those Spanish brought up horses, and then everything was on horseback."[62] He continues, "Look at those old pictures of the warriors. Those were proud men and women, Avrum, and you notice nobody's dressed like you. Every one of them is wearing cotton clothes and holding rifles. That's tradition, too."[63]

However, Owens's multivalent and complex narrative does not allow for such a quick and total rebuke of Avrum Goldberg. Within a few lines Avrum and Shorty have returned to their friendly, joking ways. Shorty *and* Goldberg take turns coming up with mocking, teasing nicknames for the anthropologist, all drawn from stereotyping Hollywood portrayals of *indians*: Doctor Dances with Endowments, Doctor Grantheart, Last of the Mo-Traditionals, A Man Called Cash, Money Highway, Plenty Yo, PocoHondas, and Pocahonkers.[64]

This ability to laugh at himself seems to mark Avrum Goldberg as something less troubling than anthropologists tend to be, especially in Native stories.[65] Indeed, while he is excessively fascinated by the concept of tradition, he still recognizes and, more importantly, participates in Native irony. When a *National Geographic* film crew comes to the reservation, Goldberg, masquerading under the name Chief Gold Bird, appears wearing "a traditional breechcloth and Apache leggings and moccasins, his torso covered by a cotton shirt and vest and his long, thinning gray hair held back by a blue headband. His face, skull, and hands, all that showed his skin, were as brown as coffee, and his stolid expression suggested both wisdom and resignation."[66]

Of course, this portrayal is laughable; it is meant to be funny. The wannabe anthropologist is dressing up as he thinks an *indian* should dress. Nonetheless, Goldberg knows that this posture is all a big joke, and Shorty notes, "You've got to admire Avrum's sense of humor, too, to go along with it."[67] Later Avrum implores, "Don't think I don't know when you're mocking me."[68] But his knowing and active participation in humor and irony, even (or especially) when he is the butt of the joke, seems to serve as a saving grace for Goldberg. He is a flawed character (all of the characters in this novel are imperfect), but he seems to fit in, to be a part of the community in a specific sense. Avrum at one point "smiled, contented now to be the eternal outsider, and knowing his value thereof."[69] What is so interesting about Owens's Goldberg is the anthropologist's understanding and humor; he gets that the joke is on him, and he still willingly plays his role. But what's more, the outsider plays an important role, pushing and playing with the boundaries of the group in the story.

Indeed, Owens's mixed-blood stories work to blur lines between Native and non-Native, a tactic that is particularly evident in the ethnic passing undertaken by Avrum and Shorty. Avrum pretends to be Apache, while Shorty is mistaken for Italian, especially because he learned Italian as an extra in

Hollywood westerns.[70] Owens addresses the simulation of Native identities noting that "anthropologists and Italians became the real Indians."[71] Jake tells Shorty, "Those white people won't believe you're Indian. . . . Your hair's too short, you blather Italian, and you dress like a white man. . . . You're not a very marketable Indian."[72] Whereas the anthropologist "looks more Indian than you do. He dresses right, knows all the stories, and has a more Indian sounding name than you do. He also speaks the tribal language better."[73] And while Jake distrusts Avrum because he is "not part of the community," the irony is that Avrum is seen at this point in the narrative as more a part of the community than Jake because the former's ties to people are stronger.[74]

This issue of varying insider and outsider status is further evidenced in the ways that home is constructed in these novels, a construction that is much more clearly settled in *Bone Game* than it is in *Dark River*. Cole feels a bond with Choctaw country, just as he feels one for California's central coast, but neither place is truly home to him. He notes, for example, "I used to pretend I might go back to live in Mississippi. . . . But I was just a visitor down there."[75] Similarly Owens has called the setting of *Bone Game*, California, "a place where I never stopped being a stranger."[76] When Abby asks if Cole will come home, he ponders and asks, "Where was home?"[77] This question speaks to the confusion that Owens's protagonists face in terms of where they "belong." Indeed, Cole remains unsure of what home means until the end of the novel when he is back in New Mexico in what he calls "Indian country."[78] However, this iteration is not prescriptive in terms of what space ought to be "home" for all Native people. Onatima tells Abby that she and Uncle Luther can't stay with them in the Southwest: "We have our own worlds, Granddaughter. We carried our people's bones a thousand days just to find a home. When so many were removed, we stayed behind. So how could we leave now? Who would talk to them out there at night if I never went home? And how would I find the path so far away? Who would tell them of their granddaughter in these strange, lightning-struck mountains?"[79] She concludes, "So the crux of the matter is that we have to go home."[80] Owens's novel shows that home is not any universal place. The implication is that it is important that some Choctaw people remain in the ancestral lands but also that movement is a crucial and historically constant aspect of Native identities. Onatima sees nothing wrong, however, with Cole and Abby staying in New Mexico. Indeed, Abby's presence there becomes a new aspect of the stories Onatima will tell. Again, we note the refusal of the story to adhere to any single narrative perspective.

In general too much emphasis has been placed on the examination of the protagonists in both these novels, as the roles of Avrum, Shorty, and Abby attest. Indeed, if these are, as I assert, stories about stories, and more specifically, stories about the way tribal stories are, can, and must be told, any focus on a single character will prove excessively myopic. And as we have seen, that individualistic myopia is ultimately the greatest shortcoming of the modernist figures central to the growth of these novels. In this sense these stories are more like de Certeau's "spatial stories" wherein "space is like the word when it is spoken[,] transformed into a term dependent upon many different conventions, situated as the act of a present[.] It has thus none of the univocity or stability of the 'proper.' "[81] These stories are inherently multivoiced, necessarily so because the concept of space and its concomitant mobility rely on interactions and intersections of stories and individuals.

We might also note a connection to the spoken word (which de Certeau implies is equally present in some literary texts) to Kimberly Blaeser's study of Vizenor's work, *Writing in the Oral Tradition*.[82] Moreover, Owens's novels focus on the storytellers, the storiers, to use Vizenor's term. Vizenor begins *Fugitive Poses* with, "Native American Indians are the storiers of presence, the chroniclers in the histories of this continent."[83] This presence, or this "present" in de Certeau's lexicon, marks a critical aspect of survivance. Since these are stories to be worked on, retold, and reinvented over and over within (though not necessarily exclusively) the community, the focus must be on the multivalence of the perspectives of the story and its storiers, and through that multivalence, Owens articulates stories of presence and of round, tricky Native figures rather than flat, tragic *indians*.

Within these novels we encounter a number of characters who rely on tactical and comic movement within space and time as well as those who proceed within very limiting and tragic conceptions of place and identity. Cole and Jake are generally static characters, and their status as such is emblematized by a beer sign in Jake's office and in Cole's general rut. Jake once received "a gift from a Choctaw guy he'd met in a bar in Alburquerque."[84] The sign, which burned out the first time Jake tried to plug it in, is supposed to show a man paddling a canoe on a river. The moving lights provide the appearance of motion. Jesse, a young man who is one of Jake's only friends, offers to fix the sign for Jake who responds, "Maybe I like it just as it is." In disbelief Jesse replies, "No way. Imagine how great it would be with all that simulated motion. I saw one of those in a bar in Flagstaff, and it was great. . . . Everything tells you this guy's going somewhere, real lifelike, but it's just illusion."[85]

Similarly Jacob looks to be in motion, always in motion, but he's not really going anywhere, except away from something. This stasis, however, is not of physical movement alone but also of a personal progress toward healing, that is, in his stubborn refusal to change, to adapt, and to heal, Jake serves as a direct contrast to the concept of survivance, a term that implies motion. Such a stasis further contrasts de Certeau's model, which focuses not only with the images we receive but with "what the cultural consumer 'makes' or 'does' during this time and with these images."[86] The focus here is on activity versus passivity, on manipulating instead of merely receiving. Cole's inaction comes from an inability to embrace chance or effect change in his life. He simply replicates the same pattern day after day. Along these lines, Alex tells Cole, "You always wear the same thing."[87] Ally also criticizes Cole for always tying the same fly, the mundane mosquito. Both Cole and Jake attempt to keep still in a world that is always in motion; those who fail to recognize that reality fail to truly know the spaces in which they live.

If Jake and Cole stand as symbols of inactivity and stasis, Jake's daughter Allison displays a certain sense of cultural mobility. Allison seeks Jesse out to guide her on a vision quest, despite the fact that vision quests are not an Apache "tradition." But Allison seeks out a diversified perspective, one that looks to other tribal practices in order to broaden her understanding and to expand her perspectives. Jesse tells Jake that she "said she could learn from our native brothers and sisters in other tribal cultures. No shit. She really talked that way."[88] Jesse later notes, "Allison chose to do this even though it's not traditional. I think she's trying to invent her own traditions."[89] Allison's approach to tradition is much more fluid than static. First, she shows an ability to imagine outside of a monolithic tribal context. Second, she recognizes the fact that traditions change and that those changes sometimes come at the hands of a few.

Jesse's approach is similarly fluid but much more tactical, and one is reminded of the theme of "situational ethics" that is repeated throughout this novel. Jesse plays the role of *indian* spiritual guide to mostly white wannabes. His business, Vision Quest Enterprises, charges two to four thousand dollars and uses the money for a tribal scholarship fund.[90] Yet while Jesse's actions may seem like an acceptance of a stereotype, they are in fact a tactical utilization of that stereotype. He is using the *indian* simulation to help real Native students, thus helping the community. Later, Jesse asks some reservation kids who Russell Means is. They respond, "That's easy man. He's that actor that was in Last of the Mohicans and Natural Born Killers. He was supposed to be a Navajo in that one. That was funny."[91] When Jake asks Jesse why they don't know about Means's role in AIM and why the latter feels no need to tell them, Jesse says, "I'm just trying to make sure the kids know their roles, develop their sense of irony so they'll know how to function, how to adapt like Russell Means."[92] Owens elsewhere calls Means "Vizenor's quintessential 'postindian warrior of survivance.'"[93] Means's ability to shift and adapt himself shows a tacit, if unconscious, acceptance of the mobility of the self, a lack of any essential and tragic image. Jesse embraces this irony, and while some have read this character as a negative portrayal of a sellout, his humor and ability to recognize the silliness of the whole venture (traits that continue even beyond his death) show the value of this tactical mobility and flexibility.

Of course, Owens's text would not be so simplistic as to show only a range of Native tactics; we also encounter Jake's former captain, Steve Stroud who now runs a survivalist business.[94] Owens notes that "the business was chock full of fake war heroes attracted by Stroud's ad in magazines like *American Survival*."[95] These survivalists are rather like the fake Indians engaged in Jesse's vision quests, and Stroud calls them "right-wing morons."[96] Both Stroud and Jesse are tactical in their constructions, giving ignorant and naïve outsiders exactly what they expect while internally mocking them and taking their money. And while LaLonde sees Stroud as actually coming to believe his own hype, I think these excerpts show that he does not.[97] His affirmations of his clients' paranoia are just for show.

Owens's story is about the ability to shift our expectations and personae in the face of an ever-changing world, one in which the bulk of us are fairly short on material power. Or as de Certeau asserts, "Marginality is today no longer limited to minority groups, but is rather massive and pervasive."[98] Likewise, Phillip Brian Harper notes postmodern decenteredness comes from "'general' culture" going through "what are thought of as socially marginal or 'minority' experiences."[99] Stroud is no different. He tells Jake that the military "made us what they wanted us to be, but now we can remake ourselves and say fuck them. We don't have to stay where they put us."[100] Stroud recognizes the importance and the liberation that can come from tactical mobility, and the destruction that comes from manifest manners and terminal creeds. Gretchen Ronnow uses the term "lost," which she places within quotation marks in order to take the word out of the negative contexts with which it is often associated; she contends that within this novel "being 'lost' or being without the parochialism of 'home' may be part of perfection."[101] In other words, a certain mobility both of body and philosophy becomes a method and mode of survivance in these texts.

These possibilities for broad Native mobilities that serve to connect Native peoples across the continent are further emphasized in *Bone Game's* chapter 5, which consists of a version of the Ohlone creation story with the addition of, "Then the ones with crosses came from the south, and the children began to die."[102] Thus the story of creation changes, although not for the better, and new people become important. The assertion then is that the story is big enough to adapt so as to include these outsiders. Part of Cole's healing comes from Uncle Luther's bringing an Ohlone doll and arrowheads that Cole and his brother Attis found when they were children.[103] These are found objects reclaimed and set within a multitribal context of healing. Uncle Luther further suggests, "Used to be boundaries. . . . Us Choctaws used to worry about them Chickasaws that was our brothers once, but we didn't know about all this other stuff. Then those Spanish come. . . . Since that time things've been getting bigger and bigger."[104] In *Dark River* Jake thinks, "So maybe . . . there was such a thing as an Indian, something that cut across the lines of Choctaw and Cherokee and Black Mountain and Lakota to make some kind of connection."[105] So while the *indian* may be a simulation, Native people across the continent, sharing to a large extent histories of displacement and survival of attempts at ethnocide, possess in common certain connections. This connection is not to say that these texts endorse any kind of pan-tribalism; they don't. Instead, they call for alliances, entities that are always similarly fluid and tactical. Christie points out that *Dark River* "negotiate[s] complex crossings between occasionally competing tribal identities, histories, and affiliations without rendering these latter formulaic or needlessly antagonistic."[106]

Of course, these are stories; what's more, like many Native texts including the novels of Momaday, Silko, and Vizenor, these are stories about stories, stories that work to make room for contemporary Native voices within tribal narratives. Indeed, for de Certeau the story itself is a tactical vehicle. The transformation comes as the reader's world "slips into the author's place" and "makes the text habitable, like a rented apartment. It transforms another person's property into a space borrowed for a moment by a transient."[107] Both novels make nearly constant references to themselves as stories; all the characters are aware of the fact that they are participants in narrative tales, the ends of which are unknown. Both are littered with images of spiders, and "Spider Woman . . . traditionally aids the lost and forgotten by weaving their stories into the broader pattern of elemental forces."[108]

Any number of other critics discuss the role of storytelling and the self-consciousness of the characters in these texts.[109] For our purposes it suffices to say that the end(s) of the novels, the false endings and the discussions of the (im)possibilities of other endings are one lesson of these stories. They tell the audience of chances, of mobility. And while the audience may be very familiar with the plots and characters in the stories we tell, these texts insist that the endings are unwritten, always being unwritten and rewritten. By ending his novels with passages that serve as the beginnings to other unwritten narratives, Owens shows what Vizenor has elsewhere asserted of Native stories: "Last words are never the end."

Within *Bone Game* and *Dark River* Owens offers stories of Native mobility and motion, stories of relocations that come by choice. The growth of the protagonists and the tactical mobility of the community of characters convey a message that moves Native people beyond tragic portrayals, static definitions, exclusive tribal nationalism, isolation, and alienation. Within these novels Owens also offers a critique of modernism as a vehicle for all of these negative cultural artifacts and effects. In their place these novels narrate a continuous and continuing Native presence, and as such, they are stories of survivance. Onatima, a character in *Bone Game*, gives a lesson to her audience: "We read their books and find out we're supposed to die. That's the story they've made up for us."[110] This story is that of the tragic *indian*, not that of the warrior of survivance. The characters of these novels insist on survival as an ongoing process. And while the idea of tradition may be extremely marketable as a marker of the vanishing *indian*, Owens refuses any such portrayal in favor of humor and adaptability. Onatima defends these positive aspects of fluid Native presence most clearly: "It's not wrong to survive."[11]

Notes

1. Clifford, *Routes*, 3.
2. Clifford, *Routes*, 7.
3. Kaplan, *Questions of Travel*, 4.
4. De Certeau, *Everyday Life*, xi.
5. I also, of course, draw on Vizenor's concepts of native transmotion and survivance.
6. Vizenor, *Fugitive Poses*, 15.
7. Lee, "Outside Shadow," 12.
8. De Certeau, *Everyday Life*, xix.
9. De Certeau, *Everyday Life*, 126.
10. Owens, *Mixedblood Messages*, 26.
11. Owens, *Mixedblood Messages*, 8.
12. Owens, *Mixedblood Messages*, 11.
13. De Certeau, *Everyday Life*, xi. De Certeau further suggests that this tactical mobility and flexibility may trace their roots to "the age-old ruses of fishes and insects that disguise or transform themselves in order to survive" (*Everyday Life*, xi).
14. De Certeau, *Everyday Life*, xix.
15. De Certeau, *Everyday Life*, 117.
16. Owens, *Dark River*, 126. Vizenor also uses this term in *Postindian Conversations*, 37.
17. De Certeau, *Everyday Life*, xix.
18. Owens, *Mixedblood Messages*, 166.
19. Owens, "Syllogistic Mixedblood," 235.
20. Bernardin, "Moving in Place," 115.
21. Cook-Lynn, *Anti-Indianism*, 177; Womack, *Red on Red*, 5–6.
22. Owens, *Mixedblood Messages*, 165.
23. Owens, *Mixedblood Messages*, 164.
24. De Certeau, *Everyday Life*, 116.
25. Owens's references to Ohlone history include a retelling of the Ohlone creation story as well as the references to Venancio Asisara and his son Lorenzo, who within *Bone Game* seems to be the first Ohlone mixed-blood. In this novel Owens refers to an 1877 interview with the latter, an interview that has recently been translated and published by Gregorio Mora-Torres in *Californio Voices*. This interview includes many

useful and interesting insights, including the facts that Padre Quintana's date of death is listed as October 12, 1812 (Columbus Day), and that the "Tulareans were the ones who played peon, a game of hidden objects; there were two pieces of bones about two inches long: one black and the other white. The white one was the one of value" (127). This interview also includes a phrase repeated throughout the novel: "Los padres españoles eran muy crueles con los indios" (94).

26. Owens, *Mixedblood Messages*, 157.

27. Owens, *Mixedblood Messages*, 164.

28. Owens, *Mixedblood Messages*, 158.

29. It is, however, somewhat disturbing that the only Ohlone character we meet in *Bone Game* is a ghost. We do not meet any living Ohlones as we do Apaches in *Dark River*. And while the numbers are different and while from an anthropological perspective the Ohlone are no more, certain Ohlone activists, Linda Yamane among them, would certainly dispute this simulation of extinction.

30. De Certeau, *Everyday Life*, 115.

31. Owens, *Dark River*, 241. Jake, of course, shares his first name with Jake Barnes, the protagonist of Hemingway's novel.

32. Owens, *Dark River*, 11. Mrs. Edwards wonders how Jake and Hemingway's characters "find pleasure in luring the underwater people into the air world that kills them" (Owens, *Dark River*, 45). Like Jake, Cole fishes the Black River (a tributary of the Salt River that divides the White Mountain Fort Apache Reservation from the San Carlos Apache Reservation) (Owens, *Bone Game*, 33). He tells Alex, "What I really want is to just go fishing. Flyfishing on the Black River" (Owens, *Bone Game*, 46).

33. Vizenor, *Fugitive Poses*, 15. Similarly de Certeau's approach means to establish "a *present* relative to time and place," a present that deals in large part with stories, with the speech act (*Everyday Life*, xiii).

34. Owens, *Dark River*, 50.

35. Bernardin, "Moving in Place," 106.

36. Owens, *Bone Game*, 39.

37. Owens, *Bone Game*, 10.

38. Vizenor, *Narrative Chance*, 3.

39. Vizenor, *Manifest Manners*, 12.

40. Kaplan, *Questions of Travel*, 4.

41. Kaplan, *Questions of Travel*, 28.

42. De Certeau, *Everyday Life*, xi.

43. De Certeau, *Everyday Life*, xi.

44. While *Dark River* closes with the sentence, "It is said that Jake Nashoba went home," it is important to note that his return comes with his death. This passage should not be read in an entirely tragic manner, but his return certainly seems less positive than Cole's.

45. Owens, *Bone Game*, 211.

46. Owens, *Bone Game*, 135.

47. Kaplan, *Questions of Travel*, 31.

48. Kaplan further notes, "It is interesting to consider the tension between location and dislocation or between nationalism and internationalism in their descriptive narratives" (*Questions of Travel*, 30). I would further assert that Owens's work is a form of Native United States internationalism.

49. Vizenor and Lee, *Postindian Conversations*, 179.

50. Owens, *Dark River*, 270.

51. Owens, *Dark River*, 218.

52. Owens, *Dark River*, 218.

53. Owens, *Bone Game*, 26. Cole calls Alex a "Navajo *Heyokah*, a sacred warrior-clown" (Owens, *Bone Game*, 27), and the latter certainly serves as a trickster figure within this novel. It is also important to note that Owens makes yet another intertribal reference, as "heyokah" is a Lakota, not a Diné word.

54. Owens, *Bone Game*, 47.

55. Owens, *Dark River*, 39.

56. Owens, *Dark River*, 39.

57. Vizenor and Lee, *Postindian Conversations*, 60.

58. Kaplan, *Questions of Travel*, 35.

59. Owens, *Dark River*, 71.

60. Owens, *Dark River*, 74.

61. Owens, *Dark River*, 212.

62. Owens, *Dark River*, 213.

63. Owens, *Dark River*, 213.

64. Owens, *Dark River*, 214–15.

65. In *Postindian Conversations* Vizenor discusses the "dead voices" of "social sciences" (137) and states, "I have not been fierce enough about anthropology. There are no measures of fierceness that could be reparations for the theft of native irony, humor, and original stories. There's not enough time to be critical of the academic enterprise of cultural anthropology" (90).

Vizenor is hardly alone in his critique of anthropology. Vine Deloria's send up of the field in "Anthropologists and Other Friends" in *Custer Died For Your Sins* inspired Biolsi and Zimmerman's *Indians and Anthropologists*. Sherman Alexie similarly lampoons anthropologists in "Dear John Wayne." Anthropology leads ultimately to what Baudrillard calls "extermination by museumification," the disappearance that comes from being categorized and studied as objects (*Simulacra and Simulation*, 10). One of Vizenor's most commonly cited examples is that of Ishi to whom Owens refers in both of these novels. Owens calls Ishi "the perfect Indian artifact" (*Dark River*, 144; *Bone Game*, 51) and refers to the crusade of Vizenor (referred to as Saint Plumero) to have a courtyard on the Berkeley campus named after Ishi. Further, Cole imagines how an anthropologist might read his cluttered office: "*As you can see, coincidental with this*

October level is a rather obvious decline in the mixedblood's socially acceptable behavioral characteristics. Notice the Mexican beer stains on the unopened envelope, indicative of low survival quotient, intense liminality, possible homophobia" (Owens, *Bone Game*, 17).

66. Owens, *Dark River*, 61.

67. Owens, *Dark River*, 64.

68. Owens, *Dark River*, 206.

69. Owens, *Dark River*, 174.

70. Owens, *Dark River*, 61.

71. Owens, *Dark River*, 63.

72. Owens, *Dark River*, 65.

73. Owens, *Dark River*, 65.

74. Owens, *Dark River*, 88. Jake goes on to ponder, "Had a moment come when the anthropologist became more Indian than the tribe he had started off studying and ended up becoming? Maybe anthropologists were the real Indians, anyway. If the whole idea of Indian was just an invention, then it made sense that an actor hired to play Indians, even if he was a fullblood like Shorty, would have a lot in common with an anthropologist who studies what his own kind had invented. Was everybody just playing some kind of role written for them by somebody else?" (Owens, *Dark River*, 92).

75. Owens, *Bone Game*, 47.

76. Owens, *Mixedblood Messages*, 144.

77. Owens, *Bone Game*, 204.

78. Owens, *Bone Game*, 242.

79. Owens, *Bone Game*, 242.

80. Owens, *Bone Game*, 243.

81. De Certeau, *Everyday Life*, 117.

82. Chris LaLonde makes a similar connection (*Grave Concerns*, 122).

83. Vizenor, *Fugitive Poses*, 1.

84. Owens, *Dark River*, 12.

85. Owens, *Dark River*, 17.

86. De Certeau, *Everyday Life*, xii.

87. Owens, *Bone Game*, 42.

88. Owens, *Dark River*, 26.

89. Owens, *Dark River*, 38.

90. Owens, *Dark River*, 25.

91. Owens, *Dark River*, 30.

92. Owens, *Dark River*, 31.

93. Owens, *Mixedblood Messages*, 154.

94. Owens plays with a contrast between these survivalists and survivance.

95. Owens, *Dark River*, 114.

96. Owens, *Dark River*, 162.

97. LaLonde, *Grave Concerns*, 10–11.

98. De Certeau, *Everyday Life*, xvii.

99. Harper, *Framing the Margins*, 12.

100. Owens, *Dark River*, 167.

101. Ronnow, "Secularizing Mythological Space," 148. It is important to ask what we make of the fact that the tactical agents meet with violent ends. I would first say that, as LaLonde very astutely points out, "Simulations can cause real harm" (*Grave Concerns*, 180). I would also note that Jesse's death is still comic, and his presence continues beyond it. Stroud, however, hitches his wagon to those who want to simulate violence and death, those who long to reproduce what should be entered into only out of necessity. These are characters who are overcome with a desire to be what they are not, and what they want to be is violent. Moreover, death in this story is not literal death (as we see from characters rising from the dead to discuss alternate endings to the novel). Death here is a story about death, which, as retold and as retellable, is never terminal.

102. Owens, *Bone Game*, 33.

103. Owens, *Bone Game*, 37.

104. Owens, *Bone Game*, 91.

105. Owens, *Dark River*, 106.

106. Christie, "Crossing the Frontier," 23.

107. De Certeau, *Everyday Life*, xxi.

108. Christie, "Crossing the Frontier," 19.

109. See LaLonde, *Grave Concerns*; Bernardin, "Moving in Place"; Helstern, *Louis Owens*; Christie, "Crossing the Frontier"; and Ronnow, "Secularizing Mythological Space."

110. Owens, *Bone Game*, 161.

111. Owens, *Bone Game*, 161.

Bibliography

Alexie, Sherman. "Dear John Wayne." In *The Toughest Indian in the World*, 189–208. New York: Atlantic Monthly, 2000.

Baudrillard, Jean. *Simulacra and Simulation*. Translated by Sheila Faria Glaser. Ann Arbor: University of Michigan Press, 1994.

Bernardin, Susan. "Moving in Place: *Dark River* and the 'New' Indian Novel." In *Louis Owens: Literary Reflections on His Life and Work*, edited by Jacquelyn Kilpatrick, 103–18. Norman: University of Oklahoma Press, 2004.

Biolsi, Thomas, and Larry Zimmerman. *Indians and Anthropologists: Vine Deloria, Jr., and the Critique of Anthropology*. Tucson: University of Arizona Press, 1997.

Blaeser, Kimberly M. *Gerald Vizenor: Writing in the Oral Tradition*. Norman: University of Oklahoma Press, 1996.

Caplan, Karen. *Questions of Travel: Postmodern Discourses of Displacement*. Durham NC:

            Duke University Press, 1996.
Christie, Stuart. "Crossing the Frontier: Hollow Men, Modernist Militias, and Mixed-
            blood Mimesis in Louis Owens's *Dark River*." *WAL* 40, no. 1 (2005): 7–31.
Clifford, James. *Routes: Travel and Translation in the Late Twentieth Century*. Cambridge
            MA: Harvard University Press, 1997.
Cook-Lynn, Elizabeth. *Anti-Indianism in Modern America: A Voice from Tatekeya's Earth*.
            Urbana IL: University of Chicago Press, 2001.
de Certeau, Michel. *The Practice of Everyday Life*. Translated by Steven Rendall. Berke-
            ley: University of California Press, 1984.
Deloria, Vine, Jr. *Custer Died for Your Sins: An Indian Manifesto*. Norman: University of
            Oklahoma Press, 1988.
Harper, Phillip Brian. *Framing the Margins: The Social Logic of Postmodern Culture*. Ox-
            ford, UK: Oxford University Press, 1994.
Helstern, Linda Lizut. *Louis Owens*. Western Writers Series 168. Boise: Boise State
            University Press, 2005.
Kaplan, Caren. *Questions of Travel: Postmodern Discourses of Displacement*. Durham NC:
            Duke University Press, 1996.
Kilpatrick, Jacquelyn. Introduction to *Louis Owens: Literary Reflections on His Life and
            Work*, edited by Jacquelyn Kilpatrick, 3–17. Norman: University of Oklaho-
            ma Press, 2004.
LaLonde, Chris. *Grave Concerns, Trickster Turns: The Novels of Louis Owens*. Norman:
            University of Oklahoma Press, 2002.
Lee, A. Robert. "Outside Shadow: A Conversation with Louis Owens." In *Native Amer-
            ican Representations: First Encounters, Distorted Images, and Literary Appropri-
            ations*, edited by Grethchen M. Bataille, 11–25. Lincoln: University of Ne-
            braska Press, 2001.
Mora-Torres, Gregorio, trans. and ed. *Californio Voices: The Oral Memoirs of José
            María Amador and Lorenzo Asisara*. Denton: University of North Texas Press,
            2005.
Owens, Louis. "As If an Indian Were Really an Indian: Native American Voices and
            Postcolonial Theory." In *I Hear The Train: Reflections, Inventions, Refractions*.
            Norman, University of Oklahoma Press, 2001.
———. *Bone Game*. Norman: University of Oklahoma Press, 1996.
———. *Dark River*. Norman: University of Oklahoma Press, 2000.
———. *Mixedblood Messages: Literature, Film, Family, Place*. Norman: University of
            Oklahoma Press, 1998.
———. "The Syllogistic Mixedblood: How Roland Barthes Saved Me from the *indi-
            ans*." In *Mixing Race, Missing Culture: Inter-American Literary Dialogues*, edit-
            ed by Monika Kaup and Debra J. Rosenthal, 227–39. Austin: University of
            Texas Press, 2002.
Ronnow, Gretchen. "Secularizing Mythological Space in Louis Owens's *Dark River*." In

Louis Owens: Literary Reflections on His Life and Work, edited by Jacquelyn Kilpatrick, 139–53. Norman: University of Oklahoma Press, 2004.

Vizenor, Gerald. *Fugitive Poses.* Lincoln: University of Nebraska Press, 1998.

———. *Manifest Manners: Narratives on Postindian Survivance.* Lincoln: University of Nebraska Press, 1994.

———, ed. *Narrative Chance: Postmodern Discourse on Native American Indian Literatures.* Norman: University of Oklahoma Press, 1989.

Vizenor, Gerald, and A. Robert Lee, eds. *Postindian Conversations.* Lincoln: University of Nebraska Press, 1999.

Womack, Craig S. *Red on Red: Native American Literary Separatism.* Minneapolis: University of Minnesota Press, 1999.

13. GHOSTS IN THE GAPS

Diane Glancy's Paradoxes of Survivance

JAMES MACKAY

It puts responsibility on me. — Diane Glancy, *The West Pole*

Diane Glancy is an author whose works could be designed as an exercise to challenge and confound critics of almost every ideological bent. Those who celebrate her work's postmodern, refracted denial of authority must either embrace or confront her born-again evangelical Christianity. Those who would see her as a strong female, indeed feminist, voice must also read her characters' occasional homilies that favor wifely subservience and male superiority.[1] And critics who would analyze her as an uncomplicatedly Native, Indian, Cherokee voice must also deal with her frequently stated distance from her heritage: "I'm also white. I want you to remember that."[2] This chapter, which intends to treat Glancy as something of an emblem of Gerald Vizenor's concept of survivance, also has to begin with such a confrontation.

I intend in this essay to argue that Glancy's work can be taken as a moral challenge to the reader to participate in a continuation of Native America that is both survival and "more than survival, more than endurance or mere response."[3] The confrontation lies in the fact that to do so, my reading must also in intellectual honesty be able to account for passages such as the following: "I need to say here the hardest thing to say. I think the sacred hoop of the Indian nation was broken because it wasn't the sacred hoop of God. It wasn't complete. It left too much to pride and self works. . . . It was broken by the white man with his terrible ways. His repeating rifles and broken treaties. . . . Yet in that imperfect vehicle came news of the light."[4]

To argue that the colonization of America with its attendant thefts and genocides is in some way redeemed by the bringing of the Christian faith to the indigenous people of the Americas or to argue that "the bison is the ark of the covenant for the Indian" and "Christ is confounding to the Jews" is to move into a missionary mode of thought altogether premodern in its Manichean binaries.[5] For Jesus to come to America, the bison had to die, and the sacred hoop had to break. For Christianity to be the Revelation, the Jewish faith must be confounded. It can be understood why Glancy immediately follows these monotheistic sentiments with the comment that "now, this is something that's going to make some people mad." And indeed, Devon Mihesuah has described some of Glancy's thoughts as "shocking."[6]

From my own position as an atheist (and Christian apostate), I cannot deny that I also find Glancy's sentiments troublesome. As a British critic who prefers to celebrate the endless possibilities of multiculturalism and for whom Christianity is at best a shadowy presence haunting the edges of my largely secular immediate society, the evangelical and fundamentalist religion that her Christian texts espouse seems alien, closed in thought, and more associated with the medieval Crusades against the "heretics" of Islam (or certain generals' remarks in the current War on Terror) than with the qualities of imagination and linguistic play so often celebrated in critiques of Native American fiction.[7] As Glancy herself remarks, "Sometimes Natives write books that are different than what readers expect."[8]

It could, however, also be argued that sometimes fundamentalist Christians write books that are different than that which an academic reader might have expected from the foregoing. Most of her texts are fractured in form, voice, or method, and usually all three together. This fracturing can be swiftly illustrated with two brief quotations.

In *Pushing the Bear* (1996):

> The Tennessee Cherokees would vent their anger against them no matter what the leaders and ministers and ᏣᎳᎩᎠᏂᏑᏓ said. Even Reverend Bushyhead preached forgiveness.[9]

And in *Stone Heart* (2004):

It's the ghost horses you
see again.
They take you from the
Shoshoni.
The horses are cutting you
in half.
You cry in a place the men
cannot see.
You see Otter Woman's
hand stretched out to you.[10]

[. . .] killed 4 men 4 women a number of boys, Sah-cah-gar-we-ah o[u]r Indian woman was one of the female prisoners taken at that time; tho' I cannot discover that she shews any immotion of sorrow in recollecting this event, or of joy in being again restored to her native country; if she has enough to eat and a few trinkets to wear I believe she would be perfectly content anywhere.

Glancy, as can be clearly seen here, regularly breaks up her texts with the wildest forms of visual experimentation. The text of the Trail of Tears novel *Pushing the Bear* regularly changes, only for a few words at a time, from the Roman alphabet into the Sequioan syllabary. Although there is in the United States a population of over ten thousand Cherokee speakers, it can be assumed that Glancy is addressing a non-Cherokee audience and that, despite the helpful inclusion of an alphabet, she does not intend this audience to learn the language.[11] Rather, as she puts it in the note following her afterword, "The [Cherokee words] can be viewed as holes in the text so the original can show through."[12] The inclusion of this non-Roman lettering serves to demonstrate that when ᏗᏓᏅᏍᎩ is transliterated (according to *Pushing the Bear*'s alphabet) as "di-da-nv-s-gi," it is *not* the same word, not having an identical feel or look or "sound" in the mind.

The holes become even clearer in *Stone Heart*, in which the text is split down the middle almost throughout, with the internal narrative of Sacajawea (told in the second-person voice and therefore constantly addressed to the reader) on the left and extracts from the journals of Lewis and Clark on the right. As in the extract above, each voice serves in part as a commentary on the other. The teller of Sacajawea's narrative allows us to experience the inner hurt not noticed by those around her and thus carries an implicit critique of the historical document. The diary entry taken from "[Lewis] Sunday July 28th 1805" not only shows the ways in which the sixteen-year-old Native female is viewed by her husband's employer but also carries a suggestion that she may be deliberately concealing what we know to be the rawest of feelings. As with many of Glancy's texts, such as "Oklahoma Land Run," this play with format gives emotional weight to blank spaces on the page, literal holes in the text, emphasizing what is not said by her characters (even in internal dialogue) and placing most power in silence.[13]

There are many other tropes of fragmentation in Glancy's work. Divorce recurs again and again: characters are either divorced (*The Mask Maker*), separating (*The Only Piece of Furniture in the House*), or wondering about separation (*The Man Who Heard the Land*). Her nonfiction works are usually cut up into small fragments, in wildly differing styles (*Claiming Breath*), or mixed genres as with DEATH CRY FOR THE LANGUAGE, which is a play, a poem, and a bilingual experimental text that cannot be read aloud.[14] Asked about this trope in an interview Glancy replied, "I know it is difficult to read, but that awkwardness, that mixing of voice and points of view is important to my writing."[15]

We have in this short examination seen polyvocalism, distrust of historical "truth" (that is, metanarratives), and textual plays to question the reader's prejudices: all classic tropes of postmodern writing and all constants in her work. And here, I believe, we return to the idea of confrontation. The more common Christian evangelical position toward postmodernism is nicely summed up by Pastor Dennis McCallum: "Postmodernism, as it applies to our everyday lives, is the death of truth as we know it."[16] By the time one reaches the end of McCallum's major collection of essays, unimprovably entitled *The Death of Truth: What's Wrong with Multiculturalism, the Rejection of Reason and the New Postmodern Diversity* (1996), it is obvious that the only "truth" to which he is referring is the divine truth of the Bible. As he states in the chapter "Evangelic Imperatives," "The object of our faith is our real and truthful God. Without truth, Christianity itself will vanish."[17]

McCallum finds himself (possibly for the only time) in agreement with Marxist critic Terry Eagleton, who states in *After Theory* (2004) that "fundamentalism is a textual affair. It is an attempt to render our discourse valid by backing it with the gold standard of the Word of words. . . . It means adhering strictly to the script. It is a fear of the unscripted, improvised or indeterminate, as well as a horror of excess and ambiguity. . . . [*Footnote:*] Fundamentalism . . . also involves a strict adherence to traditional doctrines . . . a commitment to what are taken to be the unchanging fundamental beliefs.... But literalness of interpretation is of its essence."[18]

As we have seen, Glancy's project, which is carried out across and dissolves the boundaries between novel, poetry, spiritual meditation, autobiography, and historical romance, is far from the version of biblical foundationalism on which both apologetic minister and semiotic critic can agree. Indeed, it would not seem much of an exaggeration to say that she is in love with the unscripted, improvised, and especially the indeterminate.

Although Glancy does not at any point lend absolute authority to an un- or anti-Christian narrator, her employment of traditional Native voices within a polyvocal text nevertheless ensures that such voices are regularly heard, particularly in the historical novels. In The Dance Partner (2004), indeed, she includes long verbatim passages from Natives who were witness to the Ghost Dance phenomenon.[19] As missiologist Frederick Hale points out in his able and well-researched analysis, Pushing the Bear can easily be read as a missionary novel, in that several of the characters undergo conversion experiences, all in the direction of monotheism and away from the animist belief system to which virtually all Native characters subscribe at the novel's opening.[20] But Glancy's purpose in depicting this historical reality (many Cherokee did indeed convert on the Trail) is clearly not to proselytize for her faith. As Daniel Heath Justice points out in his reading of Glancy as a writer who owes much to the Cherokee Beloved Path philosophy, "Christians are also the objects of distrust and struggle."[21] The "conjurors," or men powerful in the traditional religion, are capable of literally turning themselves into birds or striking smoke from the ground.[22] These are "real" powers that clearly owe nothing to the Christian God. Moreover, it seems unlikely that, after watching so much suffering along the way, many readers will sympathize with the Reverend MacKenzie when he assumes that the number of converts means that "'maybe the trail was worth it.'"[23] In addition to the two possibilities of Christian conversion and animist traditionalism, Justice adds the observation that "there's not always a sharp distinction between being Christian and being traditional."[24] Glancy does not give us a fixed religious message, allowing for at least as many possibilities as she has narrators.

So we have located something that has the shape and feel of a paradox, a tension or contradiction at the heart of Glancy's thought, the terminal fixities of religion yoked together with a fractured style entirely comfortable with indeterminacy. In passing it is worth theorizing (admittedly by way of caricature) that this might explain why Glancy's poetic, challenging and substantial body of work has been so little studied. To indulge in a moment's stereotype: the sort of critic drawn to Native American fiction tends not to like evangelicals, the sort of critic drawn to Christian interpretation tends not to enjoy heterogeneity of meaning, and the sort of critic drawn to postmodern texts could well be suspicious of the essentialism required for texts dependent on either the myth of ethnicity or the myths of religion. Glancy is quite possibly sui generis in bringing together such opposed strands of thought, faith, and method. But if this is a contradiction, it is far from being the only one. Glancy seems, like the Red Queen, entirely capable of believing in "six impossible things before breakfast," or at least of producing texts that hold contradictions in suspension without resolution.[25]

The best example with which to illustrate this characteristic occurs in Glancy's 2001 "green novel," *The Man Who Heard the Land* (2001). Here the eponymous protagonist, who is anonymous and who is always referred to as "the man who heard the land," is a deeply religious Christian, who remembers his father standing over him as a child when he worked on a science project "so he didn't violate the principles of God in the Bible."[26] At the novel's start the man who heard the land is an assistant lecturer in literature, specializing in ecocriticism. Having been told that he will need publications to gain tenure, he begins researching the nature of time. It is impossible to give a more accurate précis of the intended topic: the actual sentences quoted are hazy in the extreme, and the project remains nebulously vague until its eventual abandonment.

What he reads in his research flatly contradicts "the principles of God." The universe is billions of years old, not six thousand. Man evolved from animals rather than being created from a rib. Black holes open up the possibility of baby universes.[27] Of course, the multiple contradictions between scientific observation and biblical history are in reality an old problem for persons of faith, pre-dating Darwin, Galileo, or even Copernicus. But the man who heard the land does not choose either the easy path of faith (that is, "the scientists must be wrong because the Bible is Truth and cannot be wrong") or the easy path of Enlightenment-style rationality (that is, "the Bible must be wrong because there is physical evidence that it is wrong"). And Glancy's choice to have her character deal mainly with physics means that the "third way" in the evolution argument supposedly exemplified by the Discovery Institute's "Intelligent Design" theory (that is, "the scientific evidence can be made to fit with our creation stories") is also unavailable.

Instead, the man who heard the land attempts an impossibility — believing simultaneously and without contradiction in the truth of biblical and universal time: "Were there millions of years of history on earth? Was there another history before his father's six-thousand-year history since Adam? Were there several creations of the world? . . . Had dinosaurs walked with an earlier version of man? . . . How could dinosaurs and millions of years of history fit into the six thousand years since Adam? There had to be some explanation. . . . He would invent time that was shorter than it seemed."[28] Rather than choose between mutually contradictory concepts, Glancy's character chooses to embrace paradox, to posit "a time shorter than itself." An impossible equation, "six thousand *is equal to* one billion," $6,000x = 1,000,000,000x$, which can seemingly only be expressed in questions. Interestingly, Glancy gives him a third possibility, that of cyclical or repetitive time (repetition-with-difference), which strongly resembles the idea of a pan-Indian belief in cyclical time put forward repeatedly by Vine Deloria Jr.[29] Still, this is in no way privileged over the previous two possibilities: $6000x = 1,000,000,000x = 0$ (infinity): contiguous, overlapping, simultaneous models of space/time, forming a mystical double paradox.

It is not just large-scale paradoxical formulations with which the reader has to deal: single sentence contradictory formulations also form a characteristic stylistic motif throughout Glancy's writing. A few examples, each from a different text, should suffice:

> The closer she reached, the farther away she got.
>
> This is not what was but moves between the was & will & is always.
>
> Everywhere is the center of the universe. . . . Space filling with itself.
>
> They had to get. into his head to keep his thoughts. on earth.
>
> You have to understand an Indian / To see he isn't there.[30]

Of course, the last of these examples brings us back to what is probably the principle contradiction throughout the remarkably consistent work of this complex author: that of mixed and contradictory cultural heritages. Glancy's heroes are frequently mixed-bloods who are distanced from or unaware of Native culture, the historical trilogy being an obvious exception. The man who heard the land, for example, is aware of possible Native ancestry, but he does not know from which tribe he might be descended. As with John Smith in Sherman Alexie's *Indian Killer* (1996), the man who heard the land is adopted and in the act of adoption is absolutely cut off from his heritage. Indeed, it is only a theory that he has Native blood at all: "An Indian mother, possibly, as best they could guess. She left him. At the church."[31] However, unlike Smith, whose white adopted mother "bought all the children's books about Indians and read them aloud to John," Glancy's hero is brought up by his adoptive parents solely in a white, fundamentalist Christian tradition, and when he encounters Indian students, he does not "feel any particular kinship with them."[32]

Similarly the near-silent eponymous heroine of *Flutie* (1998) may experience dreams or visions of "the ghost tribe that was near the pond."[33] And she may also be told by her father about "our Indian people," but the tribe from which her great- (or possibly great-great-) grandfather came is at no point explicitly named.[34] This last is significant particularly because, asked in general about the autobiographical nature of her work, Glancy replied, "*Flutie* is personal. That is another experience that came from my years in Oklahoma, though I didn't live in Vini — but her shyness and longing for her father to tell her more of their heritage is the same."[35] And given the autobiographical elements and precise place names, this absence of a name, indeed of any tribal signifier other than the generic racial epithet "Indian," cannot be considered as anything other than a deliberate omission. The narrative makes repeated reference to the ancient Greek myth of Philomela, who was raped and had her tongue cut out, and there is a clear analogy being drawn between this physical mutilation into silence and the willed absence — willed by her father and grandfather — of one side of Flutie's heritage.

The obvious next question that might be asked is whether Flutie, Edith from *The Mask Maker* (2002), or the man who heard the land should really be considered within the context of Native or mixed-blood characters at all. Clearly they do not belong to a specific tribal background. Equally, they are not currently involved in either a tribal or pan-Indian scene: indeed, isolation, loneliness, and "an insecurity of self" are distinguishing features of much of Glancy's fiction.[36] Even if one were tempted by the sort of potentially racist and comprehensively disproved racial "science" that holds that behavior and cultural traits are genetically heritable, it would then be necessary to deal with that deliberate extra distancing wherein the man who heard the land cannot be sure of his ancestry or where it is explicitly noted that Flutie has no documentation to prove what her father tells her.[37] Glancy works extremely hard to ensure that all her protagonists (obviously excluding those in her historical fictions) walk a line at the very whitest edge of mixed-blood/white identity. This effort is why it is significant that all three novels end with their main characters gaining a new understanding of the world around them and in which Indianness plays a central role.

All of this discussion is particularly crucial, of course, in the context of a Christian author who states that, as we saw at the start of this chapter, Native religions, customs, and folkways are things of the past, dead, gone, replaced by the "Christ light" without which "all other forms of light are darkness."[38] The paradox keeps recurring: why should a world this dead matter? This is, of course, an atheistic question at heart. For a Christian there are states of being that are other than the simple binary of alive or dead: indeed, ghost worlds, unnatural life, and permeable boundaries of death can be said to lie at the very heart of the religion (heaven, the Virgin Birth, and the Resurrection). Glancy, accordingly, employs the figure of the ghost or incorporeal being many times in her fiction. Flutie sees ghost tribes. The characters of *Fuller Man* are surrounded at all times by fluttering angels.[39] *The Dance Partner* includes spirit hitchhikers and Seventh Cavalry ghosts and is in its entirety a meditation on the Ghost Dance religion. When asked about the contradiction between Christianity triumphant and a continuous Indian heritage, Diane Glancy replies, "The old world is gone. But the *ghost* of it *is still here*" (emphases added). Despite the slightly gnomic nature of this remark, it adds weight to my contention that, to seek Glancy's purpose, I must now move away from close reading to examine a philosophy of ghosts.

Jacques Derrida muses in *Specters of Marx* (2006) on the significance of the ghostly, and it is easy to see that attraction that the notion of a spectral

plane between life and death might hold for the philosopher of *différance*. Indeed, there is a surprisingly precise description of why ghosts matter in the
"Exordium":

> *It is necessary to speak* of the *ghost, indeed to the ghost and* with *it,*
> *from the moment that no ethics, no politics, whether revolutionary or*
> *not, seems possible and thinkable and* just *that does not recognize in*
> *its principle the respect for others who are no longer or for those others*
> *who are not yet . . . presently living, whether they are already dead or*
> *not yet born. . . . Without this* non-contemporaneity with itself of
> the living present *. . . without this responsibility and this respect for*
> *justice concerning those who* are not there, *of those who are no longer*
> *. . . what sense would there be to ask the question "where?" "where to-*
> *morrow?" "whither?"*[40]

Robert Eaglestone glosses this "obsession with spectres . . . ghosts, ashes,
spirits" as being part of what he labels "the philosophy of cinders": a reading that takes as its starting point the trauma of the Holocaust. Bringing out
the significance of Derrida's remark that "the thought of the incineration of
the holocaust, of cinders, runs through all my texts" demonstrates that Der-
rida/deconstruction is always already concerned with a primary insight, an
understanding of the limits of philosophy to incorporate events such as the
Holocaust while acknowledging that such events cannot be ignored.[41] This
idea is summed up nicely by Herman Rapaport as "the idea that something
always survives nonsurvival . . . something is always lost in survival."[42] For
Derrida the cinders of the incinerated bodies of Holocaust victims provide
a metaphor for this double movement of non/survival, an ineradicable trace
of eradication. Eaglestone convincingly argues that the ghost is for Derrida another word for "trace," in its turn another word for "ash" — something
that in its presence demonstrates the absence of its being *and yet* in its very
absence calls out for justice. Most importantly for my argument here, Eaglestone argues that "the trace is the appearance of the exterior that is unquan-
tifiable or unnamable by philosophy . . . the other appearing before (and so
outside) reasoned thinking." Derrida and Ferraria go further in *A Taste for the
Secret* (2001), saying that "the trace . . . is introduced to mark the limits of
the linguistic turn," in other words that it is the trace in language precisely
of the extralinguistic.[43]

In this primary case Derrida may be concerned with the six million victims of industrialized slaughter as an obscenity, a slaughter with which philosophy cannot engage directly through reasoned thought and in the face of which all textual representation falls silent, falls apart. Yet it is clear from the long passage from *Specters of Marx* above that he does not see the European Holocaust as a unique event in this regard: indeed, how could he, speaking as he is of Marxism so soon after the collapse of the USSR and subsequent exposure of the atrocities of Stalinism? The universal "respect for justice concerning *those who are not there*," the watching (spectating) specters of the disappeared or incinerated, is an ethical imperative that can be driven by the dead of Armenia, Bosnia, Rwanda, Darfur, or, of most immediate importance here, by the near-destruction of the indigenous peoples of the Americas.

To invoke (non)being, cinders, and the trace in the context of a mixed-blood author will inevitably lead us to Gerald Vizenor, theorist of *indian* presence and absence whose theoretical writings acknowledge an occasional debt to Derrida's thought. In his theoretical works Vizenor makes play with concepts of the trace, but typically supplements and supplants it with a natural metaphor and an Anishinaabe philosophy of language: "The trace is a nickname that leaves a presence in literature. The shadows are the silence in heard stories, the silence that bears a referent of tribal memories and experience. . . . The word *agawaatese* is heard in the oral stories of the *anishinaabe*. . . . The word hears silence and shadows, and could mean a shadow, or casts a shadow. The sense of *agawaatese* is that the shadows are animate entities. The shadow is the unsaid presence in names, the memories in silence, and the imagination of tribal experiences."[44]

It hardly seems contentious to suggest that the shadow, like ash, like cinders, like *différance*, like the trace, represents the unsayable, the unwritable, and thus the extralinguistic. There is no single Holocaust at the back of Vizenor's thought in the sense of a one-time act of industrialized mass slaughter. Instead, there are the uncountable genocides of five centuries of colonial oppression, the erasure of human lives on an unknowable scale. Like Derrida, Vizenor uses this horror as the basis for a deconstruction, a relimning not of history — it is easy to condemn other people's great-grandparents — but of present-day casual, systemic, and unconscious racisms.

As with Derrida, however, the centrality of this act of deletion is sometimes masked by an unwillingness to discuss the event itself. Derrida observes, "Auschwitz has obsessed everything that I am able to think, a fact that is not especially original. Least of all does it prove I have ever had anything original or certain to say about it."[45] Similarly, Vizenor's theoretical works do not often touch directly on the historical mass murders, though when they do, as when he discusses Charles Eastman's witnessing of Wounded Knee, the language is clinically direct ("massacre," "horror," and "crime"). Glancy is equally direct in depicting the historical murders: "We saw the white men killing and killing."[46] Through her engagement with the historical novel (rare among Native writers), she brings herself up against this history of violence more often than Vizenor, whose works, in keeping with his declaration that "the tragic wisdom of [native] survivance has been converted by many academics to an aesthetic victimry," generally avoid a concentration on the terminal fixity of deaths in favor of a concentration on the survivance of the living.[47]

Vizenor's theory is aimed at image makers, museum curators, fakes, anthropologists, and romanticizers (of all genetic heritages) who would seek to *historicize* the Indian, a term I take from his fictional manifesto in *Trickster of Liberty* (1988): "The trick, in seven words, is to *elude historicism, racial representation, and remain historical.*"[48] Here "historicism" must be read as an active process, a defining of Indianness that makes the Native a museum case spectacle. Vizenor proposes the shadow, the "unseen presence," as an extralinguistic *haunting* of the American narrative, a specter of an original presence that cannot be captured in words ("memories in silence") but that, like Derrida's specters (like the cinders of Auschwitz), means that the reader is always conscious of "this responsibility and this respect for justice concerning *those who are not there.*" Derrida's imagery situates him in history as the nonobservant Jew living in the shadow of the Shoah. Vizenor's also marks the peculiar horror of the American genocide, a genocide that once sought to incinerate the person of the Indian, attempted to kill "the Indian in them," and then re-created Native cultures as "inventions," hobbies for schoolchildren, sports mascots, and the sources of anthropological theory with fixed or invented customs and habits.[49] This fixity is the reason that, throughout the long opening chapter of *Manifest Manners* (1994) with its constant refrain of "this is not an Indian," there is and can be no moment of "this *is* an Indian." The tribal and especially the pantribal reality is for Vizenor a quality inherently outside language. The *written* English text in Vizenorean theory thus becomes a trace that attests to the absence of a precontact, pregenocide tribal presence but at the same time calls for the imaginative re-creation of such a presence ("imagination of tribal experiences").

Glancy similarly stages a spectral resurrection of the "old world" that is gone, although "the ghost of it is still here," in the service of an ethics of reading. Amy J. Elias, in her excellent reading of Glancy, argues, "The ideology of *Pushing the Bear* is not located in a . . . unified alternative text of Cherokee national . . . identity beneath or behind the fragmented phenomenal text."[50] The crucial word here is, naturally, "unified": the text is limned with a possibility of a "Cherokee identity" that is not the sort of static "Tradition" Terry Eagleton glimpses below *The Waste Land* and therefore does not form a stable alternative text but is rather something ungraspable, extralinguistic, "fluid, historical, and inclusive."[51]

Vizenor adopts the word *survivance*, which is the French for "survival" and has a prehistory in English as an eighteenth-century alternative form of the same (see the *Oxford English Dictionary*), but he makes a radical adaptation to its meaning, using the word as a figure for precisely the trace of presence we have observed above. Survival is textual, a matter of statistics and laws: so many members of such-and-such a tribe commanding so much terrain with so much natural resources under such-and-such laws despite such-and-such attempts at destruction by state and federal government. By contrast, "survivance, in the sense of native survivance, is more than survival, more than endurance or mere response; the stories of survivance are an active presence."[52] Survivance is a haunting of the text that alters survival, the passive process, turning it into an imaginative act wherein the reader must imagine the fluid, the unimaginable, Native ghost. Similarly we have seen in Glancy the haunting through ᏗᎪᏫᏍᏗᎥ, a figure for holes in the text "so the original can show through," and the crucial emptiness that literally runs through the middle of each page of *Stone Heart*.

It seems that in Glancy, far from the "Death of the Native" I suggested earlier, we have a repeated staging throughout her novels and essays of the "Death *and Return* of the Native," wherein the author creates a space for the unimaginable dead to haunt the present-day text, a gesture of survivance that, just as in Vizenor's theory, gives an ethical impulse to her work. This aspect of Glancy's work explains why the characters as close to the edges of Indianness as possible can gain understanding of the world through understanding or confronting their Native heritage: it is an effect of a survivance that is *more* than survival.

I would suggest that the real ethical interest of this move is in its inclusivity. In American censuses of the past three decades, the number of people listing themselves as part-Native American has been growing almost exponentially.[53] Undoubtedly the "wannabe factor" is a major factor in this growth, but it also reflects a truth that as the generations continue, indigenous peoples' genes will spread to virtually every member of the American population.[54] Miscegenation far from being "wrong" or in any way negative is an inherent part of biological existence. Indeed, in that it predates all racial identities and given that races are not species, it does not, literally speaking, exist. Glancy's method of suggesting an Indianness present in even the most marginally Indian of her characters resembles Derrida's constant presence of Holocaust cinders and Vizenor's shadows in carrying with it an ethics, a responsibility to think with the American genocides constantly in mind.

Rather than engage in destructive politics of who is or is not an Indian, Glancy's philosophy carries a moral charge that would apply to anyone who chooses to recognize their Indian heritage, whether genetic or ghostly.[55] The man who heard the land, for example, may not start with much empathy for his Native students, but he finishes by realizing that part of the voice of the land is the sorrow and anger of Indian children forced into boarding schools and into English, on the very site of the university where he now works and teaches. The realization finishes with the words "in recognition of the past, and a conscious commitment to the present."[56] As Kimberly Blaeser points out, Glancy's "theoretical stance . . . involves the supraliterary intentions of writing and a belief in the power of words."[57] The man who heard the land's epiphany stands for a moral imperative to act with consciousness of the American colonial past that bears upon every reader.

This position does not seem so far from the ethical stance of Elizabeth Cook-Lynn's "call for the writer to be encouraged toward conscience in his work" or even Devon Mihesuah's injunction to "focus on the importance of traditions, sovereignty rights, and the tribes as a whole instead of the continually repeated themes of alienation and individualism," for all that these

thinkers are often seen as the opposite end of an imaginary scale from Vizenorean theorizing.[58] Combining the ethical imperative of remembrance with
a poetry and experimental prose that focuses on silences, gaps, and awkward
breaks also brings to mind Jace Weaver's critique of hybridity. Weaver argues
that a criticism that seeks "to press everyone into a hybrid or mixed-blood
mold is to consummate finally the as yet uncompleted act of colonialism."[59]
In avoiding the smoothness of a universal model and by placing the ethical
burden on the reader through gaps in the text, Glancy, though not obviously concerned with the same nationalistic sentiments as these critics, nevertheless similarly takes aim at the narrative of colonization.

It would seem that my starting image of Glancy as an emblem of survivance indeed holds water. In conclusion, however, I would like to return to the
starting question of this chapter: how can we create a unified theory of Glancy that could accommodate the closed sentiments of religion and the open
plays of survivance?

To begin an answer, I would like to quote at length from the interview I carried out with Glancy in July 2006:

> **Mackay:** I wanted to ask about your faith. Postmodernism is usu-
> ally taken as challenging the sanctity of the written word,
> and many people, both authors and theologians
> (particularly evangelical ones), have interpreted this as
> a relativist act, in some ways being an attack on the au-
> thority of the Bible. With this in mind, I was wondering
> why you've chosen to work so much in a post-modern
> style in your fiction?
>
> **Glancy:** To me, postmodernism strengthens the Bible. It is 66
> separate books written by many different writers over
> a long period of time. Yet it holds together (for me anyway,
> as I am an evangelistic Christian). There also are denom-
> inations and many divisions within those denominations.
> I belong to a Bible study group of people in the same
> church, and we have many different interpretations and
> disagreements about scripture, and we're supposed
> to be alike. I think the Bible is a living, fluid, composite

> that has stretched across every incident of my long life.
> I don't find too much set in cement in scripture except
> that Jesus is the way, the truth, the life; no one comes
> to the Father but by him. And not everyone agrees with
> that.

Pausing briefly to note that Glancy's Bible study group must be an event rather less stultifying than those of my childhood, I would like to offer a couple of observations on the theology that she here displays. First, it can be seen that she treats of the Bible as being written by (imperfect) humans from very different historical backgrounds and of its being a book in which nothing is set in cement. (This contrasts with McCallum's belief that "the Bible is fundamentally understandable."[60]) Second, the only concrete teaching, the only nonnegotiable that she here offers, is the mystical, personal message of Christ's revelation, and indeed, the semiautobiographical *Fuller Man* records just such a Gnostic moment of personal revelation.[61] And this stance reflects the fundamental morality that we have already observed at work within her haunted texts: one that does not follow the rigid structure of *x action* = *y response* but instead relies on an extratextual, extralinguistic ethics that retains the emphasis on the reader to make up his or her own mind. The Bible is fluid, and interpretation and disagreement are positives: Christ is outside the text, atextual, understandable only through revelation.

This fits in with the mystical, apophatic tradition of negative theology, the *Via Negativa*, an ancient Christian philosophy dating back at least as far as Pseudo Dionysus, that holds that God being perfect is beyond description and therefore no positive statements can be made concerning his nature. To say that God is "good" would be to measure a divine being by a human yardstick that is inherently fallible, whereas to say that God is "not evil" is to measure only that which is not God and which can therefore be defined by imperfect humans.[62] Apophatic tradition contrasts with a cataphatic tradition we may here take to be represented by Dennis McCallum ("God is explicit: He wants us to guard our children from drowning"), who holds that God is knowable through the divine word of the Bible.[63]

John D. Caputo in *The Prayers and Tears of Jacques Derrida* (1997) considers Derrida as owing a debt to the *Via Negativa* in his explorations of the text beyond text. Derrida's motivating force, which is justice, is beyond the text and therefore not a question of laws or $x + x = y$ ethics but rather of an unknowable force that impels the text from outside the text and in doing so impels the reader to action. For Caputo "what is at issue [in Derrida] is not a cognitive delineation of some . . . *causa prima*, not some being or essence marked off by certain predicative traits, but rather something that has to do with suffering and justice."[64] This is precisely the field where cinders and survivance come together: the impulse, the particular holocaust does not matter; what matters is always and only justice, acting rightly, not according to the rules of religion but according to a force beyond linguistic capture.

Neither Vizenor nor Derrida is normally spoken of as a mystic, but what else can we label extratextual shadows and traces if not precisely the language of mysticism? This, too, is the field in which Glancy's mystical equation ($6000x = 1,000,000,000x = 0$) can be solved by a God beyond laws, words, and logic, a God that haunts her texts just as surely as they are haunted by the victims of American genocides and cultural imperialism. This aspect of her work also provides an explanation for the way her texts are so comfortable with the ever-proliferating contradictions we observed at every level of the text — such contradictions can be resolved by the imaginative understanding of the reader and by appeal to the space outside the text. And whether one calls such a nonpresent, nonembodied, nonexistent resolution to paradox and call to justice "God," "*différance*," or "the shadow of a bear" belongs, I would argue, rather more to the how-many-angels school of philosophy than to purposeful critical discourse. As with Vizenor and Derrida and as with her church group's "many different interpretations," the question is not one of rigid ethical rules but of imperatives. Glancy ultimately puts forward fragments and haunted texts that can only be unified through a nontextual Presence, with a call to justice buried within them for the reader to discover and act upon.

Notes
1. For example, see Glancy, *Only Piece of Furniture*, 122–23.
2. Glancy, *Firesticks*, 11.
3. Vizenor, *Fugitive Poses*, 15.
4. Glancy, *Claiming Breath*, 97–98.
5. Glancy, *Cold-and-Hunger Dance*, 41.
6. Mihesuah, "Finding Empowerment," 98.

7. On the term "Christian texts," *Only Piece of Furniture* (1996) and *Fuller Man* (1999) contain virtually no Native referents and are clearly intended as belonging to a white Christian discourse (despite *Fuller Man*'s cover image from Native artist Fr. John B. Giuliani). The temporary, wholly artificial boundary between "Native" and "Christian" texts that I am suggesting here is not, of course, to oppose the two (Christianity being a major religion among Native peoples today) but merely to suggest that it is reductive to insist that ethnic minority authors must always and only be read through the prism of their ethnicity if their texts do not suggest such a reading.

8. Andrews, "Conversation," 645.

9. Glancy, *Pushing the Bear*, 223. The TrueType Cherokee font, as encoded by Tonia Williams and designed by Dr. Gloria Sly, Anna Huckaby, and Lisa LaRue of the Cherokee Nation Cultural Resource Center, is available as freeware from the Cherokee Nation Web site at http://www.cherokee.org/Culture/Downloads/4/Default.aspx.

10. Glancy, *Stone Heart*, 66.

11. "The Cherokee language ᏣᎳᎩ is spoken by approximately 10,000 people in the Cherokee Nation, as well as speakers in the homelands (of the Eastern Band of Cherokee)" (see the Cherokee Nation Web site at http://www.cherokee.org/home.aspx ?section=culture&culture=language). Arnold Krupat has discovered several possible infelicities in Glancy's written Cherokee that suggest this should not be read as a bilingual text ("Representing Cherokee Dispossession," 32–34).

12. Glancy, *Pushing the Bear*, 239.

13. Glancy, *Relief of America*, 23–29.

14. Glancy, *Lone Dog's Winter Count*, 46–55.

15. Diane Glancy, e-mail interview with author, July 2006.

16. McCallum, *Death of Truth*, 14.

17. McCallum, *Death of Truth*, 249.

18. Eagleton, *After Theory*, 202. Eagleton's analysis implies a continuity between Islamic and Christian fundamentalism and privileges oral over textual religion. Unfortunately, although his work on Christian fundamentalism is constructive, his analysis of Islamic terrorism contains unpardonable errors, for instance assuming that suicide bombers are ill-educated and poor when the opposite is much more likely to be the case.

19. These passages are in their turn almost exclusively extracted from various texts by James Mooney. For the list of sources, see Glancy, *Dance Partner*, 113–14.

20. Hale, "Cherokee Traditional Religion and Christianity," 1.

21. Justice, *Our Fire Survives the Storm*, 201.

22. Glancy, *Pushing the Bear*, 216–17.

23. Glancy, *Pushing the Bear*, 212.

24. Glancy, *Pushing the Bear*, 202.

25. Carroll, *Through the Looking-Glass*, 210.

26. Glancy, *Man Who Heard*, 77.

27. Stephen Hawking's *Black Holes and Baby Universes* (1993), a popular science book, is the title quoted in the text (Glancy, *Man Who Heard*, 80).

28. Glancy, *Man Who Heard*, 121–22.

29. For example, see Deloria, *Evolution, Creationism and Other Modern Myths*, 210–11, and Deloria, *God Is Red*, 71.

30. These quotations are taken from the following Glancy works, respectively: *Mask Maker*, 135; *Claiming Breath*, 64; *Firesticks*, 46; "Landscape Painting," 207; and *Lone Dog*, 65.

31. Glancy, *Man Who Heard*, 6.

32. Alexie, *Indian Killer*, 12; and Glancy, *Man Who Heard*, 48.

33. Glancy, *Flutie*, 78.

34. See Glancy, *Flutie*, 59.

35. Glancy interview, July 2006.

36. Justice, *Our Fire Survives the Storm*, 196.

37. Atam Vetta and Daniel Courgeau provide a refutation of this sort of genetic determinism: "Heritability analysis of behaviour genetics rests on three legs: (1) the nineteenth century nature-nurture ideas of Galton, (2) Fisher's (1918) genetics and (3) Jinks and Fulker (1970). If one accepts the concept of evolution by adaptation, then many of our behavioural traits evolved when our ancestors tried desperately to adapt to the environment. That environment is gone. Therefore, Galton's idea of separation of nature and nurture effects is not realistic. . . . Fisher's genetics predates our understanding of chromosomal inheritance. His basic assumption that genes segregate independently is not correct because all genes on a chromosome segregate together. Moreover, his kinship correlation formulae are wrong (Vetta 1976a). Vetta also pointed out the algebraic errors in Jinks and Fulker (1970). Thus, none of the legs would support anything" ("Demographic Behaviour and Behaviour Genetics," 424). The assumptions that underpin the conflation of genetic inheritance (such as skin color) with cultural attributes are the same assumptions that underlie intelligence studies such as Richard J. Herrnstein and Charles Murray's *The Bell Curve* (1994). For a comprehensive analysis of the errors of this study and of the way that its racialist assumptions sustain social policies with racist effects, see Graves, *Emperor's New Clothes*, 157–72. For a general account of why popular science journalism is erroneous in its frequent use of the phrase "a gene for," see Sapolsky, "A Gene for Nothing."

38. Glancy, *Cold-and-Hunger Dance*, 81.

39. In our 2006 interview I asked Glancy whether these angels (which despite being constantly visible take no part in the action of the novel) should be seen as objectively present. She replied, "I think those are real angels there. Helpers that come to help."

40. Derrida, *Specters of Marx*, xviii.

41. Eaglestone, "Derrida and the Holocaust," 27.

42. Rapaport, *Later Derrida*, 62.

43. Eaglestone, "Derrida and the Holocaust," 31; and Derrida and Ferraria, *Taste for the Secret*, 76.

44. Vizenor, *Manifest Manners*, 72–73.

45. Eaglestone, "Derrida and the Holocaust," 27.

46. Glancy, *Dance Partner*, 48.

47. Vizenor, *Fugitive Poses*, 21. In *Fugitive Poses* Vizenor declares, "Natives have endured centuries of separation, proscription, removal by treaties and *disappearance*" (21). The italicized use of *disappearance* points to both the colonial trope of the vanishing Indian and the "disappearance" (used as a verb) of political opponents, a usage that serves to keep a contemporary focus rather than a return to a tragic past.

48. Vizenor, *Trickster of Liberty*, xi; Vizenor's italics.

49. Vizenor, *Manifest Manners*, 55.

50. Elias, "Fragments That Rune up the Shores," 205.

51. Elias, "Fragments That Rune up the Shores," 204.

52. Vizenor, *Fugitive Poses*, 15.

53. "In the 2000 Census . . . 4.1 million Americans said they were at least partly Native American, more than double the 1990 figure. Both alone and in combination with another race, American Indian population numbers are soaring far beyond anything that can be explained by birthrate" (Morello, "Census Restores Indian Roots").

54. See Graves, *Emperor's New Clothes*, appendix A.

55. For a fantastic example of exclusionary debate, see Pulitano, "Telling Stories," 43:

> **WYR:** Diane is controversial because she has just discovered her Native heritage. She has never claimed her Native heritage before; she had a book of poetry that did not sell, but when she claimed her Native heritage, she became a Native writer and then her stuff started selling.
>
> **EP:** Has she written any plays?
>
> **WYR:** Yes, she's written three plays and now she wants to be considered a Native playwright.

As we have traced in this chapter, Glancy has never made one claim to Nativeness beyond the strict marginal truth ("I was not raised with the culture" [*West Pole*, 29]): Yellow Robe's conflation of her with "fake natives" such as Nasdijj/Tim Barrus is deeply unfair. Interviewing Glancy on May 3, 2007, I read her Yellow Robe's comments. Her response was, "It does seem a little mean-spirited. I started getting published in the early '80s. My first book was *Offerings* and then *One Age in a Dream*. It was always Native issues, from the very beginning. What book didn't sell? I don't know what he means."

56. Glancy, *Man Who Heard*, 160.

57. Blaeser, "Like 'reeds through the ribs of a basket,'" 564. A broader-based "haun-tology" of Native American identity is outlined by David Murray in "Cultural Sover-eignty and the Hauntology of American Identity," positing it as a third way between the essentialism of nationalist critics and postmodern fluidity.

58. Cook-Lynn, *Anti-Indianism*, 45; and Mihesuah, "Finding Empowerment," 101. Compare Justice, "We're not there yet Kemo Sabe," 260.

59. Weaver, Womack, and Warrior, *American Indian Literary Nationalism*, 21.

60. McCallum, *Death of Truth*, 256.

61. Glancy, *Fuller Man*, 173–76.

62. Caputo offers an excellent anecdote to illustrate the double-bind of nega-tive theology: "As a good friend of mine once said, 'Of God I do not believe we can say a thing, but, on the other hand, as a theologian I have to make a buck'" (*Prayers and Tears*, 1).

63. McCallum, *Death of Truth*, 276.

64. Caputo, *Prayers and Tears*, 337.

Bibliography

Alexie, Sherman. *Indian Killer*. 1996. Reprint, London: Vintage, 1998.

Andrews, Jennifer. "A Conversation with Diane Glancy." *American Indian Quarterly* 26, no. 4 (2002): 645–49.

Blaeser, Kimberly. "Like 'reeds through the ribs of a basket': Native women weaving stories." *American Indian Quarterly* 21, no. 4 (1997): 555–65.

Caputo, John D. *The Prayers and Tears of Jacques Derrida: Religion without Religion*. Bloom-ington: Indiana University Press, 1997.

Carroll, Lewis. *Through the Looking-Glass, and What Alice Found There*. In *Annotated Al-ice*, edited by Martin Gardner, 133–288. London: Penguin, 2000.

Cook-Lynn, Elizabeth. *Anti-Indianism in Modern America: A Voice from Tatekeya's Earth*. Urbana: Illinois University Press, 2001.

Deloria, Vine, Jr. *Evolution, Creationism and Other Modern Myths: A Critical Enquiry*. Golden CO: Fulcrum, 2002.

———. *God Is Red*. Rev. ed. Golden CO: Fulcrum, 1994.

Derrida, Jacques. *Specters of Marx: The State of the Debt, the Work of Mourning and the New International*. Edited by Bernd Magnus and Stephen Cullenberg. Trans-lated by Peggy Kamuf. Oxford, UK: Routledge, 2006.

Derrida, Jacques, and Maurizio Ferraria. *A Taste for the Secret*. Edited by Giacomo Do-nis and David Webb. Translated by Giacomo Donis. London: Polity, 2001.

Eaglestone, Robert. "Derrida and the Holocaust: A Commentary on the Philosophy of Cinders." *Angelaki* 7, no. 2 (2002): 27–38.

Eagleton, Terry. *After Theory*. London: Penguin, 2004.

Elias, Amy J. "Fragments That Rune up the Shores: *Pushing the Bear*, Coyote Aesthet-ics, and Recovered History." *Modern Fiction Studies* 45 (1999): 185–206.

Glancy, Diane. *Claiming Breath*. Lincoln: University of Nebraska Press, 1992.

———. *The Cold-and-Hunger Dance*. Lincoln: University of Nebraska Press, 1998.

———. *The Dance Partner*. East Lansing: Michigan State University Press, 2005.

———. *Firesticks*. Norman: University of Oklahoma Press, 1993.

———. *Flutie*. Wakefield RI: Moyer Bell, 1998.

———. *Fuller Man*. Wakefield RI: Moyer Bell, 1999.

———. "Landscape Painting." In *Two Worlds Walking: Short Stories, Essays and Poetry by Writers with Mixed Heritages*, edited by Diane Glancy and C. W. Truesdale, 207–11. Minneapolis: New Rivers, 1994.

———. *Lone Dog's Winter Count*. Albuquerque: West End, 1991.

———. *The Man Who Heard the Land*. St Paul: Minnesota Historical Society, 2001.

———. *The Mask Maker*. Norman: University of Oklahoma Press, 2002.

———. *The Only Piece of Furniture in the House*. Wakefield RI: Moyer Bell, 1996.

———. *Pushing the Bear*. Orlando: Harcourt, 1996.

———. *The Relief of America*. Chicago: Tia Chucha, 2000.

———. *Rooms: New and Selected Poems*. Cambridge, UK: Salt, 2005.

———. *Stone Heart: A Novel of Sacajawea*. Woodstock NY: Overlook, 2004.

———. *The West Pole*. Minneapolis: University of Minnesota Press, 1997.

Graves, Joseph L., Jr. *The Emperor's New Clothes: Biological Theories of Race at the Millennium*. New Brunswick NJ: Rutgers University Press, 2002.

Hale, Frederick. "The Confrontation of Cherokee Traditional Religion and Christianity in Diane Glancy's *Pushing the Bear*." *Missionalia: The Journal of the South African Missiological Society* 25 (1997), http://www.geocities.com/Missionalia/cherokee.htm (accessed March 14, 2007).

Hawking, Stephen. *Black Holes and Baby Universes*. London: Bantam, 1993.

Herrnstein, Richard J., and Charles Murray. *The Bell Curve: Intelligence and Class Structure in American Life*. New York: Free Press, 1994.

Justice, Daniel Heath. *Our Fire Survives the Storm: A Cherokee Literary History*. Minneapolis: University of Minnesota Press, 2006.

———. "We're not there yet, Kemo Sabe." *American Indian Quarterly* 25, no. 2 (2001): 256–61.

Krupat, Arnold. "Representing Cherokee Dispossession." *Studies in American Indian Literatures*, 2nd ser., 17, no. 1 (2005): 16–41.

McCallum, Dennis. *The Death of Truth: What's Wrong with Multiculturalism, the Rejection of Reason and the New Postmodern Diversity*. Minneapolis: Bethany House, 1996.

Mihesuah, Devon. "Finding Empowerment through Writing and Reading, or Why Am I Doing This? An Unpopular Writer's Comments about the State of American Indian Literary Criticism." *American Indian Quarterly* 28, no. 1 (2004): 97–102.

Morello, Carol. "Census Restores Indian Roots: 4.1 Million Americans Say They're at Least Partly Native American." *San Francisco Chronicle*, April 15, 2001. http://www.sfgate.com/cgi_bin/article.cgi?file=/chronicle/archive/2001/04/1/MN184041.DTL (accessed March 19, 2007).

Murray, David. "Cultural Sovereignty and the Hauntology of American Identity." In *Mirror Writing: (Re-)Constructions of Native American Identity*, edited by Thomas Claviez and Maria Moss, 237–56. Berlin: Galda + Wilch, 2000.

Pulitano, Elvira. "A Conversation with William Yellow Robe." *Studies in American Indian Literatures*, 2nd ser., 10, no. 1 (1998): 19–44.

Rapaport, Herman. *Later Derrida*. London: Routledge, 2003.

Sapolsky, Robert. "A Gene for Nothing." *Discover*, October 1, 1997. http://discovermagazine.com/1997/oct/agenefornothing1242 (accessed March 19, 2007).

Vetta, Atam, and Daniel Courgeau. "Demographic Behaviour and Behaviour Genetics." *Population* 58, nos. 4–5 (2003): 401–28

Vizenor, Gerald. *Fugitive Poses: Native American Scenes of Absence and Presence*. Lincoln: University of Nebraska Press, 1998.

———. *Manifest Manners: Postindian Warriors of Survivance*. Hanover NH: Wesleyan University Press, 1994.

———. *The Trickster of Liberty: Tribal Heirs to a Wild Baronage*. Minneapolis: University of Minnesota Press, 1988.

Vizenor, Gerald, and A. Robert Lee. *Postindian Conversations*. Lincoln: University of Nebraska Press, 1999.

Weaver, Jace, Craig S. Womack, and Robert Warrior. *American Indian Literary Nationalism*. Albuquerque: University of New Mexico Press, 2006.

14. THE NAKED SPOT

A Journey toward Survivance

DIANE GLANCY

> *Showing the naked spot the ball drives through.*
> *A shiver. The coming hour, the windy grass*
> *Under the suns beyond him, these he knew.*
>
> Alan Stephens, *The Death of a Buffalo*

Part 1: A Treatise on Poetry and Rationale

More than any other writer, Gerald Vizenor and his idea of survivance has marked my work. I want to make a journey through the meaning of native poetry and the history of Vizenor's direction for it because writing is how I came to understand the layers of self and its placement between the margins of the worlds. Writing is an act of survivance. It scrapes the edges of a mixed-blood, broken heritage, leaving some of it silent and wrapped in mystery. What is this part-Indian heritage? What is this spirit moving in poetry, the breath of the people? What are the roots of native writing? What are its possibilities? What is there in the eternal springs of language that can be used to present the essence that has been covered over with something like naugahide.

Poetry is dreaming while awake. Poetry is wake-dreaming. It is a derangement of self in an accentuated landscape. It establishes the boundaries of its range. Poetry is rebound. A turn of writing. (Sur)vivance: Sur—a survival outside survival. Vivance—the vitality of it. It takes something outside survival to define it. It is a stepping away from it to look back at the surrounding vibrance.

In Charles Bernstein's *Poetics* he says that "it is only an other that, in the

final instance, constitutes the work, makes it more than a text (test), resur-
rects it from the purgatory of its productions, which is to say its production of self-sameness. Bakhtin puts it very eloquently in a 1970 interview in
Novy mir . . . : 'in order to understand, it is immensely important for the person who understands to be located outside the object of his or her creative
understanding.'"

The Native American has a tough time standing outside his or her plight.
But turning plight to *unplight* is Vizenor's stance—his pose—his *outside
location*.

I begin with my own survival. The roots of it came early. I remember feeling
unwelcome in the world. It was a feeling that began as soon as consciousness.
But there was light. The shadows of the sun through the window or curtains,
the angle of the house to the universe that moved spots of sun between the
slats of a crib. There was the writing of light that I followed with my eyes, my
attention. From it I can say poetry is a visual movement of light.

There is a description of poetry by A. R. Ammons in his introduction to the
1994 *Best American Poetry*: "Language is the medium that carries the inscription, but what is inscribed in poetry is action, not language. The body of the
ice skater is only the means to an inscription on ice. Beautiful as the body may
be, the inscription does not exist for the purpose of the body but of what the
body does, what its doings symbolize. Magnificently great about poetry is
that its action is like other actions. It stands not as an isolated, esoteric activity but as a formal and substantive essentializing of all action."

Poetry is the sealing wax that holds together. It is the outpouring of the sun
on whomever, wherever, whatever it reaches. A window pane. Inside a child of
mixed heritage desperate for the naked spots of light I remember. For me poetry begins in the visual—the movement of light through the action of a curtain, wavering, wafting—a spot of light like a little skater on ice.

I found later that I could be involved with moving spots of light through writing, changing questions, using the trickery of changing genres that remained
based in poetry. It is often where Native Americans begin to write. The poems
are the visages of breath in the struggle for survival. I began writing early in
the pages of books. I continued to write throughout my life. It was survival. I
wrote to know who I was, what I was in this unaccepting world.

I often felt a difference from others. I went to a school where there were no other Indian children except my brother three years behind me or anything like an understanding of mixed heritage. Such a heritage wasn't even realized, much less named.

I continued seeing the changing light, warping and morphing and transgressing. Establishing itself. Unestablishing. Moving to another fragment. Overgrown as the woods I remember in northeastern Oklahoma and northern Arkansas where my father's family had been. All of it juxtaposed with the stark flatland of Kansas where my mother's parents had a farm. This process of poetry I know also is based in land. The light and shadows that cross it.

Robert Pinsky in *The Sound of Poetry* says that "the vocal reality . . . is individual and distinct in ways too subtle for any terminology or system to describe completely." It is the same with poetry's patterns of light. Its individual and distinct patterns of sight are often closer to thought patterns than sound patterns. They are a floating island—a sweep of heavy clouds across a flat terrain, present but not tied down.

I had been looking for it from the beginning: a way to write according to the stance I felt. I found it in the Vizenorian tracks through an early book of his. For the roots, for the historical perspective, I backtrack to *Anishinabe Nagamon* (1965)—from it making notes: "Poetry is a scared *enclavement*. It is pictomyth. It is a long rapids, repetitive, rhythmic, broken. It is a migration trail to the sacred, a volume of words wrapped in a quiver, a map to other, to transformation, the sun reflecting on a shell, a skate blade on ice, all of it—survivance."

Vizenor pokes holes in the identity that others have given to the Indian. He finds the silence preliminary to an understanding of the old essence that waits to be called upon again. It is a term he calls "shadow survivance." In *Manifest Manners* he writes, "The shadow is that sense of intransitive motion to the referent; the silence in memories. Shadows are neither the absence of entities or the burden of conceptual references. The shadows are the prenarrative silence that inherits the words; shadows are the motions that mean the silence, but not the presence or absence of entities. . . . Shadows are honored in memories and the silence of tribal stones."

It seems to me that Vizenor hopes that native writing will be caught in the very act of refuting the identity it has been given, confounding it with myths and old stories, liberating a manifold meaning, presenting oral tradition in written form, using the English language with more elasticity than anyone thought it had, using language to show what it didn't mean to show, and taking the vacuousness of given meaning to bend existing meaning to fit its means. Native writing should be a transporter of the old world until the new world is a gauze behind which the real world moves. All of this is embedded in survivance.

To return to *Anishinabe Nagamon,*

> The sacred migis shell of the anishinabe spirit arose from the east-ern sea and moved along the inland waters guiding the people through the sleeping sun of the woodland to bawitig — the long rapids in the river.
>
> The anishinabe — the original people of the woodland — believe they were given wisdom from the sun reflecting on the sacred shell during the long migration. Five hundred years ago the migis shell appeared in the sun for the last time at moningwanekaning in anishinabe kitchig-ame — the great sea of the anishinabe.
>
> The people measured living through time in the circles on the sun and moon. Trailing the summer shores of kitchigami to the hardwoods and swamps drawing sisibakwat and gathering manomin the anishin-abe returned each winter to moningwankeaning — Madeline Island in Lake Superior.

I too have been to Madeline Island — several times in the summer. Once in the winter — driving two and half miles across a frozen inlet of Lake Superi-or from Bayfield, Wisconsin. I felt the trickster-crossing of that frozen road, only there when ice covers the inlet, back to the sudden settlements in Okla-homa, the ice-fishing houses on Minnesota lakes as soon as they freeze, the boom towns of breath in the cold, which is the Native American meaning of poem (loose translation of the meaning of *Boom Town* and *Rooms: New and Selected Poems*).

Vizenor continues,

> In the seventeenth century voyageurs and the first missionaries of the old world established a Christian fur trading post on moningwaneka-ning near the sacred community of the people. While showing the new world discoverers how to endure the long woodland winters only half

*of the anishinabe survived the first pestilence of the white man — a se-
vere smallpox epidemic.*

*Fulgurant missionaries Latinized the woodland and thundered through
the epistles that the people were only children learning the hymns of
a new civilization. The hymns were peddled like military secrets to the
voyageurs who learned the language of the woodland and enmeshed
the people in the predatory economics of peltry.*

Firearms and intoxicants. The industry of war. These gifts of the European immigrants. But Native American tribes warred before the coming of the
white man. It seems to be inbred.

Vizenor writes further that "the rhythm of the land was broken. . . . Anishinabe orators . . . were colonized and mythologized and alienated from their
woodland life and religion while the voices of the conquerors ran."

The Anishinabe did not have a written history: "the past was a visual memory and oratorical gesture of dreams plating an endless woodland identity
between the conscious and unconscious worlds of the people."

This is the Vizenorian voice of survivance that threads through the body
of Vizenor's own work from the earliest book to the latest collection of his
selected poems, *Almost Ashore*. With images of crows, moose, beaver, fox, otter, kingfisher, bear, he gives tribute to memory in his new work:

> *Blue lights*
> *ancient stones*
> *shattered*
> *on the southern*
> *pacific tracks*
> *far from home.*
>
> (from "Winter Camp")

Vizenor evokes poignancy, then douses it with manifest moteliers and other
city survivors. He tracks native storiers, who "during the great depression inspired survivance in unheated cold water rooms stained by kerosene." He also
pays tribute to freight trains, federal schools, Indian agents, reservation masters, mongrels, and treelines in the "cruel distance in cultural dominance."

This is Vizenor's pose of poetry — this in-between thinking, this relational
thinking, this voice based on sound in the crevices of the rocks, the enduring

rhythms of the roots of the witch tree on Lake Superior, and these visual cords of

> *Window ice*
> *cloud creased*
> *faces change.*
>   (from "Window Ice")

Vizenor writes that "the anishinabe hears music not only in the human voice but in the sounds of animals and trees and ice cracking on the lakes. Anishinabemowin is a language of verbal forms and word images. The spoken feeling of the language is a moving image of tribal woodland life."

In *Anishinabe Nagamon* Vizenor uses pictomyths with his words. They are visual portraitures. They are the sound of the words made visible. They are the wound of the words made visible. Original language has been wounded. It has been *killed* to some extent. But it twines in the arena of dream. It is the *sighting* that marks native poetry.

Vizenor continues with Anishinabe poetry "in sympathy with cosmic rhythms and dream songs." It is the "spontaneous rhythm of breathing."

This native stance was oppositional to the early missionary experience Vizenor writes about in "Shadows at La Pointe," from his book *Shadow Distance*:

> *Reverend Hall and his wife were separated from their culture and families in the East. The two of them seemed to be lost, without shadows, with no humor to throw at the weather. Their isolation turned into a dedication to convert the tribes. Sometimes, we whispered, it was the missionaries who needed to be saved. We lived in a world of comedies, thunderstorms, chances like a flight of passenger pigeons over the lake, and surprises, dreams about whales in a fish barrel. Some of our friends think it is strange to find pale, weak and shadowless, individual church heroes, in the middle of old woodland families. The biblical stories were fun to tell, the old men turned them over in oral tradition.*

I depart from Vizenor in that Christianity has been an underpinning to my life and writing. The Cherokee were evangelized by the Baptists. It is something that has stuck. I have felt connections to native culture in the Bible. In the first chapter of Zechariah, for instance, "I saw at night, a man riding on a red horse and he stood among the myrtle trees that were in the bottom, and behind him were red horses, sorrel and white." Zechariah asks who they are, and the man on the red horse answers that they are sent by the Lord to travel the earth. I used those images in *Designs of the Night Sky*, published by the University of Nebraska in the Native Storiers series. The *novel* is an explanation tale for written language. Patterns for written words came from stars in the night sky. The clusterings are seen as paragraphs in a story. Yet written words remain the lesser light. The greater light is still the sun, the voice. The book itself is written in broken texts as if the scattered sections were small constellations of stars in the night sky.

In *Cherokee Myth and Dance* there is an old Cherokee bear-hunting song:

> *He-e! Hayuya'haniwa, hayuya'haniwa, hayuya'haniwa,*
> *hayuya'haniwa,*
> *Tsistuyi' nechandu' yanu', Tsistuyi' nechandu' yanu — Yoho-o!*

It is the beginning form that makes *poem*. It is action as poetry. It is a call for a meeting place with a bear: in such and such a place I will be; you be there also. The place name could change — wherever the hunt took place. The hunting song was an assurance that a bear will be found during the hunt.

Hunt also works in contemporary poetry. A hunt not for a bear, but for the invariable other way, the inadvertent way, in the betrayal and flash of gorges, valleys, and ravines where poetry stalls until sung forth with the poet's words in parameter, pitch, rhythm, stress, and moving patterns of shadow and light.

In another song from *Cherokee Myth and Dance*, the singer reports,

> *The man was my lover*
> *he is dead*
> *I am lonely*
> *if I could go to him*
> *I would go —*
> *no matter how far.*

This a direct narrative. Sonorous in its tone.

Each tribe has its own rhythms and images and archetypes. Each tribe has its sidereal placement.

Frances Densmore made recordings of the Teton Sioux in her field work:

> *A wolf*
> *I considered myself*
> *but the owls are hooting*
> *and the night*
> *I fear.*

To be understood, the song/poem needs the context of a winter night on the open prairie in a blizzard, the buffalo scarce, the children crying in other teepees, the necessity of food that is not there. Sound carried between the teepees. It passed through the hides of the teepees. An Indian camp was not separate living quarters, but all slept as one.

Contemporary native poetry carries the loss of culture, the loss of a way of life, and the bare spots that annihilation and acculturation left. The rations, the military forts on the natural landscape, the scarcity of game, and the inevitability of being able to do nothing. The poverty, alcoholism, and dark ages. The Indians were led where they didn't want to go. It brings to mind John 21:18: "But when you are old, another will gird you and carry you where you don't want to go." But surrounding all that, native poetry carries the knowledge of silence and shadow outside or beyond the loss, circling back to the essence that does not die or transmute, which is survivance.

Writing is the weapon we bear as we go into the new world we did not want. It reinvents locale. It reshapes loss. Words after all have light. They are the physics of generation and regeneration, taking part of itself to make more of itself. The work of survivance transforms. It is an act of *languaging* time. It retakes the combo of events.

Survivance is formulating survival on one's own terms. It provokes the absence of meaning that is thought to be and shows the undertones of *being* — using a written language to orate what is replaced since it can't be got at otherwise. The trickster of disguise, the trickster-act of survivance, is much like the dance of the ragged, perforated edges of paper torn from a spiral notebook — using the ragged edge as parent to the serrated knowledge of the reinventive spirit of survivance.

This is the poetry that is the underpinning of all the genres I write.

Part 2: Survivance-based Discourse: An Essay on the Essay

The dichotomy that pervades native work is evident in the layers of its narrative. It inhabits contradictory spheres or definitions at once. Or the spheres inhabit the writing. Native work is sedentary and peripatetic. There is a sense of place and migration or the state of movement as place. It is definite yet *unboundaried*. Concrete and abstract. There is a duality in the root of its base, a directory for possibilities, possibilities necessary for survival, for *survivance* with meaning and prevalence — prevailence. Native work knows the *necessaryness* of alignment and imbalance. It is static and kinetic, absent and present. Native work is erased and written in the corporality of letters. The body of language is its written form.

Language is creator as well as trickster that robs meaning. It is a conduit for the other world, and yet it is imbedded in this one. Its variable units are the four directions of trick, disturb, interpret, and realign.

Native work confronts the confrontation it has confronted. Fighting the always plains narrative with the necessary variousness of other tribes.

There is texture, a geology or geography of written language as conduit.

Native writing has redistributed the distributions after conquest. It bypasses now the ear, the main receptacle of story when I read it. What remains of poetry if the voice is removed? Yet the always previous territory of sound is there. The geography of sound waves *ghost* or *spiritize* or *abstract*, the soundless written text.

The brief thief of sleep after the cavalry, the covered wagons, that resulted in a native *dark ages*.

Maker: because you are forever: provide, forgive, deliver.

Native work is tribal yet searching for individualism, unity, and separation after displacement of the outbuildings of language in the sky — stories aligned to the movement of the sky, the moving alphabet of stars. On earth as it is in heaven.

Our bread is the air of the believer. The walker of oppositional worlds — anger and spiritual confrontation or upfrontness, upfrontedness, and the differentiations in subtlety.

Native work provides a *conision* of world views. Or should it be *convision*? Ours and theirs. Ours within ours. Theirs within theirs.

Native work resees the decline of culture, the loss of spoken language from what was before the invasion. After conquestors. Native work is its own conquesting—to explore, to preserve, and to document the unknowing/knowing because its pattern reflects the nature of being.

The fulcrum in the crossroads.

The voice in regalia is its written language.

The telling of the other versions, all versions of events for a composite that history always is. An elastic band pulled over all the folds. A transgraphic change of the world, bringing into perception what is known of the visible world and the other world by its hiddeness in other.

The truth of versions, the versions of truth or truths.

In Native American writing it is the past, the ancestors, and the spirits, real as if they'd never vanished. Native American literature reinvents geographics—landscapes of life that no longer *are* in the present sense. The boundaries are elastic in this world.

There is a tribal-centered aesthetic conspiring a transreservationism, an oral traditional halved on a construction site.

A creviced language caught in its crevices. Influenced by invisible distance. Native writing is a topography of oral thinking morphed into written words.

If ever there was a nonfit. An unfit.

Straddling the outboundaries of the experience and rearrangements and realignment of letters. The outsiders and sideriders. The polyvocalism of the voices speaking an elliptical language.

A spoken *Pocanhontas* haunts us with image over the reality of nography. Why can't *just be* is? Landed from the land that was. A before feet suspended between past and soil.

The question of perception also is raised or the deceptiveness of perception. What do we see when we see? How far can one kick at categories and borders, tearing apart the rules of writing and have it still be writing?

I translate the world into a shape not its own. Feeling the language that is not translatable—translating a world into a language that cannot translate it.

I clause it instead.

Which is better?

In survivance there are the open possibilities of writing after the natives became emigrants into a new form of life. We are the spokesman for the change.

The spoken change. The words that hit the open place and create substance. The words that hit the naked spot and clothe it. Native poetry is the some-thing-that-is-there. The something-that-makes something there.

Part 3: To Understand Survivance

As usual I start from a native perspective: the something that moved there. The peripheral vision. The indirect trail. The evidence enfolded in story. The different voices that move there.

To look into the literature of another, I believe it's important to start with nothing and face the discomfort. To wander for a while. To feel awkward and not at home. But at some point there has to be connection that asks what is happening here? At some point there has to be contact that says, this is what I think it means.

I want to take a creative rather than analytical stand. I don't want to look at native literature through another's theory though that is helpful, an identi-ty in flux, which is a principle formulated by Goethe or Mikhail Bakhtin's work on a dialogue of forces or a world between consciousnesses or his pursuit of different answers to the same questions. Bakhtin also said

> history
> a dialogue about it
> should take into consideration the interpretations and heteroglossia
> the many voices of history.

I am a stranger to what I am. I have an identity in the process of being cre-ated—a theory that is a trampoline on which there is rise/fall/rise.
Or:

He came as an outvoter to speak on withdrawal of power from the coloniz-er. Non-self governing territories with their vernacular and dialect no iden-tity can form. The political founder of colonial status with political proc-lamations, thunderous collapses, lists, catalogues, prosaics, place runners, place names, on and one defined by its amplitude. An island formed estab-lishing a clump of mud on the surface of the water that dried and spread this turtle island, this America on the world. The terrible brightness of identi-ty placed against the land uniformed against intrusion, invasion, words to march and settle themselves on another with souvenirs of the dispossessed.

Verbal correlative became its own while investors take our funds for flames that remain to burn. What is the stillness here—he stops talking a moment to gather his thoughts, the former new colonist but no longer, remythologized, renamed, remapped, the territory of geographies. Locale and locale. The irreconcilable differences left in the margins told together the unit that would by sameness repopulate histories, reconstructed energies, and pull away from separatist forms. And where will we eat afterwards in this cold? This coldness. This political new land. This was ours and now is given against construction of national repoeticization with stories of translocation. I look at him talk but think how the joints of my bones hurt. Colonized by imperialists someone talks beyond what they are given or allowed to stay, but they stay there anyway. The chair in the room upholstered, the elegy of chairs and wallpaper choices, their choirs that stray off tune, the literary works defalsified. I hear the litany of self-deception, a life there, a valiance of aftermaths, mainly subtraction and being occupier of the margin, the very name of our language, a compilation of others pierced here and there, a conglomerate of bushes, sky, clouds. Reconstructed, recused, reexcused. Transmorphed by the colony transcolonized. He wanted me to go because I was the only one with a car. The decolonized loved us they would not overboard they would be grateful we withdrew, or driven maybe.

Part 4: A Creative Survivance

In boarding schools physics our tribes were together until the big bang blew us apart. Afterwards we transmuted in a colder climate, no longer what we were. An atom is a particle with electrons revolving as swallows at evening. Quarks joined in with the ducks flapping their way above the highway. Their strings of webbing forces. Mass and charge. A multiple unification theory. Their big smooth words we heard after our *reduction* were now small turbulent ones. Sometimes I looked into the air and could see the mass of strings moving. After travel I could see dark sparkles in the cold air. It is what we make of dimensions. Ours and yours. There are multiple realities. Subtractions on the blackboard of the boarding school indicated this. Broken treaties. Landscapes cut in half. General relativity and quantum mechanics on a disc. It is the sameness of the difference in the big and little worlds. They jump to different tunes while playing the same music. Our small world has gone through reduction. It has been boiled to its invisible essence. Lapping with intensi-ty. We learned the smooth orderly world of general relativity placed on the quantum mechanics of our turbulent one. The overlay of it all. A herd of buf-falo once there was not there. Our arrows disappeared into the ice hole of the target. We multiplied the four forces. We found corkscrews we didn't know how to name. The power of the new world. The old land circle. That's why strings are round. Or nearly so, bumped into their line. There are contra-dictory possibilities. And fluctuations on the highway. In this frenetic world there are particles of vibrating twine. The theories of two worlds not com-patible, but they take the same denominator — their essence is the same. Our big world compressed beyond endurance — our ultimate theory stuck to the sealing wax of the world.

15. SURVIVANCE IN THE
WORKS OF VELMA WALLIS

JAMES RUPPERT

Resistance . . . is an alternative way of conceiving human history.
Edward Said, *Culture and Imperialism*

"That reminds me of a story I think you should hear," Velma Wallis's mother said to her.[1] And so oral tradition continues for the Gwich'in Athabascans of Alaska even as it is passed on to us. Though missionaries and linguists have been collecting oral narratives for a century, only a few Athabascans have collected and published their own traditional stories. Wallis, a Gwich'in Athabascan raised in and around Fort Yukon, Alaska, is the author of three books: *Two Old Women, Bird Girl and the Man who Followed the Sun*, and *Raising Ourselves*. The first two publications are stories that she heard from her mother and that she dramatized while the last is a memoir of growing up in an alcoholically dysfunctional Fort Yukon. Wallis heard stories from her mother, and she carried them with her for many years. Her mother told the stories in order to teach Velma important lessons and to instill a sense of pride that comes from the knowledge of tradition. For mother and daughter the stories recreate a sense of identity and history, but they also reveal the essence of resistance and survivance as embodied in oral narratives.

Survival is always at stake in oral tradition. When Wallis heard these stories, she worried that the oral traditions were being lost and decided to record them. In an interview she commented, "When I handwrote *Two Old Women*, my culture and everything that we were as Native people had been latent and in limbo for a long time. We were going into assimilation into modern-style living. We were not being told who we were so we were in an identity crisis. We had massive alcoholism in the community. Many of our elders were dying of it. The stories were dying with them."[2]

Wallis decided to preserve the stories she heard because they "validated who I am" and recreated a sense of history for the Gwich'in people. She thought the stories would remind her community that "we were once a strong people. We actually have a history."[3] Clearly the Gwich'in were being blanketed by the colonial impetus to label the native as primitive and thus implicitly rob them of identity and history. Wallis believed that her writing was a reassertion of identity through oral history, a history that challenged the colonial definitions of history as a written activity whose purpose was to document Western accomplishments. She never thought of her writing as fiction, even though she fictionalized the characters and fleshed out their personalities. For her the stories were history. Wallis understood that the Gwich'in must do more than just physically survive; they must survive as a people. In the introduction to *Two Old Women*, Wallis writes that she hopes "tomorrow's generation will also yearn for stories such as this so that they may better understand their past, their people and hopefully, themselves."[4]

However, Wallis's goals are wider than mere documentation. Certainly building a sense of pride and identity are important as anticolonial activities, but the oral narratives contain something equally vital to Gwich'in survivance if not more so. The stories promote a way of thinking about the world, an epistemology familiar to the Gwich'in. To learn the stories and to think about them and to pass them on is to live with them, to allow them to influence how one sees the world. For Wallis this purpose is the deeper value in collecting and disseminating the stories. She can help revive an epistemology that colonialism has repressed and supplanted in the push toward "modern-style living."

Oral narratives create a historical consciousness that encourages intellectual interrogation. Wallis feels that they were traditionally used as an educational system that asked one to think seriously about actions, to question and weigh priorities, and to imagine effects and results — what we might call today a play of narrative meaning and signification intended to reinforce the use of a set of cultural values. This interactive sense of knowledge is not commonly associated with the Western tradition of documentation, though most usable senses of the past endorse an agenda. However, such discursive qualities are often associated with narratives in the oral tradition. Alaska Native oral narratives present a complex interaction of values and culturally moral subjects that outline an epistemological system structured around dialogism and interaction. Narrative meaning is never one-dimensional nor exhaustive. It is always in negotiation and mediation. Stories reinforce values while they question them. They are an education because they bring one's mind alive and ask one to comment, question, and respond. The listener or reader is encouraged to enter a discourse field in which response is expected. Plots serve to highlight the interplay of idea-positions; as such, they evolve and develop specific cultural conversations.

In this context we can see Wallis's written work not only documenting and partaking of oral structures but contributing to and reinvigorating oral traditions as she enters Gwich'in contemporary cultural conversations. Her books have been widely read by the Gwich'in, though not everyone has been pleased by her voice. Yet no one can doubt that she is engaged with a vital cultural discourse. Her stories articulate the discursive qualities of oral narratives as she takes positions, expects replies, and continues an emerging definition of Gwich'in identity. By engaging contemporary discourse through oral narratives, she employs an epistemological confrontation with the forces of repression and delegitimization.

Central to this oral epistemology is an engagement with competing cultural values. All of her characters — the two old women, Ch'idzigyaak and Sa', Bird Girl and the Man Who Followed the Sun — explore that space between competing cultural values. They all express some form of individuality and rebel to a greater or lesser extent against the expected cultural norms. As young women Sa' and Bird Girl did not wish to take up the expected female gender roles. They want to hunt, trap, and fish with the men. They try to live lives outside the norm. Similarly Ch'idzigyaak shows no interest in getting married, but she is forced into a wedding with an old man. Daagoo (The Man Who Followed the Sun) wishes to live the life of a traveler and explorer, but tragedy and the harsh demands of survival will not let him. Eventually, he gathers his courage and begins his remarkable personal journey.

Wallis makes it clear that the need to conform to cultural expectations is based on the understanding that survival in the arctic requires a community

and cooperation. Yet at the heart of Athabascan culture lies deference for individualism. Ron Scollon suggests that "the central aspect of the bush consciousness is respect for the individual."[5] Indeed, many others have commented on the marked penchant for individualism in Athabascan culture and its
concomitant nonintervention. Wallis acknowledges that independence may
have a high price for individuals and their families, a price that could be avoided by conformity. Athabascan scholar Phyllis Fast has identified this implicit paradox as existing between two cultural ideals: "One is a cultural idea of
individualism that directs each person to act with as much emotional, physical, and economic independence from others as possible. The other is a cultural ideal of conformity through consensus that suggests that every Athabascan somehow knows 'the' Athabascan way of thought, word, and act."[6]
And then as a matter of cultural identity and individual definition, the person must follow the unwritten code. Wallis sees such a contest of values at
the heart of her second book. In an interview she said,

> Before Bird Girl is kidnapped, she is an individual. And in tribes, indi-
> vidualism is not encouraged. The main philosophy is that you cannot
> survive without others. Bird Girl doesn't want to adhere to the rules.
> The Man Who Followed the Sun has a dream, not to support his fam-
> ily, but to travel. So I brought them together. In the end, they come
> home after all their trials. They have survived and learned the ways in
> which they do need their people, yet they have also attained their in-
> dividuality. As a modern Indian person from my area, I think I am tak-
> ing the same unthinkable journey.[7]

It is not unusual for Athabascan narratives to value both positions. Indeed,
the sense of dynamic interaction of cultural values and competing epistemological expectations informs all Athabascan narratives. The narratives force
the listener or reader to consider the situations and needs presented and
thus to weigh the benefits and outcomes. Sometimes individualistic actions
can force a new consensus or paradigm shift, though one risks shunning and
exclusion. For Wallis the narratives represent the sort of dynamic cultural vitality that colonialism has devalued. Survival as a people depends on a
sense of identity and the interplay of cultural values presented in oral narratives; consequently, they provide the best path to a culturally knowledgeable

Gwich'in identity. A people without a history are not a people. A culture without dynamics is not a culture. Wallis's contribution to preserving the narratives highlights a series of interrelated cultural subjects.

All three of Wallis's books incorporate elements of a struggle against the expectations and traditions of her community. Athabascan societies value individualism as well as traditionalism. The presentation of values and the testing of those values are common not only in trickster stories such as the Vasaagihdzak stories but in most Athabascan narratives. They often illuminate the lines of social interaction while they explore what Barre Toelken refers to as "culturally moral subjects."[8] They also engage such topics as social duties, relationships between kin, the difficulties and responsibilities of marriage, conflicting priorities between the human and spiritual world, and the necessity of cooperation or the pitfalls of relying on others. My point is that the narratives are seldom pedantic and more commonly useful for engaging important subjects that need some critical thinking rather than delivering rigid answers.

One might recall that some members of the Gwich'in and the interior Athabascan communities publicly did not support Wallis's work. Some feared that stories of abandonment and intertribal warfare would create a representation of Gwich'in society that would appear savage to the mainstream culture. The stated fear was that non-Native readers would see her work as a window on culture and generalize about Gwich'in society based on this small representative sample. However, as can be seen by reviews of Wallis's work, readers trained in Western literary aesthetic quickly grasped the sense of individualism her characters portray and saw the first two books in universalist terms as a triumph of self-reliance, perseverance, and self-realization. Yet Bird Girl and The Man Who Followed the Sun do not share in the felicitous reunion at the end of Two Old Women. Their nonconformity has had a price. Just as oral narratives do, Wallis's stories emplot around culturally moral subjects so as to bring to the forefront discussion, balance, and evaluation.

To make this narrative significant for both Native and non-Native readers, Wallis recreates the mediation of narratives that can retain tradition while interrogating it. The resolutions at the end of her books are never total, never permanent. The balance between cultural expectations and personal choices is always being negotiated. Contemporary book reviewers often miss this cultural dialog. Her texts mediate for the non-Gwich'in reader when they provide a perspective on the cultural conversation even if the non-Gwich'in reader can never completely join that conversation.

Both *Two Old Women* and *Bird Girl* are about survival within a specific cultural and physical landscape, and in each survival, there is resistance. Since the narrative presents a precolonial world, one sense of resistance is to a non-mediated view of cultural values, one that could exist inside the cultural dynamic and impose a rigid paradigm in place of a dialog on values. Any resistance to a simplistic acquiescence to one rigid set of priorities reemphasizes that competing cultural values require negotiation. However, Wallis's written versions of the oral narratives were created in a colonial period so that the recounting of the tales reminds Gwich'in readers that to assert the dynamic of Gwich'in values is to resist the colonial impetus that would simplify and invalidate Gwich'in identity and history.

Perhaps the most remarked upon cultural dynamic in which Wallis engages is her examination of the roles of women. As she grew up, she saw Fort Yukon as a community that had lost its sense of identity. Her characters are either in search of an identity or in need of reinventing one. In *Raising Ourselves* her personal life becomes a search similar to those of her characters. Indeed, her fierce independence has alienated some community members. She is quoted as saying, "I broke tradition. No one had ever told our legends in writing. Outsiders had come and written stories, and gone their separate ways, but no one in the community had ever done it. And no woman had ever reached beyond her community in this way. . . . So I have gone beyond my own tradition. I think there is good tradition and there's tradition that has grown upon people as habit. People would have been more comfortable with me if I had just been a wife with children."[9] Wallis contends that the stories that validated who she is will help validate her community, but personally, they also empower her as a strong woman just as her mother intended.

Rachael Ramsey illuminates this connection when she writes, "It is as if Wallis is admitting, not only by the similarities between her story and the ethnographic writings but by the reference to customs being handed down, generation to generation, that she is very aware of how the social organization should be challenging socially prescribed and socially accepted roles."[10] Ramsey sees in *Two Old Women* a story that hinges on Wallis's insights into issues of gender and power distribution. The two old women have lived lives that put them out of the mainstream gender expectation. Bird Girl also struggles against community expectation that she follow gender roles, and so does the Man Who Followed the Sun to some extent. For Ramsey the subjects of abandonment and intertribal warfare are less important than the questioning of gender roles. She concludes that "Wallis's exploration of female power, then, appears to question concepts of authority based on gender, challenging the traditional male/female roles."[11] Ramsey sees the negative reaction by male Athabascan leaders as an acknowledgment of the threat implied in Wallis's work.

Even Wallis links community identity and female individuation when she says, "At the same time Native Americans are coming to terms with ourselves, women are pursuing empowerment and self-realization."[12] Such interplay of individual needs and community expectations is seldom captured in the reviews that extol the virtues of freedom and self-reliance. Ramsey sums it up when she writes that "Wallis's work seems to come closer to presenting a version of a traditional tale that exposes the competing ideological struggle at work in Gwich'in culture."[13]

As Wallis's work enters into a cultural conversation, the texts, the retellings become dialogic entities in which positions are taken and responded to in the text itself as well as outside it. The narratives successfully mediate for non-Native readers, creating access to a discourse field foreign to us while engaging in a discourse familiar to us, thus satisfying Western expectations of plot, motivation, and theme. In Wallis's work narratives of power and identity are always gendered because tradition is gendered. There is always questioning, discussion, and evaluation because such negotiation is at the heart of signification in oral narratives. Resistance to internal boundaries and delegitimatization sets the groundwork for resistance to external disenfranchisement.

Wallis's project could be described by what Vizenor has called "survivance" since her work highlights how survival and resistance are allied in Native narratives: "Survivance, in the sense of native survivance, is more than survival, more than endurance or mere response; the stories of survivance are an active presence. . . . The native stories of survivance are successive and natural estates; survivance is an active repudiation of dominance, tragedy, and victimry."[14] Since Wallis's characters are taken from oral tradition, they see themselves as active agents in their destiny and repudiate victimization. Their survivals engage the active epistemological perspective of oral narratives and resist colonial representations of their Nativeness.

My last point concerns how Wallis's work engages the larger context of postcolonial and resistance literature. Surely her desire to preserve oral narratives and revive a latent culture could be seen in the context of the postcolonial project to reinscribe a nationalism lost to colonial expansion. Yet in her mind there are two traditions, one of which has grown upon the people as habit. What Wallis doesn't say but implies is that that other tradition is one of gender inequality. One doesn't have to cite Spivak or Minh-ha to wonder to what extent Wallis's work unites colonialism and sexism. Certainly *Raising Ourselves* presents a community wracked with alcoholism in transition to an "assimilation into modern-style living" with its cash economy and sexual stereotypes.

Yet Wallis's project to preserve the stories she heard repopulates a precolonial world. Bhabha suggests that such projects are prone to essentialism and nostalgia for a period that is unknowable. Indeed, most postmodern and postcolonial theory sees the postcolonial complicit with the colonial in that it is colonial oppression that spawns the anticolonial impulse. This line of theoretical discussion owes much to Foucault's insights in *The Archaeology of Knowledge*, in which he discusses how power itself inscribes its resistances and hence seeks to contain them. Many scholars would argue that the attempt by postcolonial writers to reinscribe a world before colonialism and to be free of its influence is unattainable. They would appreciate gender inequality only in its Western form at work in the text. But such a position would assume a certain transparency of meaning whose loci is the text and certainly Spivak, Minh-ha, and other scholars have labored to clarify the forms of gender inequality in existence in national cultures as well as colonial cultures.

It seems to me that Wallis's project to salvage the stories and revitalize identity would meet the criteria in an unexpected way as resistance literature, given the wide use of the term from political protest writing to feminist texts that resist male violence. Stephen Slemon defines resistance as "an act or set of acts, that is designed to rid a people of its oppressors, and it so thoroughly infuses the experience of living under oppression that it becomes almost an autonomous aesthetic principle. *Literary* resistance under these conditions, can be seen as a form of contractual understanding between text and reader, one which is embedded in an experiential dimension and buttressed by a political and cultural aesthetic at work in the culture."[15] Slemon is here concerned with more highly organized and political forms of literary resistance, but Wallis's work clearly reveals the experiential dimension buttressed by a cultural aesthetic. And while she might feel closer to insights on how gender inequality inhibits the development of identity, she does reveal resistance to communal limits on identity and individualism. All of this discussion can easily sound like a Western world view attacking parochial Native culture, but the point is that Wallis sees this whole project as affirming and revitalizing tradition and cultural identity, not tearing it down.

Oral tradition always inscribes a conversation on values not an emphasis on one moral like an Aesop's fable. Ramsey sees Wallis revealing a "competing ideological struggle at work in Gwich'in culture" because traditional oral narratives in general propel a listener or reader into a discourse field in which a continuing dialog about values is occurring. The storyteller and the audience are always renegotiating the priorities of competing values. It is, as Slemon suggests, a "form of contractual understanding between text and reader," though we should also add "listener."[16] Such a discourse is identity producing because as the Gwich'in engage in the discourse on cultural values, they also define a world view that is Gwich'in in nature, though not bound to a fossilized formation of mores.

Approaching her work from a perspective built on the dialogic nature of oral discourse and its function as survivance suggests that resistance literature does not have to be a one-dimensional political reaction aimed at a colonial Other. Seen as position taking in a discourse that expands out from the intracultural to the transcultural, we can now appreciate how resistance literature must engage multiple discourse fields. Oral narratives that enter into the realm of resistance literature can inform our theoretical understandings in ways not anticipated by those who see the term in the context of writing. Wallis's work performs a mediational task when it bridges supposed boundaries and leads us into seeing a new paradigm for the postcolonial. If, as Hayden White suggests, a discourse is a model of the processes of consciousness, then Velma Wallis's books allow us insights into a Gwich'in world view and discourse that enriches our understanding of literature and narrative art and suggests an argument that resistance texts are necessarily doubled in their cultural conversations and necessarily mediated in their social locations.[17]

Notes

1. Personal communication with author, October 1996.
2. Yost, "Telling Stories," 13.
3. Yost, "Telling Stories," 13.
4. Wallis, *Two Old Women*, x.
5. Scollon, *Narrative*, 100.
6. Fast, *Northern Athabascan Survival*, 138.
7. Yost, "Telling Stories," 13.
8. Toelken and Scott, "Poetic Retranslation," 86.
9. Yost, "Telling Stories," 13.
10. Ramsey, "Salvage Ethnography," 31.
11. Ramsey, "Salvage Ethnography," 34.
12. Yost, "Telling Stories," 13.
13. Ramsey, "Salvage Ethnography," 36.
14. Vizenor, *Fugitive Poses*, 15.
15. Slemon, "Unsettling," 107.
16. Slemon, "Unsettling," 107.
17. White, *Tropics of Discourse*, 5.

Bibliography

Fast, Phyllis. *Northern Athabascan Survival: Women, Community, and the Future*. Lincoln: University of Nebraska Press, 2002.

Foucault, Michel, *The Archaeology of Knowledge*. New York: Pantheon, 1972.

Ramsey, Rachel. "Salvage Ethnography and Gender Politics in *Two Old Women*: Velma Wallis's Retelling of a Gwich'in Oral Story." *Studies in American Indian Literatures* 11, no. 3 (Fall 1999): 22–41.

Scollon, Ron. *Narrative, Literacy and Face in Interethnic Communication*. Norwood NJ: ABLEX, 1981.

Slemon, Stephen. "Unsettling the Empire: Resistance Theory for the Second World." In *The Post-colonial Studies Reader*, edited by Bill Ashcroft, Gareth Griffiths, and Helen Tiffin, 104–10. London: Routledge, 1995.

Toelken, Barre, and Tacheeni Scott. "Poetic Retranslation and the 'Pretty Languages' of Yellowman." In *Traditional American Indian Literatures: Texts and Interpretations*, edited by Karl Kroeber, 65–116. Lincoln: University of Nebraska Press, 1981.

Vizenor, Gerald. *Fugitive Poses: Native American Indian Scenes of Absence and Presence.* Lincoln: University of Nebraska Press, 1998.

Wallis, Velma. *Bird Girl and the Man Who Followed the Sun: An Athabaskan Indian Legend from Alaska.* Seattle: Epicenter, 1996.

———. *Raising Ourselves: A Gwich'in Coming of Age Story from the Yukon River.* Seattle: Epicenter, 2002.

———. *Two Old Women: An Alaska Legend of Betrayal, Courage and Survival.* Seattle: Epicenter, 1993.

White, Hayden. *Tropics of Discourse: Essays in Cultural Criticism.* Baltimore: Johns Hopkins University Press, 1985.

Yost, Barbara. "Telling Stories That Must Not Die: A Conversation With Velma Wallis." *The Bloomsbury Review* 17, no. 1 (1997): 13, 16.

16. Writing Survivance

A Conversation with Joseph Boyden

ALLAN J. RYAN

> It takes an exceptionally intense and clear vision for a writer to per-
> suade us that there is anything new to be said about the Great War,
> now creeping steadily towards its centenary anniversary. Yet every now
> and then a book comes along . . . that rescues from the mire and car-
> nage a genuinely new perspective on the awful events of 1914–1918.
> Focussing on the rarely told stories of indigenous people enlisted into
> the Canadian army, Joseph Boyden's first novel, Three Day Road, is
> one such book.
>
> The Glasgow Herald

> There are . . . lyrical moments which possess an eerie power — especial-
> ly where Boyden writes about the northern landscape and the human
> relationship to it. He has illuminated a forgotten corner of the Great
> War, and that, in itself, is a prodigious achievement.
>
> Julie Wheelwright, The Independent

Joseph Boyden's *Three Day Road* exemplifies the idea of survivance in that it
actively brings into the present in a richness of character delineation and historic detail a little-known history of Aboriginal presence in one of the grand
master narratives of colonial construction that imagines Aboriginal experience as an absence. The novel provides a compelling counternarrative that
honors the lives and historical contributions of Aboriginal peoples and offers
entry into a world and world view foreign to many readers but made accessible through the skilful interweaving of stories that resonate with universal

human experience. Boyden inserts a Native presence and Native voices into the cultural and literary spaces of the global community. In the process he imagines new spaces for the creation and reception of stories of ongoing Aboriginal experience.

I first saw Joseph Boyden in a darkened theatre at the Canadian War Museum in Ottawa in December 2005. Several writers were gathered together on this midwinter's night for an evening of poetry, prose, and song. The proceedings opened with a hand drum song sung by Tamara Podemski, a young Ojibway/Israeli woman from Toronto. Later on, she sang Buffy Sainte-Marie's antiwar anthem *Universal Soldier*, the lyrics to which are as relevant today as they were when written four decades ago. They seemed especially poignant in that venerable setting.

Joseph Boyden cut a dashing figure in the podium spotlight that night, reading in a calm and measured voice several selections from his first novel *Three Day Road*. The story is a harrowing, epic tale of Xavier Bird and Elijah Whiskeyjack, two young Cree men from the northern Ontario bush who enlist in the Canadian army during the First World War and become celebrated snipers in the European conflict. The most riveting moment of the evening for me was Boyden's reading of the graphic and horrific description of the sniper's calculated art in which the face of a careless German soldier is reduced to a "red smearing explosion."[1] That singular image haunted my thoughts for days. The audience present was similarly moved by the author's compelling words. *Three Day Road* is unlike any other novel of the Great War, or any other narrative about Native Indians.

In conversation afterward, Joseph readily accepted my invitation to participate in a conference on Aboriginal arts that I was organizing at Carleton University in Ottawa in early March 2006. En route to the conference from his home in New Orleans, Joseph, along with his wife, fellow author Amanda Boyden, stopped off in Toronto, where *Three Day Road* was awarded the Rogers Writers' Trust Fiction Prize that came with a check for $15,000. That same week *Three Day Road* was issued in paperback by Penguin Books.

Joseph Boyden is a writer of Irish, Scottish, and Metis ancestry, born in 1966 to Raymond Wilford Boyden, the most highly decorated frontline doctor in the British Empire in World War II, and his wife Blanche, a former school teacher. One of eight children raised in north Toronto, Joseph spent his summers in and around Georgian Bay on Lake Huron, where he gained a great appreciation for the outdoors and the natural world.

Growing up, he was a voracious reader, writing "angsty" poetry in his teenage years while imagining himself as a rock star musician. The latter proved impractical since he couldn't play an instrument and was shy onstage. But he soon began to pursue poetry and writing more seriously: "Being one of so many kids I think that it's hard for you to find your own space, or express yourself in a way that stands out, so I was pretty quiet as a kid, and the idea of writing down stories was much more appealing to me than fighting for attention."[2] This activity led him to seek a degree in humanities at York University in Toronto. Several poems from his undergraduate thesis were published as a chapbook and later adapted as song lyrics by an enterprising musician who released the songs on CD. The recording is a source of great pride for Joseph, perhaps allowing him to fulfill his dreams of a career in music, if only vicariously.

In his late twenties Boyden enrolled in the MFA program in creative writing at the University of New Orleans. It was here that he found his "writer's voice." Four stories from his MA thesis were written from a Native Ojibway perspective: "Those were by far the best stories out of my thesis and I knew that's where my voice lay." Following graduation, he taught in Moosonee/Moose Factory on the west coast of James Bay, where the local Native inhabitants further inspired his writing. His first collection of short stories, framed as narratives of the four directions, was published as *Born with a Tooth* (2001). The book included the four stories from his graduate thesis. In the piece "Bearwalker" from this collection, Boyden both demonstrates, and reflects on, the power of storytelling through the voice of a contemporary character who, like one of the main protagonists in *Three Day Road*, is named Xavier Bird:

> I've had the ability to talk from the age of seven months. Full sentences in both English and Cree. I'd often, and still do, mix them up in the same sentence and not even realize it. My mother told me when I was still a young geegesh that I was on this earth to be the one to tell the tipachimoowin, the stories. This is because my mother is polite and could never get me to shut up. But her little announcement stuck with me, her saying to me, "Xavier Bird, I thought your father was a talker.

But you! You I cannot make stop your foolish talk." She actually said this, "foolish talk." In Cree it's pukwuntowuyumewin. *Maybe I remember my mother's words too fondly sometimes, more fondly than the reality. But it was her telling me that I was the talker, the storyteller, that made the biggest impression on me.*

It was Antoine Hookimaw who explained to me that the next logical step for the right storyteller is to become a shaman, a healer. "It is one thing to talk to entertain, Xavier," he told me. "But it is a more powerful menewawin, *a more powerful gift, to talk in order to teach. If you become a good teacher, you are on your way to healing some of the things that have gone wrong."*[3]

The four stories in "North: Home," the final section of *Born With a Tooth*, are interconnected and center around the suicide of a young woman in a northern community and the suicide's effect on family and community members. This interlinking of stories led Joseph to embark on a much more ambitious project, a novel with two primary points of inspiration: "My dad, number one, being involved in the war, and my growing up hearing stories of his being a war hero. His older brother was in WWI, my great aunt was a nurse in WWI, and so, growing up, I always had these myths of the war swirling around me. And then, from a very young age, I'd always heard of Francis Pegahmagabow, the Ojibway sniper from Wasauksing, right near here, and that always fascinated me too — the idea of the Indian sneaking around in the trenches and being very good at what he did."

By the time Joseph began work on his novel, he had returned to New Orleans to teach at his alma mater along with Amanda, a fellow graduate of the creative writing program whom he had married in their final year. After four and a half years of meticulous research and writing, *Three Day Road* was released by Penguin Books in the spring of 2005 to instant critical acclaim. What followed was a dizzying carousel ride of festival readings, international travel, and book releases in a variety of translations. A Cree language edition is currently in the works, as is a feature film based on the book. Joseph was living every writer's dream. In the spring of 2006 Amanda Boyden's coming-of-age novel *Pretty Little Dirty* was published by Vintage Books. Since then, the couple has had very little time to call their own. For much of the past year, they have been living out of a suitcase and longing for the time when they can return to their home in New Orleans to work on their next novels.

The geographic bedrock of sanity for Joseph and his siblings is Sandy Island, a rustic retreat the Boyden family has owned for over twenty-five years, located just off Parry Island in Georgian Bay. A popular destination for summer cottagers and tourists, Parry Island is home to the Wasauksing Ojibway First Nation and the resting place of Francis Pegahmagabow. It was to Sandy Island that Joseph invited me on the last weekend of August 2006 to interview him for this volume. That his life is now filled with people soliciting favors was not lost on me. Mine was one more request that he graciously fitted into his already busy life. As has been frequently noted by those who know him, both personally and through his writing, Joseph Boyden has a big heart.

Late on a Friday afternoon, Joseph, along with his nephew Mike met me at the Wasauksing marina and spirited me across the water to the family homestead in a small open boat. A generous gesture to be sure. Clad in a bush jacket and jeans and sporting a black T-shirt emblazoned with a bright yellow Sun Records Studio logo, Joseph seemed in his element. On the horizon an ominous band of dark blue stretched across the sky, separating the gray clouds from the gray waters, as Joseph speculated on the possibility of rain. Off to the right a group of small ducks huddled together and bobbed on the surface of the water as we passed.

The family home was a grand wooden structure with a wraparound porch that nestled in a space carved out of the bush. It was larger than a cabin but smaller and more modest than a chalet. The building was a project under constant modification and improvement, depending on which family members were around to supervise construction. The spacious main room was warm and inviting, dominated by an imposing stone fireplace that was built from local rocks and that was reminiscent of those found in medieval castles.

Upon arrival I was introduced to Joseph's fifteen-year-old son Jake, who was sharpening a brush-cutting machete by the porch; Joseph's editor, Nicole Winstanley, who was marking up a hefty manuscript she had brought with her from Toronto; and Joseph's wife, Amanda, author, photographer, and former trapeze artist, who welcomed me with a warm smile while overseeing preparations for a grilled barbecue dinner for an indeterminate number of guests.

Replacing the porch boards was the current family project, and all visitors were encouraged to pitch in and swing a hammer a few times. I willingly obliged.

Before dinner Joseph and Jake persuaded me to join them in climbing to the top of a nearby three-story wooden tower in order to savour the view before the sun set behind the trees. While unaccustomed to scaling such heights and feeling somewhat apprehensive, I must admit that the view was worth the climb. As a point of interest, I was informed that the platform at the top of this somewhat shaky tower, the tallest structure on the island, is the only place on the island that a cell phone will function.

Soon after our descent, other family members arrived, and we feasted by candlelight in the glow of a raging fire while the music of Johnny Cash, *Live at Folsom Prison*, emanated from a compact iPod console in the corner. It was a memorable evening. The threat of rain was just that, and the night passed uneventfully.

The following morning Joseph invited me to join him on the wooden dock to discuss whatever it was I had come to talk to him about. The sun shone brightly and glinted on the water, and the waves lapped at our feet. It was easy to appreciate the attraction of such a place. As we talked, Jake and a young cousin who'd arrived the night before headed off down the rocky shoreline with fishing poles across their shoulders. It was an idyllic scene some city dwellers might describe as a "Mayberry moment."

I began our conversation by asking Joseph about his father, Raymond Wilford Boyden.

> **JB:** My dad was very much a family man. He was a family doctor, the last of the kind of doctors who would make house calls. He had a lot of Chinese immigrant patients in the '60s and '70s, and he'd take payment in chickens and animals if they didn't have the money. He passed away when I was eight, but his influence continues in everything I do. He was stern, strict, and very loving. One of my greatest memories of him is he was quite sick in the last couple of years of his life, but even when he was, this one time when we were driving back from Georgian Bay to Toronto, and the car in front of us went off the road, my dad bounded out like a young man with his doctor's bag to make sure the people in the car were okay.

AJ: Can you identify specific influences from your father in your own life?

JB: Definitely a work ethic, a passion for what you do well, the idea of how important family is, empathy for others, to always care for others, to always look after others.

AJ: Many of those qualities are present in *Three Day Road*. Tell me about writing that book.

JB: Much of *Three Day Road* I wrote out longhand in a coffee shop on Magazine Street in New Orleans. Much of it. I find that writing at home is almost too quiet. I guess part of this is being one of so many children. Complete quiet almost drives me crazy sometimes, and so I started years ago going to this coffee shop in the neighborhood, and I found it really worked. There's all this activity around me, which is what I grew up with, and so I'm in a very comfortable environment.

AJ: The narrative structure of the novel is somewhat unusual, with chapters alternating between the voices of Xavier Bird and his aunt Niska and with the story beginning at the end. In an earlier draft you told the story chronologically. Why did you change it?

JB: I realized that it was not finished, there was something missing, something was bothering me. And it wasn't that I was missing anything in terms of material—actually I had too much material—it was in the telling. I was giving it a very Western linear chronological telling, and I realized that it needed to be a Native telling of the story, and so I wrapped it back in on itself, began near the end, and told the circular telling.

AJ: And you feel comfortable writing in both male and female Native voices?

JB: I'm very comfortable, especially with a female voice. A lot of male writers can't write a female voice, but I grew up hearing a woman's voice, a strong woman's voice, so it's a part of me. As for the Native perspective, I feel comfortable writing that, absolutely. It might not be the Native voice of a Mohawk person or a Sioux or some other tribe or band, but I've lived

long enough to know not to worry about the idea of appropriation, although I am Metis . . . but my heart, my world view,
lies squarely in the Native world, the urban Native world, as
much as the Native bush world. I'm very comfortable writing in that voice.

When I was writing Niska's voice, it was as if I was being
channeled. It was not my voice, and it was the easiest writing
I've ever done. It just poured out of me.

I never will say that I'm a spokesperson for a group or a clan
or a culture, but I certainly am a storyteller, and I want to always tell that story right; I want to tell that story with heart.
When my heart's in it, I feel like I'm being successful at what
I'm trying to do. I'm never going to speak for a people, but I
certainly will speak for an individual that I create who might
come from a community or a culture.

I think one of the greatest tools a writer has is the ability
to create a character that a reader will read and a reader will
become for a while or live the world through that character's
eyes. And suddenly it's not "them" anymore, it's not "Indians" — a white person reading my novel, for example — they
are the Native person, they get to see the world from a perspective that might have been very foreign to them before,
and now it's very close. That's one of the great powers that
you have as a writer that no other medium really captures.

AJ: One of your favourite narrative strategies is telling stories
within stories.

JB: It's like that Matchoiska doll, you open it up and there's another one in it, and you open it up, and there's another, and
another. But mine's almost like the inverse of the Matchoiska
doll: it's a small story; you open it up, and there's a bigger story, and you open that up, and there's an even bigger story.

AJ: Despite the gravity of this novel, you still manage to find humor in unexpected places.

JB: There is humor there for sure because Elijah is a trickster;
he likes to play. I wanted him to have at least some traits of

the trickster, a levity and an ability to tease and even the ability to teach. Even though Xavier teaches him everything he knows about the bush, he teaches Xavier both good and bad lessons about people and about relationships and about friendships. You can't escape it. If I'm going to give my character the last name Whiskeyjack, you know there's going to be a little bit of the trickster Weesakeejack in him. I wasn't writing him as just a trickster in human form, but I definitely wanted him to have aspects of the trickster in his personality because the trickster is a fascinating, multifaceted, multi-dimensional character.

I think that with humor — some of the best humor — there's a real sense of sadness just below the surface. . . . I think humor is the best way to teach too. And there's no denying how important humor is in the Native world view. I've watched friends up in northern communities who are in real bad situations be able to laugh, and it just breaks the tension.

AJ: There's also a sense of musicality in your writing, in the rhythm of the words. I'm thinking now of the Cree phrases that are interwoven throughout your novel.

JB: I love just sitting and listening to my Cree friends up in Moosonee or around James Bay talk. There's a singsong and a rhythm in the way they speak that I just love. I don't know how well I capture it on the page, but I certainly hear their voices when I am writing the way they talk.

AJ: How has the book been received by the Native community?

JB: So far, Native people have accepted it and actually liked it and appreciated it, and that's probably been the greatest part of all of this journey for me because the people I'm writing about have accepted it and are appreciative, and that's been the really, really satisfying thing.

AJ: When you were researching *Three Day Road*, did you visit any historic sites in Europe?

JB: I wasn't able to go over to the battlefields until I'd finished the first draft of my novel. I finally saved up enough money so that Amanda and I could go overseas together to see what I was writing about. I was amazed at the similarities between that part of the world and Southern Ontario — the farm fields and the hills and the lush vegetation.

AJ: Did you fine tune the manuscript after you came back?

JB: I did fine tune things after I went over. I read a lot of diaries and memoirs written by average people that give a very good description of what it looked like at the time. So I was able to picture it through them. But then getting over there and actually getting to see how the land has kind of reclaimed itself was really neat, but there's still all the scars just under the surface. My son and I found a human bone. . . . You just scratch the surface, literally, and you end up coming across stuff.

And every year farmers still pull up hundreds of tons of unexploded shells and pieces of metal and old rifles. Farmers still die by running over unexploded land shells. It doesn't go away. The people in Belgium and northern France are living with that history. And all of them have stories. People would come up to us and start talking, and they'd tell about how, when they were kids in WWII, the Germans just rolled through that place really quickly. But in WWI they had grandfathers who were there. Whole original homes were destroyed but they came back afterwards.

One of the most powerful places I've been to is the battlefields in Belgium. There's a lot of entrepreneurs there. You'd be driving down the road and you'd come to a very small town and then you'd see a sign, WWI battle site, and you'd pull off and you'd go through this person's house and into his backyard, and there's old trenches there that are still existing from WWI and all of the detritus of war — the rifles and grenades and helmets — and it's quite amazing. It's like little living museums.

AJ: Do we need historic sites to help us remember? Do we need war museums?

JB: I think we do need these kinds of places because a lot of people don't have a clue what happened in WWI or any war really. But even ninety years later, seeing the scars still in the ground leaves an impression that it must have been very intense. At Vimy Ridge you walk up to the memorial and the fields on either side are just pitted. They look like rolling hills at first but then you realize they're mine craters and shell holes and trenches and scars on the ground.

AJ: Besides honoring the dead, aren't war museums supposed to teach us lessons about peaceful coexistence to prevent atrocities from happening again?

JB: I don't know if war museums are only there for the honorable reason of teaching lessons. I think that we have an unhealthy fascination with absolute brutality. And it happens over and over again. Look at Lebanon just recently, and look what's going on in Afghanistan and Iraq. We want to make war because in a way it's easier, and in the short term it's satisfying to say "well, this guy did this to me, so let's just get him." It's very easy to say "this is the bad guy, let's go kill him" versus "this is a guy who doesn't see my way, let's figure it out by talking." War is easier, it seems.

AJ: What do you think of the Canadian War Museum?

JB: I think it's a good one. I brought my mum there not so long ago, and we walked through there. It's a very clean museum in all kinds of ways, but it doesn't capture the brutality like other museums that I've seen, especially in Europe. It's very "austere." It's very "Canadian" in its telling of our history with war. It's very well done, it's beautifully put together and run, but there was something very — I don't want to say "sterile" about it — but something very distant about it when I walked through it.

I've been to other museums. There's one in Ypres, the In Flanders Field Museum, and you walk through that, and they have the noise of the cannon, and you get a card at the beginning of a person — its either of a young soldier whose German or Belgian or English or a nurse — and there's different stations as you go along and you put the card in and find out what happened to them, these real live people. Often times, by the end of the war they died. And it brings it to life in a way that's just fascinating, that's really interactive. That to me was much more powerful than seeing the machine guns and the helmets and the barbed wire that you could actually go up and handle.

AJ: What can you tell me about the new novel you are working on?

JB: It's about grandchildren, relations of characters in the first novel. It's contemporary. It's dealing with some of the same issues and themes that *Three Day Road* explored: the idea of family and of identity is a huge part of this novel, and how one identifies oneself—and that ability to very easily not know who you are, even though you come from a very strong place. These are all things that fascinate me because this is what I often question about myself, coming from a big family, coming from a mixed background. Who am I in this world? Where am I? It's very easy to lose your footing sometimes if you're not careful. People tie themselves up with their identities very strongly, to the point that it can become a negative thing. But at the same time a lot of people that I meet who are really lost don't really have a self-identity; they can't say of themselves, "I am from here, this is what grounds me." And I think the whole idea of grounding too is very important.

AJ: Your family seems to be the grounding in your own life.

JB: The one thing that you have in the world when everything else is gone is your siblings and your parents and your memories of who you are, and that began to come out more and more strongly in this new novel. And the idea of family—even if the family is dysfunctional, which I think every family is—that's what you have, and that's what you're given, and it's how you respond to your siblings that ultimately is going to make you happy or not. I've seen so many families disintegrate under pressure and sibling fights; people never talking to each other again, and our family has always avoided that, even though we're a big family. I think it's because we know that the one great thing you have in this world is the people you come from. The idea of family is much more conscious in this new book than it was in the first one, and it's something that I feel the urge to write about.

AJ: You write about family in your nonfiction work as well; you and your son Jake at Vimy Ridge, you and Amanda in New Orleans.[4] I felt like I knew them both before I met them.

JB: To me my whole world view is defined by my family and where I fit in that family and the history of my family, and so it's something I can't really escape even if I wanted to.

AJ: You write both fiction and nonfiction. Do you have a preference?

JB: Fiction absolutely is my preference, although I do enjoy non-fiction very much. The only nonfiction I've written that's been published is almost memoir. It can never be claimed that I write thinly disguised nonfiction in my fiction. A lot of writers I know, especially younger writers, are basically writing a fictionalized version of their lives. That's something that I'm not able to do in fiction and don't have the desire to do in fiction.

AJ: Your nonfiction is written so visually with such vivid images of people in peril, people coping with traumatic situations. You describe them with great empathy. And I'm here thinking of the articles you wrote for *Maclean's* magazine about the aftermath of Hurricane Katrina.

JB: I think that goes right back to my father. I've never consciously thought about this before, but when you mention the idea of people in trouble and trauma, that's exactly what my father had to deal with for so much of his life, and I think that there's a little bit of him in me, no question, this idea of wanting to help.

I have found myself more than once putting myself into a very dangerous situation but not thinking about doing it, jumping in to try to prevent fights, for example, or helping this dying African American guy. The guy who shot him could have very easily come back and shot me, too. But I didn't think about it.[5] I guess it's wanting to live up to my father in some ways . . . especially in the war . . . the desire to help takes precedence over personal safety.

AJ: From your description of the second novel, *She Takes You Down*, it would seem that survivance will be a prominent theme. What is your understanding of this term?

JB: I have a good friend who's an actor out in Vancouver, Tahmoh Penikett, and he's on a big TV series called *Battlestar Galactica*. His mother is from up in the Yukon and his father was actually the premier of that area for a long time. His father is from England and married a Native woman. And Tahmoh has found this balance where he lives in Vancouver and has this wonderful life as an actor and is getting very well known as an actor, but he says, "God, when I need my head cleared, I just go out in the bush and I'll walk for days." That's it in a nutshell. That's survivance, I think, if I'm reading Vizenor's term correctly. It's not just survival anymore, but it's the paradigm of a Native person suddenly living in the city, and how does he adjust? Sometimes it's poorly, sometimes it's great.

AJ: Survivance can take many forms. With new technologies and the internet, stories can be circulated and exchanged throughout the global community.

JB: You might not become a famous classic book-published writer, but you certainly have the ability to put your voice out in the world now. That's one of the things I love about northern reserves that I want to write about in this new book; all my friends are now internet aficionados. They're on chat rooms with people in the southern United States, and it's just wild. I love that kind of wonderful difference.

I'm very excited to be a writer in this global community. I really feel like I showed up at a very good time in writing.

Canadian historian Pierre Berton once said of his days working as the editor of the University of British Columbia student newspaper that "they were the best years of our lives, and what's more, we knew it." When told this statement, Joseph Boyden replied, "Since I've known Amanda, I've thought to myself, these are the best times of my life, and I know it, and they're continuing on."[6]

On August 28, 2006, the first anniversary of Hurricane Katrina, Joseph and Amanda headed back to New Orleans to work on their respective new novels, while I returned to Ottawa to transform this interview into an essay and to prepare for the upcoming school term.

Notes

1. Boyden, *Three Day Road*, 88.

2. Joseph Boyden, interview with author, August 26, 2006, Sandy Island, Ontario. All other excerpts are from this interview.

3. Boyden, *Three Day Road*, 92.

4. Boyden, "The ghosts of Vimy Ridge," 114; Boyden, "The drowning of New Orleans."

5. In "The drowning of New Orleans" Boyden describes the night he and Amanda stopped their car to assist a young black man who had just been shot by another youth, who moments earlier had pointed his gun at Joseph. The wounded young man died in Boyden's arms.

6. Similar sentiments are expressed in Berton, *Starting Out*, 152–53.

Bibliography

Berton, Pierre. *Starting Out, 1920–1947*. Toronto: McClelland and Stewart, 1987.
Boyden, Joseph. *Born With A Tooth*. Toronto: Cormorant Books, 2001.
———. "The drowning of New Orleans." *Maclean's*, September 7, 2005.
    http://www.macleans.ca (accessed July 31, 2006).
———. "The ghosts of Vimy Ridge." *Canadian Geographic*, November/December 2005.
———. *She Takes You Down*. Toronto: Penguin, 2008.
———. *Three Day Road*. 2005. Toronto: Penguin, 2006.

17. A LANTERN TO SEE BY

Survivance and a Journey into
the Dark Heart of Oklahoma

JACE WEAVER

A Trip Home

In the mid-1990s I organized an all-Native conference on the environment
in Denver, an event that became my edited volume *Defending Mother Earth*.
As I stood up to convene the proceedings, my friend Thom White Wolf Fas-
sett announced in a loud voice, "I just want to go on record that there are
too many lawyers in the room, too many Cherokees, and too many people
from Oklahoma." I appreciated the jibe from a Seneca from western New York
and smiled. I replied, "Thom, I will readily agree that, with two (and me being
one), there are too many lawyers in the room. I might even agree that there
are too many Cherokees, though I don't see how that's possible. But you can
never have too many people from Oklahoma."

I am unashamed to admit that I love Oklahoma. I love the panhandle, flat
land where earth and sky are instantly discernible as disk and bowl. I like that
you can see rain falling a long way off, and I crave the storms, during which
Thunder and the Ukten' battle once more. I respect the power and unpre-
dictability of tornadoes. And I love the Cross Timbers, near where I grew up:
scrub oak forest so dense that Washington Irving likened getting over it to
"struggling through forests of cast iron." When I'm away, I miss the beef, the
best south of Alberta (though it embarrasses me to have to acknowledge
that Alberta's is better). I love the people: Natives and non-Natives who,
like my family, were tough and tenacious enough to stick it out through the
Dust Bowl—and those who were smart enough to get the hell out and build
a new life elsewhere. The red dirt of Oklahoma courses through my veins. In
Betty Louise Bell's novel *Faces in the Moon*, a Cherokee character posits that

the land "lives for Indian blood. It's taken so much blood it can't git back to its natural color."

Oklahoma is a land of stark contrasts. Writer Bill Burchardt in the *Oklahoma Monthly*, as quoted in "Glass Mountains State Park Visitors' Guide," captures this characteristic, along with something of the grip it continues to exert on me even though I have not lived there regularly for over two decades:

> *The true natives of this country of extremes . . . the quiet breeze . . . silence . . . shimmering squirming heat waves . . . incredible color . . . a bitter chilled blast of whipping flesh cutting sleet . . . snow . . . cold as hard and intractable as iron, gripping the same earth refined by midsummer's furnace heat . . . gentle, cool rain . . . a caress in spring . . . autumn's sleepy lull . . . It is apt to drive you to insanity — the insanity of wanting to live your whole life there. Its solitudes are good for a type of casual, easy living, possible only to a paradoxical people who can instantly change to cope with change; change which may be sudden, and even violent.*

I love Oklahoma. But I am acutely aware that there is a darkness at the heart of the place I cherish. My Native ancestors and their contemporary progeny are those "paradoxical people" to whom Burchardt refers — who can instantly cope with change — because they were subjected to violent change as they were uprooted and marched there against their wills. More likely, however, Burchardt was referring to those for whom migration was voluntary: "boomers" who illegally attempted to settle what were euphemistically termed the "Unassigned Lands," territory coerced away from Indians by treaty in 1866, and "sooners," those who sneaked into the territory to stake illegal claims prior to the land run of April 22, 1889. Twin criminalities that marked the beginning of the end of Native territorial sovereignty.

A few months ago, I returned home to see family and friends. As I drove west on I-40 to Elk City where I was born, I stopped as I sometimes do at Fort Reno. This outpost of empire was established in 1874 to protect the Cheyenne and Arrapahoe Agency and police the Unassigned Lands, repeatedly evicting David Payne's boomers and escorting them back to Kansas. Troops from Fort Reno fought the Battle of Sand Hills in 1875 and chased Dull Knife in 1881. They supervised the Oklahoma land run of 1889. In 1900 they were ordered to Henryetta in the Creek Nation to put down what whites called the "Crazy Snake" Rebellion. They did so by capturing its leader Chitto Harjo and sixty-seven of his followers. During World War II, the fort served as a prisoner-of-war camp for captured Germans, primarily from Rommel's Afrika Korps.

Today, Fort Reno is largely a crumbling assemblage of buildings built between 1876 and 1944. Part of the facility is used by the United States Department of Agriculture. There is a small museum and visitors' center in the former officers' quarters. Most structures are empty and forlorn. The heart of the place is the cemetery. I go there often. I am usually the only one there, except for an occasional hawk circling overhead. It is always quiet, except for the wind slapping the halyard against the empty flagpole.

There are Indians buried there: Cheyenne and Arapaho scouts like Chalk and White Elk; Moka Clark, who as a child had survived the Washita Massacre and later married scout Ben Clark; and seven of Clark's children, who died in infancy. There are some civilians, notably Wee Can Wah, a laundry worker whose tombstone identifies him only as "Chinaman." He reportedly saved his money to bring his family from China, but he was murdered before he could do so.[1]

Mainly, however, the graveyard is populated by the soldiers who served there and the families that lived and died there with them. Their tombstones serve as material testimony to the fact that the Indian Wars were not fought by the blindingly white American cavalry of John Ford westerns but by African Americans and Irish and German immigrants: Buffalo Soldiers of the Ninth and Tenth Cavalry—Clark Young (killed at Sand Hills), James Coleman and Saul Shipley (both drowned crossing a swollen North Canadian River); Walk-a-Heaps of the Twenty-Fourth and Twenty-Fifth Infantry, Edward Lee, Frank Aldrich, and Porter Webster; Robert Baker of County Cork, John Dolan, Thomas Mulcahy, and Patrick Lynch (who died fighting Dull Knife at Turkey Springs); Louis Biehl, Gustav Niebuhr, and Jacob Zellwegger.

The cemetery is bisected by a rock wall. On one side are those who were stationed at the fort. On the other are the graves of Italian and German prisoners from various internment camps: Innocent Ortelli Giovanni Bo, Emil Minotti, Klaus Bork, Johann Grundwall, Fritz Holldorf. These face each other in two neat lines as if in military formation. The United States has always prided itself that no prisoner of war in its care ever escaped, citing the fact as proof of its strict observance of the terms of the Geneva Convention. Yet most of those interred at Fort Reno had been captured fighting in a war that they had not wanted, and were a German *soldat* to escape, where would he go on the prairies of Oklahoma, Texas, Kansas, or Nebraska? What strikes me every time is that the names on one side of that dividing barrier are no different than some on the other. Sergeant Hermann Hauser of the First New York Cavalry, buried against the wall, could easily have been eighteen inches away on the other side but for the date of his death and the color of his uniform.

Heading west from Fort Reno, I swung north to visit the Glass Mountains, a range of sacred red rock mesas that jut sharply up from the Oklahoma prairie in the Cherokee Outlet near the boundary of the Cheyenne-Arapaho reservation. On the way I passed through Watonga and drove by the Diamondback Correctional Facility, a private prison owned by Corrections Corporation of Nashville. The facility houses around 2,100 inmates. About 400 of these are Native Hawaiians, uprooted from their island homeland and incarcerated on behalf of the state of Hawaii in the middle of landlocked Oklahoma. There they languish, as out of place and disoriented as Fort Reno's troopers or the GermanPOWs their successors guarded there.[2]

Oklahoma is Native America (the name itself, suggested by Choctaw chief Allen Wright in 1866, means "land of the Red people"), but there is nonetheless a strong undercurrent of anti-Indianism and racism, usually subtle, though not always.

Lynn Riggs, Writer of Survivance

I do love Oklahoma, but I also understand Oklahoma and that dark spot in its heart, a cancer deeply embedded on some ventricle and metastasized through a long history. Cherokee playwright and poet Lynn Riggs did too. Born in the Cherokee Nation and raised in the state of Oklahoma, Riggs knew how Oklahomans sounded. But he did more than hear. He saw into that dark corner of the settler-colonizer heart—and sometimes, disturbingly, that settler colonizer was Native.

Elias Cornelius Boudinot was the intellectual leader of the land-hungry boomers that Payne molded into a movement. According to biographer James Parins, for Boudinot "the battle for national sovereignty for Indians could never be won, and to resist was to fight a holding action that was doomed to eventual failure." To this point he follows in the belief of his father Elias Boudinot, one of those who surrendered Cherokee patrimony with quill and ink at New Echota in 1835. Parins continues, however, "Perhaps more importantly, for him and his family Cherokee sovereignty was not desirable unless he could somehow rise to power, and that was unlikely. Why not, then, he asked himself, try to manipulate the situation to one's own advantage and to the advantage of one's people? If this thing the whites called Manifest Destiny was going to succeed in the face of all opposition, why not align yourself on the winning side and hitch your wagon to its star?"[3] E. C. Boudinot favored allotment as early as 1871, advocated white settlement of what he first dubbed the "Unassigned Lands" in an infamous letter to the *Chicago Times* in 1879, and attempted to carve out a private empire for the Treaty Party in the Cherokee Outlet.[4]

Three generations earlier, almost twenty years before the Treaty Party's paternalistic sellout of Cherokee sovereignty at New Echota, Old Settler Cherokees — those who voluntarily emigrated prior to Removal — attacked the Osage under Chief Clermont during the Strawberry Moon of March 1818. Undertaken in retaliation for Osage raids against the Old Settlers, the attack took place at the village of Pasona at the base of a large hill on the banks of Black Dog's Creek. Often referred to as the "last battle" between the Osage and the Cherokee, the assault was, in fact, a massacre, launched against a sleeping village well after midnight when most of the young men were away on a buffalo hunt. Cherokee historian Rachel Caroline Eaton, writing in 1930 from both written sources and the oral tradition, describes the Cherokees as "transformed into a mad melee of furies . . . worked up to a pitch of passion little short of madness."[5] Men, women, and children were killed without regard. "Gone berserk with revenge and excitement," the Cherokee pursued those who fled for two days.[6] The Cherokee killed Clermont and his family. Then in an act reminiscent of rapacious white settler colonizers throughout North America, they kept a corruption of his name for both the site of the massacre and the town that grew up near by, Claremore.

Though the Cherokees certainly are culpable for the act, that it was possible at all reflects the perverse logic of American empire, according to which indigenes were displaced to make way for relocation of Indians from other lands Amer-Europeans coveted. The Osage were compelled to surrender land to make it available for Cherokees. The Caddo and Wichita were removed to permit relocation of the Creek.[7] The result was a haunted landscape.

The massacre forms an important backdrop for the Lynn Riggs's play that is most widely accepted as being Indian-themed, *Cherokee Night*.[8] The Clare-more Mound is a brooding presence throughout the drama. Eaton, "whose childhood was spent under the shadow of the historic hill," notes, "The grassy slopes and rock-rimmed summit . . . furnished a marvelous playground where romantic youth seeking adventure could salvage, with eager interest, such relics of a vanished culture as arrow heads, battered tomahawks, and bits of colored beads; could gather gorgeous wild flowers to lay with childish rever-ence on the grave of the great chief who gave his name to the Mound where he is said to have fallen fighting; or garner great handfuls of fragrant blood-red berries that ripened in such profusion on the site of the village of Pasuga in the time of the Strawberry Moon."[9] Riggs uses these recreations.

As act one opens, on a scrim is projected "a gigantic teepee," a "ghostly habitation." Voices and the "muffled thud of a drum" are heard. These fade away: "The teepee vanishes. The drum, the voices are silent." In their place, the Claremore Mound appears. A group of young, cross-blood Cherokees gather around a fire, picnicking. The group is confronted by Old Man Tal-bert, also a Cherokee. He has been driven mad by a vision he was given. It is necessary to quote his description of it at length:

> *Don't you know—whut I seen—on this hill—this un! The Chero-kees! Painted for war! A-stealin' up on the Osages asleep up there by their campfires! Fall on 'em, cut their th'oats, bury yer tomahawks in their thick skulls, let yer muskets thunder! At every Cherokee belt a row of Osage scalps—with long black hair swishin' and drippin'! I seen it—all of it—*my people! I heared the Osage groans! . . . And more*—they was *more that happened! When it was all over, they seen me. They looked at me. They come toward me down the mountain. From 'way up there—the crest of the Mound—streamin' like a river! One of 'em—the biggest one—in his war bonnet, he stood right in front of me. He looked th'ough me like I wasn't there! He was terrible! He started in to speak. "Jim Talbert," he said—"Now you've saw, you've been showed. Us—the Cherokees—in our full pride, our last glory!*

This is the way we are, the way we was meant to be!

In the gray night we walked into ice-cold water,
Our drums had no tongues,
Seven sharp turkey bones cut our flesh.

The Shaman pressed three beads into the sand,
They leaped into his hand crying the names of the chosen.

We prayed to our brothers, the hawks,
"Brothers! Hawks!
Fall from the sky into the camp of the Osages,
Strike with your wings, beaks, talons the bodies of our
enemies!"

The hawks, our brothers, came.
The Osages lie in heaps on the mountain.

But this was moons ago;
We, too are dead.
We have no bodies,
We are homeless ghosts,
We are made of air.

Who made us that, Jim Talbert? Our children — our children's chil-
dren! They've forgot who we was, who they are! You too, Jim Talbert,
like all the rest.

Talbert's vision occurred in 1905, ten years before the opening scene and two years before Oklahoma statehood erased Cherokee territorial sovereignty. The only response Talbert knows to make is to engage in the romantic, youthful adventure of Eaton's — and Riggs's — childhood. In the intervening years he has scoured the Claremore Mound for arrowheads, which he now desperately proffers to the young Cherokees before him as talismans of memory. In gathering them, he has sought not only connection to place but also to a time past.

Though Riggs hints at the brutality of the Cherokee assault, the images he conjures remain nonetheless nostalgically gauzy, reflecting Amer-European stereotypes of Indians rather than historical reality: war bonnets, tomahawks, and bows and arrows. For him this "last battle" represents a time when his people were strong and indisputably Native. He ignores the ultimate criminality of the Cherokees' action, whatever the provocation. Crime, however, is central to Riggs's oeuvre, and that crime is linked explicitly to land.

Cherokee literary scholar Daniel Justice astutely observes that "blood quantum and ethnicity, and the moral character that accompanies both in Riggs's Cherokee world, are consistently embedded within a concept of land that is central to the well-being of both individuals and cultures."[10] For Riggs the land itself works upon its inhabitants. For Natives it is a source of strength and memory — of survivance. Upon outlanders, however, it works a deleterious mojo. It debilitates and literally de-moralizes.

Riggs biographer Phyllis Braunlich describes his first full-length play, *Big Lake*, written in 1925 and produced in New York two years later: "Subtitled *A Tragedy in Two Parts*, this play is about two adolescents, Betty and Lloyd, who wander away from a school picnic and seek shelter in a dugout with an evil couple. Butch, a bootlegger, has just murdered an informer and schemes to pin the murder on Lloyd. He looks upon Betty with lust. After they escape from the situation and return to their friends, the ugly accusations of their classmates and teacher repel them. They flee out onto the lake, where death pursues them."[11] Violence and crime also play pivotal parts in *The Lonesome West*, *Rancor*, and *The Domino Parlor*. This theme is perhaps most clearly presented in *A Lantern to See By* and *Out of Dust*, the two plays telling substantially similar stories.

Like *Lonesome West* and *The Domino Parlor*, *A Lantern to See By* is set at Blackmore, a painfully transparent disguise for Riggs's hometown of Claremore, described in *Domino Parlor* as a town that "God and the oil boom forgot."[12] The brightness and light of Claremore has been blotted out. The resulting darkness, however, is that of interior landscapes rather than the external world. There is no moral clarity here.

The play takes place over a single summer, from June to September. Unlike most Riggs plays, *A Lantern to See By* does not indicate the date of the action. Internal evidence suggests a date shortly after Oklahoma statehood.[13] The play unfolds at the Harmon farm near Blackmore.

John Harmon, the family patriarch, is an arrogant, violent, bullying drunk-ard. He came to the territory from Missouri as a young man, arriving with nothing and making himself a man of substance: "two farms, a hundred an' sixty acre, thirty head of cattle, hogs, chickens, timber land, land fer grazin, land fer plowin." As Harmon himself rehearses the story:

> *An' who am I t' be denied anything? John Harmon, that's me. Borned in Missouri. A purty good slice of fat land I got — you'll have t' admit that — a hundred an' sixty acre — worked fer an' won by the stren'th of these hands. And all from nuthin! I had nuthin t' start with. Grand-pap Bradley'll tell you how I first went to work fer him a-buildin a fence through the Verdigree bottom. I wuzn't more'n a kid, a weak sleazy-lookin cotton-headed kid. But I knowed how t' work, an' I knowed how t' save. An' I did, by God!*
>
> *Years an' years of slavin! Years an' years of savin! Nen I bought my land — a hundred an' sixty acre — The hand of man hadn't touched it. It wuz all growed up an' tangled with briars, an' the woods wuzn't cleared, an no plow had ever run its snout under the sod. It was vir-gin from the Maker. An' I worked it an' planted it. I wuz man enough fer the job. An' I built me a house. An' I married as fine a womern as God ever made. I had sons then, sons I tell you! — many an' many a son! Some of em died. Six of em lived though. I'm a strong man an' a powerful. An' I got six sons — six, I tell you! More'n anybody in these parts! Six sons, one after the other, six boys a-growin up like stair-steps t' keep me alive when I dead!*

Harmon is obsessed with land. He repeatedly refers to the size of his prop-erty: a hundred and sixty acres. Daniel Justice, in discussing *Cherokee Night*, notes, "The effects of allotment are indelibly marked on every aspect of the narrative."[14] The Curtis Act had applied the General Allotment Act to Indi-an Territory in 1898. One hundred and sixty acres, a quarter section, was the size of a standard allotment. John Harmon bought some Cherokee's al-lotment, the acquisition one of many examples of the land passing from Na-tive to non-Native hands. Notice, however, how he describes his purchase: it is "virgin from the Maker," overgrown, unplowed, and unplanted. It reflects an Amer-European notion that land must be farmed to be of worth, but even more, it calls into question even the humanity of the former proprietors, since the "hand of man hadn't touched it."

As often as Harmon refers to his land, he refers to his six surviving sons. They are Heck, Nick, Pick, Dick, Stick, and Jodie. Jodie, the oldest, is mild-mannered and his mother's favorite — consequently bearing the brunt of his father's violence. As fixated as Harmon is on his property and the power it coveys, he is also obsessed with masculinity. He encourages his boys to set-tle disputes with their fists and to "make the other feller bleed" because that "shows you're a man." When he gets publicly drunk at the weekly entertain-ment at Lone Ellum (the real-life Lone Elm), his wife, Thursey, who has ar-rived late with Jodie, says, "You ain't drinkin again, air you?" He wheels on her, declaring, "You're married to a *man*, you oughta know it by this time, you'd oughta git used to it."

Things begin to unravel in act two with the arrival at the Harmon home-stead of Annie Marble, described in the stage directions as "coquettish." When Thursey is bedridden after yet another miscarriage, John hires Annie to take care of the household and prepare the meals. Unfortunately the stress of car-rying twelve children over twenty years and the daily life of a pioneer woman prove too much, and Thursey dies at the end of act two, scene one.

In the ensuing weeks Jodie falls for Annie, as she fills the void left by his mother's death. Annie, however, despises the farm life and longs to move into the "big city" of Muskogee but lacks the wherewithal. She tells Jodie,

> Well, it's money, I tell you. T' git away from here! I wanta go to Musko-gee. It don't take much. I aint even got enough fer train fare. I'm t'ard of this, t'ard! They's lights thar, an' pavements, an' people a-dancin on slick floors like they couldn't get enough. I uz thar a-visitin Ruby Dawson two summers back. I don't see why I had t' come back again. I wish I'd stayed then! 'Stid of comin here t' rot! They aint nuthin here — but clods under yer feet! An' no one t' tell you you're purty, whe'er you air or not.

When Jodie impetuously proposes, Annie almost immediately turns back to money, telling him, "Marryin's sump'n ' at costs money." If manhood is John Harmon's obsession, money is Annie Marble's. Jodie and Annie talk complete-ly at cross-purposes, and Jodie never comprehends. Jodie promises to get money somehow. She wants only to escape.

At this critical moment Lem Williams, a friend of Harmon's, shows up looking to hire younger brother Heck as a teamster in the coalfields at Collinsville.[15] Thinking this job is his opportunity to get the money Annie needs and craves, Jodie persuades his pa to allow him to go instead. He'll be gone two or three months. Before he departs, he elicits Annie's lukewarm promise to wait for him. No sooner has he exited the stage than she turns her attentions to the father, cuckolding her new "fiancé."

During act three Jodie discovers the painful truths of his situation and is moved from passivity to action. John Harmon has, unbeknownst to Jodie, indentured his son to Lem Williams, making a deal with Lem to pay *him* for Jodie's labor. When he finds out, the young Harmon beats up Lem and heads for home. As the third act begins, Annie argues with John, who is refusing to pay her the twelve dollars he owes her for six weeks' work. She accuses him of wanting "it fer nuthin, I guess. An' 'cause I said I uz goin away, you won't pay me. Jist so's I'll stay! Well, I *won't* stay. You're a lyin cheat, that's whut you air, a-doin me the way you done me! But you won't keep me here, you won't! I'll find a way! I will!"

Jodie arrives back. Once again, he and Annie talk past each other, her whole focus being herself and the money she's owed for her work and "*besides* fer workin." She tells Jodie that she's the victim of repeated rapes: "Him! Comin in my room. I couldn't help it. He uz bigger'n me, he's strong like an animal — . . . At night. More'n once. Yer Paw! Make him pay, make him!" Enraged, Jodie exacts revenge for Annie and for himself and all the violence John Harmon has visited upon him, killing the father with the same crowbar that has been directed more than once at him.

After the killing reality begins to dawn on Jodie. As he emerges from the smokehouse where the deed was done, Annie's immediate question is, "Did he pay you?" It seems her *cri de coeur*, "make him pay, make him," had to do only with money owed to her for her services. She confesses to Jodie that what transpired between her and his father was consensual, defiantly telling him, "I wanted money, money! I wanted to git away from here! I'll tell you whut fer! To live with Ruby Dawson an' some other girls. It's a house — fer men to come to — that's whut it is!" When Jodie feebly protests, the once-and-future prostitute continues, "It's better'n here! They don't kill theirselves a-workin. An' they have clothes. An' dancin! I wanted to have things! I won't now — not

ever! I'll have to go back home. It's yore fault!" Jodie lapses back into his natural passivity. As people arrive and find the crime, he promises to wait peace-
fully for the sheriff, adding, "I'm glad I done it. It's better that a-way. My mind
ud got dim. It didn't light my way so's I knowed whur I was goin. It's brighter
now—a little brighter." As the light dawns, the curtain falls.

More than twenty years after *A Lantern to See By*, violence, manipulation,
betrayal, and patricide again took center stage for Lynn Riggs. Written in
1948, *Out of Dust* was produced in Westport, Connecticut, the following
year but never made it to New York. Even so, there are many who consider
this Shakespearean tragedy to be Riggs's greatest play.[16] As I write in my introduction to *The Cherokee Night and Other Plays by Lynn Riggs*, "A reimagin-
ing of Shakespeare's *King Lear*, the play is set on the Shawnee Cattle Trail in
the Cherokee Nation in the early 1880s, years before Riggs's birth but after the time that the trail had actually ceased operation, made obsolete by
the big trails further west and the opening of the Katy railroad, which largely traced its route."[17]

William Grant, the Lear figure, is cut from the same emotionally cruel cloth
as John Harmon. In stage notes Riggs describes him as "patriarchal, and severe, bigoted, tyrannical and deeply—mystically—a troubled man. His search
has carried him through hard-won accomplishment, through greed and lech-
ery and power over men. He has dignity and authority, dimensions that are
hard to deal with." With him are his three sons, Teece (the oldest), Bud, and
Jeff, as well as Teece's wife Maudie. Grant is the trail boss, and King, a crimi-
nal just out of prison, is his subboss.

Teece, though outwardly reticent, is dissatisfied and seething. He feels
that his father has denied him his proper position, passing him over for King
and leaving him an ordinary cowhand. When he confronts the old man, telling him the trail boss job is his "by rights," the father's reply is characteristic: "Things in this world are for men who take 'em. Don't you know that?"
Though his statement seems to be about the personal situation involved in
the argument, Bill Grant is speaking more broadly, his attitude that avaricious
Anglo Oklahomans about the taking of Native lands. He continues, narrating
a personal journey closely akin to John Harmon's:

> *A man would see his way clear to get 'em, anyway. Without their bein'*
> *give to him. Was anything ever give to me? Was it? I started out without*

a sou markee *in my pocket right after the war. I come to the Territo-*
ry and took hold, put down roots, slaved and struggled and fought my
way to be what I am, to have what I've got. Do you think it was easy?
Was it ever easy for a man since the start of time? The men in the Bible
wrestled with the desert and made it bloom. They stood alone at the
head of their family, at the head of their flocks and fields, and asked
no favors. And expected none.

The reference to the desert, once again, is reminiscent of John Harmon's view of his land as virginal and untouched before his arrival. In Native hands the land is literally barren. Like the heroes of the Bible, Grant and other Amer-Europeans have taken a desert and made it bloom.

As the drive winds its way through Indian Territory, King plays upon the sons' weaknesses, inciting them to plot their father's death. Though Maudie is a more sympathetic character than Annie Marble, she has similarities to the latter as well. Maudie came to live with the family when the boys' mother died:

King: *At the time there was no one to do for you boys, to see you was*
feed and tuck keer of. So your paw found someone. Maudie. An
orphan girl, from God knows where back in the backwoods. He
brought her in and she lived there. Tuck your maw's place.
Jeff: *What'd you mean?*
King: *The things a woman will do for a man.*
Jeff: *She went on the Trail with us all to Baxter, cookin' at the chuck*
wagon, washin' our duds in the cricks we crossed, bed-din' us
down when night come!
King: *Like I said.* The things a woman will do for a man. *For your*
paw, to put it plain. From the minute she set foot in your
kitchen.

There are intimations that Grant and Maudie's sexual relationship may be on-going. King tells Teece that "a man" would kill "the man that fooled around" with his "legal property."

The boys do finally succumb to their demons and attempt to murder Grant, trying to stage it as an accident, but when that fails, King stabs the father. The arrival of Jeff's fiancée Rose, however, strikes the youngest son with a fit of conscience. She persuades him to go with her to Baxter Springs, Kansas, the northern end of the trail, and tell the federal authorities of the crime.

The other conspirators pursue the fleeing lovers to a deserted prairie shack where they have holed up for the night. In the ensuing confrontation, Rose shoots King to keep him from killing Jeff. One crime has led to another. Jeff cries out, "Lie after lie, murder on top of murder! It's got to stop. It's got to stop now." With Maudie's assistance he and Rose escape and head for Baxter Springs. Though Teece and Bud light out for Mexico, Maudie resignedly waits for the law.

Obviously these two plays have everything to do with Riggs's issues with his emotionally distant Anglo father and the son's problematic relationships with women. The descriptions of the brutal fathers in both *A Lantern to See By* and *Out of Dust* are on fours with the story of his own father—William Grant Riggs. In an "I've Got a Secret" moment, Riggs flips over all the cards and names the patriarch in the latter William Grant. The tale of Amer-European trail drivers in the Cherokee Nation may have been called *Out of Dust*, but the Cherokee playwright himself remained firmly in the closet. It is significant, though, that both dramas, unlike *Cherokee Night* and *Green Grow the Lilacs*, are clearly set among non-Natives, the drovers of *Out of Dust* and the hard-scrabble farmers of *A Lantern to See By*. Though violence is not wholly absent in Riggs's Indian-themed plays, the criminality is pointed among non-Natives in plays like these as well as *The Lonesome West*, *Rancor*, and *The Domino Parlor*.

We Are Those Who Endure

Gerald Vizenor's term *survivance*, first deployed in his 1994 book *Manifest Manners*, quickly implanted itself at a foundational level in Native American Studies. Leaning on his Anishinaabe heritage, Vizenor takes an actual French word and repurposes it. *Survivance* carries a sense of "relic," a vestige of the past. Vizenor brings both the word and Indians into the present by applying it to American indigenes, eloquently imbuing it with a sense of both "survival" and "endurance." Yet it means more than these recombinant words. In *Fugitive Poses* Vizenor writes that words in "historical dictionaries" that he employs are "used with new connotations." He elaborates, writing, "For instance, survivance, in the sense of native survivance, is more than survival, more than endurance or mere response; the stories are active presence."[18] As Vizenor makes clear, survivance has a rhetorical aspect. Native presence can perdure in story. In fact, that presence can — paradoxically — occur in absence, in the story of a lost allotment or in an abandoned homestead where whites play out family violence.

Lynn Riggs understood Oklahomans, how they talked and how they thought. But more than that, he understood what the process of colonization had done to them, its deleterious effects. He dramatized the larger crime of theft of Native land in terms of interpersonal violence and individual crimes.

Out of Dust is framed by Maudie telling her story to Osborn, the United States marshal. She says that "what happened to us on the Trail could happen to anyone." When the lawman questions that assertion, she replies, "Because we all have the same weaknesses . . . temptations . . . greeds. Somehow, we have. The same blackness is in all of us." Asked by Osborn to tell him the details of the crimes, she says, "I would hide it from you if I could! Seal the pictures up in my brain! Never look at 'em myself even — or let thought touch 'em — in day or dark night." That is Oklahomans in a nutshell: wanting to hide any memories of theft of Indian lands even from themselves. Of course, this simply reflects a larger pattern when it comes to this country's indigenes, what ethicist Donald Shriver calls "American pragmatic forgetfulness" — "our blithe national habit of trying to get on with a future unencumbered by a past."[19]

Later, during the final confrontation at the abandoned house, as Jeff argues for confessing, Teece counters, "But we can tell the same story, and make it stick! We can get out of this scot-free!" For generations Oklahomans have told themselves the same story of stalwart boomers and enterprising sooners, even singing about it at football games, until they believed it themselves. And anyone pointing out the uncomfortable contrary truth angers them. Through drama Lynn Riggs reminded them (and all Americans) in an act of survivance.

In exposing these dark, hidden secrets to light, Riggs knew the provocation he was making. In a letter to a friend in Oklahoma, written just as *Big Lake*, *Sump'n Like Wings*, and *A Lantern to See By* went to press, he wondered and worried whether people at home would be "irate Oklahomans when my plays are published — in all their fever and horror and brashness and lewdness and all the things that accumulate and throw their shadows over the inner gentility and fragility which is at their core."[20]

Journalist H. L. Mencken was fond of reminding Americans that the United States was a nation of losers. No one ever came here who was making it where they were. In his essay "On Being an American," he sums up: "All of which may be boiled down to this: that the United States is essentially a commonwealth of third-rate men. . . . The land was peopled, not by the hardy adventurers of legend, but simply by incompetents who could not get on at home."[21]

What Mencken observed for the nation as a whole is even more true of Oklahoma, the original "Last Frontier." The boomers and sooners Oklahomans celebrate in song and story were failures, drifters, grifters, and grafters—malcontents and crooks of every stripe. They were Mencken's "botched and unfit."[22] In 1928 Riggs describes them in a letter to his friend, drama critic Barrett Clark:

> And I know what makes them a little special, a little distinct in the Middle West is the quality of their taciturnity. They are voiceless, tongueless; they answer the challenging "Who goes there?" only by a flash of a lantern so quick, so momentary, that none but the acute guard sees more than a shadowy figure retreating into the darkness. There are two reasons for this: faulty education (or none at all); the other, the people who settled Oklahoma were a suspect fraternity, as fearful of being recognized by others as they were by themselves. Gamblers, traders, vagabonds, adventurers, daredevils, fools. Men with a sickness, men with a distemper. Men disdainful of the settled, the admired, the regular ways of life. Men on the move. Men fleeing from a critical world and their own eyes. Pioneers, eaten people. And their descendants have the same things in them, changed a little, grown out a bit, but there, just the same. And so they don't speak. Speech reveals one. It is better to say nothing. And so these people, who had been much admired and much maligned, have been not quite known—a shifting fringe of dark around the campfire, where wolves, perhaps, and unnamable things lurked.[23]

At the end of Out of Dust Maudie cryptically ties all that has transpired to the land. As Osborn is about to lead her away, she stops:

> **Maudie:** The thing that bothers me!: It took me so long to take hold of a stand and hang on to it! Why is a person so blind?

> *Why does he allow some other person to drag the evil out*
> *of him, drag it out into the light? And then to use it, turn*
> *it loose on the folks around him till they die and are slung in*
> *the grave! Why do we do that? Is it because we're all so*
> *vain — and lost — and afraid?*
>
> **Man (Osborn):** *Lots of people ask themselves that. The answer is yes, I reckon.*
> **Maudie:** *Yes. Stuck, like we all are — smack between heaven and hell.*
> **Man:** *In purgatory, you mean?*
> **Maudie:** *On earth, I mean. In my case — in our case — this was the*
> *earth we knowed and walked on.*

Notice the reference to evil being dragged "out into the light." In both *A Lantern to See By* and *Out of Dust*, references to light and dark are prominent — as they are in Riggs's other work as well. His is, however, no Manichean world of sharp divisions between these opposites. Lynn Riggs was a playwright of the shadows. In that same letter to Barrett Clark, Riggs refers to Oklahoma as a place of "much cruelty and darkness." Reacting to a review of his one-act *Knives from Syria* that initially pleased him but on reconsideration troubled him, he writes, "And at first I was [pleased], because I care very much about Oklahoma's seeing some justice, and some truth in my work. . . . No, the truth about those plays [his] is that here is a germ of *light*, a germ of poetry about a dark and sometimes fierce and nearly always ignorant people." He continues,

> *Some day, perhaps, all the plays I will have written, taken together, may*
> *constitute a study from which certain things may emerge and be for-*
> *mulated into a kind of truth about people who happen to be living in*
> *Oklahoma instead of South Dakota. But not now. The secret is scat-*
> *tered too widely — and, what is worse, hid away — in the breasts of too*
> *many people. Farm people, ranchers, lawyers, bankers, doctors, wait-*
> *resses, bakers, tool dressers, school teachers — there, as everywhere,*
> *unite in a desperate concealment; the beats of their hearts are mys-*
> *terious and faint; no pressure of hand or even opened vein may teach*
> *much about that guarded flow.*[24]

I love Oklahoma. But that love does not blind me to the darkness that exists at what the French would call the *triste* locales like Fort Reno and the

Claremore Mound, where there is at least some nobility in the blood that the ground has absorbed, and I love it in spite of irredeemable places like Diamondback Correctional Facility. Despite everything, Lynn Riggs loved it too. But that love rendered him neither deaf nor blind. He heard and saw Oklahomans. He knew what participation in the enterprise of empire had done to them. He dramatized the larger crime of theft of Native land in very intimate terms. It is as though he traveled up the rivers of veins of white colonizers into their heart of darkness and whispered, "The horror. The horror."

Notes

1. http://findagrave.com (accessed September 23, 2006). Besides the information that can be garnered from the gravestones themselves, a good source of information on some of those interred there is *Fort Reno Tombstone Tales* (El Reno OK: Fort Reno Visitor Center, 1999).

2. Creek writer and critic Craig Womack, who regularly volunteers and visits the Native Hawaiian inmates at Diamondback, told me that a group once asked him to draw a map of their location so that they would know where they were. Assuming they wanted to know where they were in the state, Womack drew the map. Only then did he learn that they had meant they needed to know where Oklahoma was within the United States.

3. James W. Parins, *Elias Cornelius Boudinot: A Life on the Cherokee Border* (Lincoln: University of Nebraska Press, 2006), 163.

4. Parins, *Elias Cornelius Boudinot*, 201–2.

5. Rachel Caroline Eaton, "The Legend of the Battle of the Claremore Mound," *Chronicles of Oklahoma* 8, no. 4 (December 1930): 375.

6. Eaton, "Battle of the Claremore Mound," 375–76.

7. For example, see the Fort Clark Treaty of 1808 between the Osage and the United States and the treaty concluded with the Cherokee on July 8, 1817.

8. See Lynn Riggs, *The Cherokee Night and Other Plays by Lynn Riggs*, ed. Jace Weaver (Norman: University of Oklahoma Press, 2003), 106.

9. Riggs, *Cherokee Night*, 369.

10. Daniel Justice, *Our Fire Survives the Storm: A Cherokee Literary History* (Minneapolis: University of Minnesota Press, 2006), 100.

11. Phyllis Cole Braunlich, *Haunted by Home: The Life and Letters of Lynn Riggs* (Norman: University of Oklahoma Press, 1988), 45.

12. Quoted in Braunlich, *Haunted by Home*, 61.

13. Significant offstage action takes place in the coal pits at Collinsville, which was settled in 1897 after the discovery of coal. Originally called simply Collins, the name was changed to Collinsville on June 16, 1898. In the play Blackmore is said to be

"Blackmore, Oklahoma." Claremore was in the Cherokee Nation and ergo *Indian* Territory. If it is Blackmore, Oklahoma, one may assume that this story of Amer-European farmers takes place after statehood. See George H. Shirk, *Oklahoma Place Names*, 2nd rev. ed. (Norman: University of Oklahoma Press, 1974), 56.

14. Justice, *Our Fire Survives*, 98.

15. The entry on Indian Territory in the 1896 edition of *King's Handbook of the United States* declares that "one of the chief natural endowments of the Territory is its coal-measures, covering 13,600 square miles, and producing a valuable bituminous coal, great quantities of which are mined every year." Moses King and M. F. Sweetser, *King's Handbook of the United States* (Springfield MA: King, Richardson, 1896), 248.

16. Weaver, in Riggs, *Cherokee Night*, xiv, 214.

17. Weaver, in Riggs, *Cherokee Night*, xiv.

18. Gerald Vizenor, *Fugitive Poses: Native American Indian Scenes of Absence and Presence* (Lincoln: University of Nebraska Press, 1998), 15. Inspired by Vizenor and his recreation of survivance, I coined the term *communitism*, a combination of "community" and "activism."

19. Donald Shriver, *An Ethic for Enemies: Forgiveness in Politics* (New York: Oxford University Press, 1995), 74.

20. Braunlich, *Haunted by Home*, 52.

21. H. L. Mencken, "On Being an American," in *Prejudices: Third Series* (New York: Knopf, 1922), 22–23.

22. Mencken, "On Being an American," 24.

23. Braunlich, *Haunted by Home*, 71; emphasis in the original.

24. Braunlich, *Haunted by Home*, 70–72; emphasis in the original.

18. SURVIVANCE MEMORIES

The Poetry of Carter Revard

A. Robert Lee

Survivance is more than survival.
It means redefining ourselves.
It means raising our social
and political consciousness.
It means holding on to ancient
principles while eagerly embracing
change. It means doing what is
necessary to keep our cultures alive.

The term was first put
forward by the Anishinaabe scholar
Gerald Vizenor in his book
Manifest Manners: Postindian
Warriors of Survivance *(1994).*

National Museum of the American Indian,
Jolene Richard, Cynthia L. Chavez, and Gabrielle Tayac

Poet, autobiographer, essayist, and scholar, it would be hard not to assign Carter Revard a life of literary multiples. But the cv carries a yet wider span, life-filled, various, and full of eclectic different seams. These latter embrace the Oklahoman, the farmhand, and greyhound-minder in youth; the Oxford Rhodes Scholar and Yale PhD; the Revard, also Nom-peh-wah-the, or "Thunder Person," in the dynastic naming instigated by his Osage grandmother Josephine Jump in 1952; and the Ponca gourd dancer. A scholar of the Harley Lyrics manuscript and its *fabliau* poetry and professor emeritus of medieval literature and linguistics at Washington University since retirement in 1997, Revard has also been a board member and president of the American Indian Center of Mid-America (AICMA). With international and U.S.-regional and mixed Native and white lineage and from out of a history spanning the Dust Bowl to the Bush Jr. presidency, he also belongs beyond question among the leading ranks of contemporary Native authors — his poetry not only engaging but being an often startlingly live archive.

How not to imagine that issues of survival/survivance give every pertinence both to Revard's sense of the world and to his sense of the role of his own poetry? Two observations supply working touchstones. In *Family Matters, Tribal Affairs* (1998) he writes of Osage legacy and its implications:

> In the Osage Creation Story, which was recited as part of the Naming Ceremony and therefore was heard many times by assembled families as their children were being "brought into" the tribal society, we see animals as partners, teachers and helpers welcoming us into this world, giving us ways to survive and prevail in our earthly lives. Perhaps when the Tainos thought "Columbus came from the sky," and welcomed him to this world that was new to him, they had some such belief in mind: a new group of beings, in those three ships, was coming to this world, and those already here could welcome and show them how to survive.[1]

In *Winning the Dustbowl* (2001) he expounds on the resources, especially Ponca resilience of spirit and practicality, necessary to counter setbacks of poverty and reservation-blame stereotype:

> Over a span of years in Buck Creek I've watched the deputies come for my uncles, have put up bail money for relatives, with Ponca aim cousins in White Eagle hit the floor while car-lights of what may have been a drive-by shooting moved slowly past — and ours was one of the less tough situations in that Depression-then-War-then-AIM time and Oklahoma place. In short, I grew up poor in a mixedblood family on a reservation among people like ourselves, trying to resist and survive the incoming flak from people who thought they were not like ourselves, hitting us with loud or silent messages that everything happening to us was our fault. But while some poems in this collection speak directly from that foxhole, most assume and celebrate a temporary survival, though the war has no end. One way to survive is to keep a sense of hope, of being able to find what works, what helps, the laughter and shared strength and awareness of good things and good ways.[2]

Within this compass Revard's life and writing has been one of necessary particularities. He has written with enormous verve of his French-Irish (and Scots-Irish) and Osage-Ponca extended family. Key geographies include Pawhuska, Osage capital and his Oklahoma Indian Agency birthplace; the early Revard and Jump reservation homesteads in Bird Creek, the Caney River, and near Buck Creek; Illinois's Cahokia Mounds; the Missouri of St. Louis, the city and suburbs and the university world (his poem "Outside in St. Louis" — "inside the whisper of / a soft St. Louis rain" — much applies); and Oxford (the fond memorial sequence "Homework at Oxford" in *An Eagle Nation*).[3] He writes also of the Isle of Skye (to which he pays vivid tribute in "Letter to Friends in the Isle of Skye" with its allusions to "great mossy boulders of / the pyramid island" and "waterfall's tuba" and "rock-juts") and Europe, Greece, and the Mediterranean.[4] A natural order of landscapes, in fact, supplies a connecting allusive pattern in his verse: animals, creeks, littoral, rivers, or bird and tree and ocean life. Given his interest in tribal and other Creation myths, he has long shown a penchant for exploring timelines both ecoevolutionary and modern. Native politics has meant a fund of community and cultural participation, not least those that have arisen out of Wounded Knee 1973 and that took him to the edge of AIM activism and has involved him in different marches, bail-support, and court hearings as a witness.

Throughout, Revard has kept to a steady double track of academic and creative work, though with any number of overlaps. Notably he has sought to link his Old and Middle English and language-history interests to his Native American classes and scholarship. His taste for *Beowulf*-era riddle formulae he adapts to modern voice in "Nine Beings Speak in Riddles" (*Cowboys and Indian/Christmas Shopping*), whether "The Swan's Song" with its "wayfaring soul" or "Something Inside" with "this azure eyeball" of modern TV. A further gloss is to be found in the playful essay and verse of "Some Worldly Riddles: Trinity and Skunk" (*Winning the Dust Bowl*). His interest in other Old English forms such as the kenning (*hwael*-weg, whale-way, for the sea and like) he reflects in the spaced appositions aimed to convey eagle–flight. One sees this technique in these lines from "What the Eagle Fan Says":

> *I strung dazzling thrones   of thunder beings*
> *on a spiraling thread   of spinning flight.*

It is also evident in the process of tree-into-vessel in "Birch Canoe":

> Red men embraced   my body's whiteness
> cutting into me   carved it free.[5]

To shared purpose a wide-ranging essay such as "Making A Name" (*Family Matters, Tribal Affairs*) connects the word creations of the book of Genesis to bird and human names and, above all, American place names. Two place names especially have drawn his interest: Amherst, with its naming for Lord Jeffrey Amherst, the British commander responsible for biological warfare in the form of smallpox blankets against the French-allied Ottawa (under their leader Pontiac) and other Algonquin tribes, and St. Louis, with its connection to Jefferson's Louisiana Purchase and the ethnic cleansing of Missouri River civilizations such as the originally Missouri-based Osage and which was settled from the 1760s on by Euro-America, among whom were French trappers such as Revard's own ancestor Joseph Revard. If Revard has adverted to the English and American literary canon, Chaucer, the English Romantics, Emily Dickinson, and others, he has frequently expressed an admiring sense of lineage for John Joseph Mathews, vintage Osage author, fellow Oxonian, whose *Sundown* (1933) remains a landmark in the depiction of Oklahoma as historic "Indian Territory" with its white-Osage interface, oil politics, tribal dispossession, and mixed-blood lineages.

The gloss thereby given to Gerald Vizenor's philosophy of survivance by the curators at the National Museum of the American Indian, albeit a touch short on wider implications, supplies but one of several working perspectives for Revard. The concept has, however, been of greatest importance in a poet full of heritage yet also of intimate attunement to how that heritage takes on new energy, a reliving. One body of writing that notably bears upon this sense of past into present is Revard's interstitially organized seven-part verse and prose sequence "Indian Survival" in *Winning the Dust Bowl*, each section of which is a life vignette, although none more affecting than "At Cahokia Mounds" with its eulogy to his hugely loved Aunt Jewell, Ponca elder of White Eagle, Oklahoma, and, on this occasion, "Powwow Princess."

Yet fuller overall confirmation lies in the enactive imagining of each of his verse collections, *Ponca War Dancers* (1980), *Cowboys and Indians/Christmas Shopping* (1992), *An Eagle Nation* (1993), and *How the Songs Come Down: New and Selected Poems* (2006). Taken together, they amount to the sustained exhibition of ear and eye, a poetry of sharp, often wryly comic and winningly vernacular awareness, the one or another speculative turn to do with memory or science or landscape. Above all Revard leaves no doubt of his resolved-upon witness to a Native America, Osage and Ponca, and reservation and beyond-reservation, as wholly in being against whatever odds and given to their own resilient continuity of presence.

If any one poem serves as Revard's *ars poetica*, it is likely "How the Songs Come Down," the title phrase for his most recent volume and first published nearly three decades ago in *Ponca War Dancers*. A mid-May suburban night-time supplies the opening "full moon," "starry heavens," and

> *a streetlamp mellow in the new oak*
> *leaves*

against whose backdrops two overweight lovers

> *white*
> *T-shirt wobbling with her breasts, he bulge-*
> *bellied in Bermuda shorts*

nuzzle and kiss.[6] It leads the poem's speaker to contrast watcher and watched, his own sleeping children as against the entangled pair, and "public streets" as against "private selves." How can he see the world's design, its "memories," "molecules" seeming "darkness" in this vista from his "unlit" window?

The poem moves to the song of a mockingbird ("fortissimo in the high catalpa's blossoms"), another kind of night vista. Owls are said to be

> *listening for*
> *the stir of mice on tiptoes,*

"midnight moths" to probe the leafy catalpa's blossoms "unharassed."[7] Above all, the mockingbird becomes a kind of avian hipster-musician:

> *He not only dee-Jays*
> *his own commercials, he jukeboxes*
> *the songs of all the other birds*
> *except I think for owls perhaps.*[8]

This scene is then linked to one in Skye—a roaring cataract, clouds, granite rocks, other mockingbirds, streams, "star-moss," and "luminous lichen," in all a scene

> *like time fixed*
> *on Mayan orbstones.*[9]

The poet-observer, clad in mundane weather-proofed "nylon rain-pants," feels himself close to "the earth's eyeball," Nature's "tensor calculus." The issue again arises: what is this mass called earth, life amid death, the black holes behind creation? How does the mockingbird's song illuminate a once primordial darkness?

Those contemplations bring the poet round to the memory of the "lullaby our Ponca aunt would sing" in his childhood, a song whose Ponca words in the voice of Aunt Jewell he did not understand but which speak exactly to sound over silence, life over death:

> *It was a song her blind*
> 　　*great-aunt had made up after the Poncas*
> *had been forced down from Nebraska onto*
> 　　*the Oklahoma reservation, and she made it there*
> *one night to sing her brothers when the whisky*
> 　　*was almost drowning them: its words said:*
> 　　　　*Why are you afraid?*
> 　　　　*No one can go round death.*
> *She tells her children lately now, Aunt Jewell, some of*
> 　　*those real old things.*
> 　　　　　*now that the time has come*
> *to pass them on, and they are ready*
> *to make new places for what she*
> 　　*would sing us in*
> *our moonlit darkness like*
> 　　*a bronze and lively bird.*[10]

Aunt Jewell serves perfectly as gifting past into present and present into future. One might well hear something of the darkness of a poem such as Robert Frost's "Design," something of the hope of Whitman's "When Lilacs in the Dooryard Bloom'd," or something of the dream-myth of Yeats's "Byzan-tium" diptych. But to be heard quite irresistibly and from Aunt Jewell's "blind / great-aunt" is also this Ponca wisdom, both in the name of health over self-destructive drinking and in the name not just of well-being but proportion ("*No one can go round death*").[11] To be heard is a Native sense of cycle, a song for "our moonlit darkness." The song, its own species of human bird song as it were and reflexively like the very poem in which it is remembered, carries the energy of life's "old things" transposed and "passed on" into "new plac-es," nothing less than and precisely *survivance*.

Native-themed poems, to be sure, comprise but one sheaf in Revard's over-all repertoire. The work available easily extends out to his Oklahoma youth-memory verse, as with "Free White and Fifteen" in *Ponca War Dancers*; a poet-ry of place, as with "In Kansas" and "Okies" in *Cowboys and Indians/Christmas Shopping*; or time-space philosophical verse, such as "Geode," "Sea Chang-es," and "When Earth Brings" in *An Eagle Nation*. To these pieces should be added his poems on hearing loss, reflecting Revard's own loss, as notably with "And Don't Be Deaf to the Singing Beyond," the anecdotal elegy to a "migrant Okie" uncle who dies seemingly amused at watching the moving lips of Aunt Jewell and "hearing" some voice far beyond. But, almost inevitably, the writ-ing that makes tribal reference carries an especially charged weight, "mem-ories of now" in the sense that they speak to the making and the furthering of Native signature in the world.

In this respect "Washazhe Grandmother" in *Ponca War Dancers* offers a key touchstone in looking to how Revard's own Osage grandparental lineage of family persists into a wholly contemporary America. Not the least of this poem's qualities is the avoidance of sentimentality and the careful particu-larization of feeling with place and time-then with continuance-now. Two departure points first intersect. The one borrows from Francis La Flesche's *A Dictionary of the Osage Language* (1932) to explain the vortex of meaning in the term *Ho-e-ga* as the convergence point of elk forehead and creation myth, at once encampment and cosmic gathering point. The other summons Oklahoma as both geography and history,

    allotted land

> *out west of the Agency,*

"the prairie's edge" and "the Osage hills," where his homesteading (and honeymooning) grandparents set up house.[12] Revard's contextual locale might almost in itself be a code of remembrance ("I was six"): Timber Hill, Bird Creek, deer at dusk, "dark water turning into / a spilling of light" (in the grandmother's Osage term "*ni-xe*"), a kingfisher's "blue flash" of diving, and above all the spiritually defining stillness:

> *the whole place was so quiet,*
> *the way Grandma was quiet.*[13]

That, relays the poem, was then. "Now" is the aftermath of

> *that Depression year when Osage oil*
> *still gushed to float us on into*
> *a happy future.*

It is a line whose ironic pitching makes its own kind of mark.[14] Grandmother Jump, widowed in the war, has moved to land "south of Pawhuska" to be reached by

> *a dirt road winding red and rocky*
> *across tree roots*

and in a "rumbling Buick Eight" driven by the poet's mother.[15] The older homestead has been submerged by dam water that formed Lake Bluestem, a drinking, pool, and sprinkler supply for Pawhuska. Yet as

> *big catfish*
> *grope slowly in darkness*

or "scavenge" in "Bird Creek's old channel under Lake Bluestem," so the memory holds of a bridal party, an "Indian marriage" (albeit Native and white)

> *where*
> *an Osage bride and her man came riding one special day*
> *and climbed down from the buggy in all their*
> *best finery*
> *to live in their first home.*[16]

This is stored family, past time and place yet also present time and place. Revard's touch invites every recognition, Native dynasty however apparently just out of view, kept as alive in the Pawhuska lake waters and township as in an Osage grandmother's one-time nuptials and homemaking.

A companion piece is to be found in "People From the Stars" (*Ponca War Dancers*), with a suitably attached subtitle acknowledgment of John Joseph Mathews's *The Osages: Children of the Middle Waters* (1961). If the Osage or Wazhazhe reference scheme is celebratory, not to say mythic and historic, the follow-on Las Vegas reference scheme is all uncelebration. The poem initially makes a contrast of two creation stories, that of the Osage/Washazhe as a benign union of sky and earth people in the gathering point known as *Ho-e-ga* and that of the Old Testament or Miltonic pageant of Satan's expulsion from Heaven. The Osage specifics conjure up a harmonizing kinetics of food, ceremony, dress, bestiary, bird, and thunder-myth:

> We made our fire places
> and made our bodies of
> the golden eagle and the cedar tree,
> of mountain lion and buffalo,
> of redbird, black bear, of the
> great elk and of thunder so that we
> may live to see old age
> and go back to the stars.[17]

Modern oil, however, has entered the equation ("the Europeans pay us royalties"), energy supply to light "midnight highways" and create "star-strings through the night." The exchange deal, though, has exacted more than an explicit money value. If airplanes now "enthrone" their passengers to fly over tribal land into casino Las Vegas and to play craps at the aptly named Stardust Inn, so Native people—Anishinaabe/Chippewa or Osage or any other—in the mind's eye become the distant Other, remnant exotics. The gamblers to hand can only

> talk of Indians and their Trickster Tales,
> of Manabozho up
> in Wounded Knee.[18]

Truly an ironic signification inheres within this literally flying visit, all too temporary gaming in the face of so permanent a tribal history.

"Ponca War Dancers," title-poem of its volume and four-part sequence centred fondly but again without the slightest undue sentimentality in his Uncle Gus McDonald, brother to Aunt Jewell, gives sight and sound to a key player in the family and stepfamily web set forth in detail in the text and photography of *Winning the Dust Bowl*. Uncle Gus bows in as an observer of old-time Ponca etiquette, unwilling to speak directly to his nephew Buck's new wife, an obliquity of manner necessarily to be explained by Aunt Jewell. But his presiding credential is offered anything but obliquely: "he was the greatest of Ponca dancers."[19] The voice of the poem might well recall Gus's drinking, his "heavy-bellied quick talking," and his sheer fun and japery. But that also comes with the self-upbraiding

> how come I never understood
> he was a champion.[20]

"Sixty-something," "pot-bellied but quick-footed," and in ankle bells, Gus's agility of response to the drum becomes "the Spirit's dance," the very hawk wing. He more than simply memorializes, he embodies passed-down tribal art, "the old songs" resung or reenacted. The poem's spacing shadows that art's grace, albeit with reference to being seen within a shared Native/non-Native context and to an abetting word play around Kentucky bourbon (Old Crow, if a brand, is also the Yukon township of the Vuntut Gwitchin First Nation) and Canadian Club whisky. Gus so dances

> among bleachers and tourists
> and the grave, merry faces
>   Osage and Ponca, Otoe and Delaware,
> Quapaw and Omaha, Pawnee Comanche and Kaw,
>   who saw what he was doing
>   and how he did it well even when
>   to the white eyes watching he was
>   an old Indian slowing down
>   and between dances going
>   to have another slug of
>   hell, maybe Old Crow or even
>   Canadian Club,
>   good enough for the Champion.[21]

It is Gus's residual spirit that plays into the events of the long third section set in Ponca City of 1974, a "memorial feast" a year after Wounded Knee. The poem looks both forward to when "cousins Carter and Craig and Dwain and Serena" would become AIM fugitives pursued into the Oklahoma hills by helicopter and backward to Uncle Woody, 1930s Gatsbyesque bootlegger and also an FBI fugitive. Positioned in between and in Revard's own vernacular speaker-voice is the family car en route to Ponca City and tailgated by a state patrolman:

> we weren't in trouble
> just driving all crowded up
> in my old Dart,
> with Stephanie from Third Mesa and Mickey
> from Pine Ridge,
> with Geronimo and Big Jim Jump and Mary Ann
> teaching us Cherokee and all of us singing
> Forty-Nine songs on our way to the way to the feast.[22]

Osage dancers and Ponca singers join together. Blankets and food are distributed. A small squabble breaks over Buck's woman. Amid these happenings Cousin Carter, eventually to be caught in Chicago for

> disarming (allegedly) a postal inspector
> inside Wounded Knee

and sentenced to three years in federal penitentiaries in Indiana and Missouri, turns the focus back to Gus McDonald ("Uncle Gus was the best all right").[23] In Wounded Knee as iconic history, the 1890 massacre and the 1970s AIM-FBI face off, it is Gus's spirit — dance, song, drum, grace — that the poem sees as persisting.

The fourth section is to remember Gus as both a McDonald, Celtic-American, and Shongeh-ska, Ponca kinsman, real yet also the *figura* of a people who, in life-over-death echoes of the books of Isaiah and Jeremiah as well as of equal pertinence the Gettysburg Address, "shall not perish from the earth." The poem is self-described as a

> memorial song
> to Shongeh-ska, one
> of the greatest Ponca dancers,
> to dance once more.[24]

"The songs" embodied in Uncle Gus's dance take on an inclusive meaning, with Ponca life in itself as an ongoing song-dance. It points to culture
deeded into the present not as some "Indian" show time but exemplary life
energy, an invitation to witness and learn from a people's historic measure
through and as time:

> For those who saw him dance
>   and learned from him the way,
>   he is dancing still.
>   Come to White Eagle in the summer time,
>   Indians dance in the summer time —
> He is back with his people now.[25]

This same emphasis on the carried-down resilience of Native life — which is
not to suggest Revard sidesteps setbacks, odds, and fracture — marks most
of *Cowboys and Indians/Christmas Shopping*. It is discernible in poems such as
"Making a Name," with its opening of,

> The authors of this story are
> my Ponca folks, Aunt Jewell and
> Uncle Woody;

"Where the Frontier Went" as a landscape of American time line and site
through Osage and white settlement; or one of the title poems, "Christmas
Shopping," with its vista of

> Christmas Eve
> with sunset
> in St. Louis,

in which a combination of sumptuous night sky and a zigzagging squirrel
play against the season's credit-card buying frenzy.[26] Two other poems do
duty, each at first seemingly similarly anecdotal but in fact subtly loaded in
the way tribal history is able to remake even as it revisits inherited weights
and measures.

In "Summer 1983" Ponca song — and song in its widest inclusive sense — again
enters the reckoning. The lines begin as though part of a diary, a chronicle-
in-small set on "the August prairie":

> Going up to the Sun Dance
>   at Rosebud
>   there in Nebraska they
> stopped, my Ponca cousins
>   from Oklahoma —
>   it was out there
>   by some kind of ruins
>   on the August prairie,
>   some kind of fort it may have been.[27]

Cousin Serena, Mike, and the children hear singing even though

>   there
>   was not a soul in sight.[28]

They identify it as "a victory song." It is in imaginative reality a song that carries down history, chorus, or memory, not just tribal resistance but triumph.

The encounter at issue has been that of the Cheyenne in Nebraska pinning and taunting federal troops in their fort in the wake of Colorado's 1864 Sand Creek massacre. That episode, the killing of an estimated five hundred peaceably encamped Cheyenne and Arapaho, together with leaders such as Black Kettle and Left Hand, at the orders of Colonel John M. Chivington, needs no editorializing from the poem. Rather, Revard keeps the allusion a matter-of-fact Indian killing that was all too "ordinary" throughout U.S. history:

>   that time the news got out of what
>   had been done to Black Kettle and
>   his people there under
>   the big American flag. George Bent
>   has told about it in his letters.[29]

George Bent (1843–1917), son of the prairie trader William Bent and his Cheyenne wife Owl Woman and informant on indigenous prairie culture to the ethnologist George Bird Grinnell, could not be a better name to invoke. His is the participant-witness, a voice throughout his collected letters from both histories. Whether or not the poem's ending is quite a dénouement, it once more bespeaks remembrance but also "song" as ongoing tribal sign:

I guess, Mike said,
there must have been some Poncas
 joined the Cheyenne and fought
the soldiers there.
           We recognized the song,
Serena said. It's one
           that we still sing.[30]

"The Secret Verbs" gives off a nice double play of irony and serious whimsy, a riff both on manifest destiny and on American history's naming of parts. Revard writes not a little under his role as language professor and, maybe, even with the echo in mind of Henry Reed's "Naming of Parts" as a British World War II poem that contrasts the combat rifle with Nature's flora. The tone of Revard's poem is seize-the-attention, breezy, and possessing a classroom's grammar lesson questioning to get things started:

           They're hidden right in plain sight.
      Take UNASSIGNED LANDS *for instance: what's the verb?*
           TO UNASSIGN.
           A powerful verb, in 1889 it grabbed
           almost two million acres of Indian lands
           where Oklahoma City squats, and all
           those other towns, wheat farms and ranches,
           oil wells and politicians.[31]

The poem glosses "UNASSIGN" with its own counterlexicography, its own interrogation as to the preemptive writ, not just of American colonial history but of colonial language:

           Why call them UNASSIGNED?
      Well, after the "Civil" War, the Creeks
      and Seminoles were forced to concede
      this land for settlement by freed slaves.
           Quite understandably, no one ever
            assigned the lands to slaves.
           So what the participle means is this:
           WE UNASSIGN *THESE LANDS TO BLACKS OR INDIANS,*

WE NOW ASSIGN THEM TO AMERICANS,
SO LONG AS THEY ARE WHITE.[32]

Revard's irony is well judged in a poem to repossess the narrative as much as the vocabulary of America. These "participles" and "adjectives," as he calls them, carry the very sediment of a grievous dispossession, whether land, sovereignty, or tribal language. What the poem proposes is a reexamination of how the canonical version of America secretes, and often enough outright deletes, its Native order. Mixing in some of his own word play, Revard instances other examples, as in

> the words DISCover and COVERt,
> or DISinform, or UNAmerican,
> or Unused Land.[33]

The closing lines can hardly be thought any less a wry Native time line, with tongue or memory as restorative, a lived counterlexicography indeed to play against the 1792–1992 bicentennial and the euphemisms it has entailed:

> How we UNUSE our language
> Is maybe worth a thought, in a
> CENTENNIAL year, and every year's
> centennial for something, isn't it?[34]

"Under the old names, new beings gather; within the new beings, old ways survive."[35] So runs Revard's "A Giveaway Special," his introduction to *An Eagle Nation*. Whether in truth "portentous stuff," as he self-ironically terms it, it affords a perfect gloss for the three sequences to follow ("An Eagle Nation," "Homework at Oxford," and "Sea Changes"). The dedication to

> the Wazhazhe and Ponca Nations
> and all our Relations,

moreover, in no way tempers the invitation to a wholly encompassing wider readership—"You are welcome in my books at any time."[36] It sets a congenial note but not one to suggest a dip in Revard's seriousness or vernacular dexterity in memorializing "now" as much as any time past "then"—and certainly not in issues of Native dispensation.

"Parading with the VFW" understandably has become familiar Revard. The history it carries is worn lightly, engagingly, but with great underlying edge. The evidential first-person voice beckons:

> Apache, Omaha, Osage, Choctaw, Micmac, Cherokee, Oglala . . .
> Our place was ninety-fifth.[37]

There is a note of credible ease and chat about the army howitzer muzzle ("'Hey, Cliff,' I said, 'haven't seen guns that big since we were in Wounded Knee'").[38] A nice swerve of irony enters as a troop of cavalry joins the parade in Civil War–style uniforms with the insignia of "the 7th Cavalry, George Custer's bunch."[39] Walt tells Cliff that the cavalry have him marked as Sitting Bull even as Sherry laconically warns about horse droppings:

> Us women walking behind the trailer
> will have to step around it all
> so much, they'll think we're dancing.[40]

This one latter-day VFW parade, accoutred in due irony, the imagery kept at the proper temperature, perfectly takes up the history behind it: Indian and overseas wars, tribe, ribbon shirt, "traditional dresses," gun, dance, horse, and U.S. cavalry.

In the verse paragraph to follow, this same history carries right into the contemporary. A city yellow line guides the parade participants. Both "fake war-whoops" and applause greet word of the coming powwow in, paradoxically of all places,

> Jefferson Barracks Park,
> where the dragoons were quartered for the Indian Wars.[41]

The judging done, shawls and clothing stored in the car, Kentucky Fried Chicken purchased, the group — appropriately enough, given the occasion — head to the Indian Center. As to the chicken, it too is neatly tied into historical freight, a welcome good taste

> given the temporary
> absence of buffalo here in the
> Gateway to the West, St. Louis.[42]

Revard marshals the poem with quite unobtrusive skill, image segues into image, its "parade" a possession of the tribal present as much as past.

A similar play of time eras, and with them time myths, operates in "Close Encounters." The juxtaposition is of Osage creation story on the one hand and on the other Spielberg movie title to indicate a Frontier Airlines landing in Las Vegas. As to the former the poem respectfully, knowledgeably, turns first upon the sky-messengers who taught the making of the body and

> how to make ourselves a nation,
> find power to live, to go on

and to pursue the sun into night and back into the light.[43] That same sun in a quite matching radiance of image then becomes in the course of the Osage Naming Ceremony exquisitely and beautifully transformed into the

> white eagle plumes in the hair
> of children as we give them names.[44]

Revard's ensuing lines just as radiantly fill out this topography of belief. The messengers enter and become the shared animate world of Thunder, Mountain Lion, Red Bird, Cedar Tree, Black Bear, and Golden Eagle. They cause a showering of seeds and acorns, thereby creating sources of daily bread and oak. The arboreal oak leaves in turn become a species of a creative musical score ("the sun caught / among leaves moving / around its light"), both tribal imaginative and Whitmanesque, the perfect analogues of subsequent written leaves:

> It will not end, we sang,
> in time our leaves of paper will
> be dancing lightly, making a nation of
> the sun and other stars.[45]

No ending, no Vanishing American ethos, holds for the Osage or for any other tribal legacy lived—and unforgetfully—sung and danced: that is, existence never yields to defeat. For as Revard has his poem trace out the Creation Story to hand and its ceremonial namings, he also signifies survival/survivance as story, the very sustenance for futurity.

The second part's veer into time-now—what more so than Las Vegas,

"city of dice and vice"?—once more recognizes an American round of ironies, whether Frontier Airlines, Stardust Inn, or Nevada as Warhead Testing
site. The poem's speaker, almost but not quite Revard *in propria persona*, is
due to deliver a Rocky Mountain MLA chapter paper on Trickster Tales. On
the October dawn flight out and well above the "neon and krypton lights,"
he looks down to what has become of a world whose center is Lake Mead and
its tributary waters. Las Vegas has transformed into "eyeball" and "monster,"
its world typified in a San Diego security guard's lost billfold of credit cards
and "sole identity card." A nearby wren flies away. An orange flower carried
to St. Louis wilts. Trickster rules turn his MLA paper into life:

> That trickster, he always carries
> lost identity cards and desert flowers
>   and finds himself
> surrounded by dawn.[46]

In the closing stanza the poet's song enlarges the contrast, moving it back
to "the white sails of Columbus" and to "Cortez and the Pilgrims." "Cards and
dice on the sand" are to be set against "the rainbow ghosts of waterfalls."
Above all, Las Vegas hotel signs flash

> *VACANCY*
> *VACANCY*
> up to the dancing stars,

the empty glut of casino land as opposed to the sustaining fullness of Native creation.[47]

In the title poem "An Eagle Nation," Revard manages one of his strongest accomplishments, a eulogy to Aunt Jewell, an eagle praise-poem, and a rewords-
ing of Ponca and Osage tradition in the form of a family visitation to a "*Red
Earth* powwow" with a stop-off at the Oklahoma City Zoo. The opening looks
back to "this little Ponca woman," athletic and lithe in her best year, able to
run for the horses at a tribal marriage. That speed the poem adapts to the
quickness of her tact or wisdom in the way of surviving:

> Now she's the eldest of her clan, but still the fastest
>   to bring the right word, Ponca or English, sacred or

> *profane, whatever's needed to survive she brings it, sometimes in*
> *a wheelchair, since her heart*
> *alarms the doctors now and then.*[48]

There follows a story line about Aunt Jewell, family, and multiple grandchildren from Ponca City and White Eagle going to "the Oke City Zoo" en route to the powwow. Barbecue, words English and Ponca, play, and picnic tables supply a first staging for the zoo itself, a huge animal assemblage of

> *snow leopards and black jaguars, seals and dolphins, monkeys and*
> *baboons, the elephants and tigers.*[49]

For Aunt Jewell the presiding creature is a bald eagle with "eyes closed and statue-still." A placard explains that it was found wounded and *"will never fly again."* Before her watching family, she speaks to the eagle, her words taking on the intimacy of kinship, respect, and love:

> *Aunt Jewell, from her wheelchair, spoke in Ponca to him,*
> *so quietly that I could hardly hear*
> *the sentences she spoke.*
> *Since I know only*
> *a few words of Ponca, I can't be sure*
> *what she said or asked, but I caught the word*
> Kahgay:
> Brother, *she said.*[50]

In response the silent eagle moves toward her and "makes a low shrill sound," to the amazement of a kindly nearby white couple as much as to the poem's speaker.

> *I knew she was saying good things for us.*
> *I knew he'd pass them on,*

he observes, an epiphanous moment as the juncture of two languages, two versions of time-space, and with Aunt Jewell as their human connection.[51]

What follows is to be glossed, keyed, to this moment. The powwow charges admission, to Aunt Jewell's dismay ("That's not our way"), even if "the thousands of Indian people" watching, the twelve drums, and the "fourteen hundred dancers" and family relatives who are to perform lift her spirits. She remembers her own trips seventy years ago from White Eagle to the Gray-horse Osage Dances. For his part the narrator remembers Uncle Woody's re-membrance of Aunt Jewell as a Ponca beauty, the migrations of his "Irish and Scotch-Irish folks" from Missouri into Ponca country,

> how all the circles
> had brought us into this Oklahoma time,

and

> what
> had passed between cage and wheelchair.[52]

The dancers dance, a mobile pageant of tribal art and identity, yet another kinetics of drum and

> swirling rainbow of feathers and
> bells and moccasins.[53]

For the speaker it is a lineage that connects sky to earth, the one time to the other. The eagle serves as an icon, liberating avian spirit of that connection:

> So whatever the placards on
> their iron cages may have to say, we the people,
> as Aunt Jewell and Sun Dancers say,
> are an EAGLE NATION, now.[54]

Survival or survivance, the effect is to confirm a world, a culture, not only pledged to but actually about the very life of its own hard-won continuity, be it that of Revard's own diverse white-tribal dynasty or that of a larger Native America. To remember "then" in this way could not make it more possible to remember "now." In these respects "An Eagle Nation" can also be said to do larger duty, a measure of the imagination, whether Native-centered or otherwise, of Revard's overall poetry.

Notes
1. Revard, *Family Matters*, 153.
2. Revard, *Winning the Dust Bowl*, xiv–xv.
3. Revard, *How the Songs Come Down*, 62.
4. Revard, *Eagle Nation*, 57–59.
5. Revard, *Eagle Nation*, 87.

6. Revard, *Ponca War Dancers*, 49.

7. Revard, *Ponca War Dancers*, 50.

8. Revard, *Ponca War Dancers*, 50.

9. Revard, *Ponca War Dancers*, 52.

10. Revard, *Ponca War Dancers*, 52.

11. Revard, *Ponca War Dancers*, 52.

12. Revard, *Ponca War Dancers*, 46.

13. Revard, *Ponca War Dancers*, 47.

14. Revard, *Ponca War Dancers*, 47.

15. Revard, *Ponca War Dancers*, 47.

16. Revard, *Ponca War Dancers*, 48.

17. Revard, *Ponca War Dancers*, 45.

18. Revard, *Ponca War Dancers*, 45.

19. Revard, *Ponca War Dancers*, 53.

20. Revard, *Ponca War Dancers*, 53.

21. Revard, *Ponca War Dancers*, 54.

22. Revard, *Ponca War Dancers*, 56.

23. Revard, *Ponca War Dancers*, 58.

24. Revard, *Ponca War Dancers*, 59.

25. Revard, *Ponca War Dancers*, 59.

26. Revard, *Cowboys and Indians*, 57.

27. Revard, *Cowboys and Indians*, 42.

28. Revard, *Cowboys and Indians*, 42.

29. Revard, *Cowboys and Indians*, 42.

30. Revard, *Cowboys and Indians*, 43.

31. Revard, *Cowboys and Indians*, 44.

32. Revard, *Cowboys and Indians*, 44.

33. Revard, *Cowboys and Indians*, 44.

34. Revard, *Cowboys and Indians*, 44.

35. Revard, *Eagle Nation*, xi.

36. Revard, *Eagle Nation*, xix.

37. Revard, *Eagle Nation*, 13.

38. Revard, *Eagle Nation*, 13.

39. Revard, *Eagle Nation*, 13.

40. Revard, *Eagle Nation*, 13.

41. Revard, *Eagle Nation*, 14.

42. Revard, *Eagle Nation*, 14.

43. Revard, *Eagle Nation*, 25.

44. Revard, *Eagle Nation*, 25.

45. Revard, *Eagle Nation*, 26.

46. Revard, *Eagle Nation*, 27–28.

47. Revard, *Eagle Nation*, 28.
48. Revard, *Eagle Nation*, 31.
49. Revard, *Eagle Nation*, 32.
50. Revard, *Eagle Nation*, 32.
51. Revard, *Eagle Nation*, 33.
52. Revard, *Eagle Nation*, 34.
53. Revard, *Eagle Nation*, 34.
54. Revard, *Eagle Nation*, 34.

Bibliography

Arnold, Ellen, ed. *The Salt Companion to Carter Revard*. Cambridge, UK: Salt Publishing, 2006.

Bruchac, Joe, ed. *Survival This Way: Interviews with American Indian Poets*. Tucson: University of Arizona Press, 1987.

Hyde, George E. *Life of George Brent: Written from His Letters*. Norman: University of Oklahoma Press, 1968.

Mathews, John J. *The Osages: Children of the Middle Waters*. Norman: University of Oklahoma Press, 1961.

———. *Sundown*. New York: Longmans, 1933.

———. *Wah-kon-tah: The Osage and the White Man's Road*. Norman: University of Oklahoma Press, 1932.

Rader, Dean, and Janice Gould, eds. *Speak To Me Words: Essays on American Indian Poetry*. Tucson: University of Arizona Press, 2003.

Revard, Carter. *Cowboys and Indians/Christmas Shopping*. Norman OK: Point Riders Press, 1992.

———. *An Eagle Nation*. Tucson: University of Arizona Press, 1993.

———. *Family Matters: Tribal Affairs*. Tucson: University of Arizona Press, 1998.

———. *How the Songs Come Down*. Cambridge, UK: Salt Publishing, 2006.

———, ed. *Native Heritage: American Indian Literature*. Lincoln: Nebraska English and Language Arts Council, 1993.

———. *Nuke Chronicles*. New York: Contract II Publications, 1980.

———. *Ponca War Dancers*. Norman OK: Point Riders Press, 1980.

———. *Winning the Dust Bowl*. Tucson: University of Arizona Press, 2001.

Shanley, Kathryn W., ed. "Native American Literature: Boundaries and Sovereignties." Special issue, *Paradoxa: Studies in World Genres*, no. 15 (2001).

Studies in American Indian Literature, Carter Revard issue, 15, no. 1 (2003).

Swann, Brian, and Arnold Krupat, eds. *I Tell You Now: Autobiographical Essays by Native American Authors*. Lincoln: University of Nebraska Press, 1987.

Wilson, Norma Jean Clark. *The Nature of Native American Poetry*. Albuquerque: University of New Mexico Press, 2000.

Wilson, Terry P. *The Osage*. New York: Chelsea House, 1988.

CONTRIBUTORS

Susan Bernardin is associate professor of English at SUNY College at Oneonta. She is a coauthor of *Trading Gazes: Euro-American Women Photographers and Native North Americans, 1880–1940* (2003) as well as articles on contemporary and foundational Native writers, including Louis Owens, Mourning Dove, and Gertrude Bonnin. She is a two-time recipient of the Western Literature Association's Don. D. Walker Award for Best Published Essay in Western American Literary Studies. Currently she is working on an expanded edition of *In the Land of the Grasshopper Song: Two Women in Klamath River Indian Country, 1908–09,* an account of two field matrons living in Karuk communities in northwestern California.

Helmbrecht Breinig is professor and chair emeritus of American studies, University of Erlangen–Nürnberg and founding director of the Bavarian American Academy in Munich. He has published widely in the fields of nineteenth- and twentieth-century American fiction and poetry, intercultural and inter-American studies, Native American literature, and cultural theory. His latest books are the edited volumes *Imaginary (Re-)Locations: Tradition, Modernity, and the Market in Contemporary Native American Literature and Culture* (2003) and *Poetischer New York-Führer* (2005).

John Gamber is assistant professor of English and American studies at the College of William and Mary. He received his BA from the University of California–Davis, his MA from California State University–Fullerton (both in comparative literature), and his PhD in English from the University of California–Santa Barbara. He has coedited *Transnational Asian American Literature: Sites and Transits* (2006) and published an article about Gerald Vizenor's *Dead Voices: Natural Agonies in the New World* in PMLA (January 2007). His current project examines the role of waste and pollution in late-twentieth century U.S. minority literature.

Diane Glancy, who holds an MFA from the University of Iowa, is a professor at Macalester College in St. Paul, Minnesota, where she formerly taught Native American literature and creative writing. She currently is on a four-year sabbatical, part of an early retirement program. She will hold the Richard Thomas Chair at Kenyon College in the spring semesters of 2008 and 2009. She was awarded a 2003 National Endowment for the Arts Fellowship and the 2003 Juniper Poetry Prize from the University of Massachusetts Press for *Primer of the Obsolete* (2004). Her recent collections of poetry are *The Shadow's Horse* (2003) and *Rooms: New and Selected Poems* (2005). A new collection of poems, *Asylum in the Grasslands*, appeared in 2007. Glancy's novels include *Stone Heart: A Novel of Sacajawea* (2003), *The Mask Maker* (2002), *The Man Who Heard the Land* (2001), *Designs of the Night Sky* (2002), and *Pushing the Bear: The 1838–39 Cherokee Trail of Tears* (1996). She also has published several collections of short stories, nonfiction, and drama. Her latest story collection is *The Dance Partner, Stories of the Ghost Dance* (2005). Her essay collections include *In-between Places* (2005), *The Cold-and-Hunger Dance* (1998), and *Claiming Breath* (1992). Glancy has won several fellowships for drama from Native Voices at the Autry. In 2006 her play *Stone Heart: Everybody Loves a Journey West*, adapted from her novel, was produced at the Autry National Center in Los Angeles, at the Smithsonian Museums of the American Indian in New York City, and on the Mall in Washington DC. Glancy is of Cherokee and German/English descent. She was awarded the Thomas Jefferson Teaching and Scholarship Award from Macalester College, a Cherokee Medal of Honor, and Distinguished Alumni Awards from the University of Missouri and the University of Central Oklahoma. She currently lives in Shawnee Mission, Kansas, where she writes, travels, and helps care for three small grandchildren. Her current work-in-progress is *The Reason for Crows*, a novel about Kateri Tekakwitha.

Linda Lizut Helstern is an assistant professor of English at North Dakota State University. She is the author of *Louis Owens* (2005) and essays on contemporary Native and Caribbean writers as well as Ernest Hemingway and Willa Cather, and she was named a 2006–7 North Dakota Humanities Council Larry W. Remele Memorial Fellow for her project "Revisiting Hiroshima, Reclaiming History: Gerald Vizenor's Crossblood Vision and Japanese-American Cultural Exchange." Helstern has also received recognition as a poet, holding residency fellowships at the Vallecitos Retreat and the Virginia Center for the Creative Arts. Her poetry cycle *Beyond Dreaming* with set by Darcy Reynolds premiered at the Unity Chamber Concert Series in San Francisco. She formerly served as the engineering college relations officer at Southern Illinois University, Carbondale.

Karl Kroeber is Mellon Professor in the Humanities at Columbia University. His recent publications include *Ishi in Three Centuries* (2003), *Artistry in American Indian Myths* (1998), *Ecological Literary Criticism: Romantic Imagining and the Biology of the Mind* (1994), and *Retelling/Rereading: The Fate of Storytelling in Modern Times* (1992). He is also editor emeritus of *Studies in American Indian Literature*.

Arnold Krupat has published widely in a number of critical journals, and his essays have been included in many anthologies. He has edited (with Brian Swann) *I Tell You Now: Autobiographical Essays by Native American Writers* (1987, repr. 2005) and a follow-up volume, *Here First: Autobiographical Essays by Native American Writers* (2000). He has also published, among other books, *Ethnocriticism: Ethnography, History, Literature* (1992), *The Turn to the Native: Studies in Criticism and Culture* (1996), and *Red Matters: Native American Studies* (2002). For 2005–6 he was a recipient of a Guggenheim Foundation Fellowship, which allowed him to complete a new book, *All that Matters: Native Studies* (forthcoming). He has published a novel, *Woodsmen, or Thoreau and the Indians* (1994), and he is the editor for Native American Literatures for the *Norton Anthology of American Literature*. He teaches literature as a member of the Global Studies Faculty at Sarah Lawrence College in New York.

A. Robert Lee, formerly of the University of Kent at Canterbury, UK, is professor of American literature at Nihon University, Tokyo. Recent publications include *Designs of Blackness: Mappings in the Literature and Culture of Afro-America* (1998); *Postindian Conversations* (with Gerald Vizenor) (1999); *Multicultural American Literature: Comparative Black, Native, Latino/a and Asian American Fictions* (2003), which won the 2004 American Book Award; and *Gothic to Multicultural: Idioms of Imagining in American Literary Fiction* (2008), as well as the essay collections *Other British, Other Britain: Contemporary Multicultural Fiction* (1995), *Loosening the Seams: Interpretations of Gerald Vizenor* (2000), and *China Fictions/English Language: Literary Essays in Diaspora, Memory, Story* (2008).

Joe Lockard is assistant professor of English at Arizona State University, where he teaches nineteenth-century American literature and early African American literature. He obtained his PhD in English from the University of California–Berkeley in 2000, then taught at the University of California–Davis as a UC presidential fellow from 2000 to 2002. He has also taught at Mills College, Palacky University (Czech Republic), Bet Gordon, and Seminar Ha'kibbutzim teachers colleges in Israel. His publications include *Watching Slavery: Witness Texts and Travel Reports* (2008), *Brave New Classrooms: Democratic Education and the Internet* (2007), a historicized edition of Griffith's *Autobiography of a Female Slave* (1998), and numerous journal articles on American literature, Internet culture, and cultural studies. He directs the Antislavery Literature Project (http://antislavery.eserver.org), where he has published over seventy annotated digital editions from the literature of slavery.

James Mackay is completing his doctorate at King's College–London. His thesis critically examines publications by post-1968 writers who adopt a spurious Native American identity. Other published works include "Chancers and the Native American Campus Novel" in *Gerald Vizenor: Profils américains* (2007) and "Google Scholarship, WikiScholarship" in *Resources for American Studies* (2007). Mackay is an active member of the British Native American Research Studies Network and a regular reviewer for the *Journal of American Studies*.

Deborah L. Madsen is professor of American literature and culture at the University of Geneva and is also currently president of the Swiss Association for North American Studies. In 2007 she hosted the inaugural international conference of the UK Native Studies Research Network. She has published on such Native American writers as Gerald Vizenor, Michael Dorris, Louise Erdrich, Leslie Marmon Silko, and Joy Harjo and is the author of more than a dozen books, including *Allegory in America: From Puritanism to Postmodernism* (1996), *American Exceptionalism* (1998), and *Understanding Contemporary Chicana Literature* (2000). She edited *Visions of America Since 1492* (1994), *Beyond the Commonwealth: Expanding the Postcolonial Canon* (1999), and *Beyond the Borders: American Literature and Post-Colonial Theory* (2003). She is currently completing a monograph, *Understanding Gerald Vizenor*, for the University of South Carolina Press's Understanding Contemporary American Literature series.

James Ruppert is the President's Professor of Alaska Native Studies at the University of Alaska Fairbanks. He is a past president of ASAIL and a frequent contributor to publication on Native American oral and written literature. His most recent books include *Mediation in Contemporary Native American Literature* (1995), *Nothing But the Truth: An Anthology of Native American Literature* (2001), and *Our Voices: Native Stories of Alaska and the Yukon* (2001).

Allan J. Ryan is an associate professor of Canadian studies and art history and holds the New Sun Chair in Aboriginal Art and Culture at Carleton University in Ottawa. Since 2002 he has hosted an annual interdisciplinary conference on Aboriginal arts at Carleton University. Among his publications is *The Trickster Shift: Humour and Irony in Contemporary Native Art* (1999), recipient of an American Book Award for its contribution to multicultural literature. He is also cocurator with Zena Pearlstone of the exhibition *About Face: Self-Portraits by Native American, First Nations and Inuit Artists*, shown at the Wheelwright Museum of the American Indian in Santa Fe, New Mexico, in 2005–6. In 2007 he was invited to lecture in China on Canadian Aboriginal art and cinema. In former lives he has worked as a graphic designer, television satirist, singer-songwriter, and recording artist.

Takayuki Tatsumi, PhD, is professor of English at Keio University, Tokyo; president of the Tokyo American Literature Society; and editor of both *American Review* (Japanese Association for American Studies) and *Mark Twain Studies* (The Japan Mark Twain Society). His major works include *Cyberpunk America* (1988), the winner of the 1988 American Studies Book Prize; *New Americanist Poetics* (1995), winner of the Yukichi Fukuzawa Award; and *SF Controversies in Japan: 1957–1997* (2000), winner of the 21st Japan SF Award. Coeditor of the New Japanese Fiction issue of *Review of Contemporary Fiction* (Summer 2002), he also published a variety of essays in a number of journals, among them *Critique, Para*Doxa, Extrapolation*, and *American Book Review* on subjects ranging from American Renaissance to postcyberpunk fiction and film. He recently published "Literary History on the Road: Transatlantic Crossings and Transpacific Crossovers" in PMLA (January 2004) and *Full Metal Apache: Transactions between Cyberpunk Japan and Avant-Pop America* (2006).

Alan Velie is David Ross Boyd Professor of English at the University of Oklahoma. He studied at Harvard and earned his doctorate at Stanford University. Velie is the author of more than eight books, including *Shakespeare's Repentance Plays: The Search for an Adequate Form* (1972), *Four American Indian Literary Masters* (1982), *American Indian Literature* (1991), *The Lightning Within* (1991), and *Native American Perspectives on Literature and History* (1995). He has also published more than thirty essays and chapters in books on Shakespeare and Native American Indian literature.

Gerald Vizenor is a professor of American studies at the University of New Mexico, and professor emeritus at the University of California–Berkeley. He is an enrolled member of the White Earth Reservation in Minnesota. Vizenor is the author of many books and essays on Native histories, critical studies, and literature, including *The People Named the Chippewa: Narrative Histories* (1984) and *Manifest Manners: Narratives on Postindian Survivance* (1994). He won the American Book Award for *Griever: An American Monkey King in China* (1987) and received a Distinguished Achievement Award from the Western Literature Association. His most recent books include the study *Fugitive Poses: Native American Indian Scenes of Absence and Presence* (1998); two novels, *Chancers* (2000) and *Hiroshima Bugi: Atomu 57* (2003); the narrative poem *Bear Island: The War at Sugar Point* (2006); and poetry collection *Almost Ashore* (2006). Vizenor is series editor of American Indian Literature and Critical Studies for the University of Oklahoma Press and, with Diane Glancy, series editor of Native Storiers: A Series of American Narratives for the University of Nebraska Press.

Jace Weaver is professor and director of Native American studies at the University of Georgia with nine books to his credit that cover Native literature, law, and religious traditions. He is the author of *That the People Might Live: Native American Literatures and Native American Community* (1997) and *Other Words: American Indian Literature, Law, and Culture* (2001). In 2003 he edited *The Cherokee Night and Other Plays* by Lynn Riggs.

Ying-Wen Yu is pursuing her PhD in English at National Taiwan Normal University, where she is completing her dissertation on the published works of Gerald Vizenor. Her research interests include Native American literature, American ethnic writers, and postmodernism. Her recent publications include "That the People Might Laugh: Comic Holotropes in Gerald Vizenor's Hiroshima Bugi," *Chung Wai Literary Monthly* (2005), and *(Alter)Native Survivance: Postindian, Comedy and Motion in Gerald Vizenor's Hotline Healers* (MA thesis).

INDEX

Jewish faith, 248
Joaquin Murietta (Yellow Bird), 26
Johnson, Mark: *Metaphors We Live By*, 13
Johnson, Samuel, 147
Joseph, Victor, 137
"Journeys" (Allen), 214
Joyce, James, 28
Jump, Josephine, 333, 340
Jump homesteads, 335
Justice, Daniel Heath, 251, 320, 321

Kaiko, Ken: *Nippon Sanmon Opera*, 205
Kalevala, 150
Kamuf, Peggy: *A Derrida Reader*, 21
Kansas, 273, 314
Kaplan, Caren, 228, 229, 231, 241n48; *Questions of Travel*, 222
Katy railroad, 324
Keeshkemun (Anishinaabe), 12
Keio University, 204
Kennedy, John F., 176, 193, 194
Khrushchev, Nikita, 194
King, Thomas, 99
King (in *Out of Dust*), 324
King Kong, Major (in *Dr. Strangelove*), 191, 195–97
King Lear (Shakespeare), 324
King Philip (Wampanoag), 103–5, 110–11, 118n35
King Philip's War, 118n34
King's Handbook of the United States, 331n15
Kingston, Maxine Hong, 98
Kiowa Indians, 148
Kitsutsuke (in *Hiroshima Bugi*), 182, 183, 201
Knives from Syria (Riggs), 329
Komatsu, Sakyo: *Nippon Apatchi Zoku*, 205
Konkle, Maureen, 109
Koukkanen, Rauna: "'Survivance,' in Sami and First Nation Boarding School Narratives," 19
Kroeber, Alfred, 3, 32
Kroeber, Clifton: *Ishi in Three Centuries*, 34, 38n2, 38n4
Kroeber, Karl: *Ishi in Three Centuries*, 34, 38n2, 38n4
Kroeber, Theodora, 3–4, 38n2; *Alfred Kroeber*, 3
Krupat, Arnold, 79, 264n11
Kubrick, Stanley, 191, 194–97, 204–5

Kurosawa, Akira, 200–201
Kyoto, Japan, 181
Kyushu, 201

LaCapra, Dominick: "Trauma, Absence, Loss," 65
Ladinos. *See* mestizos
LaFlesche, Francis, 143n13, 339–42; *A Dictionary of the Osage Language*, 339
Lager, 216, 217
La Junta (town), 170
Lake Bluestem, 340
Lake Huron, 299
Lake Mead, 350
Lake Superior, 12, 274, 276
Lakoff, George: *Metaphors We Live By*, 13
LaLonde, Chris, 230, 236, 243n101
land allotment, 10, 321
Landfill Meditations (Vizenor), 69, 70, 71
landscape: and Carter Revard, 335, 339–40, 344; and Diane Glancy, 273, 279–82; in *From Sand Creek*, 169, 177, 187; in *Hiroshima Bugi*, 167, 187; and history, 164–65
language: and Carter Revard, 335, 351; of colonialism, 346–47; in *Crown of Columbus*, 77; intercultural, 41–43, 76; and loss, 27, 278–80; and manifest manners, 91; and metaphor, 13; and native worldviews, 129, 279; and poetry, 272–74, 276–78; and survivance and survival, 19, 20, 35–36, 39, 57; in *Three Day Road*, 305; and trauma, 64, 68–69; and tribal identity, 100n6; use of, by Gerald Vizenor, 27–30, 51–54; and visual reminiscence, 3; and Wounded Knee, 258; of Yahis, 34. *See also specific languages*
A Lantern to See By (Riggs), 320–24, 326, 327, 329
Larry (in *From Sand Creek*), 169, 173
Last Supper triptych panel, 131
Las Vegas NV, 341, 349–50
Laub, Dori, 64
Lazarus, Emma, 159
Leatherstocking series (Cooper), 153
Lee, A. Robert, 73
Lee, Dorothy: *Freedom and Culture*, 18
Leech Lake, 151, 152, 155, 158
Left Hand (Arapaho), 345

CPSIA information can be obtained
at www.ICGtesting.com
Printed in the USA
LVHW03s2106020718
582515LV00025B/265/P